BAKHTIN AND THE HUMAN SCIENCES

No Last Words

edited by

Michael Mayerfeld Bell and Michael Gardiner

SAGE Publications

London · Thousand Oaks · New Delhi

First published 1998

Published in association with *Theory, Culture & Society*,
Nottingham Trent University

 SAGE Publications Ltd
6 Bonhill Street
London EC2A 4PU

SAGE Publications Inc.
2455 Teller Road
Thousand Oaks, California 91320

SAGE Publications India Pvt Ltd
32, M-Block Market
Greater Kailash – I
New Delhi 110 048

British Library Cataloguing in Publication data

A catalogue record for this book is available from the British
Library

ISBN 0 7619 5529 1
ISBN 0 7619 5530 5 (pbk)

Library of Congress catalog card number 98–060406

Typeset by Type Study, Scarborough, North Yorkshire
Printed in Great Britain by The Cromwell Press,
Trowbridge, Wiltshire

CONTENTS

PART IV ETHICS AND EVERYDAY LIVES

CONTRIBUTORS

Michael Mayerfeld Bell teaches social theory and environmental sociology at Iowa State University, USA. He is the author of 'Deep fecology: Mikhail Bakhtin and the call of nature', which appeared in *Capitalism, Nature, Socialism* (1994), and several books, most recently, *An Invitation to Environmental Sociology* (1998).

Courtney Bender (Princeton University, Department of Sociology) recently completed her dissertation (1997), entitled 'Kitchen work: the everyday practice of religion, cooking, and caring for people with AIDS'. In it, she develops ethnographic methods that apply Bakhtian theories of answerability and dialogue to the study of everyday life interaction. Her interests also include US religious and non-profit organizations.

Michael Bernard-Donals, Associate Professor of English at the University of Missouri-Columbia, USA, is the author of *Mikhail Bakhtin: Between Phenomenology and Marxism* (1994), *The Practice of Theory: Rhetoric, Knowledge, and Pedagogy in the Academy* (1997), and co-editor, with Richard Glejzer, of the forthcoming *Rhetoric in an Antifoundational World*.

Michael Billig is Professor of Social Sciences at Loughborough University, UK, and a founder member of the Discourse and Rhetoric Group at Loughborough. His interests include social psychological theory, rhetoric, nationalism and psychoanalysis. Amongst his recent books are *Arguing and Thinking* (1996), *Banal Nationalism* (1995) and *Talking of the Royal Family* (1992).

Ian Burkitt lectures in sociology and social psychology in the Department of Social and Economic Studies at the University of Bradford, UK. He is the author of *Social Selves: Theories of the Social Formation of Personality* (1993).

Michael Gardiner is Assistant Professor in Sociology at the University of Western Ontario, Canada. He is author of *The Dialogics of Critique: M.M. Bakhtin and the Theory of Ideology* (1992), as well as numerous articles on Bakhtin, ethics, utopianism and social theory. He is currently working on his second book, to be entitled *Critiques of Everyday Life*.

Peter Hitchcock is a professor of literary and cultural studies at Baruch College and at the Graduate School and University Center (GSUC) of the City University of New York, USA. Among his books are *Dialogics of the Oppressed* (1993) and *Oscillate Wildly: Space, Body, and Spirit of Millennial Materialism* (forthcoming).

Hwa Yol Jung teaches political theory at Moravian College, Bethlehem, USA. His academic interests cover phenomenology, hermeneutics, postmodernism, comparative cultural studies, literary criticism, and ecophilosophy. His recent publications include *The Question Of Rationality and the Basic Grammar of Intercultural Texts* (1990), *Rethinking Political Theory* (1993), and 'Phenomenology and body politics' which appeared in *Body and Society* in 1996.

Raymond Morrow is Professor of Sociology and Adjunct Professor of Educational Policy Studies, University of Alberta, Canada. Recent publications include *Social Theory and Education* (with C.A. Torres, 1995) and *Critical Theory and Methodology* (1994).

Greg Nielsen is Associate Professor and Director of the Concordia Centre for Broadcasting Studies, Canada. He is on leave from the Sociology Programme at York University's Glendon College in Toronto where he is also a member of the Graduate Programme in Social and Political Thought. His first publications on Bakhtin date from 1984 and his most recent, 'Bakhtin and Habermas: toward a transcultural ethics', appeared in *Theory and Society* in 1995.

Jennifer de Peuter is completing her doctorate in sociology at Carleton University, Canada. Her dissertation explores the implications of a dialogical perspective for theories of narrative identity. Jennifer lives in Calgary, Alberta, and works as a freelance life historian. She has published in the *Journal of Social Psychology*.

Barry Sandywell is Senior Lecturer in Sociology in the Department of Sociology at the University of York, UK. He is the author of *Logological Investigations* (1996), a multi-volume work on the history of reflexivity: *Reflexivity and the Crisis of Western Reason* (volume 1), *The Beginnings of European Theorizing* (volume 2) and *Presocratic Reflexivity: The Construction of Philosophical Discourse* (volume 3).

John Shotter is a professor of interpersonal relations in the Department of Communication, University of New Hampshire, USA. His long-term interest is in the social conditions conducive to people having a voice in the development of participatory democracies and civil societies. He is the author of many books, most recently *Conversational Realities: The Construction of Life through Language* (1993).

Dorothy E. Smith is in the Department of Sociology and Equity Studies at the University of Toronto, Canada, and is the author of *Writing the Social* (forthcoming), *The Conceptual Practices of Power: A Feminist Sociology of Knowledge* (1990), *Texts, Facts, and Femininity: Exploring the Relations of Ruling* (1990) and *The Everyday World as Problematic: A Feminist Sociology* (1987).

PREFACE

We begin this preface on the day after we first met in the flesh, or, to use more Bakhtinian vocabulary, in chronotopic co-presence. Although we had recently sent the first draft of this manuscript off to Sage for review, and had become close colleagues and collaborators over many months of working together, until this point we had met only in cyberspace. Such are the delights of the Internet and the work of Bakhtin that scholars find themselves plunging into intimate and excited conversation despite being thousands of miles and a national border apart – in this case, the distance and the national border between St John's, Newfoundland and Ames, Iowa.

This meeting consummated a project that had grown out of a correspondence between us on the philosophy of nature in Bakhtin's writings. We both recognized a gap in the literature on alternative appropriations of Bakhtin – in the area of ecology, and in other domains in the social and human sciences as well. Michael Gardiner suggested that we co-edit a volume that would bring together some of the diverse strands of the new scholarship on Bakhtin, drawing not only on established scholars in this area, but also authors who are newly discovering his rich and suggestive writings. We were delighted that our solicitations by letter and by electronic means generated an enormous, perhaps even overwhelming, response – an embarrassment of riches. As the volume took shape, certain thematic configurations of this new scholarship began to suggest themselves. And, in the end, we selected the thirteen chapters that, as we saw it, best reflected the promise of a Bakhtinian legacy for the human sciences.

But, again, we had never met, nor even spoken on the phone. Our relationship was entirely virtual, and hence curiously decorporealized – yet not undialogical. To be sure, there is a lack of immediacy in a dialogue lacking full co-presence. Some textual and biographical evidence suggests that Bakhtin himself was suspicious of electronically mediated communication, and that, like Martin Buber, he considered the face-to-face encounter to be the most genuine manifestation of dialogue. Certainly, a purely electronic relationship tested the meaning and limits of dialogue, both as a metaphor and in terms of the practicalities of linguistic interchange.

A series of contingencies, however, has happily brought us together on this hot summer day in July, on an island in the St Lawrence River, where we are jointly composing this preface on a laptop computer in Mike Bell's boathouse. And even this briefest of chronotopic encounters confirms Bakhtin's main insight: that dialogue is not only unfinalizable, but that it always retains an element of surprise, of a loophole in time and space, of something that remains yet to say. This open-endedness is what nourishes the will to dialogue – which, of course, is the central theme of this volume.

The portion of the book written by us is dedicated to our respective families – Rita Gardiner, Diane Mayerfeld, and Samuel Bell. We would also like to acknowledge in particular Chris Rojek, whom we initially approached with this idea, and Robert Rojek, for being such an exemplary and enthusiastic editor, and for helping to nurture this project from its earliest phases to its eventual completion. We also recognize the work of Pascale Carrington, Teresa Warren and Melissa Dunlop at Sage, and the anonymous external reviewers. And finally, of course, the contributors to the volume are to be congratulated for their patience, attention to detail, and fidelity to various deadlines. To all we offer our thanks and hopes for future communions of, as Bakhtin would have put it, 'participatory thinking'.

MB
MG

30 July 1997, Tar Island, Ontario, Canada

Amended, mid-October, 1997, in Cyberspace

1

BAKHTIN AND THE HUMAN SCIENCES: A BRIEF INTRODUCTION

Michael Gardiner and Michael Mayerfeld Bell

[T]ruth itself, in its uttermost, indivisible, 'atomic' kernel, is dialogue
– Vladimir Bibler[1]

By anyone's standards, the life of the social philosopher and cultural theorist Mikhail Bakhtin was an extraordinary odyssey, during a period of Russian history not noted for its uneventfulness. Trained as a classicist and philologist in St Petersburg, his promising academic career was cut short by the cataclysmic revolutionary events of 1917. The ensuing terror and civil war even split his family asunder, as his older brother, also a scholar of high repute, rejected Bolshevism and fought for the Whites.[2] Bakhtin's own initial cautious support for the new Soviet regime was eventually replaced by intellectual dissent, prompted by the termination of the relatively open New Economic Policy (NEP) era and Stalin's consolidation of power in the late 1920s. Official banishment to Kazakhstan for ideological reasons; the disappearance of friends, family, and colleagues; continual harassment and censorship by state authorities; physical deprivation and chronic illness – these were the defining moments of a personal narrative that paralleled the plight of countless others during the darkest days of the former Soviet Union.[3]

Miraculously, however, Bakhtin was granted a second lease on life – and scholarship. Partially rehabilitated by the regime in the 1950s during the Khrushchevite thaw and allowed to return to the Moscow area, he was once again able to engage in active theoretical work. This, in turn, led to the rediscovery of his writings by a new generation of Soviet intellectuals and subsequently by the West. This rediscovery yet continues.

The reasons for Bakhtin's renaissance are compelling. Despite the difficult vicissitudes of his personal life, Bakhtin managed to prosecute a highly successful intellectual career that encompassed a prodigious range of topics, which survives today as a challenging, complex, and many-hued body of work. If we include the writings of the Bakhtin circle as well as Bakhtin's own undisputed single-authored texts,[4] such an *œuvre* could be said to encompass, as a partial list, the following areas: an existential phenomenology that focuses on human perception, the body, and intersubjectivity; the aesthetics of cultural creation; the philosophy of language; literary theory; the revolutionary potential of humour; social ecology; the temporal and spatial constitution of human life; critical interrogations of Freudianism, Marxism, Russian formalism, and Saussurean linguistics; and the ethical and moral implications of all of the foregoing. These interventions were supplemented by a series of more programmatic reflections on the nature of the human sciences, mainly written in the post-war era and collected in the posthumous volume *Speech Genres and Other Late Essays* (1986), as well as various applications of his theoretical and philosophical insights to textual and linguistic analysis, European literature, and cultural history. Bakhtin's death in 1975 was a significant event within Russian dissident and academic circles, and, aided by the openness of the *perestroika* period, his reputation grew dramatically in subsequent years, both in his native land and abroad.

The sheer breath, complexity, and conceptual richness of Bakhtin's intellectual legacy has much to offer to a panoply of academic disciplines. Judging from the current international interest in Bakhtin's ideas and the upsurge of articles and books that evoke his concepts and theoretical vocabulary, it might appear, at least on the surface, that this promise has been largely fulfilled.[5] Curiously, however, the impact of Bakhtin's ideas has remained somewhat asymmetrical and selective, with the possible exception of that increasingly nebulous domain generally referred to as 'cultural studies'. In spite of his repeated insistence that his project was an inclusive and open-ended one, with broad relevance for all the human sciences – centring around an approach that has been variously termed 'dialogism' or 'translinguistics'[6] – the majority of scholarly work using Bakhtin can still be located in the realm of literary theory and textual analysis.[7] Disciplines like sociology, philosophy, political science, and so forth have been slow to recognize the potential of Bakhtin's ideas.

Indeed, despite his growing international notoriety, there remains considerable resistance to the development of Bakhtinian-inspired theoretical frameworks within many academic spheres.[8] The reasons for this situation are complex and multifarious. At least in part, it has to do with the fact that Bakhtin's texts were made available to Western audiences in an oddly haphazard fashion. For instance, his early philosophical works are only now being published in English, whereas the literary and textual analysis from what is often termed his 'middle period' work, and best represented by the influential study *Rabelais and His World* (written in the late 1940s), has existed in English translation for nearly three decades.

And these well-known middle-period works, which are far more than literary criticism, have been mis-framed by many potential readers from other disciplines – which is not to belittle the importance of literary criticism. But there has been a problem of intellectual cataloguing. Bakhtin's project was too complex, too interdisciplinary – to raise that much-used and much-abused and rarely fulfilled term – to be contained on only one bookshelf. Despite suggestions from many quarters that disciplinary confines are now undergoing a process of irreversible dissolution, academic boundaries in Western post-secondary educational institutions still retain a depressing resiliency, and works like Bakhtin's continue to be rejected out-of-hand or consigned to a single box by the potato-sorters.[9]

Also, it must be noted that much of what Bakhtin wrote during his life-time was never intended for publication, and was hence written in a cryptic and highly allusive style that has not encouraged a wide, multidisciplinary readership or promoted a broadly synthetic approach to the appropriation and extension of his ideas. This has, of course, been further complicated by the exigencies of translation and the reception of translated texts within particular national and linguistic intellectual cultures.[10] And then there is the sheer density of some of his writing, particularly the early philosophical works. Nevertheless, Bakhtin was a good, and highly quotable, writer – as the chapters in this book attest – and an extraordinarily rewarding partner in the dialogue of reading.

Finally, for many years, the reception of Bakhtin's work was tainted by ideological differences fostered by the lengthy post-war geo-political stale-mate between the state-socialist Eastern bloc and the liberal-capitalist West. This encouraged a very proprietorial attitude towards Bakhtin's legacy and a number of fierce, and sometimes unhelpful polemics, especially between Slavicist interpreters of Bakhtin, who have tended towards the conservative side of the political spectrum, and those who have favoured the utilization of Bakhtinian ideas for a progressive sociocultural critique and praxis, including feminists, Marxists, poststructuralists, and others (Hirschkop, 1986; Shepherd, 1993). Equally proprietorial was the debate in the West over whether Bakhtin was a Marxist, which for a number of years preoccu-pied some scholars and probably alienated some others. This kind of intel-lectual tribalism is, of course, distressing and regrettable, but also seems now to be waning. Perhaps the time is upon us when Bakhtin can be evalu-ated in a fresh light, without the distorting influence of academic boundary-making and cold war clichés and platitudes.

For these and other reasons, the result is that Bakhtin is generally associ-ated with literary studies by individuals working in other academic areas. When he *has* been recognized as a figure of note outside literary criticism, Bakhtin has often been (quite inaccurately) lumped in with the 'new wave' of mainly French poststructuralist and postmodernist thinkers, represented by the likes of Derrida, Foucault, Kristeva, and Lacan. One effect of this conflation is that Bakhtin has been absorbed willy-nilly into the modernity versus postmodernity debate, and held up as an iconic figure to be either scorned or celebrated, depending on one's theoretical and ideological con-victions. Such selective enlistment has often obscured the originality of Bakhtin's project and the complex nature of his relationship to postmodern thought. This, in turn, has militated against the creative utilization of his ideas by a wide range of intellectual domains, as a fecund source of inspi-ration for theorizing about and responding to current sociopolitical and cul-tural developments.[11]

It could also be noted that the recent publication in English translation of some of Bakhtin's earliest writings – including *Art and Answerability: Early Philosophical Essays* (1990) and *Toward a Philosophy of the Act* (1993) – adds impetus to the suggestion that his ideas have considerable relevance outside literary studies proper. (It seems there are still more manuscripts of these early works currently being prepared for publication in Russia.) These texts, written when he was only in his mid-twenties, are best described as philosophical and social-theoretical works that address a wide range of key issues in the human sciences, including aesthetics and the nature of cultural creation, the ontology of intersubjective life and the lifeworld (centring around a phenomenology of the 'deed' or 'act'), interhuman ethics, the process of value construction in sociocultural life, and the critique of an abstract, formalized rationality. Although written before he developed his characteristic metalinguistic paradigm in the late 1920s, these formative studies contain *in nuce* Bakhtin's ideas about the dialogical character of language, culture and selfhood, the open-ended or 'unfinalizable' nature of such phenomena, and the central importance of ethics and responsibility in human life. They also reveal more clearly some of his key formative influences, including Bergson, Husserl, Kant, Nietzsche, and Schopenhauer, all of whom can be regarded primarily as philosophers and social thinkers. These writings reveal a quite different side to Bakhtin, one that has received much less attention to date than his later texts, which contain such by now familiar concepts as 'carnival', 'polyphony', and 'heteroglossia'. They demonstrate conclusively that he is a *social* theorist in a very significant and profound sense. The debate over this aspect of Bakhtin's work and its contribution to theoretical development in the human sciences is only at a very embryonic stage.

Thus far, we have argued for the potential importance of Bakhtin's ideas for the human sciences, with respect to the chronotope of our present-day consumer society. But, in more specific terms, why should Bakhtin interest contemporary sociologists, philosophers, political theorists, psychologists, historians, geographers, social ecologists and so forth? Eschewing a general exegesis of Bakhtin's central ideas, a function that has already been admirably discharged by a number of existing studies,[12] we will focus on briefly situating Bakhtin *vis-à-vis* the current climate of theoretical work.

First, Bakhtin is of topical interest because, in a quite remarkable fashion, he anticipated a number of later developments within poststructuralist and postmodernist theory which have been part of the broad assault on the axioms of Western science and rationality in recent years. It is significant to note, for example, that he was at the forefront of the 'linguistic turn', perhaps the defining feature of twentieth-century social thought, in that he early identified communicative and symbolic practices as the *locus classicus* of human life. All sociocultural phenomena, according to Bakhtin, are constituted through the ongoing, dialogical relationship between individuals and groups, involving a multiplicity of different languages, discourses, and symbolizing practices. In prioritizing the relation over the isolated, self-sufficient monad, his ideas dovetail neatly with present attempts to supersede what is often called 'subject-centred reason'. As Wald Godzich puts it, Bakhtin offers us 'an alternative conception of the constitution of the subject to the prevailing one that is anchored in the theoretic and produces the familiar dyad of subject and object' (1991: 10). Furthermore, Bakhtin is no less incredulous than Jean-François Lyotard regarding the metanarrative. He is fully sensitized to the domineering potential of abstract Reason, and he strives to resist the seductive blandishments of Hegelian-style dialectics. As such, Bakhtin, like his postmodernist counterparts, privileges the marginal, the de-centred, the contingent, and the unofficial. In highlighting the dialogical relations between different symbolic systems and practices that have generated the kinds of 'heteroglot' and composite cultural forms that we are becoming increasingly familiar with today in the wake of a pervasive globalization process, a Bakhtinian model holds considerable promise with respect to the theorization of such phenomena as the new media, popular cultural forms, 'hybridization' and multiculturalism, and the emergence of post-colonialist discourses, just to name a few (Featherstone, 1995; Young, 1995).

Secondly, Bakhtin's work parallels the current reawakening of interest in the everyday lifeworld, and with the nature of 'intercarnal' and intersubjective experience, as opposed to the theorization of general 'laws' of sociohistorical development (Dallmayr, 1991). Throughout his investigations, Bakhtin was concerned with a number of interlocking phenomena that are only now receiving sustained attention in social and cultural theory – such as the body, the chronotopic organization of 'lived' time and space with respect to the constitution of social experience, the nature of 'primal' or pre-reflective intersubjectivity, the role played by value, affect, and desire, and many others. Bakhtin's approach indicates a pronounced hostility towards transhistoric and deterministic theorizing, such as Saussure's structural linguistics and orthodox Marxism, not only because such theories ignored or denigrated the sphere of everyday sociality, but also inasmuch as they violated his stress on the open-endedness of history and the 'unfinalizable' nature of the thoughts and actions of the human subject with respect to what he liked to call the 'event of Being'. In this sense, Bakhtin's work has considerable relevance with respect to the recent upsurge of research on sexuality, gender issues, everyday life studies, body politics, new social movements, postmodern identities, spatiality and temporality, and so forth.

Thirdly, there is a significant ethical component to Bakhtin's thought that runs through all of his writings. Ethics, as well as the nature of sociocultural value, has recently emerged as a central topic in social theory and philosophy, as evinced by the writings of Habermas, Derrida, Levinas, and many others (Bauman, 1993; Connor, 1992; Seidman, 1994). For Bakhtin, ethics is interpreted as a primordial concern for the other and an unequivocal recognition of difference, which is linked inextricably to the experience of alterity, the self/other relation, which constitutes the basis of his dialogical outlook. In developing such a conception of the necessarily ethical character of human life, one that is rooted in everyday sociability and the dialogical encounter between subjects, Bakhtin avoids the twin extremes of moral absolutism and an 'anything goes' postmodern relativism. As such, he manages to adumbrate a moral vision that is highly apropos for our times.

Finally, this preoccupation with ethics raises another significant feature of Bakhtin's thought: that although there are broad affinities between his ideas and recent developments in postmodernist and poststructuralist theory, Bakhtin is not easily assimilated to the latter. Sharply critical of ego-logical reason and the philosophy of consciousness, Bakhtin is nonetheless clearly at odds with those who would celebrate the fragmentation or disso-lution of the subject. For Bakhtin, the self is an embodied entity situated in concrete time and space, and which is constituted in and through its dia-logical relations with others and the world at large. This subject is certainly 'decentred', but not erased altogether, for Bakhtin places a considerable premium on human creativity, responsibility, and agency. We relate to lan-guage and other social processes dialogically, as practices that are simul-taneously structured and structuring; hence, human beings are not simply 'effects' of linguistic systems or apparatuses of power/knowledge, as many postmodernists would have it. In developing this stance, Bakhtin attempts to reconcile the false dichotomy between objectivism and subjectivism, and to sidestep the limitations of the anthropocentric and hubristic tendencies of modernity, no less than the extreme 'post-humanism' of a Baudrillard or Deleuze. Hence, Bakhtin's social thought holds considerable potential for the development of a new humanistic outlook that is not centred in the monologic, self-contained subject but on the boundary between self and other, or what Augusto Ponzio has usefully termed a *'humanism of other-ness'* (1991: 3). In focusing on the realm of the 'interhuman', Bakhtin's thought displays numerous affinities with Martin Buber, Emmanuel Levinas, and many feminist approaches (Gardiner, 1996).[13]

Bakhtin therefore retains a more nuanced, and indeed more social, view of modernity than most postmodernists, which has at least some parallels with Jürgen Habermas's defence of a 'radicalized modernity'. Cognizant of its considerable capacity for violence and domination, Bakhtin is also keenly aware of a strong potential in the postmetaphysical age for an expan-sion of participatory democracy and dialogue. He would seem to have con-siderable empathy with what Agnes Heller and Ferenc Fehér (1988), as well as one of us (Gardiner, 1997), have called a 'radical tolerance'. This is not a form of tolerance that simply allows us to 'put up with' the existence of a multiplicity of forms of life and world-views. Rather, it aims at mutual recognition and co-understanding in a manner that opens up each such form of life to a diversity of reciprocal influences and points of view.[14] This is why Bakhtin regards 'truth' as something that is constituted dialogically and intersubjectively. In short, he envisages the widening and deepening of the public sphere, again anticipating recent developments in social theory, most notably those advocated by Habermas in this case (Hirschkop, 1990; Nielsen, 1995). In taking this position, Bakhtin does not abrogate the need for ideological criticism, as have numerous postmodern theorists, and he continues to entertain Utopian alternatives to existing sociopolitical conditions, most notably in his writings on carnival. All of his works bespeak of the necessity to overturn structures of domination, to challenge illegitimate curtailments of human freedom, and to establish more just and equitable relations of power between individuals and groups. In short, it is possible to read Bakhtin both with and against the grain of postmodernist modes of thinking, although it is clear that his work provides little succour for what Ben Agger terms 'establishment' postmodernism.[15] If this is postmodernism, then it is *practical* postmodernism – postmodernism we can do something with.[16]

The goal of the present collection is to provide a focal point for some of the diverse new scholarship that is beginning to emerge on Bakhtin from a wide range of disciplines, and to extend the concept of 'dialogue' from linguistic communication in the narrow sense to a multiplicity of different social, cultural, and ecological phenomena. It is our feeling that this volume will help to fulfil a pressing need to resituate and foreground Bakhtinian problematics *vis-à-vis* the current debate over the nature and direction of critical theoretical inquiry within the human sciences, and to extend his ideas into new research domains. Much of the existing literature has been characterized by a superficial appropriation of Bakhtinian tropes or neologisms, to the neglect of a serious philosophical engagement with his core ideas and a sustained reflection on their implications for contemporary theoretical practice. The intent of this anthology is, therefore, to go well beyond the 'add Bakhtin and mix' mentality that sometimes prevails in the existing academic milieu. The various chapters included here strive to explore the theoretical and philosophical roots of Bakhtin's dialogical imagination, to engage his concepts with a plethora of figures and intellectual developments, and, finally, to enlist Bakhtinian ideas for the project of developing genuinely post-Cartesian human sciences.

In the pages that follow we offer four manners of exploration, engagement, and enlistment – four means of congress between Bakhtin and the human sciences. We have designated these means *Dialogics*, *Carnivals*, *Conversations*, and *Ethics and Everyday Lives*, and bunched together the anthology's thirteen chapters along these plural and permeable lines. The lines are plural in their names, but also, we hope, in their encouragement of other responding voices, their inducement to sociability, and, ultimately, their stimulation of the eclipse of any implied singularity of the printed word. The lines are permeable in their receptivity, we hope, to other ways of understanding Bakhtin's work – and, we hope, as well in the receptivity of other ways to what is offered here. This book is not comprehensive, far from it. Nor would we want it to be, for that would suggest that there is nothing left to say on Bakhtin and the human sciences, beyond these pages. Rather, the book is intended to suggest something of the scope and potential of what could be said, while simultaneously increasing that scope and potential. More is neither possible nor desirable. Indeed, more would in the long run be less.

The first section, *Dialogics*, contains four such suggestions, concentrating on the utility of Bakhtin's concept of dialogics for sociology and psychology. The first, by John Shotter and Michael Billig, asks what a dialogic psychology would look like; the other three, by Jennifer de Peuter, Michael Mayerfeld Bell, and Dorothy E. Smith, ask the same question of sociology, exploring themes of identity, culture, and disciplinary practice, respectively. The second section, *Carnivals*, shelters a rumination on the often painful bodily boundaries of the cyborg life by Peter Hitchcock, an examination of the body's politics by Hwa Yol Jung, and a discussion by Michael Bernard-Donals of how we might welcome those who are unheard into the carnival of the human sciences. *Conversations*, the third section, presents creative engagements between Bakhtin and Merleau-Ponty, Mannheim, and Bourdieu, hosted, in turn, by Michael Gardiner, Raymond A. Morrow, and Ian Burkitt, and emphasizing how such engagements might speak to the problem of knowledge and problem of the author. The concluding section, *Ethics and Everyday Lives*, houses a chapter by Courtney Bender on a Bakhtinian approach to everyday life, drawing primarily on the early Bakhtin; a chapter by Barry Sandywell on the complex ethical and phenomenological connections between our experience of time, communication, and the other; and a final chapter by Greg Nielsen on answerability, the ethical foundation of Bakhtin's notion of dialogue.

This is obviously only the briefest of introductions to the chapters. (An examination of the table of contents would tell nearly as much.) We have refrained from the editorial hubris of providing a reader's digest of the chapters, as is often done in collected volumes, finding these prevent engagement more than they encourage it by giving the impression that there is no real need to proceed further. But we hope to have indicated the diversity – or, better put, the polyphony – of the collection, and to have provided an invitation to join us in the café as we converse, confer, contest, and confabulate over what Bakhtin has suggested we all consider.

In bringing together such wide-ranging readings of Bakhtin, we hope to make readers more aware of the rich promise of utilizing dialogical theory in the human sciences. Vladimir Bibler, a prominent Russian scholar, has argued that '*Bakhtin has outlined the transition from cognizing reason to dialogic reason whose mode is mutual understanding*' (Akhutin and Bibler, 1993: 356 original emphasis). It is our belief that it would be unwise not to reflect on the immense significance this paradigmatic shift represents.

Notes

1 Quoted in Akhutin and Bibler (1993).

2 One of the characters in Terry Eagleton's novel *Saints and Scholars* (1987) is Nikolai Bakhtin, Mikhail's brother. See also his 'Wittgenstein's Friends, in *Against the Grain* (1986).

3 For a full-length biography of Bakhtin, see Clark and Holquist's *Mikhail Bakhtin* (1984).

4 Opinion for many years has been divided as to whether Bakhtin actually wrote *Marxism and the Philosophy of Language* (1986), *Freudianism: A Marxist Critique* (1976) (both

originally attributed to V.N. Voloshinov) and *The Formal Method* (1985) (attributed to Pavel Medvedev), or whether Bakhtin was simply a major influence on these texts, both stylistically and intellectually. In their comprehensive study *Mikhail Bakhtin: Creation of a Prosaics* (1990), Morson and Emerson argue convincingly that the evidence that Bakhtin did in fact write these works is anecdotal and unconvincing, and many Bakhtin scholars have of late come around to accepting this position.

5 For instance, a series of highly successful biennial international symposiums on Bakhtin is now in its second decade. The 1995 gathering, which coincided with the centenary of Bakhtin's birth, was celebrated in Moscow amid considerable fanfare and a high level of international scholarly interest. Scholarly articles mentioning Bakhtin number in the thousands, and in 1996 *Rabelais and His World* (1984) was the second most cited text in the *Humanities Citation Index*. Recently, the University of Sheffield has sponsored the establishment of a 'Bakhtin Centre', together with a website, electronic newsletter, and on-line database. A number of Bakhtin pages and discussion groups, both 'official' and 'unofficial', have sprung up on the Internet. A new Russian edition of Bakhtin's complete writings is in the works, and an interdisciplinary journal called *Dialogism: An International Journal of Bakhtin Studies*, edited by David Shepherd, the Director of the Bakhtin Centre, will begin publication in 1998.

6 Michael Holquist defines dialogism as 'a pragmatically oriented theory of knowledge' that seeks to 'grasp human behaviour through the use human beings make of language' (1990: 15), whereas Tzvetan Todorov designates 'translinguistics' as 'the discipline that studies the stable, non-individual forms of discourse' (1984: 82).

7 It is worth pointing out that Bakhtin has long been considered as a philosopher and social thinker in Russia, as opposed to the West. To quote the Russian critic Anatolii Akhutin:

> [I]t is very easy to confine [Bakhtin], so to speak, within the field of literary studies. That is, to think of him as a gifted, interesting, original – but still quite traditional literary critic; or (more imaginatively) to conceive of him as a structuralist, a semiotician. . . . Bakhtin has certainly made a name for himself in these fields by taking notice of such things as the significance of the dialogic structure of texts, the necessity of taking into account all those components of a text that determine its specific genre, etc. But his *philosophical* intention – and the fact that his intention was first and foremost *philosophical* – this remains unnoticed by the great majority of his Western commentators. (Akhutin and Bibler, 1993: 357)

8 This is not to say, of course, that no significant work has appeared on Bakhtin outside literary studies in the last two decades. Rob Shields (1991), for instance, has productively utilized Bakhtinian notions in the area of cultural geography, as has Mireya Folch-Serra (1990). Indeed, many of the contributors to this volume have already sought, in other works, to extend Bakhtin beyond literary criticism. We would call attention to Bell (1994, 1998), Bender (1997), Billig (1991, 1997), Gardiner (1992, 1993, 1996), Hitchcock (1993a, 1993b), Sandywell (1996), and Shotter (1992).

9 For an example of one such recent suggestion, see Seidman (1994: 325).

10 On this score, it is highly instructive to consult the fifth edition of *The Bakhtin Newsletter* (Ed. Lee and Thomson, 1996), which is devoted to how Bakhtin's ideas have been received within particular national cultures and intellectual traditions, including Germany, Russia, Israel, and many others.

11 Wall and Thomson's observations on this point are illuminating:

> [I]f there was ever an intellectual profile that would prompt us to go beyond the chronotopes represented *in literature* and to venture into the chronotopes in which and through someone's ideas might be connected to the contemporary problems and issues generated by our consumer societies, Bakhtin must surely represent such a figure. At the very least, any practical use of ethical philosophy would compel us to transcend the bounds of the literary text. (Wall and Thomson, 1993: 75)

12 This would include, in addition to the Clark and Holquist (1984) biography and Morson

and Emerson's encyclopedic *Mikhail Bakhtin* (1990), such works as Gardiner (1992), Holquist (1990), Stam (1989), and Todorov (1984).

13 For a good introduction to feminist approaches to Bakhtin, albeit from a mainly literary point of view, see Horne and Wussow (1994).

14 In other words, Bakhtin's dialogical principle must be central to the interrelationship of different forms of life in the postmodern era, in which each interlocutor is open to modifying one's own viewpoint through a dialogical engagement with the other. 'The person who understands must not reject the possibility of changing or even abandoning his already prepared viewpoints and positions. In the act of understanding, a struggle occurs that results in mutual change and enrichment', as Bakhtin puts it (1986: 142). Classical liberalism, no less than the extreme forms of postmodernism – although they pay lip service to the value of tolerance and inclusiveness – are not really open to transforming their own position through dialogical contact with the other. Symptomatic of this is Lyotard's (1984) contrual of postmodern society as a collection of discrete and incommensurate forms of life.

15 According to Agger (1992: 294–302), there is a distinction to be made between what could be termed a 'critical' postmodernism, one that is aware of the limitations of absolute Reason and the aporias of modernity, but which continues to hold out the possibility of a progressive political praxis and non-dogmatic critique, and 'establishment' postmodernism, which favours a purely ironic or satirical relationship to the *status quo* and has thus made its peace with consumer capitalism.

16 For an analysis of a social movement that advocates a practical, or pragmatic, reading of postmodernism's insights, see Bell et al.'s (1997) account of the dialogical development of sustainable agriculture in the Midwest of the United States of America.

References

Agger, Ben (1992) *The Discourse of Domination: From the Frankfurt School to Postmodernism*. Evanston, IL: Northwestern University Press.

Akhutin, Anatolii and Bibler, Vladimir (1993) 'Bakhtin's legacy and the history of science and culture: an interview with Anatolii Akhutin and Vladimir Bibler', *Configurations*, 1 (3): 335–86.

Bakhtin, Mikhail M. (1984) *Rabelais and His World*. Trans. Hélène Isowolsky. Foreword by Krystyna Pomorska. Bloomington, IN: Indiana University Press.

Bakhtin, Mikhail M. (1986) *Speech Genres and Other Late Essays*. Ed. C. Emerson and M. Holquist. Trans. V.W. McGee. Austin, TX: University of Texas Press.

Bakhtin, Mikhail M. (1990) *Art and Answerability: Early Philosophical Essays by M.M. Bakhtin*. Ed. M. Holquist and V. Liapunov. Trans. and notes V. Liapunov. Austin, TX: University of Texas Press.

Bakhtin, Mikhail M. (1993) *Toward a Philosophy of the Act*. Ed. M. Holquist. Trans. and notes V. Liapunov. Austin, TX: University of Texas Press.

Bakhtin, Mikhail M. and Medvedev, Pavel N. (1985) *The Formal Method in Literary Scholarship: A Critical Introduction to Sociological Poetics*. Trans. Albert J. Wehrle. Cambridge, MA: Harvard University Press.

Bauman, Zygmunt (1993) *Postmodern Ethics*. Oxford: Blackwell.

Bell, Michael M. (1994) 'Deep fecology: Mikhail Bakhtin and the call of nature', *Capitalism, Nature, Socialism*, 5 (4): 65–84.

Bell, Michael M. (1998) *An Invitation to Environmental Sociology*. Thousand Oaks, CA: Sage.

Bell, Michael M., Bauer, Donna M., Jarnagin, Susan and Peter, Greg (1997) 'Postmodernism on the farm: toward a pragmatic sociology of sustainable agriculture'. Paper presented at the annual meeting of the Society for Agriculture and Human Values, Madison, Wisconsin.

Bender, Courtney (1997) 'Kitchen work: the everyday practice of religion, cooking, and caring for people with AIDS'. PhD dissertation, Princeton University, Princeton, NJ.

Billig, Michael (1991) *Ideology and Opinions: Studies in Rhetorical Psychology*. London: Sage.

Billig, Michael (1997) 'The dialogic unconscious: psycho-analysis, discursive psychology and the nature of repression', *British Journal of Social Psychology*, 36: 139–59.

Clark, Katerina and Holquist, Michael (1984) *Mikhail Bakhtin*. Cambridge, MA and London: Harvard University Press.

Connor, Steven (1992) *Theory and Cultural Value*. Oxford: Blackwell.

Dallmayr, Fred (1991) *Life-World, Modernity and Critique: Paths between Heidegger and the Frankfurt School*. Cambridge: Polity Press.

Eagleton, Terry (1986) *Against the Grain: Selected Essays*. London: Verso.

Eagleton, Terry (1987) *Saints and Scholars*. London: Verso.

Featherstone, Michael (1995) *Undoing Culture: Globalization, Postmodernism and Identity*. London: Sage.

Folch-Serra, Mireya (1990) 'Play, voice, space: Mikhail Bakhtin's dialogical landscape', *Society and Space*, 8: 255–74.

Gardiner, Michael (1992) *The Dialogics of Critique: M.M. Bakhtin and the Theory of Ideology*. London: Routledge.

Gardiner, Michael (1993) 'Ecology and carnival: traces of a "green" social theory in the writings of M.M. Bakhtin', *Theory and Society*, 22 (6): 765–812.

Gardiner, Michael (1996) 'Alterity and ethics: a dialogical perspective', *Theory, Culture & Society*, 13 (2): 120–43.

Gardiner, Michael (1997) 'A postmodern utopia? Heller and Fehér's critique of messianic marxism', *Utopian Studies* 8 (1): 89–122.

Godzich, Wald (1991) 'Correcting Kant: Bakhtin and intercultural interactions', *Boundary 2*, 18 (1): 5–17.

Heller, Agnes and Fehér, Ferenc (1988) *The Postmodern Political Condition*. New York: Columbia University Press.

Hirschkop, Ken (1986) 'The domestication of M.M. Bakhtin', *Essays in Poetics*, 11 (1): 76–87.

Hirschkop, Ken (1990) 'Heteroglossia and civil society: Bakhtin's public square and the politics of modernity', *Studies in the Literary Imagination*, 23 (1): 65–75.

Hitchcock, Peter (1993a) *Dialogics of the Oppressed*. Minneapolis, MN: University of Minnesota Press.

Hitchcock, Peter (1993b) 'Exotopy and feminist critique', in D. Shepherd (ed.), *Bakhtin: Carnival and Other Subjects*. Amsterdam: Rodopi. pp. 196–209.

Holquist, Michael (1990) *Dialogism: Bakhtin and His World*. London: Routledge.

Horne, Karen and Wussow, Helen (eds) (1994) *A Dialogue of Voices: Feminist Literary Theory and Bakhtin*. Minneapolis, MN: University of Minnesota Press.

Lee, Scott and Thomson, Clive (eds) (1996) *Bakhtin around the World: The Bakhtin Newsletter*, no. 5. Sheffield: University of Sheffield Press.

Lyotard, Jean-François (1984) *The Postmodern Condition: A Report on Knowledge*. Minneapolis, MN: University of Minnesota Press.

Morson, Gary S. and Emerson, Caryl (1990) *Mikhail Bakhtin: Creation of a Prosaics*. Stanford, CA: Stanford University Press.

Nielsen, Greg (1995) 'Bakhtin and Habermas: towards a transcultural ethics', *Theory and Society*, 24 (6): 803–35.

Ponzio, Augusto (1991) 'Humanism of the other man in Bakhtin and Levinas'. Unpublished manuscript.

Sandywell, Barry (1996) *Logological Investigations* (3 vols). London: Routledge.

Seidman, Steven (1994) *Contested Knowledge*. Oxford: Blackwell.

Shepherd, D. (1993) 'Introduction: (mis)representing Bakhtin', in D. Shepherd (ed.), *Bakhtin: Carnival and Other Subjects*. Amsterdam: Rodopi. pp. i–xxxii.

Shields, Robert (1991) *Places on the Margins: Alternative Geographies of Modernity*. London and New York: Routledge.

Shotter, John (1992) 'Bakhtin and Billig: monological versus dialogical practices', *American Behavioral Scientist*, 36: 8–21.

Stam, Robert (1989) *Subversive Pleasures: Bakhtin, Cultural Criticism and Film*. Baltimore, MD: Johns Hopkins University Press.

Todorov, Tzvetan (1984) *Mikhail Bakhtin: The Dialogical Principle*. Manchester: Manchester University Press.

Voloshinov, V.N. (1976) *Freudianism: A Marxist Critique*. Eds I.R. Titunik and N. Bruss. New York and London: Academic Press.

Voloshinov, V.N. (1986) *Marxism and the Philosophy of Language*. Trans. L. Matejka and I.R. Titunik. Cambridge, MA: Harvard University Press.

Wall, Anthony and Thomson, Clive (1993) 'Cleaning up Bakhtin's carnival act', *Diacritics*, 23 (2): 47–70.

Young, Robert (1995) *Colonial Desire: Hybridity in Theory, Culture and Race*. London and New York: Routledge.

PART I

DIALOGICS

2

A BAKHTINIAN PSYCHOLOGY: FROM OUT OF THE HEADS OF INDIVIDUALS AND INTO THE DIALOGUES BETWEEN THEM

John Shotter and Michael Billig

It is an unfortunate misunderstanding (a legacy of rationalism) to think that truth can only be the truth that is composed of universal moments; that the truth of a situation is precisely that which is repeatable and constant in it. – Mikhail Bakhtin[1]

'Language lives', says Bakhtin, 'only in the dialogic interaction of those who make use of it' (1984: 183). Thus the move to the dialogical in psychology leads us more towards a focus on people's social practices, rather than on what is supposed to be occurring within their individual heads. Our attention is drawn both to the responses of others to what we do as well as to our own embodied responses to them and to our surroundings – that is, we are confronted once again with the question of whether it matters that we exist in the world as living bodies in a society with a culture and a history, rather than as isolated inanimate mechanisms. But more than just reminding us of our embodiment and our living relations to each other and to our surroundings, the turn to dialogue also confronts us with something else quite remarkable, for something very special occurs when one human voice addresses another: 'An utterance is never just a reflection or an expression of something already existing and outside it that is given and final. It always creates something that never existed before, something absolutely new and unrepeatable, and, moreover, it always has some relation to value (the true, the good, the beautiful, and so forth)' (Bakhtin, 1986: 119–20). In other words, dialogical events always give rise to something unique and unrepeatable. And, as we shall argue, it is in these only 'once-occurrent event[s] of Being' (Bakhtin, 1993: 2), in these brief and fleeting moments, that we not only express ourselves and 'show' each other the nature of our own unique 'inner' lives, but we also shape our living relations both to each other and to our surroundings. It is in these unique, dialogical, or relational moments also that we can reshape (in some small degree) the already existing historical and ideological influences at work in spontaneously and routinely shaping our ways of relating ourselves to each other and our surroundings.

In their work, in their own distinctive ways, Bakhtin and Voloshinov extensively explore the special, dialogical relations present among all the influences at work in such moments – relations which have long been repressed in our Cartesian, mechanistic ignoring of both our living bodies and of our everyday social lives together.[2] And through their dialogical formulations (of the dialogical phenomena in question), they help us to become sensitive to everyday discursive phenomena that until now have passed us by. In this chapter, then, we want both to explore the dialogical nature of these events, as well as to discuss what such a focus will imply for our investigatory practices in psychological research (Shotter, 1992). For the focus on unique events and on 'little, fleeting details' suggests that our current methods – concerned as they are with seeking regularities and repetitions – will be entirely unsuitable.

The Practices of a Social, Social Psychology

Bakhtin's and Voloshinov's work, then, points to a radical relocation of the topics of psychology: individual psychology is first transformed into social psychology, and then social psychology is rooted in the study of people's dialogical utterances. Indeed, their work contains two basic assumptions about the nature of psychological phenomena, both of which stand at variance with the theory and methodological practice of current mainstream academic psychology. The first is, as we have seen, that mental processes are created within our language-intertwined social practices, within our languaged-activity. The second is that since languaged-activity is predominantly dialogical, then human thinking is also predominantly dialogical and, therefore, also marked by an internally complex two-sidedness. We shall briefly outline the thinking behind these two assumptions, and then go on to suggest that both these assumptions are shared by the new discursive and rhetorical social psychologies which have recently emerged and which, in effect, are realizing the Bakhtinian–Voloshinovian project for a radically new kind of psychology.

(1)   In contrast to traditional, individualistic, monological psychology, which assumes that speech is a reflection of inner, unobservable processes of thought, the first assumption suggests that thinking is an aspect of our languaged-activity. Indeed, not only does Voloshinov claim that 'the reality of the psyche is the same reality as that of the sign' (1986: 26), but both

Bakhtin and Voloshinov also describe solitary thinking as 'inner speech'. The theoretical implications are most clearly outlined by Voloshinov in *Marxism and the Philosophy of Language* (1986). In that work, he suggests that: 'A word is a bridge thrown between myself and another. If one end depends on me, then the other depends on my addressee' (86). And since the word is *'the semiotic material of inner life – of consciousness* (inner speech)' (1986: 14; original emphasis), then, as Voloshinov recognized, 'the processes that basically define the content of the psyche occur not inside but outside the individual organism, although they involve its participation' (1986: 25).

As words are not abstract entities of grammar, but the speaking of words (utterance) is a living social process – in which each and every word expresses the 'one' [addresser] in relation to the 'other' [addressee] (1986: 86) – then people's 'inner lives' are to be seen as particular and concrete social constructions. Indeed, rather than as expressions of, or as referring to, already existing inner mental states, those of our utterances in which we declare things of ourselves – 'I think . . .', 'I feel . . .', etc. – should primarily be seen both as *doing* and as *expressing* very precise and specific things just at the time of their utterance: in their use, they are individual, social, and ideological all at the same time. Indeed, as Voloshinov emphasizes: 'The individual consciousness is a social-ideological fact' (1986: 12). And he goes on to comment that: 'Not until this point is recognized . . . will it be possible to construct either an objective psychology or an objective study of ideologies' (1986: 12). Because psychological and ideological phenomena are socially created through the practical use of language, a psychology of consciousness necessarily should be a socio-ideological psychology, which is rooted in the study of our communicational or languaged-activities. Thus, for Voloshinov:

> Social psychology in fact is not located anywhere within (in the 'souls' of communicating subjects) but entirely and completely *without* – in the word, the gesture, the act. There is nothing left unexpressed in it, nothing 'inner' about it – it is wholly on the outside, wholly brought out in exchanges. . . . Social psychology exists primarily in a wide variety of forms of the 'utterance,' of little speech genres of internal and external kinds – things left completely unstudied to the present day. (Voloshinov, 1986: 19–20)

Indeed, as we shall go on to argue, in focusing only on what is stable, regular, repeatable, and thus systematic, not only are these unique 'little things' presently left unstudied, but our current methods actually preclude their study.

In this methodological respect, Bakhtin's and Voloshinov's psychology is as anti-systematic and anti-structuralist as their theory of language. Just as they argue that the life and reality of language lies in the actual movement of speech activity as it unfolds, moment-by-moment, rather than in completed speech acts or in an assumed underlying grammatical structure, so their psychology also disclaims the reality of internal mental structures. The psyche is not to be sought within unobservable, internal mental structures of representation, but it is displayed or constituted 'in' observable acts of communication – as Searle (1992) might put it, our sense of our own and other people's mental states exists only 'in' the *internal relations* within such acts. Thus if Bakhtin and Voloshinov are correct, psychologists and linguists should be analysing what is observable, rather than chasing the inherently unobservable. But what is involved in us actually doing this, is something to which we shall have to return in a moment. For why we should pay more attention to the observable is our next topic.

(2)   The speech acts, the utterances occurring within our languaged-activities, which Bakhtin and Voloshinov claimed should be the topic of social psychology, are not simple or uniformly constituted. As each utterance is responsive both to other utterances and to the rest of our surroundings, and itself provokes further responsivity, every utterance is shaped by other utterances, both actual and anticipated. This is why, in practice, the meaning of an utterance cannot be sought in the internal psyche of an individual speaker: it must be understood in its concrete, particular, rhetorical and dialogical context at the moment of its occurrence. Not only is 'a word in the mouth of a particular individual person' a product of 'the living interaction of social forces' but the word itself is inherently complex: 'each word, as we know, is a little arena for the clash and criss-crossing of differently oriented social accents' (Voloshinov, 1986: 41). Each word reflects and refracts other words, and 'our' words, reflect and refract not merely 'our' thoughts, but also the thoughts of those with whom we might be disagreeing – indeed: 'All words have the "taste" of a profession, a genre, an age group, the day the hour. Each word tastes of the context in which it has lived its socially charged life . . .' (Bakhtin, 1981: 293).

Bakhtin (1981) expands on the rhetorical implications of this position in the following way: As he sees it, communication is in continual tension between contrary forces, especially between what he calls 'centripetal' and 'centrifugal' forces. Centripetal forces push towards unity, agreement and monologue, while the centrifugal forces seek multiplicity, disagreement and heteroglossia. In a point of profound significance, he stresses their inseparability, not just within an utterance but even within single words: 'Every concrete utterance of a speaking subject serves as a point where centrifugal as well as centripetal forces are brought to bear. . . . It is possible to give a concrete and detailed analysis of any utterance, once having exposed it as a contradiction-ridden, tension-filled unity of two embattled tendencies in the life of language' (Bakhtin, 1981: 272). There are crucial psychological implications in the idea that 'the authentic environment of an utterance, the environment in which it lives and takes shape, is dialogized heteroglossia, anonymous and social as language, but simultaneously concrete, filled with specific content and accentuated as an individual utterance' (1981: 272). If the psyche is structured like our utterances and our utterances contain contrary tensions, then human thinking is itself inherently 'two-sided': we can agree and disagree, question and answer, criticize and justify (Billig, 1996a). Bakhtin's insight is not merely that we can perform contrary tasks (broadly speaking, both distinguishing and relating, particularizing and categorizing, centrifugal and centripetal operations), but that we can do so simultaneously. As we speak (and think internally) so our utterances (and thoughts) are marked by a dialectic tension between centrifugal and centripetal tendencies, tendencies towards merging and unity, and towards separation and multiplicity. In consequence, our languaged-activities, and thereby our psyches, are marked by a detailed complexity and inherent two-sidedness which is overlooked by traditional structural linguistics and psychology. We need to be aware of these possibilities in our studies of people's talk.

Thus both assumptions (1) and (2) play an important role in the new discursive-rhetorical psychologies. Discursive psychologists stress the social and linguistic constitution of psychological phenomena, arguing that many of the phenomena, which have traditionally been taken as the topics of psychology, are socially constructed in the course of dialogic activity (for example, Antaki, 1994; Billig, 1991, 1996a; Edwards and Potter, 1992; Harré and Gillett, 1994; Potter and Wetherell, 1987; Shotter, 1993a, 1993b). The use of video and sound recording-machines permits not only a far finer-grained analysis of conversation than Bakhtin and Voloshinov would have imagined, but the repetition of what in the normal course of events is fleeting and unrepeatable. Thus events can be scanned many times, to study many different dimension of variation. And discursive psychologists, adopting methods derived from conversation analysts and ethnomethodology, have shown how micro-pauses and barely audible overlaps, intakes of breath and facial expressions, gestures and other bodily movements, can all have significant dialogical, and thereby psychological, meanings.

Memory and Attitudes

The Bakhtinian–Voloshinovian flavour of discursive psychology can be briefly illustrated in relation to two psychological topics: memory and attitudes. (For more details, see Billig, 1996b.) Both topics have been extensively studied within orthodox social psychology, and both have been addressed recently by discursive and rhetorical psychologists. They have sought to relocate these topics, traditionally assumed to be hidden 'inner' processes occurring inside individuals, in the outward communicative activities occurring between them, in just the way prefigured by Bakhtin.

The so-called cognitive revolution in psychology has seen a great deal of research into the topic of memory. Much effort has been devoted to the project of detailing the inner cognitive processes, which supposedly produce memory. Researchers conduct laboratory experiments in the hope that the results will indicate how information is retained, stored, and recovered by subjects. Discursive psychologists, on the other hand, dispute the usefulness of supposing the existence of such 'inner mental processes' (Edwards, 1997; Harré and Gillett, 1994). Instead of searching indirectly for essentially unobservable processes, discursive psychologists examine what people are actually doing when they are said to be remembering (for example, Billig and Edwards, 1994; Edwards and Potter, 1992; Middleton and Edwards, 1990). And as Bakhtin and Voloshinov would have predicted, discursive psychologists have drawn attention to the importance of languaged-activities, to the relational and strategic roles of memory claims, and to the rhetorical functions served by their different formulations. In consequence, remembering is shown to be a social, rather than individual, activity. For instance, discursive psychologists have examined mothers teaching children about what should be considered 'memorable' (Edwards and Middleton, 1986); families discussing 'unforgettable' events such as royal weddings (Billig, forthcoming; Billig and Edwards, 1994); and political arguments about the recall of sensitive, and rhetorically pointed, information (Potter and Edwards, 1990). All these studies underline the basic point that when people talk of remembering in everyday life – when they make 'memory-claims' – they are rarely, if ever, simply describing or reporting an internal process or mental state: they are engaging in the rhetorical, and often contentious, activity of social life, and telling of, or expressing, something of their own position in the current scheme of things in relation to the others around them.

The discursive study of attitudes points even more directly towards the rhetorical and two-sided nature of human thinking, and to the ways in which individuals put this two-sidedness to their own uses. Traditionally, social psychologists have assumed that individuals possess 'attitudes', and that such 'attitudes' are internal mental structures which determine an individual's reactions to 'attitudinal objects'. 'Attitudes', just like cognitive processes, are presumed to be fixed, unobservable, hypothetical constructs: one cannot see or hear an attitude, but one can, according to attitude-theorists, measure its consequences. Rhetorical and discursive psychologists have disputed whether people actually hold – and indeed whether they could possibly hold – 'attitudes' as described by the traditional theories (see, in particular, Potter and Wetherell, 1987). Instead of pursuing these ghostly entities, discursive psychologists have studied the dialogical activity of expressing attitudes or giving opinions. The results of such studies indicate the complexity of 'attitude-language'. For instance, when people say 'I think that capital punishment is wrong' or 'I feel that the government is at fault', they are not describing inner states. They are typically engaging in complex rhetorical activity, for an attitude is not so much an internal psychic structure, but the expression of a rhetorical stance or position on an issue of public debate (Billig, 1991, 1996b; Van Dijk, 1996). As such, attitude-talk is inevitably dialogical, and is typically marked by the sort of rhetorical complexity which, as we have seen, Bakhtin broadly described in terms of the dialectic between centripetal and centrifugal forces.

Ideology and the Dialogic Unconscious

There is a further dimension to consider: the ideological. As we noted above, Voloshinov (1986) wrote that consciousness is a social ideological fact, and elsewhere, he notes that 'any human verbal utterance is an ideological construct in the small' (Voloshinov, 1987: 88). Yet much recent work in conversation analysis has tended to overlook the ideological aspects of language, concentrating on what, broadly speaking, could be termed the more interpersonal or proximal dimensions of the emerging social constructions. Such work tends to focus on how particular utterances are occasioned by the immediate dialogical context, and to ignore the more long-term ideological influences at work in a speaker's society at large.

Crucial to Bakhtin's and Voloshinov's work in this sphere is their distinction between established systems of ideology and what they call a society's *behavioural ideology*. As they see it, a 'behavioral ideology is that atmosphere of unsystematized and unfixed inner and outer speech which endows our every instance of behavior and action and our every "conscious" state with meaning' (Voloshinov, 1986: 91). And it is from out of the sea of a people's lived behavioural ideology – 'made up of multifarious speech performances that engulf and wash over all persistent forms and kinds of ideological creativity' (1986: 19) – that the materials relevant to the official ideologies of ruling elites are selected, and others excluded. In other words, here again we can note the power of centripetal forces pushing towards unity and order, while those of a centrifugal kind, which push outward towards multiplicity and diversity, find it difficult to gain a voice in our official ideologies: *whose* words we can use in expressing ourselves is not entirely up to us, for even as we speak, we must anticipate the responses of our listeners to what we are saying. Indeed, as Voloshinov notes, 'the wider and deeper the breach between the official and the unofficial consciousness, the more difficult it becomes for motives of inner speech to turn into outward speech (oral or written or printed, in a circumscribed or broad social milieu) wherein they might acquire formulation, clarity, and rigor' (1987: 89). If we feel those around us will not play their dialogical part in building the appropriate relational-bridges between us, then we will feel inhibited in voicing our utterances in words to which we know they will not respond appropriately.

Indeed, at this point, we find ourselves inhibited in a somewhat similar way, for although we have emphasized Bakhtin's and Voloshinov's claim that there is nothing left unexpressed in our utterances, we want to contest that claim to an extent, by talking of a 'dialogic unconscious'. Of course, what Freud claimed to be conflicts within an individual's 'unconscious mind', and theorized in asocial, ahistorical, biological terms, Bakhtin and Voloshinov saw as occurring out in the everyday world between people. As a result, they both tended to avoid talk of 'an unconscious', seeing it as opening the door yet again to supposedly 'hidden' influences and the invention of mysterious theoretical entities to represent them. Yet, given that consciousness is dialogically constructed, there is still point, we feel, in talking of the unconscious – as long as it is talk of a 'dialogic unconscious'. We see it as operating, not within the heads of individuals, but in our use of certain words at certain times in certain ways, while repressing or ignoring the use of others. In such a view, there would be a dialectical relationship between consciousness and unconsciousness, for, as the very words we use in our dialogues with others draw attention to certain issues, it is drawn away from others. As dialogic consciousness, or attention, is focused on particular aspects of language, so others slip by, as it were, unnoticed.

Indeed, if ideology is reproduced through the unconscious aspects of language, then analysts should not only pay attention to the 'big' words, which carry obvious ideological meanings (for example, words such as 'democracy', 'freedom', 'equality', etc.); they should also pay attention to the 'little' words, whose presence is necessary for communication, but which are rarely the objects of conscious awareness in the course of dialogue. These are words which operate in the service, as it were, of the big words, and as such are the unobtrusive servants of dialogue. As always, the most powerful forms of ideology operate in the actions of the servant class as they unconsciously fulfil the tasks required of them by their masters. Discourse analysis is well suited to examining the role of these 'little words'. For example, Billig (1995) looked at the way in which the nation state is reproduced as an imagined community, daily and banally, in the lives of the contemporary citizen. This is not accomplished so much in the grand themes of national rhetoric, which invite the citizen to wave the flag in displays of patriotic fervor. It is done unobtrusively on the margins of conscious awareness by little words, such as 'the' and 'we'. Each day we read, or hear, phrases such as 'the prime minister', 'the nation' or 'the weather'. The definite article assumes deictically the national borders. It points to the homeland: but while we, the readers or listeners, understand the pointing, we do not follow it with our consciousness – it is a 'seen but unnoticed' feature of our everyday discourse (Garfinkel, 1967: 41). In this way, we, the readers or listeners, continue to be 'we, the nationals', especially as our attention is directed on to other matters.

The dialogic unconscious operates at other, perhaps deeper, levels of unawareness. The concept of a dialogic unconscious attempts to reinterpret the Freudian notion of repression dialogically, by assuming that language is both expressive and repressive (for further details, see Billig, 1997b). The expressive and the repressive can operate simultaneously, rather as Bakhtin described the simultaneous operation of centripetal and centrifugal forces. Indeed, for the very accomplishment of everyday, intelligible speech, certain impulses need to be routinely curtailed and driven from moment-by-moment awareness. Conversation depends upon ritual following of intricate codes, detailing what are considered appropriate responses in terms of pitch, speed, hesitation and so on. So, infractions, even minor ones, are considered to be breeches of a morality implicit in language use. We cannot just say anything anywhere. Impulses to rudeness, which are visible in the talk of three-year-olds (Dunn, 1988), must be repressed for the conventional accomplishment of adult talk.

Rhetoric is crucial for the operation of a dialogic unconscious, which is dialectically related to the sort of dialogic consciousness of which both Bakhtin and Voloshinov wrote. Ideology provides the person with multiple ways of talking, genres, voices and discursive repertoires. Given the hetero-glossic (or dilemmatic) nature of ideology, it is necessary that speakers possess the rhetorics of disagreement (Billig et al., 1988). In fact, language would not be language without the grammar, syntax, and rhetorical forms for disagreeing (Billig, 1996a). In this sense, rhetoric provides the faculty for opening up debate, and thereby the faculty for dialogical thinking. Yet, as in all matters of utterance, rhetorical forms are two-sided. The forms which open up debate can be used to close down talk, or to shift the topic to other matters. We can argue by changing topics, avoiding discursive traps and so on; and these same rhetorics can be used to avoid argument. This is particularly important for certain ideological issues. For example, study of white speakers, approaching topics of racial sensitivity, shows the speakers failing to ask questions, projecting their prejudices on to 'others', and using complex rhetorics of discursive avoidance in order to protect themselves from the unspoken accusation of 'prejudice' (Billig, 1997a). If consciousness is constituted through dialogue, then the avoidance of themes in the very words we use will constitute a dialogic unconscious.

To study the dialogic unconscious, the analyst must examine what is routinely said, together with the dialogic routines which make the saying possible. In addition, it is necessary to study what is routinely not being said, and how the routines of saying accomplish routines of not-saying. These routines are more than routines of talk: they are, as both Bakhtin and Voloshinov realized, routines of consciousness and thereby also routines of dialogic repression. In the gaps between and within words, including the dialogic gaps filled by the little unnoticed words, ideology inserts itself and so is reproduced while speakers direct their dialogic consciousness on to matters where the dialectics of justification and criticism can be safely limited. It is to the noticing of these small, fleeting, and usually unnoticed events, and the implications of their noticing, that we would like to devote the rest of this chapter.

The Dialogical and its Existence in 'Little Things'

Noting the 'orientation toward unity' central to most academic approaches towards philosophical and linguistic thought, Bakhtin (1981) points out how this has concentrated attention 'on the firmest, most stable, least change-able and most mono-semic aspects of discourse . . . [and as a result] a whole series of phenomena have therefore remained almost entirely beyond the realm of consideration: these include the specific phenomena that are present in discourse and that are determined by its dialogic orientation'

(1981: 274–5). The distinctive 'sensings' we get when involved in our discourse-intertwined everyday activities with others – the responsive understandings in terms of which we judge whether it is our turn to speak or not, whether others are questioning us or requesting something of us, or are acting sincerely, or ironically, and so on – lack 'proper theoretical recognition and illumination', suggests Bakhtin (1981: 274). And if Bakhtin and Voloshinov are correct (as clearly, we think they are), then it is precisely our 'inner lives' – which are 'displayed in' or 'carried in' the small but uniquely distinctive ways in which we express the normatively identical forms of our language in our languaged-activities – that have been ignored.[3]

Thus in the approach we are advocating here, rather than attempting to provide models of supposed cognitive structures in the head of the isolated, individual thinker, we are much more concerned to point out often unnoticed features of our ongoing social practices. For, to repeat, as we see it, our inner lives are not so much inside us geographically, so to speak, as 'in' the temporal unfolding of those of our activities in which we relate ourselves to our surroundings – which, of course, are out in the world for us all to see, if only we can become responsive to them. Thus, if we can increase our sensitivity to those aspects of our discursive activities which, although fleeting and utterly unrepeatable are nonetheless uniquely tailored to the circumstances of their expression, then we can begin to understand how it is that, as unique individuals, we can express the unique nature of our inner lives to each other. Indeed, the consequences of us recovering a comprehensive sense of our embodied connectedness to, and embeddedness in, our surroundings, are, we believe, very radical, not only for psychology, but for all aspects of social theory in our attempts at understanding our social lives together.

In what follows below, then, we shall explore in brief some of the consequences of shifting our attention in our psychological inquiries away from mental representations (supposedly inside people's individual heads) and towards the complex mixture of influences at work in unique, momentary, ephemeral events occurring in the discourses between them as they unfold. But as a first move, we must go further into the details of the special – and strange! – nature of our living, dialogically responsive understanding of each other, and how it differs from the representational-referential kind of understanding to which we are familiar.

Two living, embodied human beings cannot exist juxtaposed for long without affecting each other in a living way. We cannot, like dead and inanimate things, remain utterly inert when in one another's presence; neither can we not be responsive to aspects of our surroundings in some way. Thus, as a result, we are always in a living relation of one or another kind, both to the others around us and to features in the rest of our surroundings. But further, because the actions of a first person in the presence of a second are to an extent responsively shaped by those of that second person (and vice versa), and because the first responds in anticipation to what the actions of a second person point or gesture towards, our actions are always a complex mixture of influences both from within ourselves and from elsewhere. They are never wholly our own! Indeed, an other or otherness around us can always 'call out' utterly unique, unpredictable, never-before-performed responses from us. Thus, says Bakhtin:

> An act of our activity, of our actual experiencing, is like a two-faced Janus. It looks in two opposite directions: it looks at the objective unity of a domain of culture and at the never-repeatable uniqueness of actually lived and experienced life. But there is no unitary and unique plane where both faces would mutually determine each other in relation to a single unity. It is only the once-occurrent event of Being in the process of actualization that can constitute this unity. (Bakhtin, 1993: 2)

An important aspect of the dialogical stems, then, from our felt, sensuous involvement in social practices, in our languaged-activities: for, although we may not always be able to articulate in any explicit way what people are doing in their activities, or why they are doing it, from our responsive involvements with them, we can nonetheless gain a sharply nuanced, practical understanding of a quite remarkable kind to what is 'displayed' or 'carried' in the *specific variabilities* of their activities.[4] As Bakhtin notes, and as is confirmed by work in conversational analysis, 'we sensitively catch the smallest shift in intonation, the slightest interruption of voices in anything of importance to us in another person's practical everyday discourse. All those verbal sideward glances, reservations, loopholes, hints, thrusts do not slip past our ear, are not foreign to our own lips' (1984: 201). And we in turn show our stance to what they do or say also in fleeting bodily reactions, facial expressions, sounds of approval or disapproval, etc. Indeed, even in the continuously responsive unfolding of non-linguistic activities between ourselves and others – in a dance, a handshake, or even a mere chance collision on the street, say – we are acutely aware of whether the other's motions are, so to speak, 'in tune' or 'at odds' with ours. And in our sense of their attunement or lack of it, we can sense their attitude to us as intimate or distant, friendly or hostile, deferential or arrogant, and so on. Similarly, in the back-and-forth flow of a conversation, all involved (almost always) keenly sense the moment when the speaking turn should pass from one to another, such that both faster and slower take-ups than normal are of special significance (see Goffman (1967) for a discussion of 'involvement offences').

Such living involvements are crucial. 'Even if I know a given person thoroughly, and I also know myself, I still have to grasp the truth of the unitary and unique event which links us, and in which we are participants' (Bakhtin, 1993: 17). If we are to engage with each other, as unique, living, and responsible individuals in ways appropriate to the actual nature of our uniquely shared circumstances, we cannot locate ourselves in generalized abstractions. We cannot live by putting theories into practice, or by trying to follow explicitly formulated principles. If we do, we shall find ourselves not living out our own lives, but lives set out for us by the abstractions' original authors.

Given such an interactional focus, on the momentary living events out in the 'space' between us, if we now move to the plane of language use we find something similar, and perhaps equally surprising, to do with our use of words – their meaning cannot be simply 'in' our words themselves (as we have assumed in many cognitive theories of language):

> ... emotion, evaluation, and expression are foreign to the word of language and are born only in the process of its live usage in a concrete utterance. ... Neutral dictionary meanings of the words of a language ensure their common features and guarantee that all speakers of a given language will understand one another, but the use of words in live speech communication is always individual and contextual in nature. (Bakhtin, 1993: 87–8)

But neither is their meaning in our intentions as speakers (Austin, 1962; Searle, 1969) – for we cannot just use our words as we ourselves please: 'In point of fact', claims Voloshinov, *word is a two-sided act*. It is determined equally by whose word it is and for whom it is meant' (1986: 86; original emphasis). And furthermore, any word we voice has already been voiced by someone else:

> The word in language is half someone else's. It becomes 'one's own' only when the speaker populates it with his own intention, his own accent ... adapting it to his own semantic and expressive intention. Prior to this moment of appropriation the word does not exist in a neutral and impersonal language ... , but rather it exists in other people's mouths, in other people's contexts, serving other people's intentions: it is from there that one must take the word, and make it one's own. ... [But] expropriating it, forcing it to submit to one's own intentions and accents, is a difficult and complicated process. (Bakhtin, 1981: 293–4)

We can only fill other people's words with our own meanings to the extent that we can 'shape' them in their use – in how we intone them, place them at the moment of their use in relation to other words, to other events in our surroundings, and so on. It is in the 'specific variabilities' [see note 3 again] that they allow, that we can express our own unique position in existence. And the basic task of those around us – who must understand the unique way in which things are for us – to repeat what we have already said, 'does not basically amount to recognizing the form used, but rather to understanding it in a particular context ... *i.e.*, it amounts to understanding its novelty and not to recognizing its identity' (Voloshinov, 1986: 68).

Thus the kind of understanding indicated here is not of a cognitive, representational-referential kind, but is a practical, dialogical kind of understanding, a kind of understanding that is 'carried' in our ongoing languaged-activity, and is continually updated, utterance by utterance, as it unfolds. About this kind of what we might call a relational-responsive understanding, Bakhtin remarks:

> All real and integral understanding is actively responsive, and constitutes nothing other than the initial preparatory stage of a response (in whatever form it may be actualized). And the speaker himself is oriented precisely toward such an actively responsive understanding. He does not expect passive understanding that, so to speak, only duplicates his own idea in someone else's mind. (Bakhtin, 1986: 69)

Rather, speakers expect their utterances to be responded to with yet further meaningful activity of some kind: agreement, sympathy, elaboration, objection, supplementation, and so on. This is what understanding in practice is: it is not the grasping of a picture or an idea, but simply the practical continuation of the exchange in an intelligible manner – if the sharing of a 'mental-picture' or an idea is at stake, then that can only be achieved by people testing and checking each other's talk to establish whether they are in fact in agreement or not. Where even what it is for them to agree and to arrive at a shared understanding, like so much else in conversation, has itself to be constituted dialogically. Indeed, it is these kinds of dialogically shared, practical, relational-responsive understandings that pre-exist and, so to speak, underwrite all our more individualistically intelligible understandings. Without the continual immersion in such a background flow of dialogically responsive activity occurring between us and both the others around us and the rest of our surroundings, we simply could not be the kind of self-conscious, rational and autonomous individuals that we are. We can say that our involvement in its flow is constitutive of the kinds of person we are, culturally and historically, while its 'specific variabilities' are what allow us to express our own unique meanings from within it.

It is in this sense, then, that we should understand Voloshinov's (1986) claim that it is a mistake to separate language and life, and to think of us as learning a language in the same way as we learn pre-existing bodies of knowledge handed down to us by our teachers in schools and colleges:

> Language cannot properly be said to be handed down, it endures, but it endures as a continuous process of becoming. Individuals do not receive a ready-made language at all, rather, they enter upon the stream of verbal communication; indeed, only in this stream does their consciousness first begin to operate.... [I]t is in their native language that they first reach awareness. (Voloshinov, 1986: 81)

And it is in this sense also that we should understand him emphasizing that: *'not only can experience be outwardly expressed through the agency of the sign* . . . , but also, aside from this outward expression (for others), *experience exists even for the person undergoing it only in the material of signs.* . . . Thus there is no leap involved between inner experience and its expression, no crossing over from one qualitative realm to another' (Voloshinov, 1986: 28; original emphasis).

Yet, for us to grasp this academically, as the already linguistically constituted, socially and culturally aware individuals we are, we must not simply carry over the same individualistic, representational forms of understanding we have employed in coming to a grasp of the other bodies of knowledge of importance to us. We must recognize that if people do 'display' their 'inner lives' or 'psychological states' in the temporal organization of their behaviour, then we need the same kind of socially shared, relationally responsive, perceptual understanding in our studies as we employ them in our daily lives together. And this requires us as academics to relate ourselves to those we study in a way quite different from our present monological and centripetal modes. In focusing only on what is repeatable and essentially timeless, we talk of ourselves as studying events occurring independently of ourselves; we study, we say, the form or pattern of a person's or thing's objective behaviour. Such a one-way mode of 'observation' as this does not require any living, dialogical involvement with the persons or things we study. However, if we are to focus on the unique, unrepeatable ways in which a person's behaviour unfolds in time – with the aim not of observing them, but of understanding their 'inner' lives – then we can only do that from within a dialogical involvement with them: 'We do not see or feel an experience – we understand it . . .' (Voloshinov, 1986: 36) – indeed, in a dialogical psychology, understanding would be prior to observation.

Indeed, when it come to the source of people's expressions, the sphere within which they express their 'inner lives' and within which it receives its 'shape', 'the location of the organizing and formative center is not within . . . but outside. It is not experience that organizes expression, but the other way around – expression organizes experience. Expression is what first gives experience its form and specificity of direction' (Voloshinov, 1986: 85) – our activities, or forms of life, precede our beliefs about them.

But the few issues we have so far mentioned are just the beginning of the uncanny and extraordinary consequences of recognizing the dialogical nature of the interwoven flow of the living, responsive, relational, lan-guaged-activity between us. Because of the mixed nature of its moment-by-moment unfolding outcomes, and because each participant acts, not just simply in response to the immediate actions of another but also in response to each momentary circumstance thus created, we do not act simply in terms of a single order of connectedness between us, but we embody in our speak-ings ways of orchestrating the flow of our energies, a rhythm of acting, shaping, stopping, reflecting, switching positions, revising, looking back, looking forward and sideways, and so on; we embody *ways* or *styles* of responsively relating ourselves to our circumstances in different ways at different moments. In so doing, we act in relation to a whole *situation*, our situation, a 'landscape of possibilities' which, although we have created it collectively between us, we as individuals simply experience ourselves as existing 'within' it, along with all the others around us. And, in offering us only certain, limited ways in which we can act within it, 'our situation' seems to affect us more than we can affect 'it'. Indeed, as Bakhtin puts it:

> Each dialogue takes place as if against a background of the responsive under-standing of an invisibly present third party who stands above all the participants in the dialogue (partners). . . . The aforementioned third party is not any mysti-cal or metaphysical being (although, given a certain understanding of the world, he can be expressed as such) – he is a constitutive aspect of the whole utterance, who, under deeper analysis, can be revealed in it. (Bakhtin, 1986: 126–7)

In other words, what is special about dialogical activity – and, against the background assumption inculcated within us by the natural sciences of us as surrounded by an inert, inorganic reality, really rather peculiar – is that when we are involved in it, it is to an extent as if we are living our lives, not within an inert, dead, physical reality, but only as a bodily part of a larger organism, a collective agency, a living 'we'. Taylor puts it like this: 'An action is dialogical . . . , when it is effected by an integrated, non-individual agent.

This means that for those involved in it, its identity as this kind of action essentially depends on the agency being shared' (1991: 311). Thus, what we do, how we act, how we make sense of our experiences, how we talk of ourselves as positioned in relation to the others around us, or talk of our thoughts, our being, and so on, depends on the living circumstances, the momentary 'dialogical reality' within which we find ourselves placed. And it is against or within such a background as this that the unique, momentary, and unrepeatable aspects of our utterances can be understood.[5]

Conclusion

Dialogical phenomena constitute a third sphere of events, distinct from both action and behaviour: (i) they cannot be accounted simply as *actions* (for they are not done by individuals, thus they cannot be explained by giving a person's *reasons*); neither (ii) can they be treated as simply 'just happening' *behaviour* (to be explained by discovering their *causes*); (iii) they occur in a chaotic zone of indeterminacy or uncertainty in between the other two spheres. And as such, although containing aspects of each, occurrences in this sphere do not seem amenable to any clear characterizations at all. Indeed, although not wholly unspecified, it is their very lack of any final specificity, their lack of a completely pre-determined structure, and thus their openness to being specified or determined further by those involved in them, in practice (without, as we have already suggested, any awareness of them so doing), that is their central defining feature. And it is precisely this that makes the sphere of dialogical activity of especial interest to us. But it is precisely the fleeting, relationally responsive events in this sphere that our current referential-representational forms of rationality render invisible to us, and exclude from both rational discussion and attention. Why is this? It is the urge towards both *mastery* and *control* implicit in all our current methodologies that leads us 'to banish particularized perceptions by ordering them into comprehensible and "meaningful" regularities', suggests Kahlberg (1980: 1159–60, quoted approvingly by Bernstein, 1992: 41). Only if we are prepared to change our hierarchically ordered centripetal ways, and to dialogically balance them with ones of a more centrifugal and relational kind, can we ever hope to arrive at a psychology properly respectful of the 'little details' of people's 'inner lives', and to overcome some of the seemingly basic ideological motifs of our time: 'a *sui generis* fear of history, an ambition to locate a world beyond the social and the historical, a search for this world precisely in the depths of the organic . . .' (Voloshinov, 1987: 14).

Notes

1 Bakhtin (1993: 37).

2 We both feel that the texts written by Bakhtin and Voloshinov are different texts, for they focus on really quite different spheres: for while they both have important things to say about

people's inner lives, Voloshinov seems to focus broadly on social, political, historical, and ideological issues, while Bakhtin emphasizes the more subtle details in individual and ethical matters.

3 In this respect, Bakhtin's and Voloshinov's aims are similar to Wittgenstein's (1953): 'The aspects of things that are most important for us are hidden because of their simplicity and familiarity. (One is unable to notice something – because it is always before one's eyes). . . . To this end we shall constantly be giving prominence to distinctions which our ordinary forms of language easily make us overlook' (nos 129 and 132).

4 '. . . the constitutent factor for the linguistic form, as for the sign, is not at all its self – identity as a signal but its specific variability; and the constituent factor for understanding the linguistic form is not recognition of "the same thing", but understanding the proper sense of the word, *i.e.*, orientation in the particular, given context and in the particular, given situation – orientation in the dynamic process of becoming and not "orientation" in some inert sense' (Voloshinov, 1986: 69). Here, as above, we can find an affinity with Wittgenstein's (1953) comment that: 'A philosophical problem has the form: "I don't know my way about" ' (no. 123).

5 See Katz and Shotter (1996) and Shotter (1998) for studies of such 'fleeting moments' in medical diagnostic interviews.

References

Antaki, C. (1994) *Explaining and Arguing: The Social Organization of Accounts*. London: Sage.

Austin, J. (1962) *How to do Things with Words*. London: Oxford University Press.

Bakhtin, M.M. (1981) *The Dialogical Imagination: Four essays by M.M. Bakhtin*. Ed. M. Holquist. Trans. C. Emerson and M. Holquist. Austin, TX: University of Texas Press.

Bakhtin, M.M. (1984) *Problems of Dostoevsky's Poetics*. Ed. and trans. C. Emerson. Minneapolis, MN: University of Minnesota Press.

Bakhtin, M.M. (1986) *Speech Genres and Other Late Essays*. Eds C. Emerson and M. Holquist. Trans. V.W. McGee. Austin, TX: University of Texas Press.

Bakhtin, M.M. (1993) *Toward a Philosophy of the Act*. Ed. M. Holquist. Trans. and notes V. Lianpov. Austin, TX: University of Texas Press.

Bernstein, R.J. (1992) *The New Constellation*. Cambridge, MA: The MIT Press.

Billig, M. (1991) *Ideology and Opinions: Studies in Rhetorical Psychology*. London: Sage.

Billig, M. (1995) *Banal Nationalism*. London: Sage.

Billig, M. (1996a) *Arguing and Thinking: A Rhetorical Approach to Social Psychology*. (2nd edn). Cambridge: Cambridge University Press.

Billig, M. (1996b) 'Discursive, rhetorical and ideological messages', in C. McGarty and A. Haslam (eds), *The Message of Social Psychology: Perspectives on Mind in Society*. Oxford: Blackwell. pp. 36–53.

Billig, M. (1997a) 'Keeping the white queen in play', in M. Fine, L. Weis, L. Powell and M. Wong (eds), *Off-White*. London: Routledge. pp. 149–57.

Billig, M. (1997b) 'The dialogic unconscious: psycho-analysis, discursive psychology and the nature of repression', *British Journal of Social Psychology*, 36: 139–59.

Billig, M. and Edwards, D. (1994) 'La Construction sociale de la mémoire', *La Recherche*, 17: 161–81.

Billig, M., Condor, S., Edwards, D., Gane, M., Middleton, D. and Radley, R. (1988) *Ideological Dilemmas*. London: Sage.

Dunn, J. (1988) *The Beginnings of Social Understanding*. Cambridge, MA: Harvard University Press.

Edwards, D. (1997) *Discourse and Cognition*. London: Sage.

Edwards, D. and Middleton, D. (1986) 'Joint remembering: constructing an account of shared experience through conversational discourse', *Discourse Processes*, 9 (4): 423–59.

Edwards, D. and Potter, J. (1992) *Discursive Psychology*. London: Sage.

Garfinkel, H. (1967) *Studies in Ethnomethodology*. Engelwood Cliffs, NJ: Prentice-Hall.

Goffman, E. (1967) *Interaction Ritual*. Harmondsworth: Penguin.

Harré, R. and Gillet, G. (1994) *Discursive Psychology*. London: Sage.

Kahlberg, S. (1980) 'Max Weber's types of rationality: cornerstones for the analysis of rationalization processes', *American Journal of Sociology*, 85: 1145–79.

Katz, A. and Shotter, J. (1996) 'Hearing the patient's voice: toward a "social poetics" in diagnostic interviews', *Social Science and Medicine*, 43: 919–31.

Middleton, D. and Edwards, D. (1990) 'Conversational remembering: a social psychological approach', in D. Middleton and D. Edwards (eds), *Collective Remembering*. London: Sage. pp. 23–45.

Potter, J. and Edwards, D. (1990) 'Nigel Lawson's tent: attribution theory, discourse analysis and the social psychology of factual discourse', *European Journal of Social Psychology*, 20: 405–24.

Potter, J. and Wetherell, M. (1987) *Discourse and Social Psychology: Beyond Attitudes and Behaviour*. London: Sage.

Searle, J.R. (1969) *Speech Acts*. Cambridge: Cambridge University Press.

Searle, J.R. (1992) *(On) Searle on Conversation*. Eds. H. Parret and J. Verschueren. Amsterdam/Philadelphia: John Benjamins.

Shotter, J. (1992) 'Bakhtin and Billig: monological versus dialogical practices', *American Behavioral Scientist*, 36: 8–21.

Shotter, J. (1993a) *Cultural Politics of Everyday Life: Social Constructionism, Rhetoric, and Knowing of the Third Kind*. Milton Keynes: Open University Press.

Shotter, J. (1993b) *Conversational Realities: Constructing Life through Language*. London: Sage.

Shotter, J. (1998) 'Social construction as social poetics: Oliver Sacks and the case of Dr. P.', in B.M. Bayer and J. Shotter (eds), *Reconstructing the Psychological Subject: Bodies, Practices and Technologies*. London: Sage.

Taylor, C. (1991) 'The dialogical self', in D.R. Hiley, J.F. Bohman and R. Shusterman, (eds), *The Interpretative Turn*. Ithaca, NY: Cornell University Press. pp. 304–14

Van Dijk, T.A. (1996) 'Discourse, opinions and ideologies', in C. Scheffner and H. Kelly-Holmes (eds), *Discourse and Ideologies*. Cleveden: Multilingual Matters.

Voloshinov, V.N. (1986) *Marxism and the Philosophy of Language*. Trans. L. Matejka and I.R. Titunik. Cambridge, MA: Harvard University Press.

Voloshinov, V.N. (1987) *Freudianism: A Critical Sketch*. Bloomington, IN, and Indianapolis: Indiana University Press.

Wittgenstein, L. (1953) *Philosophical Investigations*. Oxford: Blackwell.

3

THE DIALOGICS OF NARRATIVE IDENTITY

Jennifer de Peuter

The language of the storied self is spoken across an eclectic array of disciplines; cognitive and social psychologists, literary critics, poststructural and postmodern social theorists among others have followed the interpretive turn in recent decades to postulate the textual self, the discursive self, the narrative and the mythical self. In the wake of hermeneutic and structuralist projects of the 1960s and 1970s, which bordered, for some, on the eclipse of a meaningful discourse on subjectivity and agency, a diverse collection of theoretical and substantive studies on the textual as site of agency and meaning-making is now available. What may be loosely termed the paradigm of narrative identity is in particular moving from the margins of interdisciplinary studies to gain legitimacy as an alternative to both the reductionism of structuralism and the psychological atomism of mind-oriented models of personhood.

While we have become unsettled by reductionist accounts, we have also become suspicious of the assumptions about modern Western personhood largely informing both scholastic and common sense thought since the Enlightenment. Unveiled as political, cultural and historical peculiarities are the ideals of individualism, autonomy and centralization, and self-integration, authenticity and progressive intelligibility. Surprisingly, however, one finds little discursive interaction between, for example, feminist and postmodernist attempts to destabilize such ideals, and theoretical accounts of the narrative self. While the latter indeed decentre the 'traits' of personhood from the Cartesian model of mind to the organizational schema of narrative, there is little indication that narrativists are prepared to engage in the kind of self-reflexive scrutiny of foundational assumptions that could destabilize the ideals of Western personhood and, in turn, call for their critical reconstruction.

Yet we do find on the margins of mainstream narrative models of the self several works of Bakhtinian orientation which convey a textual understanding of the self, precisely by reinterpreting the 'ideals' of Western personhood. Drawing on the ethics, philosophical anthropology and literary criticism of Mikhail Bakhtin and Bakhtin scholars, these works suggest a dialogical conception of the self, a conception which, by recasting the dominant model of personhood, has the potential to inform our narrative theories of self so that the latter may begin to deconstruct, and rebuild, the basic assumptions of personhood.

By challenging the ideals of Western personhood and making innovative use of the implications of such a challenge, a dialogical perspective can, quite literally, speak through and dialogue with theories of narrative identity, to bring the latter into the domain of critical social analysis. Dialogism and narrativity share a common foundation of relationalism, choosing a subject-centred, anti-individualistic, relationship-oriented perspective. The dialogical alternative, however, departs from the monologics of mainstream narrative-identity theory, where integration, cohesion and coherence of self are privileged, to honour the equal viability of the forces of synthesis and dispersion, unity and fragmentation, or the centripetal and centrifugal forces which produce the dynamic tensions of selfhood. It is also through the 'boundary constitution' of self that the dialogical alternative constitutes an important voice in the efforts to challenge the way we, as theorists and as everyday selves, comprehend the contemporary person.

This chapter is structured by three objectives. I want to refer to the historical contexts of what the modern West takes for granted as the natural conditions of selfhood, or the states of being towards which 'normal' or desired selves strive. The secularization of the self marks a major break in dominant beliefs, in the source of origin and locus of control of self-characteristics, if not necessarily in their privileged status. With even a cursory historical orientation as that presented here, one will become sensitive to the contingency and peculiarity of modern Western beliefs. Secondly, I want to consider in some depth a few of these traits, and in doing so I will raise the question of whether their alleged 'demise' in wake of the postmodern condition is, as some argue, best understood as a symptom of a new social order, or whether the collapse in our faith of traditional ideals is better understood as a result of an intellectual sensibility capable of accommodating the logics of contradiction, incoherence and the unfinalizable. The third objective is to evaluate the extent to which a narrative foundation of personal identity relies on the reification of modern ideals of personhood, and then to recast the narrative logics of selfhood in terms of a viable dialogical alternative. Particular attention will be given throughout to the potential of Bakhtinian scholarship to challenge the contemporary foundations of the textualities of selfhood.

The Secularization of the Self

Intellectual thought on the self has as long a history as philosophy itself. Pythagoras initially turned the philosophical enterprise from objects of the cosmos to the concept of the human self; Euripides was driven by the quest for self-knowledge; Socrates privileged the contemplation of the goals of an individual life while Plato and Aristotle sought the metaphysical structure of the self; and Augustine sought to know himself so that he might better know God (Oliver, 1992). Indian philosophy originated as 'Adhatma Sastra', or the science of the self, and Chinese philosophy was shaped by the words of Lao Tzu: 'He who knows others is clever; He who knows himself has discernment' (Lao Tzu, 1963: 92).

If, in early philosophy, the self was defined through one's relationship to God, the ideals of medieval personhood were also defined by the relationship of the individual to theological doctrine. Continuity of personal identity was ensured by the ontological permanence of the Soul; coherence, authenticity, and unity of the self inhered in the divine plan for one's life. With the Enlightenment hegemony of rationalization and scienticism, the modern, secularized self took the form of a human ideal. As the origin and locus of control of the ideals of personhood shifted from the will of God to the rational mind, self-understanding ceased to be primarily a means to understanding God. Premised on Cartesian mind/body and self/other dualisms, the self-defining, self-determining, centralized and disembodied ego strove for worldly mastery and control (Gergen, 1991; Hermans and Kempen, 1993; Oliver, 1992). Rationality, agency and ethics came to be understood as minded manifestations of inner beliefs, desires and moral principles rather than collective agreements of theological origin (Taylor, 1989). With the fragmentation of totalizing religious belief systems, the decline of social consensus on basic truths and ultimate values (McAdams, 1993), and the decline of social ascription of identity after 1800 (Goldstein and Rayner, 1994), individualistic ideologies premised on the pursuit of personal freedom and autonomy began to substitute for faith in the divine plan for the life. The Enlightenment oppositional dichotomies of subject/object and self/society for example, formed the cornerstone of the ideology of liberal individualism. Bentham, Mill and Rousseau posited the ontological priority of the individual over society, saw society as the aggregate of individuals striving to maximize self-interest, and perceived the social as a threat to authentic, independent self-realization. In Mill's most pessimistic prediction, individuality would submit to the collective will; artificial, lifeless conformity would co-opt and negate the novelty and originality of authentic being.[1]

Thus we find with the secularization of the self the persistence of idealized traits of Western personhood, including the continuity of personal identity, the coherence, unity and integration of the self, and the authentic, singular and progressive core self. At the same time, the discovery of their historical contingency in terms of perceived origin and locus of control leads us to approach these traits as cultural *ideals*, and to emphasize their valuative, political designations over their 'descriptive truth' (Sampson, 1993). It is through the deconstruction of the ideals of Western personhood that we may begin to evaluate critically not only their participation in the social construction of contemporary identity, but also the various theories which develop to explain late- or post-modern selfhood. If, as a Bakhtinian reading suggests, selfhood becomes through the dialogues of synthesis *and* dispersion, unity *and* multiplicity, or the centripetal *and* the centrifugal, is it sufficient to understand the 'postmodern' self (a fragmented, multiple, inauthentic self) as a product of the postmodern condition alone? Are the 'modernist' traits of selfhood (cohesion, singularity, authenticity) threatened by the collapse of modernity, or are they in question also because our present mode of intelligibility and, some argue, our ethics, can no longer permit the centripetal forces of self to masquerade as the 'inherent' defining characteristics of personhood? While the latter is subject to debate in some quarters, it is largely a neglected premise within the sociology of the self generally, and the study of the narrative self in particular.

In what follows I articulate the entrenchment of mainstream sociological discourse on the self in the ideals of modern personhood to argue that, with some exceptions (including versions of feminist and postmodern thought), the normative social self is reified as continuous, integrated, singular and authentic. I will draw on what has been termed the 'relational' paradigm to present a social theory of self which deconstructs these ideals as Enlightenment biases and, in turn, reconstructs the social self by giving new meaning to the 'properties' of persons. Because the relational assumptions of theories of narrative identity presuppose precisely this kind of deconstruction, the latter will serve as a point of departure for the instantiation of critical reconstruction. Yet, as I will attempt to demonstrate, the critical potential of contemporary perspectives on the narrative self is also limited by implicit biases towards synthesis, integration, progress and authenticity. These limitations may be at least partially overcome by reinterpreting the logics of narrative through some key principles of dialogical thinking. I will draw on theories of the dialogical self (Hermans and Kempen, 1993; Sampson, 1993), as frameworks ontologically and ethically suspicious of the Western myth of the centripetal self, to suggest the reconstruction of the narrative framework of identity. In doing the latter I hope to show how the concept of the contemporary Western self may be liberated from the modernist ideals of centripetal tendencies on the one hand and from the postmodernist ideals of centrifugal tendencies on the other.

The Ideals of Personhood: Modern Western Perspectives

Continuity

The concept of identity has been most debated in discourses on the philosophy of the person, and the greatest point of contention since Locke (1632–1704) has been the continuity of personal identity. Locke (1964 [1690]) located continuity in the certainty of rational mind-properties; it is because the self is recognized through self-reflection that the thinking person is a continuous person, or the same person over the course of a life. Contemporary critics emphasize the un-sustainability of the memory criterion, not by destabilizing mind-properties as the source of the self, but by contending that memories lapse and are partial, fragmented and discontinuous (Madell, 1981). The general absence of contemporary critics of the Lockean bias towards the mind as the source of the self suggests a continued desire to conceive of the individual as owner of 'inner' qualities, or put differently, to reify the metaphor of the mind as container of the self.

Coherence, Unity, Authenticity

Coherence, unity and authenticity of the secular self are also idealized in Enlightenment discourse as individual mind-states, the property and responsibility of self-contained individuals. Formerly regarded as manifestations of divine will, Enlightenment discourse locates these traits in the rational mind; once thought to reside in the fixed, enduring Soul, these properties become contingent on one's capacity for rational self-reflection. In short, the source of coherence, unity and authenticity is sought in rational cognition as the Soul becomes unintelligible under logico-positive authority.

Equilibrium

The idea[1] that selves are to master fragmentation and self-contradiction is further a bias of the domination of associationist thinking in Western cultures. Under 'normal' conditions the various aspects or parts of the self are thought to perform a specific function and thus contribute to the overall harmony and equilibrium of the self (Organ, 1987). One need only consider the idealization of harmony, equilibrium, coherence and non-ambiguity in Western understandings of self-change to appreciate the extent of influence of this paradigm. Part of the psychotherapeutic programme is to de-pathologize the life by creating a coherent life story; in the words of McAdams, '[t]o make meaning in life is to create dynamic narratives that render sensible and coherent the seeming chaos of human existence' (1993: 166). Self-fragmentation is approached as a condition of personal crisis, and may be medicalized and disciplined through techniques of psychiatric medicine (McAdams, 1993: 46). We believe that to recognize ourselves and to be recognized as distinct selves with personal identity we must experience and exhibit some degree of self-integration. When we hold conflicting opinions or beliefs, we seek resolution. When we enact contradictory roles, we practise role-distancing, taking one or more enactments as the 'not really me'.

It may be argued that our entrenchment in the centripetal tendencies of selfhood is destabilized by the emergent postmodern condition. If the ambiguous, incoherent self is one uncertain about meanings and intentions, the 'postmodern self' may embody the shift in characteristics from unity, cohesion and authenticity to dispersion, multiplicity and contradiction. Because the postmodern self is over-saturated by social stimulation and exposed to an unprecedented plethora of possible meanings, significances and ways of being, its centre of organization, and hence its certainty and concreteness, may threaten to disintegrate (see Gergen, 1991). From a dialogical perspective, however, this line of thought remains grounded in the Enlightenment hegemony of the minded self; the rational mind confronts irreconcilable contradiction and thus selfhood collapses into fragmentation and multiplicity. In this discourse, 'modernist' ideals of continuity, coherence, non-ambiguity and authenticity are reified as prior ontological truisms and their passing is mourned (see for instance, McAdams, 1993).

Centripetal Biases of the Sociology of Self

While theories of the postmodernization of the self may represent the most recent attempts to reconcile changes in social organization with emergent forms of being, they are certainly not the first to do so. Early twentieth-century sociology of the self emerged in reaction to the Enlightenment ideals; an understanding of the relatedness of persons and a dialectical model of self and society motivated, for example, the pragmatism of William James and G.H. Mead's early interactionism. James countered the Cartesian mind/body dualism by relating the body to the 'I', and both opposed the self/other dualism with the relationality of 'I' and 'me'. The work of Mauss (1985 [1938]) also demystified Western ideals by attributing concepts of the self to forms of social organization in cross-cultural contexts.

We have in many ways sought to overcome the isolating effects of individualism, the belief in self-ownership and self-responsibility which discourage cooperation and community, and the inward-turning of ethics, or ethical decision-making based on inner moral principles (Gergen, 1991). And yet while the dismantling of the ideals of liberal individualism is rightly the task of sociological sensibilities, the extent to which these ideals have been unveiled as social, historical and political constructs by mainstream self-oriented sociology is questionable. The reification of the ideals as ontological certainties and normative desires is due in part to our preoccupation with categorical identity (Greenwood, 1994; Somers, 1994). Research has generally focused on social labelling, group membership and taxonomic identity as exemplified by the infamous Twenty Statements Test. Conceptualized here is neither personal identity nor the social self, but practices and consequences of *identification*: who we identify with, and how we describe ourselves as a result (Weinreich, 1993, in Greenwood, 1994). Assumptions of individualism, autonomy and self-ownership stem also from our bias towards cognitive constructions of self-definition. Symbolic interactionism's definition of the situation, ethnomethodology's focus on natural language and accounts, and the dramaturgical emphasis on the (rational) presentation of self adhere to the primacy of the self as a minded activity housed, in part, in the person.

Indeed, there are cases in which the ideals are challenged: Hinchman (1990) theorizes the social mediation of individuality, but argues that we discover a true and essential self through (culturally informed) self-examination; others acknowledge an unprecedented fragmentation of identity, but explain it as a product of multiple role-occupancy (see Potter and Weath-erell, 1989, in Sampson, 1993). As Sampson (1993) points out, we experi-ence role conflict precisely because we hold an a priori belief in a core, integrated, non-contradictory self. Role diversity and conflict are less evi-dence of a new sensibility of fragmented subjectivity than attestation to the belief that modern forms of social organization threaten what we were in the past and should seek to preserve: the unified, integrated, core self.

The often subtle and implicit assumptions about modern Western per-sonhood, including the belief in a unique self as superior to the over-social-ized person and the belief in a core, cohesive self as the normative state towards which non-pathological selves strive, may be restated as the privi-leging of centripetal forces of synthesis and integration over centrifugal forces of dispersion and fragmentation. It is a celebration of equilibrium, coherence and control over disequilibrium, incoherence and the chaotic. Generally absent from our dialogues are attempts to unveil the social and political construction of our celebratory stance towards the centripetal and our desire to discipline and manage the forces of dispersion.

The Case of Narrative Identity Theory and the Limits of Relationalism

In the seventeenth century John Locke proposed that the self inhered in rational self-reflection; he built his case not by disproving the existence of the Soul, but by deeming it *unknowable* within the Enlightenment scientific paradigm. Today we propose that the self inheres in our sociality, and those who describe a postmodern condition of social saturation (Gergen, 1991) and the decline of systems of integration and order suggest a new kind of self: the Mutable person (Zurcher, 1977) or the Protean self (McAdams, 1993). I think it is useful to follow Locke in understanding the self so-conceived not only as the result of a new social order, but as the discursive construction of a new kind of dialogue, a paradigm shift through which we develop the modes of intelligibility by which to destabilize the ideals of modern Western personhood. Our new sensibilities are populated by the critiques of the masculinization of the secular self (Harding, 1986; Marshall, 1991); by the appropriation of deconstructionism and postmodern literary criticism (M. Bakhtin and J. Kristeva); and by the emerging dialogues of Eastern and Western philosophies (Oliver, 1992). Broadly, it is the frame-work of relationalism, premised on an inclusive, sociocentric, non-individ-ualistic concept of the person that informs and is informed by this turn.

Perhaps the most well-defined body of relational theory and research devoted to the social self is that of narrative-identity study. In 1986 the cog-nitive psychologist Jerome Bruner drew a distinction between paradigmatic or logico-scientific and narrative modes of cognitive functioning, each of which, he theorized, provides a different way of constructing reality. During the past decade microsociologies of the self have taken up Bruner's thesis to rebuild themselves on new epistemological ground, to stake a claim in a distinctly social and relational concept of the person (Brown, 1994; Bruner, 1987; Gergen, 1991; Gregg, 1991; McAdams, 1993; Rosenwald and Ochberg, 1992; Somers, 1994); in doing so they have produced 'a small revolution with potentially large consequences' (Somers, 1994: 613).

Early narrativists, such as Gordon Allport and George Bernard Shaw, used autobiography as a window to the life events and experiences of story-tellers (Rosenwald and Ochberg, 1992). Narrative was thought to represent the objective features of life, and truth was thought to inhere in the accuracy of facts. With the dismantling of the realist position we now understand narrative as the organizational framework by which selves are accomplished and known (Goldstein and Rayner, 1994). Our lives and selves are thoroughly storied with beginnings, middles and endings; we identify settings and characters and develop and follow plots, climaxes and resolutions. The relationships among social acts, settings and persons and among history, biography and selfhood are given definition, organization and articulation through loosely structuring narrative schema. Selfhood is spoken through the voices of others; prototypical plots such as the heroic, warrior and caregiver (McAdams, 1993) and community narratives mediate the storied-self (Rappaport, 1993). We are neither sole authors nor owners of situated, storied, relational and hence contingent selves (Maines, 1993).

Narrative theory is premised broadly on a rejection of the Cartesian model of self-identity as the outcome of unmediated self-reflection. Social beings are embedded in and interpret the world and themselves through mediating frameworks of collective interpretive discourses. Narrativists reject the Enlightenment belief in internal 'properties' of self awaiting discovery through painstaking self-examination; rather, it is precisely the ambiguity of the self that enables the myriad of possible situated self-interpretations (Gregg, 1991). The ideology of individualism is unveiled as a value-laden, political discourse; the model of the self-contained individual is exposed as a cultural myth and the ideals of Western personhood as products of semantic structures and narrative modes of intelligibility (Bruner, 1987) which frame, direct, absorb and recast our desires and interpretations and encode our expectations and explanations.

While the ideals are decentred from rational mind to contingent text, and as their source of origin and locus of control are recast, we remain hesitant to re-evaluate their meaning. We attribute the reproduction of self-sufficiency, coherence, authenticity and singularity of the self to the narrative mode of intelligibility, but fail to assess critically their value. Narratives are said to provide unity and purpose for a life; 'progressive' personal narratives are thought to develop towards coherence, credibility, reconciliation and integration (McAdams, 1993: 110). Some emphasize narrative as 'a cognitive process that organizes human experience into temporally meaningful episodes' (Polkinghorne, 1988: 1), bringing a sense of history and of future to the self (Rappaport, 1993). And we continue to accept Erikson's premise that self-stories contribute to the belief in self-sameness over time (Erikson,

1968, in Rosenwald and Ochberg, 1992), without re-thinking what it means to be 'self-same'.

Our persistent desire to credit narrative structure with the function of integration, coherence and the authenticity of self is exemplified by McAdams's (1993) study of 'personal myths'. McAdams challenges the belief in the individual mind as container of the self, but continues to privilege the ideals of unity and intelligible life-purpose, suggesting that the 'natural' construction of the personal myth renders the self knowable and unique. Selves for this author aspire to create heroic narratives in which opposing characters or selves are integrated as a harmonious whole. While the myth 'is embedded in the complicated series of accounts' (McAdams, 1993: 20), a single, central story is thought to underlie life episodes and provide the life with unity and purpose. The fragmented self, on the other hand, is referred to as a 'psychiatric disorder of the self' (McAdams, 1993: 46) which may be depathologized through the creation of a coherent life story.

McAdams's (1993) discourse reproduces the modern Western primacy of order, synthesis and progress, and attributes the production of these ideals to the organizational schema of narrative identity. Let us consider briefly what becomes of the ideals when recast in relational terms, using 'autonomy' as articulated by the feminist relationalism of Marshall (1991) to illustrate. Unlike the production model wherein autonomy is celebrated as independence from the object world, the relational model privileges subject relations and defines autonomy as the denial of human interdependence. In this framework autonomy is undesirable as it limits the capacity for selfhood, and unethical because it denies the interdependence of persons (Marshall, 1991); exposed as a contingent ideal dependent upon abstract individualism, autonomy is ontologically suspicious and ethically undesirable.

I want to suggest that the ideals of autonomy, integration, coherence and authenticity may, like the concept of identity itself, be re-constructed as situated, joint productions, defined on the boundary of identity and difference and constituted by the equal forces of synthesis and dispersion, order and disarray. We must fully overcome the Cartesian self/other dichotomy to understand 'properties' of selves as liminal, in neither the mind nor the text, but *between* interlocutors, real or imagined, and allow for the often-silenced centrifugal partners in the dialogues of selfhood. In what follows I will clarify this dialogical articulation of selfhood and re-consider the ideals of personhood through dialogical lenses. In doing so I hope to make clear how a narrative/dialogic partnership of intelligibility can aid in the reconceptualization of the contemporary relations of selfhood.

The Dialogic Alternative

Bakhtin departs from the logics of the self-contained individual by developing a theory of the transgredience of identity (Todorov, 1984). This theory challenges the supremacy of the interiority of selfhood by reinterpreting the concept of 'boundary' from that which excludes otherness to the active site of dialogue and definition of the self. Selfhood is less a property of mind than it is a joint production, a dialogue on the boundaries of selfhood and otherness. The dialogical self, then, is one among a plurality of interdependent consciousnesses (Bakhtin, 1986: 106; 1990: 90–7), an ongoing dialogue between rather than within interlocutors, real or imagined.

The subject participates and experiences itself becoming in the world as 'I-for-myself' (Bakhtin, 1990: 10) or 'spirit' (*dukh*) (1990: 32). Because the I-for-myself is a process in flux, it derives its capacity for self-perception and self-definition only through relations with others, thus existing also as 'I-for-others' (1990: 32). The other's 'outsidedness' to the subject gives the former an 'excess of seeing', however relative and contingent, which is inaccessible to the I-for-myself (1990: 22–4). The outsidedness of the second consciousness thus gives the subject a finalizing, valuative vision or 'rhythm' of itself. The subject is bestowed with a 'given, presently existing' inner whole, 'constituted in terms of aesthetic categories; the I-for-others is the I-for-myself the way it looks *from outside*, in the other' (1990: 100). While we watch for our reflection on the consciousness of the other, self-awareness requires the duality of rhythm (soul; I-for-others) and loophole (spirit; I-for-myself).

Because the self is liminal, 'becoming' on the boundaries of self and other, identity and difference, otherness cannot be mastered and overcome in the search for self; the voices of others are equal partners in self-dialogues. The dialogical viewpoint thus rejects the Enlightenment's 'identity thesis' in favour of the 'difference thesis' where, following Derrida, '[p]resence is built on absence; identity on difference' (Sampson, 1993: 90). As Sampson writes, 'concealed within any positive statement of meaning is an absent, other meaning, suggesting that difference rather than identity is necessary to our understanding' (1993: 89). 'Essential' identities defined through mastery of difference are unveiled as monologic voices of domination. Because the self is on the boundary of, and hence defined through relations of identity and difference, self and other, addressor and addressee, the 'ownership' of selves and their 'traits' is but a political fiction.

Dialogism moreover rejects the Western bias towards synthesis, order and progress by privileging the co-articulation or *dialogue* of centripetal and centrifugal forces. Recast as the multiplicity of inner voices or 'microdialogues' (Bakhtin, 1973 [1929]: 59), the dialogical self knows itself through the responses of real, imagined, historical and generalized others. Self-stories are double-voiced; words are directed at both an object of speech and the words of the other, or the voices that resonate from our multiple 'conversational communities' (Sampson, 1993: 125). Selfhood moreover is multi-voiced, populated by the voices or 'I-positions' of competition and cooperation, conflict and consensus. Where narrativists, for example, interpret inconsistency in the life story as an interpretive problematic to be overcome (see Maines, 1993), dialogism understands consistency and inconsistency as equal dialogical partners, co-defining one another through relations of interdependence.

Thus the dialogic alternative gives equal status to forces of synthesis and dispersion, order and disorder, as voices in dialogue on the boundary of self and other, voices made meaningful through relations of identity and difference in situated dialogical contexts. If dominant discourses favour particular ideals, they do so by constructing their opposing forces as 'serviceable others' (Sampson, 1993: 4): the other (incoherence, fragmentation, fiction, multiplicity) is defined so as to construct the desired identity of the ideals, and as a result the status of the other as a unique, separate standpoint is denied. By reconciling opposing tendencies, traditional narrative theory turns dispersion into synthesis and the unintelligible into coherence through the monologues of authorship. Dialogism, on the other hand, recasts the 'ideals' and their oppositional counterparts as equally viable value-orientations (Sampson, 1993: 22), deconstructing self-celebratory monologues to identify silenced voices and 'the nature of their otherness' (Sampson, 1993: 14). By re-conceiving narratives as active dialogues, relationship is privileged over authorship; the multiple centres of organization of the self and their relationships, pursuing on the boundaries of self and other, identity and difference, may be celebrated rather than silenced, thus ensuring the dynamic tensions among opposing forces which in turn enable the dialogical self to be unfinalizable, emergent and ongoing (Bakhtin, 1973 [1929]: 26).

Because the voices of the self populate multiple story-worlds, because self stories are multi-voiced, and because the self functions 'as a multiplicity of positions that are located at different places in an imaginal landscape' (Hermans and Kempen, 1993: 58), linear or modernist narrative *form* is also unsustainable as an ethical mode of self-intelligibility. In his seminal text *Narrative Knowing and the Human Sciences* (1988), Polkinghorne locates meaning in a typically modernist narrative form: life stories have beginnings, relations of cause and effect, and intelligible conclusions. Narrative meaning, derived from emploted relationships among events, gives 'form to the understanding of a purpose to life' (Polkinghorne, 1988: 11). The narrative scheme 'displays purpose and direction in human affairs and makes individual human lives comprehensible as wholes' (1988: 18). The plot generates integration and cohesion; logical continuity renders the story intelligible. Narratives seek internal coherence, and conclusions must be acceptable to the reader.

The dialogic/narrative model, on the other hand, draws on advances in literary criticism and postmodern novelistic literature which expand the possibilities for storied selfhood. The 'architectonic novel' (Spencer, 1971, in Hermans and Kempen, 1993), for example, abandons traditional narrative, defined as the continuous, coherent ordering of events from the perspective of a single author, in favour of the juxtaposition of multiple plots, time–space chronotopes and voices. Linearity and order are disrupted as the subject is exposed from multiple perspectives; oppositional value-orientations co-exist, producing dynamic tensions which seek neither resolution nor assimilation. The rhythm of combined fragments is privileged over narrative coherence; separateness is privileged over unity, multiplicity over singularity, discontinuity over continuity. Taken to the self-narrative, the model of the architectonic novel illuminates the dialogical movement of separate, contrasting I-positions. It privileges multi-voicedness, the dialogical relationships among different voices, and rejects the myth of the absolute, omniscient author, the myth of the unified self narrating accounts from a centralized position.

To examine the implications of dialogism for narrative identity theory in greater detail it is useful to consider the ideals of unity, coherence and authenticity. Situating each in an historical context, I will attempt to bring forth the contingency of these 'traits', critique the limitations of the narrativist focus on centripetal tendencies, and reconstruct these value-orientations as equally viable voices in the ongoing dialogics of selfhood.

The Ideals of Personhood Reconsidered

The Unity of Personal Identity

Narrativists argue that the self is unified by an integrated set of 'strong evaluations' or conceptions of the good (Taylor, 1989), by beliefs, values and commitments (White, 1991), and/or by life plans, projects, and moral careers (Greenwood, 1994). Dis-unification is attributed to the lack of an integrative narrative or insufficient opportunities for narration, or to the postmodern condition of 'social saturation', the unprecedented plethora of possible ways of being and competing ideological frameworks by which we render the self intelligible. My concern with these causal explanations is the extent to which they depend on the implicit, largely modernist and peculiarly Western assumption of an enduring and stable core self which *can* be threatened by narrative fragmentation or particular forms of social organization. The dialogical challenge is to expose the monologue of centripetal superiority as an interpretative discourse constructed in the service of Western domination, and to unveil the construction of the centrifugal 'other' as a *serviceable* other. By privileging the integration of value-orientations, theories of narrative self construct fragmentation and contradiction as conditions to be overcome. Yet it is by defining centrifugal tendencies as forces to discipline and manage that centripetal forces gain their definition and privileged status. If we define fragmentation on its own terms, articulate its unique and equally viable standpoint in the dialogics of self, and if we destabilize the implicit standard of comparison for the judgement of integration, we might be better positioned to understand the 'nature of its otherness'.

If forces of dispersion are symptomatic of the postmodern social condition, the dialogical self may be that of an historically unprecedented multiplicity of voices; if we seek in self-narratives the logics of synthesis and order and reify the ideal of mastery of dispersion, we risk silencing the dynamic tensions which, from the dialogical perspective, ensure the unfinalizability of selfhood.

The Authenticity of Personal Identity

Early modern concepts of the 'true' self were dominated by essentialist definitions of identity, the Cartesian model of self-awareness as the foundation of all knowledge, and the Rousseauesque project of discovering the enduring, authentic character of the self. The source of the true self shifted from the divine will of God in the Middle Ages to conscious acts of self-reflection with the Enlightenment. Secularization, rationalization, and the ideology of individualism have contributed to the dominant contemporary Western belief that the true self resides within, and is hence the possession and responsibility of the person.

Yet the collapse of realism and essentialism and the destabilization of categorical oppositions such as fact and fiction render the belief in, and search for, an innate, inherent and essential self suspicious. Self-deception is no longer defined by the lack of commitment to the self with which one was born, the essential self awaiting realization and fulfilment. The contemporary Western project is the search for situational authenticity; for the right and ethical obligation to define and be recognized for who one authentically is in a particular life-historical context. The catch-phrase of motivationalist Anthony Robbins is symptomatic: 'The past does not equal the future': we believe that authentic self-discovery is not dependent upon but is inhibited or limited by our past beliefs of who we 'really were'. This is not to suggest that the authenticity of identity has declined in social importance. Goldstein and Rayner (1994) suggest that the success (or demise) of social movements is based largely on the success or failure to gain public recognition of authentic identity. While movements may gain material concessions, the denial of authentic identity is murderous and the involuntary surrender of authentic identity is 'a kind of spiritual suicide' (Goldstein and Rayner, 1994: 368). Moreover, Taylor (1989) observes an historically unprecedented desperation and urgency in the search for authentic identity; our fear of the meaningless life defines our age and feeds the cultural desire for the legitimation of our claims to authenticity, now affirmed in our methods of daily living (1989: 14). Others argue that postmodernity reduces the availability of shared measures for identity claims; collectively honoured and valued definitions by which the authenticity of identity may be judged dissolve, and individuals bear greater responsibility and experience greater difficulty in claiming, gaining, and sustaining recognition for their authentic character (Goldstein and Rayner, 1994).

Thus, where Rousseau's project of reflexivity was meant to uncover the authentic self, reflexivity in late modernity appears to destabilize the self; self-reflexivity is overpopulated by the mediation of cultural information, thus evoking a continuous reformulation of the self. The outcome is not the discovery of the essential or authentic self, but is the 'Mutable' self or the Protean person, the 'self that has no permanent essence but continuously reinvents itself' (Goldstein and Rayner, 1994: 370).

Goldstein and Rayner question whether the plethora of social dialogues which give birth to continual self re-definition render the possibility of an authentic, core self obsolete (1994: 376). Those who believe in the possibility of a true, authentic self and mourn its loss with the passing of modern social order share a belief in the authenticity of personal identity as a human ideal, a universal right and an ethical obligation. Reichmann's (1985) version of the philosophy of the person, for instance, suggests that the permanence and stability of the 'I' allows us to identify ourselves as separate from our actions; the self in this account is necessarily stable, core or authentic. Belief in the authentic self also informs existential sociology of self, where authentic communication alone expresses the 'true' self and identity masks worn in inauthentic interactional performances may hide and protect the authentic existential self. Dramaturgical sociology explains the self as an expression in performances of daily life, and holds that we identify more or less with the roles we play. Behind our roles we perceive a true or 'truer' self, which may be expressed when we embrace roles that coincide with who we believe ourselves to 'really be'. In his version of narrative-identity theory, McIntosh (1994) argues for a theoretical distinction between the self we believe, hope and fear ourselves to be, and the person one actually is, or the 'objectively real' self seen from the perspective of the lifeworld (1994: 3). Authenticity, in this discourse, is defined by the dichotomy of subject and object, where the distortion of the self is a function of discrepancies between the two visions of who one may authentically be.

The criteria of authenticity for most narrativists inhere not in the ability of selves to adopt the perspective of the other, but in the terms set forth by Taylor (1989): authenticity inheres in the continuity of personal commitment to projects, evaluations, beliefs and commitments. The fictional or inauthentic self is insincere, deceptive or distorted, or, more often, is said to lack the narratives which would permit the realization of authentic self-expression.

From the relational view, the ideal of authenticity is difficult to sustain; from the dialogical perspective it is ethically suspicious. If individuals neither author nor own narrative selfhood, can the constellation of shared, situated narrative practices produce a storied self authentic to any one individual? How can there be a 'really me' when selfhood is an ongoing dialogue? To pose this question is not to deny that we experience ourselves as more or less authentic, that we feel ourselves to put on 'acts' to impress or otherwise influence others (and our selves), or that we interpret our relations with others to allow or inhibit the expression of our 'true' and 'truer' selves. It is meant as a point of departure for a theory of the self as enacted through multiple centres of organization and multiple systems of valuation. Because 'authenticity' from the dialogic perspective is defined by the ability of voices to retain and articulate their own particular specificity

(Sampson, 1993), authenticity is threatened not when the 'true' or 'truer' self or primary group associations are denied, but when forces of domination silence one or more of the dialogical partners. Cultural models whose logics dictate the resolution of disequilibrium and reconciliation among opposing valuations and systems of belief are, in dialogical terms, a greater threat to 'authentic' being than are the centrifugal forces of multiplicity and contradiction. The ethics of authenticity hinge not on the overcoming of these forces, but on the opportunities for their legitimation and articulation.

We have thus moved from definitions of authentic identity grounded in the inherent, essential and pre-social self to situational authenticity couched in the logics of self-change. I have suggested that the latter remains embedded in a cultural desire for singularity, non-contradiction and integration of identity; and I have drawn on the dialogicity of selfhood to redefine authenticity as the equal viability of and respect for both the centripetal and centrifugal voices of the self. Let us briefly consider a final ideal: the coherence of personal identity.

The Coherence of Personal Identity

The significance of a dialogical alternative for narrative theories of the self is most notably the deconstruction of Western monologues of centripetal superiority in favour of dialogical tensions among equally viable opposing forces of synthesis and dispersion. The centripetal bias of theories of the narrative self is further apparent in the definition of incoherence of identity as a state to be overcome through the production of narrative intelligibility. Dominant in the narrative model is the celebration of linear and progressive self-clarification, where coherence is an interpretive project structured by the organizing properties of narrative. Yet again, if the self is populated by multiple opposing voices or I-positions, each with unique value-orientations, narrative coherence is attained by virtually silencing the forces of incoherence and reconciling contradiction. Rather than approach coherence as an ideal 'state' achieved through narrative organization, the dialogical perspective understands coherence as a possible temporary outcome and as a resource in situated dialogues, and incoherence as the immutable defining presence of intelligibility.

Conclusion

Narrative and dialogical theories of the self are both premised on the principles of relationality, yet each takes a unique point of departure. While both are premised on the narrative mode of intelligibility and the textuality of meaning, interpretation, agency and suffering, theories of the narrative self are particularly wed to the ideals of modern Western personhood. Characteristics of selfhood are neither innate nor ideal types; once situated in the ongoing dialogics of historical antecedents and intellectual climates, ideals of the self are revealed as contingent, politicized textual constructs. The dialogic alternative situates these ideals in relation to their equal dialogic partners, to deconstruct the incoherent in coherence, the dispersion in unity and integration, the disarray in order. Further, where the theory of narrative identity seeks the structuring properties of the self in narrative organization, dialogism seeks the liminal self: the self on the boundary of identity and difference.

I have suggested that the model of narrative identity too often reifies the unattainable ideals of order and the centripetal. Integration, authenticity and coherence are privileged over fragmentation, dispersion and incoherence. Narratives are taken as the source of unification, integration, order and synthesis of the self, rendering selfhood intelligible and coherent. Those who posit a postmodern condition of social saturation and the resulting escalation of possible ways of being are particularly wed to the idea that self-narratives function to organize and reduce the potential meanings of selfhood.

Dialogism discloses the ideal of personhood in Western culture – the centralized self in equilibrium, in mastery and control of the environment – as an historically contingent cultural and political bias. It challenges the biases which privilege our taken-for-granted conceptions of order and coherence by decentring 'order' from the singularity to the multiplicity of voices and by giving equal status to centripetal and centrifugal forces. The dialogical-narrative self is not a fixed text, but is a multitude of situated, dialogic re-interpretations, re-ordered with each telling and hearing in changing social contexts. Order and coherence cannot reside in the mind of the rational human agent, but rather must be sought within and between the textual interplays of dialogic voices. The dynamics of situated dialogics call for the equal treatment of both synthesis and fragmentation; integration, authenticity and coherence are understood as highly contingent movements, as indebted to the forces of dispersion and fragmentation as to synthesis and integration.

Dialogism does not deny that narratives configure particular ways of being; rather, it is critical of narrativists' bias towards a centripetal configuration as functional for personal identity. The dialogic perspective suggests that narratives pursue on the boundaries of centripetal, ordering tendencies and centrifugal forces of dispersion and incoherence. Selfhood is enacted liminally, on the boundaries of self and other, identity and diversity, good and evil, instinct and reason, and so on, with each dialogic partner defining the other through varying degrees of situational power (Sampson, 1993). From this perspective a narrative theory which privileges one partner in dialogue over another as more 'functional' for personal identity is unsustainable.

Note

1 Self-society dialectics emerged in the late nineteenth and early twentieth centuries in reaction to the ideology of liberalism. It was most notably the Romantic movement and the German expressionists who, while retaining a self-celebratory stance, stressed the interdependence of self and society for creativity, passion and the cultivation of the inner self. Without

fully negating the possibility of a divine plan, Goethe for instance emphasized the worldly unfolding and social mediation of the self (see Hinchman, 1990).

References

Bakhtin, Mikhail M. (1973 [1929]) *Problems of Dostoevsky's Poetics*. Ann Arbor, MI: Ardis.
Bakhtin, Mikhail M. (1981) *The Dialogic Imagination: Four Essays by M.M. Bakhtin*. Ed. M. Holquist. trans. C. Emerson and M. Holquist. Austin, TX: University of Texas Press.
Bakhtin, Mikhail M. (1986) *Speech Genres and Other Late Essays*. Eds C. Emerson and M. Holquist. Trans. V.W. McGee. Austin, TX: University of Texas Press.
Bakhtin, Mikhail M. (1990) *Art and Answerability: Early Philosophical Essays by M.M. Bakhtin*. Eds M. Holquist and V. Liapunov. Trans. and notes V. Liapunov. Austin, TX: University of Texas Press.
Bandlamudi, Lakshmi (1994) 'Dialogics of understanding self/culture', *Ethos*, 22 (4): 460–93.
Brown, David D. (1994) 'Discursive moments of identification', *Current Perspectives in Social Theory*, 14: 269–92.
Bruner, Jerome (1987) 'Life as narrative', *Social Research*, 54 (1): 11–32.
Butler, Joseph (1975 [1736]) 'Of personal identity', in John Perry (ed.), *Personal Identity*. Berkeley, CA: University of California Press.
Cahill, Spencer E. (1986) 'Language practices and self definition: the case of gender identity acquisition', *The Sociological Quarterly*, 27 (3): 295–311.
Cascardi, Anthony J. (1992) *The Subject of Modernity*. Cambridge: Cambridge University Press.
Denzin, Norman K. (1989) Interpretive Biography. Sage University Paper Series on Qualitative Research Methods, Vol. 17. Beverly Hills, CA: Sage.
Deutsch, Eliot (1992) 'The comparative study of the self', in Leroy S. Rounder (ed.), *Selves, People, and Persons: What Does it Mean to be a Self?* Notre Dame, IN: University of Notre Dame Press.
Fox, Christopher (1988) *Locke and the Scriblerians: Identity and Consciousness in Early Eighteenth-Century Britain*. Berkeley, CA: University of California Press.
Gergen, Kenneth J. (1991) *The Saturated Self: Dilemmas of Identity in Contemporary Life*. New York: Basic Books.
Giddens, Anthony (1986) 'Action, subjectivity, and the constitution of meaning', *Social Research*, 53 (3): 529–45.
Goldstein, Jonah and Rayner, Jeremy (1994) 'The politics of identity in late modern society', *Theory and Society*, 23 (3): 367–84.
Greenwood, John D. (1994) 'A sense of identity: prolegomena to a social theory of personal identity', *Journal for the Theory of Social Behaviour*, 24 (1): 25–46.
Gregg, Gary S. (1991) *Self-Representation: Life Narrative Studies in Identity and Ideology*. New York: Greenwood Press.
Hanson, Karen (1986) *The Self Imagines: Philosophical Reflections on the Social Character of Psyche*. New York and London: Routledge & Kegan Paul.
Harding, Sandra (1986) *The Science Question in Feminism*. Ithaca, NY and London: Cornell University Press.
Herman, David (1994) 'On the semantic status of film: subjectivity, possible worlds, transcendental semiotics', *Semiotica*, 99 ($1/2$): 5–27.
Hermans, Hubert J.M. and Kempen, Harry J.G. (1993) *The Dialogical Self: Meaning as Movement*. San Diego, CA: Academic Press.
Hinchman, Lewis P. (1990) 'The idea of individuality: meaning, and political significance', *Journal of Politics*, 52 (3): 759–81.
Holland, Ray (1977) *Self and Social Context*. London: Macmillan.
Holzner, Burkart (1978) 'The construction of social actors: an essay on social identities', in Thomas Luckmann (ed.), *Phenomenology and Sociology*. New York: Penguin Books.

Jones, R. Kenneth (1978) 'Paradigm shifts and identity theory: alternation as a form of identity management', in Hans Mol (ed.), *Identity and Religion: International, Cross-Cultural Approaches*. London: Sage.

Lao Tzu (1963 [sixth century BC]) *Tao Te Ching*. Trans. D.C. Lau. London: Penguin.

Lauritzen, Paul (1994) 'The self and its discontents: recent work on morality and the self', *Journal of Religious Ethics*, 22 (1): 189–210.

Locke, John (1964 [1690]) *An Essay Concerning Human Understanding*. Ed. A.D. Woozley. Cleveland, OH: Meridian Books.

Locke, John (1975 [1694]) 'Of identity and diversity', in John Perry (ed.), *Personal Identity*. Berkeley, CA: University of California Press.

McAdams, Dan P. (1993) *The Stories We Live By: Personal Myths and the Making of the Self*. New York: William Morrow.

McCall, Catherine (1990) *Concepts of Person: An Analysis of Concepts of Person, Self and Human Being*. Aldershot: Avebury.

McIntosh, Donald (1994) 'Language, self, and lifeworld in Habermas's theory of communicative action', *Theory and Society*, 23 (1): 1–33.

Madell, Geoffrey (1981) *The Identity of the Self*. Edinburgh: Edinburgh University Press.

Maines, David R. (1993) 'Narrative's moment and sociology's phenomena: toward a narrative sociology', *The Sociological Quarterly*, 34 (1): 17–38.

Margolin, Uri (1995) 'Changing individuals in narrative: science, philosophy, literature', *Semiotica*, 107 ($^1/_2$): 5–31.

Marshall, Barbara L. (1991) 'Re-producing the gendered subject', *Current Perspectives in Social Theory*, 11: 169–95.

Mauss, Marcel (1985 [1938]) 'A category of the human mind: the notion of person; the notion of self', in Michael Carrithers, Steven Collins and Steven Lukes (eds), *The Category of the Person: Anthropology, Philosophy, History*. Cambridge: Cambridge University Press. pp. 1–25.

Noonan, Harold W. (1989) *Personal Identity*. London and New York: Routledge.

Oliver, Harold H. (1992) 'The relational self', in Leroy S. Rounder (ed.), *Selves, People, and Persons: What Does it Mean to be a Self?* Notre Dame, IN: University of Notre Dame Press. pp. 37–51.

Organ, Troy Wilson (1987) *Philosophy and the Self: East and West*. Selinsgrove: Susquehanna University Press.

Parfit, Derek (1975 [1971]) 'Personal identity', in John Perry (ed.), *Personal Identity*. Berkeley, CA: University of California Press.

Plummer, Ken (1990) 'Herbert Blumer and the life history tradition', *Symbolic Interaction*, 13 (2): 125–44.

Polkinghorne, Donald E. (1988) *Narrative Knowing and the Human Sciences*. New York: State University of New York Press.

Rappaport, Julian (1993) 'Narrative studies, personal stories, and identity transformation in the mutual help context', *Journal of Applied Behavioral Science*, 29 (2): 239–56.

Reichmann, James B. (1985) *Philosophy of the Human Person*. Chicago: Loyola University Press.

Reid, Thomas (1975a [1785]) 'Of identity', in John Perry (ed.), *Personal Identity*. Berkeley, CA: University of California Press.

Reid, Thomas (1975b [1785]) 'Of Mr. Locke's account of our personal identity', in John Perry (ed.), *Personal Identity*. Berkeley: University of California Press.

Rosenwald, George C. and Ochberg, Richard L. (eds) (1992) *Storied Lives: The Cultural Politics of Self-Understanding*. New Haven, CT: Yale University Press.

Rouner, Leroy S. (ed.) (1992) Selves, People, and Persons: *What Does it Mean to be a Self?* Notre Dame, IN: University of Notre Dame Press.

Sampson, Edward E. (1993) *Celebrating the Other: A Dialogic Account of Human Nature*. Boulder, CO: Westview Press.

Somers, Margaret R. (1994) 'The narrative constitution of identity: a relational and network approach', *Theory and Society*, 23 (5): 605–49.

Strauss, Anselm (1995) 'Identity, biography, history, and symbolic representations', *Social Psychology Quarterly*, 58 (1): 4–12.

Taylor, Charles (1989) *Sources of the Self: The Making of the Modern Identity*. Cambridge, MA: Harvard University Press.

Todorov, Tzvetan (1984) *Mikhail Bakhtin: The Dialogical Principle*. Manchester: Manchester University Press.

Valverde, Mariana (1991) 'As if subjects existed: analysing social discourses', *Canadian Review of Sociology and Anthropology*, 28 (2): 173–87.

White, Stephen L. (1991) *The Unity of the Self*. Cambridge, MA: MIT Press.

Zurcher, Louis A. Jr. (1977) *The Mutable Self: A Self-Concept for Social Change*. Beverly Hills, CA and London: Sage.

4

CULTURE AS DIALOGUE

Michael Mayerfeld Bell

What is culture? This is a question we have answered many ways. Culture is 'the total way of life of a people'; the 'webs of significance' we ourselves spin; 'an ensemble of texts, themselves ensembles, which the anthropologist strains to read over the shoulders of those to whom they properly belong'; a 'toolkit' of practices, stocked with 'the publicly available symbolic forms through which people express and experience meaning'; a 'perspective', a 'standpoint', an 'interpretive community'. Ways, webs, texts, practices, toolkits, perspectives, standpoints, and communities: Powerful metaphors all.[1] Or, to go back further, culture is *culture* – that which we create out of nature – the metaphor upon which the others comment, the unmoved metaphor at the end of the line.[2]

I would like to suggest another metaphor for this metaphor, not as a replacement for these others but as another comment on the original, as well as a comment on the other comments. My point is not to argue that I have solved the problem of culture and have hit upon the perfect description of what it is, a description capable of sinking all other contenders, triumphantly blowing them out of the waters of theory. As will become apparent, such a militaristic conception of scholarship would be appallingly contradictory, not just to what scholarship ought to be but also to the argument about culture I want to make. Moreover, no metaphor represents experience perfectly; all metaphors are stretched. Culture is ways, webs, texts, practices, toolkits, perspectives . . . is it really? Perhaps a melting-pot, a salad bowl, a landscape, a technology . . . perhaps. The only perfect representation of a thing is the thing itself, which is no representation at all. Although metaphors never capture experience perfectly, we would have no way to relate and to reflect without them.[3] Relation and reflection require representation, and probably the best solution to the necessary distortion that this involves is to have many ways of representing the same experience, many metaphors or understanding it, comments upon comments upon comments.

In this spirit of commentary I make the central comment of this chapter: that it is also useful to consider culture as dialogue.

The metaphor of dialogue is broadly applicable to the question of culture, I believe. Or should I say the *questioning* of culture – and the possibility of studying it – which is so current today. There are the objectivist critiques. Is culture a thing, stable, isolatable, describable, categorizable, a social force?

Can anyone, in their straining, ever catch more than a glimpse of the Other's text, a text which the Other never displays all of and constantly changes besides? And if it isn't a thing, how can (and why should) a social science study it? Then there are the subjectivist critiques. Can the study of culture ever be anything more than the culture of study, one more interested perspective peering out from its fortress of tradition and prison of institutions? Isn't it rude – or worse – to read over someone's shoulder, moreover to interpret and to critique, and thus necessarily to judge, what it is that one sees there? What right, therefore, do we who study culture professionally, we cultural experts, have to say and write what we do – and get paid for it?

These are the by-now familiar, polarizing, and perhaps tedious contemporary contentions with culture. Anthropologists in recent years have been wallowing in the subjectivist contentions, leading to a genre of work which David Chioni Moore (1994: 354) recently termed 'anthro-apology'. Sociologists, with their greater investment in a self-conception of themselves as practitioners of positive science, have tended to respond to such relativisms with more impatience and less hand-wringing. ('When I hear the word relativism I reach for my ...' Parsons? Weber? Marx?) Yet there has also developed of late a literature of socio-apology (for example, see Kleinman, 1993; Lofland, 1993; Snow and Morrill, 1993), a genre to which I, as a cultural sociologist, may be contributing now.

But I hope not. In the pages to come, I offer what I believe to be affirmative responses to these questions through a dialogic conception of culture. I sketch out three implications of this metaphor: first, for understanding cultural change; secondly, for understanding resistance to cultural change; and thirdly, for understanding the culture of study in which we study culture. I claim no special originality in doing so. A vigorous scholarly dialogue on dialogue has sprung up of late, and my thoughts have developed in interaction with the works of many, among them Martin Buber (1970 [1922]), Jürgen Habermas (1984, 1991), Patricia Hill Collins (1990), Don Levine (1995), but most especially Mikhail Bakhtin (1981, 1986, 1993) – an ongoing seminar whose participants have gathered from across the boundaries of literary theory, feminism, psychology, sociology, critical theory, and more. I make my arguments with their help, sometimes explicit, often implicit. And if my arguments do not settle these questions (as I very much suspect will be the case) I will not be dismayed, nor even displeased – as long as I have offered something worth talking about.

Dialogue and Cultural Change

Struggle as we might with our theories, it is very hard to avoid a conception of culture that treats it as, at least to some degree, a thing. Part of this reification is political. As a cultural sociologist, for example, one is committed to making the case that culture has some sociological consequence, that it is worthy of the attention of sociology – sociology as a way of looking at the world and as the profession in which one works. Culture therefore has to *be* something and to *do* something, something significant. But it is also an intellectual matter: we are seeking concepts to describe experience, and concepts must be of something. This something may not have existed before the concept, as social constructionism has taught us about trees falling in forests – at least it does not exist for *us*. Yet this something, once conceptualized, is nevertheless now some thing: a matter of interest. It is and therefore it does, for everything that is does something, if only take up conceptual space.

Reification, however, presents an immediate tension over the question of change. In order for something to be, it must have some kind of identifiable permanence and stability. This stability in turn makes it possible to identify a particular thing as a source of doing, as a teleological force initiating movement or resisting it, in good Newtonian fashion. How could we regard something as a force if the thing, and thus the force, were constantly changing? Thus, in order to say that culture is and does something, we find epistemological (and probably institutional) attractions in arguing for some kind of stability in it, leading to a degree of hammer-and-nails reification.

But say that we note that, as the hammer of culture comes down, it turns into a plumber's wrench before it strikes the nail's head. (The stuff we label 'culture' is, after all, often changing.) It would be hard to argue in such a case that the cultural hammer drove the nail, for it was no longer a hammer by the time it actually struck the nail's head. (An additional complexity would be if in the meantime the nail turned into a screw.) One common conceptual solution is to argue that the stable cause that drove the nail was neither the hammer nor the wrench, but rather whatever it was on the outside that did the swinging or created the occasion for it – the economy, say – turning culture into, at most, the kind of unstable epiphenomenon that many sociologists of culture, among others, have struggled to prevent it from becoming.

If we are to regard culture as significant, many cultural theorists have recognized, we ought to have more than an epiphenomenal argument. A favourite theoretical tactic is to find some way to lump the hammer and the wrench into the same category so that what appeared to be change in fact was not, or at least not much, such as Max Weber (1958 [1904–5]) ingeniously did almost a century ago in *The Protestant Ethic and the Spirit of Capitalism*. (In this wise and still hotly contested book, Weber suggests that the capitalist spirit of hard work and accumulation derives to a large degree from early Protestant asceticism.) After all, both a big hammer (the Protestant ethic) and a big wrench (the spirit of capitalism) can drive a nail (and probably, if you hit it hard enough, a screw as well). It is still the same basic 'strategy of action', as the practice view of culture would describe it.

Strong arguments for the significance of culture can be made with such an approach, emphasizing culture's stable influence across a period of change. But we should also consider the possibility that cultural *change* makes a teleological contribution to the dynamics of social life. It seems to me that we have been so worried about establishing culture as a thing, a matter worthy of scholarly attention, that we have emphasized its stability, its dull compulsions, over its social creativity. This emphasis may, among other things, lead us back to the epiphenomenal dilemma. Without an account of culture's creativity, we are left with no understanding of culture's origin, except as a response to that which is external to culture – which runs the serious risk of reducing culture to an epiphenomenon again, albeit an epiphenomenon with a bit of inertial Weberesque lag.

Take the practice view for culture, which I mention above, a valuable metaphor that many (myself included) have used. In her renowned article introducing the closely related 'toolkit' metaphor, Ann Swidler makes the case for culture's significance through its stability, not its dynamism – through the way culture as tradition and common sense 'provides a reper-toire of capacities' for 'strategies of action' during 'settled' periods of social life, and through the way culture as ideology shapes 'new habits of action' during 'unsettled' periods, until these too become tradition and common sense (Swidler, 1986: 279, 284). Change is either external to culture or unexplained. Swidler offers no account of what unsettles social life (could it be culture itself sometimes?), just the observation that life often is that way (as it certainly is), and suggests that 'ultimately, structural and historical opportunities determine' which of the new habits of action that somehow emerge 'succeed' – the epiphenomenal lag (Swidler, 1986: 284). Pierre Bourdieu's vision of culture as practice also externalizes cul-tural change. The *habitus*, the 'system of dispositions' which Bourdieu (1977 [1972], 1984) usefully suggests forms in response to our life experi-ences, primarily our early ones, gains its shape from the forces that pattern those experiences, primarily class – not from the *habitus's* own creativity. Berger (1995) presents a view of culture that runs along similar epiphe-nomenal lines (although Berger is more explicit about his epiphenomenal views).

Regarding culture as dialogue, however, can make the *creativity* of culture a topic for social analysis, at the same time as acknowledging culture's regularities and responses to external change. *Culture, in this view, is the conversations we have and which we expect to have with various people in various places at various times; it is also the conversations we have which we did not expect with these various people in these various places at these various times.* This definition is another reification, of course, as indeed any definition must be, but one that I believe is more conscious of itself as a reification for it acknowledges both the conversations we have which we expect and the conversations we have which we do not expect as equally cultural phenomena. Seeing culture as dialogue, as having its own internal dialectic of conversation, also allows us to acknowledge its some-times enchanting and sometimes upsetting, sometimes graceful and some-times awkward, sometimes rapid and sometimes glacial spontaneity. It allows us sometimes to see culture as collective agency in the face of fre-quently bad odds.

Conversation is never completely predictable. Imagine that you and I are talking together. I do not know what words I am going to say to you before I say them, at least not exactly. And even if my lines are well-studied, my performance will vary in ways that I cannot predict, in large part because I cannot predict exactly what your reaction and your response will be. The same must be true of your performance, however well-studied it may have been, however well you may have tried, and felt necessary, to constrain it ahead of time. I, at least, find myself constantly surprised, elated, depressed, and yet nearly always stimulated in some direction, degree, and manner by conversation. But conversation – whether it be verbal, written, tactile, or imagined – is not random. It will indeed have constraints and regularities; some we will be conscious of and some likely we will not. One can usually guess reasonably well what kind of conversation there will be before it begins, and one strategy of action each of us have is to choose our conversations in ways we think helpful. We each seek out particular kinds of conversations with particular action concerns in mind. And our hope will be that some kind of change results, some kind of collective agency – that we will be and will do something different than was the case beforehand.

Difference is central to the conversations we expect and hope to have. The various people with whom we converse at various times and places are different people in different places and times. Our conversations are with, between, among, and probably always about difference, at the same time that notions of difference imply similarities within their boundaries. Cultural understanding, as many have noted, depends upon drawing boundaries, constructing categories and differences (Erikson, 1966; Nippert-Eng, 1996; Zerubavel, 1991). But it also depends upon transcending those boundaries, as Erikson and Nippert-Eng have observed, both in order to find out where the boundaries are to begin with and to find out if the time has come when it makes sense to change them. In conversation, we discover our boundaries and transcend them as we interact with difference – that is, with each other – in a collective act of dialogic improvisation.

A degree of sameness, and a commitment to it, is also central to our cultural conversations. A word, as Mikhail Bakhtin and V.N. Voloshinov put it, is 'territory shared' (Voloshinov [Bakhtin], 1986 [1929]: 86).[4] Although the speaker's meaning may not be the same as the hearer's, and so too for the hearer's response, the hearer will *take into account* an understanding, however flawed, of the speaker's meaning in formulating a response. Correspondingly, the speaker will choose his or her words in ways that take into account an understanding, however flawed, of what the hearer's meanings might be – if in fact there is a dialogue taking place, and not, as Bakhtin put it, a monologue. *Taking into account the words of others is the principal phenomenological requirement of dialogic interaction.*[5] In a conversation, we do not say just anything about anything. We negotiate, we discuss, we mistake, we mislead, and we otherwise stumble to a jointly creative response to the conditions of our understandings and misunderstandings.

Dialogue and Resistance to Cultural Change

Dialogue – conversations with difference, through sameness – seems to me a fair description of social experience. What we spend most of our lives doing is talking to each other, or imagining such conversations in our minds, our writings, our art, and our other works. We speak, we argue; we shout, we explain; we harangue, we advise; we chat, we (as Midwesterners say) visit; we inquire, we interrogate. We consult, confer, counsel, confabulate. We discuss, debate, deny, dispute. We laugh, we cry; we smile, we frown. We quiz, query, question. We criticize. The list of words we have to describe conversation, and what goes on during it, is, of course, enormous, which suggests to me something about the significance it must evidently have for us. No great insight here. My argument, though, is that we ought to acknowledge the significance of this interactive experience of difference and sameness in our theories of culture.

If we are having a dialogue, however, for often, it must be recognized, this is not the case – at least not much of a dialogue. A striking thing about the conversation of culture is how often we lose our interest in dialogue and close ourselves off to it. The *problem of monologue* – the problem of speaking without taking into account what others have to say – ought as well to be central to cultural analysis, for reasons both theoretical and, as I'll come to, moral. We need to account for the conditions that impede dialogue, and that thereby impede culture as dialogue.

Let me immediately be cautious, though, about over-stating what I, following Bakhtin in the main, mean by monologue, and by implication dialogue. There is no pure monologue (at least among the living): all statements have some raconteur, however imagined, in mind. In Bakhtin's words, 'The word is born in a dialogue as a living rejoinder within it: . . . every word is directed toward an *answer* and cannot escape the profound influence of the answering word that it anticipates' (quoted in Morris, 1994: 76; original emphasis). Consequently, few speakers, if any, are completely impervious to the dialogic transcendence of their boundaries. As Bakhtin put it, in one of his most widely cited lines, 'There is neither a first word nor a last word and there are no limits to the dialogic context . . .' (1986: 170).

In other words, actual talk necessarily has the characteristics of both dialogue and monologue, in varying degrees. (Let not the very categories for describing the conditions of dialogic transcendence be impervious themselves to that transcendence!) And in the ultimate inescapability of dialogue, I will suggest below, there is reason for some considerable cultural hope.

But although dialogue is ultimately inescapable, we often try to escape it, and with some success. Let us consider the conversational positions that favour attempts to create monologue. It seems to me that there are three conversational positions which, when carried to their dichotomous extremes, are equally capable of shutting down dialogue: *objectivism*, *subjectivism*, and what I will ungraciously call *subjectivo-objectivism*. By objectivism I mean when someone says that my statement is the final and unalterable truth, proved through science, god, philosophy, economics, or some other external firmament: the last word on the subject. I don't need to take into account what you say. By subjectivism I mean when someone says that I have my perspective – my standpoint, my bias, my experience – which is just as good and authentic as any other, so I don't have to listen to or take into account yours. Everyone is entitled to their own opinion, after all. By subjectivo-objectivism I mean a monologic position which draws on both subjectivism and objectivism.[6] I have in mind here the person who claims, based solely on personal experience, to know the last word on the topic. The personal experience of others is simply wrong. Such a position gains the authenticity of subjectivism in combination with the foundationalism of objectivism. Objectivism (through denying difference), subjectivism (by saying difference is all there is), and subjectivo-objectivism (by saying that difference doesn't matter) each make further dialogue – further conversation with difference, through sameness – difficult and unlikely.

Much of the gripe with positivist science, of course, has been its objectivism, the way it established claims for truth that were institutionally removed from where other claims could be heard, or, perhaps better put, where they seemed worth listening to – worth taking into account. Few, I imagine, fully support that Olympian vision of science anymore. It may well be that few ever really did. But in any event, the institutional arrangements and the topics of conversation – the social conditions of talk – have changed such that the objectivist position is now scarcely tenable among those listening to what social scientists have to say, and it is not uncommon today to hear mention of 'the death of objectivism' (for example, Moore, 1994: 354). Such a pronouncement seems premature, however, especially in light of the constant little objectivisms of common conversation which, in certain social conditions of talk, could well become – and it seems to me often do become, or contribute to – the kind of conversation-stopping objectivism that positivism once was.

But critiques of objectivism seem to flip into its opposite, or so we fear (as is often the case with absolutisms). The study of culture, we imagine it being said, is no more than the culture of study, one more biased position, one more manifestation of power-knowledge, one more interested standpoint in a world of self-interest, no more valid and authoritative than any other. All standpoints are relative, and their standards of validity are incommensurable. Science is in no position to judge other cultural perspectives, nor are any cultural perspectives in a position to judge any others. Consequently, there is nothing to talk about, except that we evidently have nothing to talk about.

But we are, in fact, generally wary of such dichotomies – postmodern critiques of modernism and modernist critiques of postmodernism to the contrary notwithstanding. Hardly anyone says such starkly polarized things and really means them (except, perhaps, in graduate social theory courses and other social conditions conducive to exploring the extremes of human thought).[7] Yet although rarely is anyone so subjectivist, or so objectivist, we often worry that someone might be.[8]

This is a good sign. It is a sign of our general commitment to dialogue, despite all our own personal forays into little objectivisms and little subjectivisms, and sometimes larger ones, and despite all our suspicions that others are currently making similar forays. We apparently want to talk to each other, as Jürgen Habermas and Martin Buber have argued.[9] But given the frequency of larger degrees of objectivism and subjectivism, we are apparently as well often scared of talking to each other.

And what are we afraid of? *Critique* – another word for the spontaneous creativity of culture's dialogic improvisation. It seems fairly obvious why: critique is powerful stuff, capable of recasting the social conditions of talk even as those social conditions shape what is talked about within culture.

A paradox of culture is that, although critique often frightens us, it is only through critique that our fears are ever truly relieved.

Dialogue and the Culture of Study

What does all this suggest about how those who study culture should go about their business? My recommendation is that we see research itself as dialogue, as a public conversation with difference, through sameness – a conversation that is neither objectivist nor subjectivist (nor subjectivo-objectivist) but instead is dedicated to keeping the public conversation going by avoiding these tendencies for monologue. Let us study dialogue with dialogue. We need to drop our objectivist pretenses, though, if we have not done so already. The study of culture does indeed have its own culture of study. But admitting this does not necessarily plunge us into subjectivism. Instead, it provides an opportunity to widen our conversation with others, increasing the dialogue of knowledge, and thus avoiding subjectivism as well as objectivism.

The lack of a clear line between the culture we study and the culture in which we study is part of what makes the study of culture both theoretically and morally possible. There is a sameness here, through which we may come to talk about difference. But to say that all is difference, and that there is little possibility of, or right to, interchange with the culture of the Other, is to commit quite a large subjectivism, closing off the conversation we apparently often, and I believe rightly, want. Sociologists, anthropologists, historians, humanists, and others who study culture should not be rude about it, or authoritarian; we should not force people to participate in conversations they do not want to participate in. For one thing, if we do force them, chances are we really will do little better than to glimpse their texts – to glimpse what James Scott (1990) has called 'hidden transcripts' – little better than to hear forced conversation. My bet (if Jürgen Habermas (1984) and Martin Buber (1970 [1922]) are right) is that, given the opportunity, people will want to participate in the dialogue of culture, that they will want to talk to others, including scholars.[10] The critical interchange (what Anthony Giddens (1984) has called the 'double hermeneutic') that results will lead to a more informed study of culture, and thus a more informed culture.

Fredrik Barth puts it well:

> I am urging that we should not seek a fictitious cultural authority in others – we should engage them in an *interchange of knowledge and judgment*. That also means being willing to critique the validity, instrumentality, and morality of their ideas and actions and to being thus criticized ourselves. Our relativism should be located in the humility to learn and to engage within the contexts of knowledge and practice that frame our interaction with people – not in bracketing the other's ideas and behavior to remove them from moral, rational, and human judgment, thereby undermining the honesty of our engagement with them. (Barth, 1995: 67; added emphasis)[11]

The question becomes, then, how do we as scholars of culture conduct ourselves in a way that allows that interchange of knowledge and judgement to flourish in the least monologic way possible – how do we conduct ourselves in a way that allows mutual critique to flourish? In closing, I'll suggest a few guidelines for such flourishing.

Charles Darwin, I once read somewhere, suggested that science is different from everyday manners of thought in only one regard: science is done with more care. Now, I am not trying to add the flag of science to my cause here. Nor am I trying to burn it for my cause. The fight over possession and dispossession of this heavily laden word is one I will avoid. But I do believe that this idea of case may be helpful to the conception of research as dialogue I am advocating for the study of culture. What is distinctive about the study of culture is not its method: we study culture with culture, dialogue with dialogue. Rather, what is distinctive – in part, as I'll come to – is the care with which research is carried out, a care that, as professionals, some are paid to undertake. We professional scholars of culture therefore have time to talk through these things more than most other people do.

And if we are to study dialogue with dialogue, we must also commit ourselves to taking into account what others have to say. Let us be open, although not in an uncritical way, to their words. Call it consideration; it is considerate to consider what others have to say, as well as better scholarship. Recognizing that the basic intellectual methods of the study of culture are the same as that of culture itself is a good place to begin, for such a recognition invites others to listen and respond to the dialogue of scholarship, as well as inviting scholars to listen and respond to others. Participatory methods of research, such as those currently being worked out among extension sociologists at land grant universities and among others engaged in sociological practice, hold much potential for increasing the openness of scholarly dialogue (see, for example, Collins, 1986; Gaventa, 1993; Park et al., 1993; Stoecker and Bonacich, 1992). When farmers, dancers, street vendors, rap musicians, school teachers, and steel workers begin appearing regularly as co-authors, and perhaps even authors, in scholarly journals, and when our writings become more accessible and attentive to the concerns of these potential participants in our dialogue, these will be signs that the invitation to listen and respond has been sincere.

We need as well, it goes nearly without saying, to maintain the traditional commitment to honesty and responsibility in research if our scholarly conversations are to appeal to others, although I think we could be more straightforward about our politics than we have generally been in the past.

These, then, are five of the guidelines I would recommend for the flourishing of dialogue in research. The participants in this dialogue need to speak with care, consideration, honesty, straightforwardness, and a sense of responsibility (another form of speaking with care). Perhaps the most important reason to do so is because, when we speak in this way, we open up the conversational space for a sixth feature of dialogic talk: the collective agency represented by dialogic criticism – criticism that is careful, considerate, honest, straightforward, and responsible, and thus more likely to be seriously engaged rather than walled off through monologue.[12]

Who knows? The dialogic improvisation that results may help bring culture closer to research, and research closer to culture, as each takes the other into account. At least it seems to me to be worth trying. Indeed, I imagine most of those who participate in our studies would say this is the reason why the study of culture is worth trying in the first place.

I do not offer these guidelines as original or unusual thoughts. They seem to me part of the common culture of dialogue – the social conditions of dialogue – as opposed to the monologic cultures of objectivism, subjectivism, and subjectivo-objectivism. Indeed, I would be tempted to call these dialogic guidelines banal except for one stunning feature of them: the common disregard for the social conditions of dialogue within the community of scholarship. Care, consideration, honesty, straightforwardness, responsibility – few scholars would disagree with such homey ideals, I imagine. But where is the dialogue? Where is the participation? Why are most professional scholarly works as yet so uninviting – uninviting in tone, language, and sometimes even topic – even to other professional scholars, let alone potential lay scholars? Why are there so few serious efforts to involve those without PhDs as authors and co-authors, readers and co-readers (by which I mean people with whom we discuss what we read), in our books and journals? Why do we professional scholars regularly find ourselves a bit embarrassed when our neighbours and friends ask us about our work, unable to explain it in ways that are understandable and yet serious enough to warrant the salary and prestige we receive for doing it?

Perhaps it is because we have for so long constructed our scholarly institutions on more monologic grounds – on the belief that subjectivism (and subjectivo-objectivism) must be neutralized through objectivism – that we have not yet been able to confront fully these questions. We know now, however, that monologue in all its forms is, in the end, both impossible (as Bakhtin, among others, has helped make clear) and immoral (as Bakhtin, among others, has also helped make clear, and as we all generally believe, or so I gather from the ordinariness of the dialogic guidelines I suggest above).[13] And yet we continue to study dialogue with monologue, and thereby encourage the solidification of cultural discussion into the hardened atomic lumps of subject and object, laity and academy, local and expert, those who are spoken of and those who speak. This is all so clearly unnecessary, unwanted, and unpleasant.

So let's be done with it. In abandoning the objectivist's need to establish the study of culture as a different way of knowing, as different practices of knowledge, we need not fear that scholarship dissolves into the chaotic sea of mere opinion (and that professional cultural scholars will therefore all lose their jobs). Scholarship is opinion, of course, and its ways of knowing are not extraordinary, but it is nevertheless a distinctive kind of opinion, formed in a distinctive culture, a distinctive kind of conversation. The study of culture takes place within a culture of study. And what ought to be the prominent feature of the culture of study in which we study culture is the high degree of our commitment to creating the social conditions of dialogic talk.

The goal of a dialogic conception of culture is not mere discourse or conversational analysis (although it by no means rejects these methods of studying culture). What I am really talking about here is democracy.[14] A dialogical approach has, if nothing else, the not inconsiderable side-benefit of promoting what I believe to be the basic moral mission of cultural research: building the social conditions of a more democratic culture.

I hope, at least, that I have helped promote these conditions here. And I also hope that what I have said is not the last word on the subject. Rather, I hope what I have offered is the *next word*. The study of culture should aspire to nothing more, and to nothing less.

May the seminar never end!

Notes

This chapter about dialogue is as well the product of dialogue. I thank Laura Bell, Joshua Bell, Mitch Duneier, Mustafa Emirbayer, Sue Jarnagin, Diane Mayerfeld, Ernie Mayerfeld, Alan Rudy, Joan Weston, the staff at the Centre for Rural Economy of the University of Newcastle upon Tyne, and the students in my Fall 1995 Qualitative Methods and Spring 1996 Contemporary Sociological Theory classes for their contributions to whatever collective agency this chapter may represent. I dedicate this chapter to the memory of my friend Iverson Griffin, a great sociologist and a great conversationalist.

1 I quote, in succession, Kluckhohn (as cited in Geertz, 1973a: 4), Geertz (1973a: 5, claiming the mantle of Weber), Geertz (1973b: 452, claiming his own mantle this time), Swidler (1986: 273), and any of a variety of contemporary writers.

2 See Williams (1976) for the best overview of the origins of that most complex of cultural terms: 'culture' itself.

3 For enlightening discussions of the necessity of metaphor, see Lakoff (1987), Lakoff and Johnson (1980), and Johnson (1987).

4 This work is attributed by some to Bakhtin, but seems to me to be itself territory shared, the product of dialogue between Bakhtin, Voloshinov, and others in their intellectual circle in

the St Petersburg of the 1920s. For a review of the debate over the attribution of these works, see Dentith (1995).

5 Students of social theory will hear in here, correctly, echoes of – a taking into account of – Mead's idea of role-taking. Taking into account, however, is broader and more open to the possibility of our critical understanding of the other. Although we take the other's role in taking into account their words, we do not necessarily completely agree with those words or share in the projects which motivated them. Taking into account does not necessarily lead to the formation and solidification of a generalized other; there is a possibility for critique, the topic of the next section.

6 I thank my colleague Sue Jarnigan for pointing out this third monologic position and how very common it is.

7 The journal *Social Text* may be one such condition, as the Sokol affair suggests. But then, Sokol himself did not really mean what he wrote, as he himself has explained (Sokol, 1996).

8 Indeed, this is why Sokol's *Social Text* article generated such interest and controversy.

9 Habermas and Buber make closely related arguments from which I am borrowing liberally here. Habermas suggests that in addition to our instrumental interests, what Habermas (1984) terms 'action oriented toward success', we also have an interest in communicating with each other, what Habermas terms 'communicative action'. Buber (1970 [1922]) similarly distinguishes between 'I-it' attitudes and 'I-Thou' attitudes, arguing that humans have both objectifying tendencies in their relations with others as well as an 'instinct for communion' – pretty much the same point, albeit more essentialized by the term 'instinct' than sociologists typically feel comfortable with. Despite this essentialism, I find myself closer to Buber. Habermas's communicative action is in part an instrumentality oriented towards success; thus, it seems to me that communicative action and instrumental action cannot be separated in the way he suggests. My point is not all is interest; otherwise life would be a tautology. I argue elsewhere (Bell, 1998) for an interactive distinction between 'interests' and 'sentiments'. Communicative action pertains to our instrumental actions oriented towards both. Buber reserves the term dialogue for only what goes on in 'I-Thou' relations, making dialogue more or less synonymous with the 'I-Thou', but nevertheless an instrumentality – and yet not an objectivism, not an 'I-it'. I depart from Buber in arguing for the equally problematic status of subjectivism, what might be called, in Buber's terms, 'I-me' attitudes, and subjectivo-objectivism – 'I-me-it' attitudes.

10 See my discussion of Habermas and Buber in note 9.

11 Barth offers this dialogic thought as part of his argument for recognizing '*knowledge* as a major modality of culture' (1995: 66; original emphasis). My closely related focus is on the *interchange* of knowledge and judgement that Barth himself discusses, albeit more briefly.

12 I depart here from Habermas's model of the 'ideal speech situation' in that dialogue makes no requirement for setting aside interests or power relations. Rather, the central purpose of dialogic critique is to discuss our interests and power relations, and to engage us all in the project of democratic conversation, as I indicate below. Habermas's model seems paradoxically to propose the hypothetical overcoming of the necessity for democratic conversation in the creation of the very conditions that make it possible. A dialogic conception of critique suggests that, with difficulty and with commitment and with time, we can talk *about* power *across* power.

13 In this regard, also see Gardiner (1996) and Nielsen (this volume).

14 I thank Alan Rudy for pointing this out to me, and I thank Joan Weston for asking the question that led to this observation.

References

Bakhtin, Mikhail M. (1981) *The Dialogic Imagination: Four Essays by M.M. Bakhtin*. Ed. M. Holquist. Trans. C. Emerson and M. Holquist. Austin, TX: University of Texas Press.
Bakhtin, Mikhail M. (1986) *Speech Genres and Other Late Essays*. Eds C. Emerson and M. Holquist. Trans. V.W. McGee. Austin, TX: University of Texas Press.

Bakhtin, Mikhail M. (1993) *Toward a Philosophy of the Act*. Ed. M. Holquist. Trans. and notes V. Liapunov. Austin, TX: University of Texas Press.

Barth, Fredrik (1995) 'Other knowledge and other ways of knowing', *Journal of Anthropological Research*, 51 (1): 65–8.

Bell, Michael M. (1998) 'The dialectic of solidarity, or, why the lion spared Androcles', *Sociological Focus*, 31 (2): 181–99.

Berger, Peter (1995) *An Essay on Culture: Symbolic Structure and Social Structure*. Berkeley, CA: University of California Press.

Bourdieu, Pierre (1977 [1972]) *Outline of a Theory of Practice*. Cambridge: Cambridge University Press.

Bourdieu, Pierre (1984) *Distinction*. Trans. Richard Nice. Cambridge, MA: Harvard University Press.

Buber, Martin (1970 [1922]) *I and Thou*. New York: Scribner.

Collins, Patricia Hill (1986) 'Learning from the outsider within: the sociological significance of black feminist thought', *Social Problems*, 33 (6): s14–s32.

Collins, Patricia Hill (1990) *Black Feminist Thought: Knowledge, Consciousness, and the Politics of Empowerment*. Boston, MA: Unwin Hyman.

Dentith, Simon (1995) *Bakhtinian Thought: An Introductory Reader*. London and New York: Routledge.

Erikson, Kai T. (1966) *Wayward Puritans*. New York: Wiley.

Gardiner, Michael (1996) 'Alterity and ethics: a dialogical perspective', *Theory, Culture & Society*, 13 (2): 120–43.

Gaventa, John (1993) 'The powerful, the powerless, and the experts: knowledge struggles in an information age', in Peter Park, Mary Brydon-Miller, Budd Hall and Ted Jackson (eds), *Voices of Change: Participatory Research in the United States and Canada*. London and Westport, CT: Bergin and Garvey. pp. 21–40.

Geertz, Clifford (1973a) 'Thick description: toward an interpretive theory of culture', in *The Interpretation of Cultures*. New York: Basic Books. pp. 3–30.

Geertz, Clifford (1973b) 'Deep play: notes on the Balinese cockfight', in *The Interpretation of Cultures*. New York: Basic Books. pp. 412–53.

Giddens, Anthony (1984) *The Constitution of Society: Outline of the Theory of Structuration*. Cambridge: Polity Press.

Habermas, Jürgen (1984) *The Theory of Communicative Action*. Boston, MA: Beacon Press.

Habermas, Jürgen (1991) *Moral Consciousness and Communicative Action*. Cambridge, MA: MIT Press.

Johnson, Mark (1987) *The Body in the Mind*. Chicago: University of Chicago Press.

Kleinman, Sherryl (1993) 'The textual turn', *Contemporary Sociology*, 22 (1): 11–13.

Lakoff, George (1987) *Women, Fire, and Dangerous Things: What Categories Reveal About the Mind*. Chicago: University of Chicago Press.

Lakoff, George and Johnson, Mark (1980) *Metaphors We Live By*. Chicago and London: University of Chicago Press.

Levine, Donald N. (1995) *Visions of the Sociological Tradition*. Chicago: University of Chicago Press.

Lofland, Lyn H. (1993) 'Fighting the good fight – again', *Contemporary Sociology*, 22 (1): 1–3.

Moore, David Chioni (1994) 'Anthropology is dead, long live anthro(a)pology: poststructuralism, literary studies, and anthropology's "nervous present"', *Journal of Anthropological Research*, 50 (4): 345–65.

Morris, Pam (1994) *The Bakhtin Reader: Selected Writings of Bakhtin, Medvedev, and Voloshinov*. London: Edward Arnold.

Nippert-Eng, Christena E. (1996) *Home and Work: Negotiating Boundaries through Everyday Life*. Chicago: University of Chicago Press.

Park, Peter, Brydon-Miller, Mary, Hall, Budd and Jackson, Ted (eds) (1993) *Voices of Change: Participatory Research in the United States and Canada*. London and Westport, CT: Bergin and Garvey.

Scott, James C. (1990) *Domination and the Arts of Resistance: Hidden Transcripts*. New Haven, CT: Yale University Press.

Snow, David A. and Morrill, Calvin (1993) 'Reflections on anthropology's ethnographic crisis of faith', *Contemporary Sociology*, 22 (1): 8–11.

Sokol, Alan (1996) 'A physicist's experiment with cultural studies', *Lingua Franca*, May/June: 62–4.

Stoecker, Randy and Bonacich, Edna (1992) 'Why participatory research? Guest editor's introduction', *The American Sociologist*, 23 (4): 5–14.

Swidler, Ann (1986) 'Culture in action: symbols and strategies', *American Sociological Review*, 51: 273–86.

Voloshinov, V.N. (1986) *Marxism and the Philosophy of Language*. Trans. L. Matejka and I.R. Titunik. Cambridge, MA: Harvard University Press.

Weber, Max (1958 [1904–5]) *The Protestant Ethic and the Spirit of Capitalism*. New York: Charles Scribner.

Williams, Raymond (1976) *Keywords*. London: Fontana/Croom Helm.

Zerubavel, Eviatar (1991) *The Fine Line*. New York: Free Press.

5

BAKHTIN AND THE DIALOGIC OF SOCIOLOGY: AN INVESTIGATION

Dorothy E. Smith

If we begin as ourselves, active in the local settings of our living, we know sociology as we live it as its readers, writers, speakers and hearers. We are in the middle of it, in our reading in a library, in an office, at home. Our reading is active, responsive, attentive to possible uses, reactive to what we identify as error, anger sometimes, pleasure sometimes. It is also part of a course of action projecting into what comes next, teaching, writing, speaking at a conference. Writing social science, too, engages actively with the discourse; it references and is in dialogue with our reading. Explicit references are only a small part of it; it is deeply embedded in, and draws on, language uses as they come to hand already determined historically by their uses in multiple disciplinary sites. And beyond a particular discipline. For, of course, a social scientific language isn't clean. It is contaminated in multiple ways by its dialogue with the heteroglossia of the society. Sociology, for example, the discipline I know best, pulls language in to do its discursive work, language that trails with it a debris of meaning from its original site. Reciprocally, the language of sociological discourse goes out into the world and is taken over to do work other than the sociological discursive.

This chapter draws on Mikhail M. Bakhtin's theory of the novel, of language, and of speech genres to investigate discourse as social organization. It takes up this project as an investigation into sociology as a discourse because I know this discourse as an 'insider'; I am a participant; I know it as a local practice in my own life (and it is this that provides the main resource for this investigation). In this I move away from Foucault's (1972) conception of discourse, displacing the traditional 'unities' of the history of thought and substituting a conception of a field 'made up of the totality of all effective statements (whether spoken or written), in their dispersion as events and in the occurrence that is proper to them' (Foucault, 1972: 27). Brilliant as it is, it accredits the stasis of the text. Here, by contrast, I want to explore discourse as local practices in which people are active. In a sense, I want to lift the discourse off the page and pull it into life; I want to step outside the artifice of the text's stasis and rediscover discourse as a local organization of consciousness, as part of life.

In this I am helped by Bakhtin's differentiation between utterances in and of direct encounters between people and those mediated by texts. The latter he calls 'secondary speech genres' (Bakhtin, 1986a), a term that corresponds closely to Foucault's concept of 'discourse' and my usage of the latter term here. Bakhtin, however, is clear that speech genres 'originate' in 'spheres of activity'. Indeed, the concept of 'speech genres' reflects a textual separation of utterances from locally situated speakers and writers, hearers and readers participating in a social act. It is from the standpoint of the already 'in-text' that speech genre can be conceptualized as distinct from 'spheres of activity'. Secondary speech genres/discourses are also just as much spheres of activity as the speech genre of pickpockets as David Maurer (1981) has described it. Precipitated out of its textual security, sociology too is a sphere of activity. Sociologists are reading, writing, teaching, learning sociology; going to conferences and listening to sociologists; worrying about their sociological competitors; getting together in departments to defend the sociological enterprise against administrative marauders; participating in networks, orienting to leaders, deciding who's in and who's out. All this is not apart from its texts, for its texts are produced and read as part of these activities as local events coordinating the local practices of this sociologist here with those of others who appear to her only as the virtual participants of discourse.

The Dialogic of Social Science

I have written of texts as 'active' (Smith, 1990). I mean to see them as like a speaker in a conversation; one who is deprived of the possibility of hearing and responding to us, but nonetheless is present and active and 'speaking' to us in our reading. Our reading activates or operates the text. The artifice of the text detaches it from the local historicity of living. It was made by someone and read by someone in some definite setting, taking actual time in its reading and as a moment in a course of action or in dialogue with the intertextuality of a discourse. The texts of social scientific discourse are active in just this way.

Mikhail Bakhtin, in theorizing language and the novel, insists that the meanings of words have already been given determination as they have been used in multiple local settings; they enter local utterances trailing debris of meaning from the past, 'tasting', to use Bakhtin's (1981: 293) term, of the settings and intentions of their use elsewhere and when. The speaker has to work with the uses others before them have made of a word. They make a word 'their own' 'only when the speaker populates it with his [*sic*] own intention, his own accent, when he appropriates the word, adapting it to his own semantic and expressive intention' (Bakhtin, 1981: 294). Thus to speak or write is always essentially dialogic. A given utterance (Bakhtin's general term comprises both speech and writing) is intrinsically dialogic in its reworking of terms that have already been given determinate, if essentially transitory, meaning elsewhere in the utterances of others.

Bakhtin's theory of the novel builds on this notion of dialogue. Our every-day use of language appropriates meanings shaped in a multiplicity of set-tings. Hence meaning is not determined by individual intentions, but is social, a property of groups and relations. Speech genres arise in spheres of activity. Styles of usage are established among groups or forms of organiz-ation, professions, bureaucracy, trades, in social circles, social movements, generations, or regions, and so on. The novel's distinctive project draws such speech genres into a dialogue within the text. Its themes orchestrate diverse speech genres, bringing them into dialogic relations with one at different levels of the novel's organization. The diversity of voices in dia-logue is not only in the representation of different voices as speakers in the text, and in reported speech, but in hybrid sentences in which the author's voice draws in and subdues another's speech, in irony where the author's voice reflects on others, in movements between one voice and another in narrative sequences so that one reflects on (is in dialogue with) another.

In Bakhtin's thinking, the novel as a literary form is of, and embedded in, a society of diverse forms of speaking and writing. The many voices of the society are the resources on which the novel writer draws. The author relies on them and determines how they will be presented in the order of the text. Their dialogic forms and relations (tensions, conflicts, hierarchies) are at the author's disposal to be given determinate thematic value in the text created. The text creates a new dialogic ordering among the speech genres of the society.

Social science, too, is embedded in the heteroglossia of a diverse society. Sociology, the social science I know best, relies on and writes into its texts and hence draws into its discourse (as the text-mediated conversation among sociologists) a diversity of voices. It relies on the same resources as the novel does; indeed, sociologists have recognized this kinship though not knowing quite what to do with it. Covertly or explicitly, sociology draws into the discourse the social organization carried by the 'speech genres' of the people it has made its object or resource. It brings into the text not just a language but a linkage back into the 'sphere of activity' in which the lan-guage originated.

Imagine sociologists reading newspapers, magazines, novels, poetry, biographies, history, and watching television and going to see films, as well as doing our proper sociological reading. We participate in the multi-discoursed relations of ruling and are competent practitioners of the speech genre bearing the social organization of our place of work. There is constant leakage from the multi-voiced society in which we do our work into that work. More than that, however, is the discourse's necessary dialogue with its subject matter. It is full of voices, though often they are unrecognizable as such because before they even arrive at the threshold of sociology, they have already been transformed into textual products, for example, in the demographic data produced by the state census procedures or the legally mandated procedures for registering births, deaths, and marriages, and so forth. The dialogic of the interchange between state and people, who are the originals of the data, enters, sidling into the sociological text. Sociologists listen to conversations, record them and analyse them after converting them into texts as tape or video-recorded voices and then as written transcripts; we talk to people out there in what we call the 'real world' in contradistinction to the world we generate in our texts which is not real; we ask them questions and bring their answers home with us to build representations of those with whom we spoke which subdue them to the speech genres of the discourse. Some script the dialogue between sociology and respondent so that the latter's voice is heard only as a refraction of the sociological discourse; other methods, such as oral history or ethnography, expose sociologists to the native speaking of the society, leaving it for their later work, after they have brought their notes, recordings, etc., back to home or office, to subdue the original genres abstracted from their sphere of activity to the magisterial language of the discipline. Within sociological texts themselves we find traces and presences of diverse voices: passages quoted from interviews, passages from field notes giving accounts of what was said and done on a particular occasion, texts of a variety of kinds used for what the sociologist thinks they might be able to tell about what was on the other side of the text in the real world.[1] And, of course, recommendations and prescriptions for regulating these dialogues appear in the endless publications on methods of 'qualitative' research.

Sociology's dialogic has the potential for eroding from within the discursive coherence on which sociology's existence *as a discipline* depends. The speech genres drawn into its texts carry their own intentions, perspectives, experience and social organization – 'there are no "neutral" words and forms'. Hence language is 'a concrete heteroglot conception of the world' (Bakhtin, 1981: 293). In some sense, sociology is exposed to capture by ways of seeing and representing the world that are those of the speech genres other than its own. In such ways, sociological discourse is everywhere fractured with a diversity of voices that are methodologically regulated through formalized accounts of interviewing procedures, protocols provided for interviewers specifying the sociological script for their part in dialogue with respondents; procedures for coding that impose the disciplinary meaning on the original speech; and the like.

Sociology does not have a material technology to produce its differentiation from the world which is its object. Its tenuous separation is an achievement of its discursive order. In contrast with the novel, as Bakhtin theorizes it, its 'stylistics' rather than preserving the 'inserted genres' and the 'speech of characters' have been regulated theoretically so that the framing of diverse speech genres or voices that appear directly in the text is standardized discursively. Dialogue is subdued to the monologic or unitary language which Bakhtin contrasted with dialogized interplay of voices in the novel.

> Monologism, for Bakhtin, describes a condition wherein the matrix of ideological values, signifying practices, and creative impulses which constitute the living reality of language are subordinated to the hegemony of a single, unified

consciousness or perspective. Whatever cannot be subsumed under this transcendent consciousness is regarded as extraneous or superfluous. In other words,
monologism denies the 'equal rights of consciousness *vis-à-vis* truth (understood
abstractly and systematically)'. (Gardiner, 1992: 26)

Foundational to sociology are rules such as Durkheim's that specifically
suppress the presence of actual people (Smith, 1989). Durkheim's constitutional rules formulate for sociology 'types of conduct or thought [that] are
not only external to the individual but are, moreover, endowed with coer-
cive power, by virtue of which they impose themselves upon him, independent of his individual will' (Durkheim, 1964: 2). Constitutional rules of one
kind or another 'objectify' sociology's phenomena, producing a discursive
universe in which the people's utterances and other actions can appear as if
there were no actors. So far as sociology is concerned, there is an ambiguity
in Bakhtin's notion that monologism can displace dialogue,[2] since sociology's monologisms subdue or bury but do not do away with its necessary
dialogue with other voices. Nonetheless the notion of an *imposed* monologism suggests a regulatory device. It cannot be a particular author's since it
is a monologism standardized for a discourse rather than an individual and
adopted by individual participants of the discourse as a 'single, unified consciousness or perspective' (Gardiner, 1992: 26) that all know how to practise as their sociological competence. This device, I suggest, is sociological
theory.[3]
    Sociological theory regulates discourse. It subordinates the intentions
and perspectives of the original speakers to the 'order of discourse'
(Foucault, 1981), regulating the intra-textual dialogues, supplanting the
original intentions of the 'subjects' with an authorized system of discursive
intentions. It standardizes the local interpretive practices of its participants
and sets up a unitary organization of subject positions, determining how
the reading sociologist (or other reader) can enter into the dialogic
relations of the text. Its regulatory operation can be seen in a paper by
Hilary Graham and Ann Oakley (1981)[4] called 'Competing ideologies of
reproduction: medical and maternal perspectives on pregnancy'. Two
different and conflicting 'perspectives' on childbirth are described, that of
obstetrician and that of women in childbirth: 'Specifically, our data suggest
that mothers and doctors disagree on whether pregnancy is a natural or a
medical process and whether as a consequence, pregnancy should be
abstracted from the woman's life-experiences and treated as an isolated
medical event' (Graham and Oakley, 1981: 52). But obstetricians and
patients are not observed arguing with one another. The conflicts are
'between medical and maternal frames of reference' (Graham and Oakley,
1981: 56). The 'perspectives' or 'frames of reference' are constructed *in the
text* from rather different kinds of material: the obstetricians' perspectives
are inferred from observations obtained during consultations with patients;
[5] the mothers' perspectives, on the other hand, from extensive open-ended
interviews – the respondents speaking directly to the researcher. The
theory of ideology selects a lower-level set of categories, 'perspective',

'frame of reference', and so on, that transform the original stuff of observations and interviews into the stuff of ideology. Utterances recorded from the original setting are cited as 'manifestations' (Graham and Oakley, 1981: 56) of an underlying reality. What people said is thereby subdued to the monologism of sociological theory. Here then is the regulatory operation of theory in constituting for the discourse what Gardiner (1992: 26) calls the 'transcendent consciousness' (see above).

The 'work' of sociological theory in regulating the potentially destabilizing dialogues of sociological discourse with people is also a local practice of sociologists. Its monologism claims universality, even though that claim may be made for a variety of different theories. Sustaining the dominance of a particular standpoint as universal calls for practices of exclusion in sociology's dialogue with the world full of other voices that it is its business to bring to discursive order. The following section explores observations of my own local practices of reading a passage of sociological theory and discovering theory's regulatory capacity as it organized the dialogic of my encounters with voices from other sources.

Theory Regulates the Local Dialogic of Reading: Analysis of a Specimen

In this section I report analysis and observation of my experience of reading a passage from an essay on sociology by Anthony Giddens. A footnote to the essay tells us that it was originally written for presentation to the assembled members of Cambridge University. It can be read therefore as a dialogue between sociology and the dons and fellows of Cambridge University, in which Anthony Giddens plays in a kind of ambassadorial role, acting as sociology's representative and champion.

At the time of my reading, I was living in an apartment very close to the University of Oregon; I was on leave and had time to read eclectically and for other than strictly sociological purposes. I was, as other readers of this text, an eavesdropper. The text is not directed to me. And yet, of course, it is. The theoretical text, appearing in a collection entitled *Social Theory and Modern Sociology* (1987), is meant to be 'overheard'. Whatever the original settings of the papers in the collection, they are subordinated to their new appearance within sociological discourse in general. Just as conversations are in and of the settings in which they were 'found', the text of the essay is in and of sociological discourse as the setting in which it is 'found'.

The ethnomethodological device of writing 'of and in settings' preserves ethnomethodology's insistence that activities occur in settings and cannot be treated independently of them *and* that settings themselves are constituted *as* settings through members' activities. In the present context, the setting has a dual organization. On the one hand, the setting is sociological discourse and the paper is both in and of the discourse. The discursive setting is signalled by the title and by the stylistics of the essays it contains.

The discourse comes into play in reading the text as the reader 'activates' or 'operates' the text, deploying a how-to knowledge of methods of reading in the discursive genre in which Giddens writes, but also in the reading sociologist who brings her own sociological projects, as well as resources of memory and attention. On the other hand, there is the local discursive setting in which the text is activated by a particular reader who takes up as agent the organizing instructions it provides for local relevances of her life.

For the reader, the text pursues its remorseless way regardless of the impassioned marginal notes, the exclamation points or question marks, the underlinings, through which the reader tries to force dialogue on it. The dialogue internal to the text goes on untouched by the dialogue between text and reader. The text scripts her part in it and, in the order of reading, she has no choice. Still a silent dialogue of text and reader goes forward. It may accompany the reading or appear as afterthoughts, supplements, additions, a return to particularly troubling passages, or connections between the dialogic of the text and other texts or talk that the reader is engaged in. When I was reading and reflecting on something I found troubling in Giddens's writing, the following passage went to work in me:

> It is intrinsic to human action that, in any given situation, the agent, as philosophers sometimes say, could have acted otherwise. However oppressively the burden of particular circumstances may weigh upon us, we feel ourselves to be free in the sense that we decide upon an action in the light of what we know about ourselves, the context of our activities and their likely outcomes. This feeling is not spurious for it is arguable that it is analytical to the concept of agency that the actor in some sense 'could have done otherwise' – or could have refrained from whatever course of action was followed. (Giddens, 1987: 3)

The author has a dual role, or perhaps better, is present at different levels of the text. He is participant with us in the text as a member of the 'we' to whom all these scripted determinations of subjectivity apply; he is also puppet-master behind the scenes, creating the dialogue, and speaking in the magisterial voice of theory and philosophical principle. The magisterial voice is more than just the voice of the sociologist. He is not alone; one sentence bears an internal dialogue – a hybrid utterance to use Bakhtin's term. Giddens starts out on a proposition: 'It is intrinsic to human action . . .' and then detours to summon the philosophers to support his assertion that the agent 'could have acted otherwise'. The text here creates a visible intersection of discourses; the sociological discourse summons the support of (as well as affirming its reference to and dependence on) philosophical discourse. Philosophical discourse is pulled into the text here, and again later when 'could have done otherwise' is 'quoted' in the second sentence. The appeal is to the discourse that formulates rules, principles and procedures for thinking and inquiry for other discourses. Thus the 'we' is expanded to summon as subjects-in-the-text a circle of readers wider than the sociological.

This move enables a direct scripting of our participation in the text. 'We' are accorded properties of consciousness: 'we feel ourselves to be free'; 'we' 'decide on a course of action in the light of what we know'. As reading subject I am entered into the text as a local course of action. I become an agent of the text. Its sentences are to be mine. The text pre-empts control of the reader's consciousness – 'we feel ourselves to be free . . .', [we] 'decide on a course of action in the light of what we know'. The power of this device is such that in reading we wouldn't ordinarily stop to check out whether we do indeed feel free, etc. or whether indeed we can be sure of what 'feeling free' feels like. The autonomy of the subject's consciousness is suspended in favour of the text. '[W]e feel ourselves to be free . . .' repeats (and specifies) the theoretical 'the agent . . . could have acted otherwise', establishing the application of what philosophers sometimes say to she who reads. She is brought into the presence of virtual others. She is/I am among those who feel free.

The subject thus positioned in the text participates in a scripted dialogue with the magisterial voice that judges and asserts. 'We feel ourselves to be free . . .' we intone and antiphonally the magisterial voice assures us 'this feeling is not spurious'. 'Our feeling' is legitimated theoretically: 'It is analytical to the concept of agency that the actor . . ."could have done otherwise".' Our textually scripted subjective states are properly authorized.

Under this mapping of my consciousness I began, in those days in Eugene, Oregon (I remember the curiously lumpy orange–brown carpet in my furnished apartment) to set up dialogue between Smith as Giddens's local surrogate and other texts. Here intertexuality is transposed from its primarily literary, and hence static, force to explore a particular reader's local practice of dialogue among texts, escaping from the text into the lived actuality, into discourse as a sphere of activity, and taking on the text's part in a dialogue with other texts.

Here, for me, the concepts of 'agent' and 'agency', and of 'freedom' to choose a course of action, select and collect beyond the terms of the text, hooking into other and subversive discourses. The disk head skitters over time, pulling out examples from later reading and setting up arguments against the constant and impervious text. It picks out passages from newspapers, books, what people say. I recall Jessie Bernard's (1973) early feminist critique of the agentic assumptions of sociology, and my use of that to reflect on my own experience as a woman *who did not choose* (Smith, 1987), or, I suppose, had chosen a form of marriage that relinquished choice.

'We feel' locates us, readers/audience, as members of the class of human agents, summoning us to join the text's course. Yet in retrospect I think the pronoun creates a rent in the text which a more impersonal form might have avoided. The formulation claims universality that the pronoun subverts. Anyone can become a member of this 'we', but not everyone feels free. My intertextual dialogue, thinking about Giddens and reading eclectically over several days, engaged with more than one passage in which people wrote or were recorded as saying they do not feel free. In a study of women and depression (Jack, 1991), I encounter women who lacked a sense of themselves as agents: one of the women says 'that the traditional sort of role that

I played in my marriage was almost like an automatic pilot' (Jack, 1991: 73); another said, 'Most of my feelings about what a woman is are tied directly into a man. A woman isn't anything by herself' (Jack, 1991: 116). I remember a woman speaking in a group of 'psychiatrized' women (the self-naming of women who have been hospitalized for mental illness). She described herself as having been taught as a girl that she was *not* an agent, that she did not have the power to decide anything for herself, that she existed purely as an extension of, means to men's doings, men's actions, men's projects. How can their experience be 'claimed' by this theory of human action and agency?

I had just read Marcia Dimen's experiential and analytic account of 'domination'. Giddens's text singled out a passage that also registered as an exception. Dimen writes of 'the loss of one's sense of and wish for autonomy, as a result of processes that play on one's doubts about the reality and validity of one's self, one's perceptions, and one's values' (Dimen, 1989: 37). Her experiential account is more powerful still. It begins with an incident where she is followed by a man on the street telling her he wants to fuck her; it recounts the responses of her mother who criticizes her manner of dress, her father who wants to beat the man up, her conscience echoing many voices. An uncle, not himself blameless in such matters, tells her to ignore the man. To the last of these she replies in the text:

> *My mind doesn't work as rationally as yours How can it? My brain hears, my desire is stirred, I lose control of my body. On the street my body is theirs. I am a body on the street. Two tits and no head and big ass. I am a walking rohrschach. My body becomes a cunt and I am sore from this semiotic rape.* (Dimen, 1989: 73; original emphasis)

I remembered also a passage in Zora Neale Hurston's *Their Eyes Were Watching God* (1986). Nanny tells her granddaughters 'Ah was born back due in slavery, so it wasn't for me to fulfill my dreams of whut a woman oughta be and to do' (Hurston, 1986: 31–2). Slavery deprived slaves of freedom. They did not cease to be human or indeed to act. What sense of agency or freedom to choose applies here? Reading the *Iranian Labor Newsletter* that I then subscribed to, I located another instance. An article in it tells me that, under Iranian labour law, 'the worker is considered a minor and the employer as the owner of the society'. '[A]ny worker who reads this law carefully will say to himself or herself: This law considers me part of the means of production, without a tongue or will of its own' (Saber and Hekmat, 1992: 1). The law is enforced by the police and courts. The employer's will is sustained with beatings, jail, and sometimes by death. Iranian workers do not have, they want, the freedom to decide.

As the text's agent, the theory-in-the-text organizes my practices of remembering, noticing, looking out for, passages that bear upon it, that it bears upon. Though the input is subversive, it is the text's theory as organizer of my attention and reflection that structures the intertextual dialogue.

The text provides me/the reader with instructions on how to handle instances that 'come to mind' of people who have not felt free. It is not the feeling that validates the generalization. Not any old feeling can be admitted as relevant. The parameters of admissible feelings of freedom are laid out. It is the theory that validates the feeling and validates it selectively. As agents acting for the text we know how to discard the relevance to the argument of the voices of those who declare that they are not, and do not feel, free. What is validation here? It is not simply the text's work, but an implicitly dialogic aspect of the reader's work as agent of the text. The text lays out theory's command of relevance, but the reader must assent and activate it as a validation of the feeling of freedom of those who can enter the 'we' of the text in preference to the feelings of those others. What in the hearer/reader can be treated as properly accountable to the text?

The text's trap is that its dialogue with the reader is reader-activated. In becoming an agent of the text, they take on the text's organizing powers as their own. Just knowing how to read it enables the text to creep into their consciousness and take over (Smith, 1990). It is the special competence of the theoretical text to instruct readers in how to interpret other texts. Giddens's text in my consciousness singles out passages read or recalled; it also instructs me how to subdue them to it. Can it not be said of any of the instances I adduced that the 'actor in some sense "could have done otherwise" – or could have refrained from whatever course of action was followed?' (Giddens, 1987: 3). An Iranian worker could choose to do otherwise and risk death. 'However oppressively the burden of particular circumstances may weigh upon us, we feel ourselves to be free in the sense that we decide upon an action in the light of what we know about ourselves, the context of our activities and their likely outcomes' (Giddens, 1987: 3). Hurston's grandmother could choose within 'the context of [her] activities' (Giddens, 1987: 3) as a slave. I have to contort the others, discounting the women with depression (they are 'ill') and treating Dimen's text as metaphor. So long as I undertake to act as its agent, the text remains impregnable.

Giddens has been careful to define what feeling free might mean. While we, who feel free, are validated – *our* feeling is not 'spurious', those who do not feel free drop outside the circle of shared subjectivity constituted in the text–reader dialogue. For within that circle it seems that 'however oppressively the burden of particular circumstances may weigh upon them, they could have refrained from whatever course of action was followed' (Giddens, 1987: 3).

Here is demonstrated theory's capacity to control the bolt-holes through which the meaning of other texts might escape its regime. And the printed published text has this powerful organizing effect of making the same 'instructions' available to any reader who knows how to activate it. Any such reader becomes its agent. Just as I became agent of Giddens's text in my reading, others, reading his text in this, may find themselves saying, as a colleague of mine did when she read a draft of this chapter, 'but doesn't she see that they [my collection of other voices] don't apply?' Another might move to a larger scope of the hermeneutics of discourse to point out that I have misinterpreted the issue: Giddens surely is addressing the traditional problematic of the regional moral discourse of Western European philosophy since the Enlightenment, namely that of free will versus determinism: 'Smith has missed the point altogether.' Here is theory at work in the social organization of discourse.

There is a work of repression here. Whatever way I turned, my collection of stories from people who do not feel free cannot engage with the text or enter the circle of authorized subjectivity it constitutes. The dialogue interior to the text excludes it; the reader cannot find purchase for their counter-examples. They will not fit and cannot be spoken, without discursive shift such as I've made in this chapter to reposition the subject by making the text–reader dialogue. Trained readers of texts such as this know how to suspend their own or others experience as a challenge within the dialogic of the text. They know how to take up instructions provided by the text to subdue the intrusive and potentially disruptive other voices.

In validating the feeling ascribed to the reader by virtue of their participation in the 'we' of the text, what people may actually feel is excluded. Within the theory-regulated dialogic order of the text, the possibility of feeling otherwise, perhaps not free, perhaps not really feeling either one or the other, is not open. The reader who feels a disjuncture here has also been given instructions to bracket the sources of disjuncture emerging for them from the actualities of their own life, or from their participation in other discourses. No feeling other than that prescribed is admissible to the dialogue within the text and the reader as agent of the text is enforcer of that rule.

Theory is beyond the particular discursive instance in which it is deployed. It is the rule of discourse that Giddens relies on and draws into his text. The reader receives its authority for them in how they take it up as interpretive instructions. Thus theory organizes the reader's practices of reading, how they will take up what the text does and says next, how they can locate themselves to the text and what it speaks of, how, instructed by the text, they activate, selectively assemble, and authorize or discount their resources of knowledge and memory. These resources may appear, as I write of them, as individual, subjective, but in fact they are mapped into the fields of discourse in which they/I participate.

It is here we find theory's part in organizing the discursive exclusions that are the local practices of monologism. I don't think Giddens would have felt comfortable telling an audience of Iranian workers that 'we feel ourselves to be free', when 'we' is intended to include them. They would be indifferent, perhaps enraged. I imagine Zora Neale Hurston's grandmother turning away in contempt and disgust too profound for rage. The cogency of Giddens's passage is at least in part sustained by the lack of disjuncture between the reader's/audience's feelings of freedom and the subjective state it assigns them. . . . They/we do feel free, or at least don't feel strikingly unfree. 'We' (men and women of European origin and middle-class) have no sharp history of recent slavery; we have not experienced being confined to a ghetto; 'we' who are men do not experience masculine sexualization of women's public life as a young woman might; we are not Iranian workers, and so on. Here's where an organization of class, race and gender subtends and is written out of the text.

The override clause that specifies the sense in which we feel free relies for its operation on our being able to centre ourselves where the text centres us, setting up instructions for its exclusionary work in our consciousness. It relies on the lack of specification of who this 'we' is, and on our knowing how to participate in it and adopt the enclosures it calls on us to inscribe. There is no space, operating under the text's instruction, for an alternative 'we' offering a contentious identity. The stylistics of theory universalize and she or he can find no ground within the text enabling her or his speech. The participant as agent of the text adopts the instructions for their local practices of inclusion and exclusion. And they are not alone. Others, also readers of the theoretical texts, are observing the same boundaries. Our local practices of interpretation are, in this fashion, coordinated.

Here also we find the part we play in them as agents of the text. Though the theoretical passage had the capacity to subdue divergent texts, it could do so only as I acted as its agent. This, in part, is an artificial product of the development of this analysis. I have not recorded the dialogic of my original reading of any of them, for I certainly did not read them in the first place to pursue my dialogue with Giddens. In this way, I suggest, at least some forms of sociological theory regulate the local practices of sociological discourse, aligning the practical exercise of consciousnesses of those who participate in its order. Perspectives and voices presenting alternative standpoints are subdued to expressions or examples of the theoretical reading. The stylistics of universality are preserved against the threat of fragmentation and disorder, a threat sociology cannot evade in its dialogue with society. All this, of course, is the work of participants in the discourse who take up the theory and become its agents, making its monologic organization of dialogue their own. The sociological reader as agent of theory polices both their own and the utterances of other sociologists for their propriety as expressions of the discourse.

I did not know when I started on this analysis that I was going to discover how a passage such as this may inscribe as its hidden subject a white, male-dominant, European intelligentsia. I discovered it in finding out how I operated it to exclude others. There is no strident assertion of whiteness or masculinity. Rather being white and male emerges as complementary to the others whose voices it excludes: it is the not-female, not-African-American, not-Iranian worker. The subtextual subject is constituted in the reader's theory-governed dialogue with the various voices threatening its claim to universality. Here theory can be seen in action as regulator of sociology's dialogue with other voices, inhibiting their capacity to intrude and disrupt the consolidation of a unitary 'we' among members of a discourse.

Discussion

I have taken issue here with theories of discourse, whether Foucault's or Bakhtin's (of secondary speech genres), that live inside the text and adopt the virtual separation text-based discourses constitute between text and life or text and reality. This chapter has drawn on Bakhtin's thinking to develop less a theory of discourse than a method of 'observing' discourse as a regulator of its local practice. Sociological discourse, I have argued, participates in the same heteroglossic society as does the novel, and is also essentially dialogic. Its subject matter can never be contained to achieve the quiescence that the term 'subject matter' suggests. The speech genres of spheres of activity other than sociology are at work in, and always potentially disruptive of, the discourse's ability to create the unitary or monologic consciousness on which its claim to knowledge must rely. I have proposed that sociological theory has been the keystone of sociology's discursive order in this respect, coordinating the local practices of sociologists working in many different sites in different regions and countries. As a method of textual analysis, the notion of an interplay between sociology's monologic and its necessary dialogue with speech genres other than itself can explicate some peculiar features of sociological texts, such as the transformations of actual utterances into ideology in Graham and Oakley's (1981) text described above. My interests here, however, have also been in discovering how to observe theory at work regulating the local dialogic practices of a sociological reader. I have made use of a particular occasion of reading a passage from an essay by Anthony Giddens to explore how a theoretical text entered into and organized my own consciousness, entrapping fragments of other texts representing other speech genres into a dialogue organized by the relevances of Giddens's text. I discovered, and I stress that it was indeed a discovery, through these observations how I took on the role of agent of the text in this dialogue and, working with the instructions it provided, preserved the monologic of the theoretical text against the marauding, subversive, and alien voices that engaged, through me, with the order of sociological discourse. As Bakhtin says, ' the authoritative discourse itself does not merge with these [other types of discourses] . . . it remains sharply demarcated, compact and inert (Bakhtin, 1981: 343).

Drawing on Bakhtin's work, the chapter develops a method to explore, examine and specify the actual coordinative practices of discourse in how texts bear and replicate them across local settings. Observing theory's capacity to regulate the necessary dialogic of sociology in a particular local setting has uncovered, for a particular theoretical formulation, practices of exclusion as the local theoretical practice of a sociological reader. We saw how she/I acted as theory's agent and enforcer of its monologism. From the observation of the local practices of reading one theoretical passage, we cannot, of course, make inferences to the varieties of sociological theory in this respect. What is offered here is not intended as an indictment of theory in general as an exclusionary practice. It is, however, intended to display the local production of monologism as a/this reader took up a text that is the 'same' as for any other of its sociological readers/any other participant in the discourse and reinstitutes, under the text's instructions and for this occasion, the order of discourse.

Notes

This chapter was originally prepared for the Annual Meetings of the Canadian Sociology and Anthropology Association, Montreal, 1995. This version abridges a longer version to appear in the author's forthcoming book, *Writing the Social: Critique, Theory and Investigations*.

1 There is another level of dialogic organization in the sociological text on which this chapter does not focus: other sociologists appear as characters in the text; they are cited as authorities; attributed theoretical positions; attacked; quoted to support a position taken by the writer, or to illustrate the writer's interpretation. The sociological text positions itself inter-textually within the discourse, locating and relying on the formulations, theories, positions, methodological procedures of the discourse; it may draw similarly on related discourses such as those of cultural theory, or philosophy.

2 Indeed there is a fundamental ambiguity in Bakhtin's concept of monologism, since in his view utterances are intrinsically dialogic.

3 I do not mean that all sociologists share the same theory, though it is generally true that courses in sociological theory, covering a pretty standard array of sociological theorists, are required for undergraduate majors and graduate degrees in sociology. However, variants of sociological theory that are foundational to particular sociological enclaves, such as symbolic interactionism, claim general discursive status and are exclusive in the sense that they do not 'recognize' other monologic standpoints.

4 An example I used in an earlier paper (Smith, 1989) as part of a critique of constitutional theories in sociology.

5 '... [S]ome of the ways in which the differences between them [the two frames of reference] are displayed in antenatal consultations and women's experience of having a baby' (Graham and Oakley, 1981: 52).

References

Bakhtin, Mikhail.M. (1981) *The Dialogic Imagination: Four Essays by M.M. Bakhtin*. Ed. M. Holquist. Trans. C. Emerson and M. Holquist. Austin, TX: University of Texas Press.

Bakhtin, Mikhail M. (1986a) 'The problem of speech genres', in M.M. Bakhtin, *Speech Genres and Other Late Essays*. Eds C. Emerson and M. Holquist. Trans. V.W. McGee. Austin, TX: University of Texas Press. pp. 60–102.

Bakhtin, Mikhail M. (1986b) *Speech Genres and Other Late Essays*. Eds C. Emerson and M. Holquist. Trans. V.W. McGee. Austin, TX: University of Texas Press.

Bernard, Jessie (1973) 'My four revolutions: an autobiographical history of the ASA', in Joan Huber (ed.), *Changing Women in a Changing Society*. Chicago: University of Chicago Press. pp. 11–29.

Dimen, Marcia (1989) 'Power, sexuality, and intimacy', in Alison M. Jaggar and Susan R. Bordo (eds), *Gender/Body/Knowledge/ Feminist Reconstructions of Being and Knowing*. New Brunswick, NJ: Rutgers University Press. pp. 34–51.

Durkheim, Emile (1964) *The Rules of Sociological Method*. New York: Free Press.

Foucault, Michel (1970) *The Order of Things: An Archaeology of the Human Sciences*. London: Tavistock.

Foucault, Michel (1972) *The Archaeology of Knowledge and the Discourse on Language*. New York: Pantheon Books.

Foucault, Michel (1979) *Discipline and Punish: The Birth of the Prison*. New York: Vintage Books.

Foucault, Michel (1980) *Power/Knowledge: Selected Interviews and Other Writings, 1972–1977*. New York: Pantheon Books.

Foucault, Michel (1981) 'The order of discourse', in Robert Young (ed.), *Untying the Text: A Poststructuralist Reader*. London: Routledge. pp. 51–78.

Foucault, Michel (1988) 'Technologies of the self', in Luther H. Martin, Huck Gutman and Patrick H. Hutton (eds), *Technologies of the Self*. London: Tavistock.

Gardiner, Michael (1992) *The Dialogics of Critique: M.M. Bakhtin and the Theory of Ideology*. New York: Routledge.

Garfinkel, Harold (1967) *Studies in Ethnomethodology*. Englewood Cliffs, NJ: Prentice-Hall.

Garfinkel, Harold (1972) 'Remarks on ethnomethodology', in Dell Hymes and John J. Gumperz (eds), *The Ethnography of Communication*. New York: Holt Rinehart and Winston. pp. 309–24.

Garfinkel, Harold, Lynch, Michael and Livingston, Eric (1981) 'The work of a discovering science construed with materials from the optically discovered pulsar', *Philosophy of the Social Sciences*, 11: 131–58.

Giddens, Anthony (1987) *Social Theory and Modern Sociology*. Stanford, CA: Stanford University Press.

Graham, Hilary and Oakley, Ann (1981) 'Competing ideologies of reproduction: medical and maternal perspectives on pregnancy', in H. Roberts (ed.), *Women, Health and Reproduction*. London: Routledge & Kegan Paul. pp. 50–74.

Hurston, Zora Neale (1986) *Their Eyes Were Watching God: A Novel*. London: Virago.

Jack, Dana Crowley (1991) *Silencing the Self: Women and Depression*. Cambridge, MA: Harvard University Press.

Maurer, David W. (1981) 'The argot of pickpockets', in Allan W. Futrell and Charles B. Wordell (eds), *Language of the Underworld*. Lexington, KY: University of Kentucky Press. pp. 234–56.

Oakley, Ann (1981) 'Interviewing women: a contradiction in terms', in H. Roberts (ed.), *Doing Feminist Research*. London: Routledge & Kegan Paul. pp. 30–61.

Saber, Mostafa and Hekmat, Mansour (1992) 'Labour law against workers' rights: a critique of labour law', *Labour Solidarity*, Jan/Feb: 4.

Smith, Dorothy E. (1987) *The Everyday World as Problematic: A Feminist Sociology*. Boston, MA: Northeastern University Press.

Smith, Dorothy E. (1989) 'Sociological theory: writing patriarchy into feminist texts', in Ruth Wallace (ed.), *Feminism and Sociological Theory*. Newbury Park, CA: Sage. pp. 34–64.

Smith, Dorothy E. (1990) 'The active text', in Dorothy E. Smith, *Texts, Facts and Femininity: Exploring the Relations of Ruling*. London: Routledge. pp. 120–58.

Voloshinov, V.N. (1986) *Marxism and the Philosophy of Language*. Trans. L. Matejka and I.R. Titunik. Cambridge, MA: Harvard University Press.

PART II

CARNIVALS

6

THE GROTESQUE OF THE BODY ELECTRIC

Peter Hitchcock

> We must share each other's excess in order to overcome our mutual lack.
> – Michael Holquist

I begin with Bakhtin's leg; or rather, its manifest absence. I will begin by singing Bakhtin's body electric, the materiality of his body and the body-image that, in true historico-allegorical fashion, move across the borders of theory and practice.[1] I commence, therefore, with the practical experience of Bakhtin's body. Bakhtin, a consummate theorist of the body, begins with the unconsummated nature of his own tissue, a body that for most of his life painfully reminded him of its fleshly imperfections. From an early age Bakhtin suffered from osteomyelitis, a bone disease that can set light to nerve endings as easily as it can kill them. The disease takes a variety of forms but in its chronic manifestation it causes inflammation around the bones (especially the long bones of the arms and legs) and secondary infections that often require high doses of anti-biotics. Common symptoms when present include sinus tract drainage which often emits a foul odour, bony sequestra, and non-healing ulcers. Although much about Bakhtin's health remains somewhat murky, there is no doubt that osteomyelitis played a crucial role in the decision to amputate his right leg in 1938. People do not write about the body merely because their body appears in permanent revolution against them but one might take on the possibility that Bakhtin's excessive body, its grotesque order of pain, has a pertinent and permanent inscription in his theorization. By the time Bakhtin is considering the borders of answerability in Vitebsk, the osteomyelitis has spread to his left shin, a hip joint, and to his right hand (Clark and Holquist, 1984). His body, weakened by the relentless nature of the disease, then suffers from a bout of typhoid, which further inflamed the bone marrow in his right leg and, in 1921, required an operation. Clark and Holquist note:

As a result of the operation on his right leg, Bakhtin was subject to periodic inflammation of the hip joint, which flared up several times a year, giving him acute pain and high temperatures and obliging him to spend as much as a month or two in bed. The fever was so high that his wife had to change his bedshirt several times a night. The pain was so great that he conducted his classes while lying on a couch. (Clark and Holquist, 1984: 51)

It is likely that the periodic inflammation addressed here was again a product of chronic osteomyelitis but was exacerbated by typhoid. In his correspondence, Bakhtin comments, 'It was a very grave operation: they chiselled through my leg, across the hip, they even chiselled through my shin'.[2] Within the architectonics of answerability Bakhtin is at least attempting to answer the painful demands of his flesh. He is the author, and what Other confronts him as he lays upon the couch? Much more, of course, can be said about the value of Bakhtin's body in history. In general I am interested in Bakhtin as 'a constant meditator on the meaning of borders' (Holquist, 1990: xix), but particularly where the borders of the body exceed themselves. Architectonics is not a simple compensation or displacement device for the wholeness that Bakhtin does not feel; it is, rather, an attempt to understand the logic of work in effecting wholeness. It is not a theory on the perfectability of 'Man' but a detailed exegesis on the will to construct a human differently. True, in the early philosophical manuscripts Bakhtin will often discover an aesthetic solution to what is properly a sociopolitical problem (itself perhaps an allegory of Bakhtin's misgivings about the solutions posed in terms of Soviet Marxism at the time), but even when he finds that the artist and art 'as a whole create a completely new vision of the world, a new image of the world, a new reality of the world's mortal flesh' this whole is not solace from the mortal world but a 'new plane of thinking about the world' (Bakhtin, 1990: 191).

Diseases work in mysterious ways. In 1924, Bakhtin returns to Leningrad because the severity of his illness disqualifies him from officialdom's definition of the physically able: he is awarded a state pension (second class) and is no longer required to work. The paradox of illness is that a great deal of the world's most significant art and thinking would not have been possible without it (and one should add that a socialist outlook towards disability – or 'socialized' medicine for those who wish to overlook what Marx would call the rational kernel for its mystical shell – has played an enduring role in this realm of possibility). While one could argue that authorial will will overcome any obstacle, Bakhtin's pension provided him with a vital resource: time. This is by no means an endorsement of Soviet social relations of the 1920s. The same system that produced state pensions threw Bakhtin in jail in January 1929 (as part of a general purge of intellectuals). Again, however, his body intervenes, as if its persecution was better than the state's. The effects of osteomyelitis killing his right leg were compounded by paraphrenitis in the kidneys. Thus, in June 1929 Bakhtin's condition was 'upgraded' to Category Two which rewarded him with a hospital bed rather than a prison cell. In addition to an appreciable campaign to release Bakhtin from the thrall of political persecution, Bakhtin himself sent an application to the Commissariat of Health for official confirmation of the severity of his illness (he believed at this time that he was to be sentenced to several years at the dreaded prison camp on the Solovetsky Islands – easily a one-way ticket for someone in his condition). In a somewhat apposite interpretation of Derrida's work on the Pharmakon as poison and cure, one could say that what was killing Bakhtin was also preserving him. He was sentenced to exile in Kustanai, Kazakhstan, which, while no holiday, greatly improved his chances of survival.

Of course, the major medical event in Bakhtin's life took place on 13 February 1938 in Savelovo. The osteomyelitis had become so severe that Bakhtin's right leg was amputated. He would use crutches or a stick for the rest of his life. But, more importantly, he would experience the borders of the body in a different way, as a zone of prosthesis and image. I would argue that if the concept of the cyborg is founded on the body's shadowy exist-ence between its fictional and fleshly self, then this notion came to write itself into Bakhtin's very being. In Savelovo Bakhtin would begin his most significant statement of the body's function in art and life, his 'dissertation' on Rabelais. As he struggled with his own carnivalized body, Bakhtin writes one of the twentieth century's most provocative works on the culture of the body. The cyborg confronts the grotesque.

Bakhtin as cyborg? This will require some qualification. The cyborg remains a symptom more than a reality – a concept with enough liminal being to provide both radical critical possibilities and conservative techno-deter-minist appropriations. We can, on the one hand, celebrate the cyborg for its guerilla epistemology because, in challenging dualisms of various kinds in the representation of the body, it explodes some of the trusted 'truths' of contemporary social formations (this, indeed, has been its particular allure for a developing corporeal feminism, of which more below). On the other hand, the cyborg embodies (sometimes literally) a deeply problematic thesis about the role of advanced technology with 'actually existing' transnational capitalism so that its very status as bodily enhancement or interface of flesh and technology is the last frontier of social control (and who gets what form of cyborganic being is also a direct integer of brute economic power). For some, the contradictions of the cyborg are a badge of faith in the undecid-ability of the moment: it is a symptom, therefore, of the nervousness with our system. Yet one wonders whether theory cedes too much in represent-ing the cyborg as an inevitable symptom and that what results from this fatalism with fantasy is to pre-programme the future, and indeed the body, with a logic that is itself an instantiation of corporate lore (like Ford's famous quip about a choice of colours for a car that had only one)? Rather than simply read the cyborg as an allegory about the perfectability of 'Man' gone wrong (say, 'from thesis to prosthesis'), we will explore the contours of its counter-logic, the conditions of its knowledge for body politics. On one level, these will be read (as I have already suggested) in relation to the tortuous labours of the body for Bakhtin. On another, these conditions, while fashionably eliding the absolute, suggest why the human in the cyborg says 'no' to the corporate logic that demands its obeisance. They are the conditions, I will contend, of the grotesque in body, action, and mind. They are the embodiment of imperfections and of pain.

This, too, should be clarified, for one could easily argue that whatever the conditions of knowledge in the concept of the cyborg, good old plodding techno-capitalism can still make robots of us all. Yet this misses the point. It is not enough to locate the radical potential of the cyborg in its shadowy being, then go on to admit that, after all, cybernetic developments will occur under the aegis of corporate capital or not at all (this is precisely Donna Haraway's intervention in her 'Manifesto for cyborgs' (1985) – of which more below). The initial explorations of a properly cyborganic imagination (redolent, for instance, in Mary Shelley's *Frankenstein*) pick up on a narrative of what makes a human, human, and link this to a horrific encounter of nature and science. The discovery is not the truism that when science plays god 'Man' is denatured (although the progressive politics in and around the formulation should not be disparaged): the crux of the matter is whether greater understanding of what makes a human, human, under historically specific conditions actually renders the domination of techno-capitalism impossible. In this sense (and sense perception is part of the argument), the cyborg is not the scene of carefully contrived discursive duplicity, but a 'real contradiction' with socio-economic portent. Could it be that the paradox of progress is that Marx's famous gravedigger of capitalism will be a machine-human composite who putatively at least was meant to be the ideal worker?[3]

I want to connect (or, more appropriately, reattach) Bakhtin's body to his concept of the grotesque in a way that inflects the determinate being of the cyborg. The subtext of the critique is the link between Bakhtin's experience of the liminality of his own body and the thesis of grotesquery that is coterminous with it. The symptom here is not the mere correspondence of biographical details (Bakhtin's lifelong battle with osteomyelitis) with certain theoretical formulations (the grotesque as excessive body and as an imaginative plane), but rather that Bakhtin's body is *inextricably implicated* in the grotesquery he elucidates in a way that emphasizes the material conditions of the body's question for the social. Indeed, it is the sublation of a conventional theory/practice split that makes Bakhtin's concept of the grotesque a vital contribution to materialist thought.[4] Bakhtin (like Mary Shelley in this regard) explores the condition of the cyborg without ever naming it. And this is where the imaginative field of the grotesque, of the monstrous, of the excessively human, has its revenge on exploitative forms of rationality.

The first being to be termed a cyborg was a white rat in the 1950s, a fact with enough symbolic overtones to make an argument in itself.[5] What is a cyborg? Conventional wisdom tells us that it is shorthand for a cybernetic organism, an expanding and problematic interfacing of human and machine. It can also represent the constructed wholes of separate organic systems. In recent years the definitions have multiplied which, while it has greatly expanded the borders of 'Borg culture, has tended to blur its potential for socio-critique. For instance, since we all interact with machines of various complexity, humanity is always already cyborgian by some accounts (all humans are 'soft' cyborgs or low-tech cyborgs). If one reduces cyborgian phenomena to the fact that machines are extensions of the self, then the specificities of integration may well be elided, as well as the more nefarious logic that makes the self an extension of the machine (the factory system within industrialization has consistently rationalized the latter). Let us say that the cyborg as a sign, as an arena of (class) struggle (to borrow from Bakhtin/Voloshinov) constructs its own hierarchies of significance according to ideologies of power, but these, from low-tech to advanced, do not define the real foundations that are their genesis. The plethora of definitions, therefore, should not obviate the need to analyse what conditions their possibility, including their function as ideology. The original development of cyborgs was fostered by the needs of the military-industrial complex: the quest for a sophisticated 'man-machine weapon' was as much a staple of the Cold War as it is of more recent high-tech 'low intensity' conflict (the representation of the Gulf War as a video game on CNN is, for the Pentagon, a triumph of cybernetic systems development). Of course, not all cyborganic development is military, but even otherwise benign technical advances in replacement body parts move in symbiosis with military conflict ('refinements' in anti-personnel mines have clearly intensified research and development in prosthetic limbs, whose fleshly counterparts are torn asunder in ever-increasing numbers from Vietnam to Afghanistan). The cyborg as killing machine crops up all over popular culture (*Terminator*, *American Cyborg*, etc.): this kind of cyborg is the Id of the military mindset, the 'what if' of technology's destructive self. On one level then, the grotesque cyborg is merely the name for obscene violence.

I have suggested that the chief representation of cyborg reality, however, is its function as symptom and, if we are to understand Bakhtin's profound contribution to the field of the cyborganic, this must be explained. There are many reasons why Donna Haraway's 'A manifesto for cyborgs' (1985) has become a classic statement on cyborg Being, and they all in varying ways advance key theses on the cyborg as symptom.[6] First, cyborg politics are posited as a powerful rhetorical device. There is an endearing playfulness in Haraway's approach which is, as she notes, girded by an 'ironic political myth' (1985: 65) that the cyborg inspires. How so? The cyborg exists in a form of nether-world between fiction and reality, just as its subjectivity is caught in the contradictory hybridity of machinery and flesh. What Haraway does is pose this border being as a symptom of specific political dilemmas. To read the cyborg, in and of itself, as the solution to political problems in feminism or socialism (the subtitle of Haraway's essay is 'Science, technology, and socialist feminism in the 1980s') is to misunderstand her ironic stance. Thus, when Haraway boldly declares that 'the cyborg is our ontology; it gives us our politics' (1985: 66), it is irony that saves the formulation from crude technological determinism. The stress is on a Being at or beyond 'our' normative Selves. And, as Haraway emphasizes, one must come to terms with the chimerical components of our existence if we are to reformulate a properly radical political agenda.

The manifesto's second intervention is an extension of the first, for to embrace the rhetorical strategy of foregrounding the cyborg as an historical agent is to confront the possibility that its transgressive boundaries might form a political space for new tactical alliances. Obviously, the danger in this move is that the cyborg may be interpreted realistically rather than ironically and that activists may be dutifully miffed that the cyborg elbows its way into the political arena as a substitute for the delineated struggles of race, gender, ethnicity, class, and sexuality (to name just a few of the areas of social conflict with their own theories of ontology and politics). Nevertheless, in demonstrating the logic of what she calls the 'informatics of domination' (1985: 79), a logic that is predicated on oppressive dualisms or false dichotomies, Haraway shows how the advent of the cyborg offers new combinatory potentials in oppositional work. Again, for the uninitiated the difficulty is in seeing beyond the shorthand cyborg of popular culture (the T1000 of *Terminator 2: Judgment Day* seems to offer only an ontology of death) yet even then the popular embodies elements of the counter-narrative that Haraway is at pains to elucidate. The second intervention, then, proposes the cyborg as a heuristic device: it is a way to learn about the forms of politics possible at the end of the twentieth century.

The most important reason for the continued relevance of Haraway's strategy *vis-à-vis* cyborganic politics is in its lessons for feminism's critique of science. There are many other examples of feminist polemic against the patriarchal structures of supposedly neutral scientific thought (including the work of Sandra Harding, whose debate with Haraway over the status of the cyborg for feminist politics would provide a separate argument in itself), but few have so deftly raised the banner of feminism against the scientific rationalism busily fulfilling promises of an avaricious world system. True, Haraway has since significantly qualified her initial statements (which is as much a register of the dangers of irony as anything else), but her analysis of how cyborganic systems directly impact and are transformed by woman as subject remain a prescient critique of science's failure in the modern era. Technology may offer the cyborg, so says Haraway, but it cannot determine in advance all the forms of hybridity that its liminal being may make possible and this can be a touchstone for feminism's transgression of woman's objectification in scientific 'development'.

What is feminist about Haraway's intervention is also what is Bakhtinian in this instance. First, cyborg imagery is deployed to displace the obsession of reproduction with regeneration: the bio-politics of birthing are carnivalized by the non-originary theses (or prostheses) of cyborganic being. Clearly, the psychoanalytic valorization of the Name of the Father must be continually challenged; Haraway's attempt is through the transgressive body boundaries of the cyborg with its hope of a 'monstrous world without gender' (1985: 67). The prerequisites of this monstrous world are the conditions of the monstrous body. Bakhtin suggests that 'the grotesque body is a body in the act of becoming. It is never finished, never completed; it is continually built, created, and builds and creates another body' (Bakhtin, 1984: 517). True, Bakhtin will often use images of procreation and birthing to elaborate 'becoming', but only because in his reading of Rabelais these are instances of the body opening out. For Bakhtin, as for Haraway, the body does not end with the skin. The cyborg exists in Bakhtin to the extent that becoming is the very ground of augmentation and reconstruction.

Haraway's feminist challenge is also Bakhtinian in the way it elaborates a constructive strategy of responsibility. Arguing away from models of victimhood that pose technology and science as smothering human agency, Haraway instead offers feminism the challenge of embodied power. While the cyborg is an image of the pleasure of confused bodily boundaries, a cyborg body politic stresses responsibility in the articulation of such transgression. Certainly this is not answerability in the precise terms that Bakhtin elaborates it. Yet Bakhtin, I believe, would not have found Haraway's stress on the agency of the transgressive body anathema to his philosophy of the deed. According to his architectonics of answerability, Cartesian dualism fails to understand the body's axiological dependence on the Other in constituting value. Bakhtin develops this principle in relation to aesthetic acts, but it is clear that the material realization of the body as value-constituting makes answerability a general concept of challenging the idea of the body as a monad. For Bakhtin, crossing normative notions of body boundaries implies ethical responsibility: it is the mode in which agency is situated.

The strongest affinity between Haraway's ironic vision of cyborg politics and Bakhtinian critique is the stress on a radical heterogeneity in discourse and language. Haraway ends her argument by suggesting that, 'Cyborg imagery can suggest a way out of the maze of dualisms in which we have explained our bodies and our tools to ourselves. This is a dream not of a common language, but of a powerful infidel heteroglossia' (Haraway, 1985: 106). We recall that Bakhtin used heteroglossia to refer to the contextual specificity of meaning in the utterance, the radical heterogeneity of the utterance in its centrifugal and centripetal elements. Its infidelity is not to meaning, then, but to any abstract systematicity in linguistics or indeed formalism in discursive critique. Both Haraway's and Bakhtin's interpretations of heteroglossia can be challenged for their extravagance. For instance, clearly the pleasures of heteroglossia (responsible or not) do not in themselves negate the powerful cyborgian imagery in the informatics of domination. And the more one states the positive inclinations of heteroglottic border-crossing, the more one risks reinventing a dualism *vis-à-vis* monoglossia. The weaknesses in Bakhtin's argument are legion: from the tendency to hypostatize the novel as heteroglossia's most privileged aesthetic form, to the confusing shifts between heteroglossia as the 'normal' condition of languages *and* as the historically specific instance of one language in particular. There are counter-arguments available, but let me stress the positive confluence of the concept in Haraway and Bakhtin. If we accept the boundary-breaching condition of cyborg ontology, the task is continually to concretize the context of this event. Bakhtin allows for all kinds of possible influences on the 'eventness' of heteroglossia's distillation in discourse and the I/Other relations of subjectivity. Surely cybernetics is a science of contexts in this light – an approach to the field of connectivity and integration in differing environments? What the problem of the cyborg demands in Haraway's rhetorical 'dream' is an infidelity to normative claims of rationality as currently construed, for the latter fail, socially and philosophically, to understand the ways in which the body and body image get articulated in heteroglottic profusion. I will mention two of these aspects here: the grotesque and the phantom limb.

The body in revolt is often a revolting body. The grotesque is not a tribute to the embodiment of technological will, but rather it is the scene of its *mise en abyme*. The body constantly contradicts the pretensions and ideologies of perfection in its defecation, sneezing, farting, belching, and bleeding. Bakhtin is impressed by Rabelais's celebration of these bodily functions because they simultaneously transgress and destabilize the ideologies of the medieval world order. If god made 'Man' in his own image, then he must have had a sense of humour. Just as Rabelais characterizes the belly laughter of a world turned upside down and inside out, so religion is made to see the comedy in its bodily imagery (this takes many forms in Bakhtin's critique, but the discussion of the grotesque in religious relics, particularly those of dismembered bodies of the saints, is pertinent in this regard). The body's materiality, especially the materiality of what Bakhtin calls its 'lower stratum', conspires against the codes of order and rationality issued by its 'head'. It wants nothing of 'discipline' and 'regularity'; it prefers, inestimably, the excessive processes of waste, procreation, and decay.

But of course, the body needs its head, even if we know that it can survive without it (for instance, in madness and in the cyborgian stasis of the brain-dead on life support). What interests Bakhtin in the grotesque, however, is its meaning within Renaissance thought, principally as an index of 'Man's' inscription in a much broader cosmology, one where the body is in the world and not separate from it, one in which the body is open to organic processes that 'hold no terror for him' (Bakhtin, 1984: 365). To laugh at our bodily imperfections is not base or gross in Bakhtin's theory of the grotesque: it is an affirmation of our extraordinary material being.

I will not detail all of the elements of the grotesque that Bakhtin outlines, but several are clearly appropriate to the present discussion. First, the grotesque life of the body is not a pure negativity but a warning about any system of thought that renders the body either abstract or easily perfectable.

The process or 'becoming' of the body resists its codification: it answers hypostatization with hyperbole, excellence with excrement. For the French humanists of the Renaissance the body provided endless fascinations – even Rabelais performed a public dissection to underline a non-disciplinary philosophical disposition in the medical science of the time. Indeed, the body itself is simultaneously a sign of 'interchange' and 'interorientation' (Bakhtin, 1984: 317) with the world, but also a catalyst for radical thinking about that world. Clearly, this is a lesson that Bakhtin wants to be read into his world, a place where the righteous and the regulative were in danger of sucking the spontaneous and festive from a revolutionary spirit. For those, however, who willy-nilly make the carnivalesque and the grotesque trans-historical categories, it is worth reiterating that they are both radically historicized in Bakhtin's conception. Ever attentive to the material conditions of thought and practice, Bakhtin will even go as far as suggesting that Rabelais's *Pantagruel* inflects the weather that accompanied its genesis: a heatwave and drought in which 'men actually walked with their mouths open' (Bakhtin, 1984: 326). He later remarks that a plague, too, marks the eventness of this tome because this, like the drought, had awakened the people's 'cosmic terror and eschatological expectations' and Rabelais's book was 'a merry answer to these fears and pious moods' (Bakhtin, 1984: 339). My point here is to draw attention to the material conditions of the production of *Bakhtin*'s own book. But while other studies have focused on the carnivalizing tendencies of Bakhtin's intervention *vis-à-vis* the terrors and errors of Stalinism, I would argue that the material and materialist manifestations of this work can also be understood in terms of the evidence of Bakhtin's own body.

For instance, on several occasions in *Rabelais and His World* Bakhtin lists key elements of grotesque imagery in male speech: 'Wherever men laugh and curse, particularly in a familiar environment, their speech is filled with bodily images. The body copulates, defecates, overeats, and men's speech is flooded with genitals, bellies, defecations, urine, disease, noses, mouths, and dismembered parts' (Bakhtin, 1984: 319). Most of these elements are either the site or the process of bodily functions but two in particular need further explanation. The body is naturally prone to disease either as a potential or as an embodiment from birth (something genetically prescribed), but if you subtract disease from these elements few would argue that the body represented would be abnormal. To put this a slightly different way: the inclusion of disease disrupts the series of bodily attributes – it is not parallel in the way that a nose or urine may be. A similar point could be made about 'dismembered parts' which, again, is something done to the body and does not stand in the same relation of bodily functions as say a belly or defecation. This occurs again later in Bakhtin's argument where he suggests, 'In the oral popular comic repertory we also find everywhere the reflection of the grotesque concept of the body: specific obscenities, debasing parodies, abuse and cursing, and dismembered parts'

(Bakhtin, 1984: 354). Here the false series is even more glaring: the list begins by ennumerating forms of comic repertory but ends with a *subject* of that repertory. Why did this particular component of grotesque anatomy suggest itself?

Diseases, of course, play a key function in grotesquery. It is not just the way they can deform the human body (although that is of great interest here), but also that they are the body's classic manifestation of fallibility. This does not make Bakhtin fatalistic; on the contrary, what he admires in Rabelais is that he interprets disease as an opening out of the body, that disease regularly and insistently transgresses the body's boundaries with the world, integrating it with the lively complexities of an entire cosmology. For this reason, Bakhtin is particularly taken with the philosophy of the 'Hippocratic anthology' (Bakhtin, 1984: 357) which elaborates the symptoms of life and death along the same continuum. When we say that someone is living with disease rather than dying from it we are stating a cornerstone of Renaissance cosmology *and* the grounds for Bakhtin's rearticulation of it. To excise Bakhtin's theorization from his experience of his own body seems to me to misunderstand profoundly his reading of the carnivalesque and grotesque. Bakhtin's body was also the 'epitome of incompleteness' (Bakhtin, 1984: 26).

To the extent that every writer's corpus is dictated by his corpus there is nothing particularly inflammatory in invoking the materiality of Bakhtin's body, yet it has a specific prescience given his unique contribution to our sense of the body's possibilities in culture and politics. Evidence suggests that Bakhtin may have developed osteomyelitis from as early as nine years of age. From that point he could no longer exercise or indeed play with other children. For those who marvel at the fact that he read Kant's '*Kritik der reinen Vernunft*' at the age of twelve one might add that his remarkable self-education was due in part to the isolation that came with his disease.[7] As I have mentioned, some bouts of the disease were more debilitating than others but, typically perhaps, the disease had positive and negative valences. Bakhtin's relative immobility and official status as a disabled person allowed him inordinate time to read and write. With his wife, voluntarily or not, reduced to the role of servant and secretary, Bakhtin could spend days on end in fervent contemplation. Yet it is important to keep in mind that there were as many days of excruciating pain and no day when a manifestation of grotesquery did not threaten what passed for a modicum of well-being. As I look at a photograph of Bakhtin bedridden with osteomyelitis in March 1930 (Clark and Holquist, 1984: 144), just before his exile to Kazakhstan, I am reminded of what Bakhtin calls a 'remarkable excerpt' from the 'Prognostics' of the Hippocratic anthology:

> In acute diseases it is necessary to make the following observations: first of all as to the patient's face: does it resemble or not the face of persons in good health, and especially does it resemble itself? For the latter sign should be considered the best, and the lack of this resemblance presents the greatest danger. The face will then offer the following aspect: sharp nose, sunken eyes and hollow temples, ears

cold and taut, the ear-lobes twisted, the skin on the forehead taut and dry, the color of the face greenish, dark or leaden. (Bakhtin, 1984: 358)

Bakhtin uses this example to illustrate the Hippocratic focus on the face as an integer of 'death's proximity or remoteness'. It is hard to find a photograph of Bakhtin where this drama of life and death is not drawn across his face. After his leg was amputated, Bakhtin was quite proud of the fact that he could move around on crutches at least as much (or as little) as before. There was also an attempt to fit Bakhtin for a prosthesis. Unfortunately, because the amputation was so high on his leg, almost to the groin itself, he did not have enough stump to wear a prosthesis comfortably. Indeed, the pain of using a false leg was almost as great as the pain provided by its fleshly counterpart.[8] Even the use of crutches took its toll. The cartilage in his eft leg was progressively weakened by his dependence on it and made even assisted movement a painful experience.

I have suggested that there is a strong connection between Bakhtin's health and his approach to the grotesque. Bakhtin begins his work on Rabelais around the time of the amputation of his leg, and to underline the significance of this I want to elaborate more of his right leg's afterlife in the theorization of that tome. To do this I want to borrow from what we know of the phantom limb. Briefly, the phantom limb refers to an experience of a body part after its removal, an experience that confirms that humans live with an image of their body's exteriority – their body's existence in a specific time and space. The phantom limb is experienced by almost all people who have endured the amputation of moving, functioning, extremities (the most notable exceptions are young children and the mentally impaired). It can also be experienced by people who have had internal organs removed. Typically, the phantom appears almost immediately after amputation, but it can take up to two years to manifest itself. It is important to note that the phantom limb is an image of what was amputated, not a copy of it. Indeed, the body phantom is often distorted, as Elizabeth Grosz explains:

> The phantom is invariably shorter than the limb; often the proximal portions of the phantom are missing; it is commonly perceived as flatter than the healthy limb; it usually feels light and hollow; and the perception of its mobility is extremely impaired ... losing its ability to perform finer, more nuanced acts of dexterity which the intact limb was able to undertake. (Grosz, 1994: 71)

The phantom limb is the scene of a trenchant cognitive confusion: the reality of the stump is co-extensive with the reality of the phantom; that is, one indicates a manifest absence in the same time/space relations as that which indicates a manifest presence. Thus, the phantom limb asks the first question of grotesquery: where does your body end?

When Bakhtin writes of the grotesque open character of the body he is not just reading a wild sixteenth-century narrative: he is articulating the coordinates of his own experience of the liminality of flesh. If he may be deemed nostalgic for a certain symbolic destruction of authoritarian grants and then administer them under one common set of grant conditions and administrative requirements. Three years after enactment, an OMB study found that actual implementation of the act was "virtually negligible." By 1979, only approximately 30 national joint-funded projects existed.[36] According to OMB, federal agencies have not made a commitment to implementation, and there is widespread ignorance of the process at both the national and regional levels. The implementation of joint funding also is restrained by the voluntary nature of the process for federal agencies.

Circular A-95. A more widespread reform is OMB's Circular A-95, implementing the Intergovernmental Cooperation Act of 1968. Circular A-95 established a Project Notification and Review System for state and local agencies to review and evaluate grant applications from area governments. This reform, sparked by pleas from elected officials and their generalist staffs, creates clearinghouses, usually state or regional planning agencies, where the review of grant applications can take place. One problem is that the large volume of applications handled by clearinghouse agencies limits the analysis and comments that are then passed along to federal agencies. Also contributing to the problem is the large number of A-95 notifications that must be processed in a relatively short time.

One result of A-95 is that it reduces the frequency with which program managers bypass elected officials in their search for federal aid. A-95 helps to establish systematic, regular, regional assessment of federal grant activities. It does not necessarily improve coordination among the federal agencies that are asked to consider clearinghouse comments during the review process. Federal managers, as well as many state and local officials, generally view A-95 certification as another hurdle to be jumped before funds can be obligated.

In summary, A-95 serves as a valuable tool for the exchange of information among levels of government. However, the circular's thrust is to coordinate state and local responses to federal programs rather than to forge coordinative links between federal agencies. The ACIR notes, "A-95, as presently conceived, is an alternative to Federal interagency coordination rather than a spur to it." [37]

None of these efforts to coordinate domestic assistance programs—the FRCs, joint funding, A-95 review—yields anything beyond limited or case-by-case results. Program managers, who are accountable to congressional subcommittees and dependent upon national interest groups for support, have few incentives to streamline their requirements and coordinate programs. Top agency managers focus on their individual program, not on that program's effect on the federal system. Presidential staff members and OMB personnel recognize the problem, but lack the incentive or commitment to improve grants management— more dramatic issues and crises drive grants reform off their agendas. The result is that special interests stoutly defend each program's requirements, and no one aggressively monitors the existing reforms to make them work. In short, few actors at the federal level have the time and interest to attempt to sort out a confusing aggregation of grants and regulations.

FEDERAL OVERSIGHT AND EVALUATION

Does the federal government enforce grant-in-aid regulations? Do federal programs regulate subnational governments or do they serve subnational governments? Actually, federal grants implementation accomplishes a bit of each goal. Under many circumstances, however, federal agencies deploy resources and monitor their use in order to develop a constituency relationship; as a result grantees are in a position to use federal programs to serve local goals. State and local officials can exercise influence over federal actors at this phase of the implementation process.

The Politics of Oversight

At the core of federal grants management is the fact that HUD, EPA, DOT, and other agencies operate within a federal system. Every cabinet secretary or agency administrator is responsible to Congress— which represents local interests. As legislators expand their casework activities and service orientation, direct relationships are forged between legislative staff and federal central office and field personnel. Congress often makes it difficult for administrators to set performance standards because the drive to enact legislation means expanding the list of goals and objectives. Often it is not clear whether grants programs are designed to impose federal objectives or underwrite state programs. As a result, legislation represents compromises between advocates and opponents of federal action. According to Phillip Monypenny:

> The opponents of a given federal action may lose out because they are not quite as powerful in Congress or in the federal executive as they are in the state legislative or in the governor's office. They are never without some influence in Congress, if only through their own state Congressional representative.[38]

This directly restricts administrators attempting to hold states and localities accountable for performance.

One result of the above condition is that subnational officials frequently view the purpose of federal grants as the improvement of existing programs. For example, President Johnson pushed a National officialdom, then he might also be combating a more personal nostalgic manifestation in his present. Interestingly, the phantom limb expresses a desire for the complete body that is not, but this is not a thesis, or prosthesis, that neatly fits Bakhtin's outlook. Indeed, if he experienced a phantom limb, he embraced its shadowy existence, as if the horror of his own body were the positive symbol of the grotesque incarnate. Let me be clear on this: there is no evidence extant in which Bakhtin discusses either his health or his body in any great detail. What I am suggesting is that the imagery of the grotesque body he elucidates is symptomatic of imagery with a real foundation in his existence.

Grotesque imagery, like the phantom limb, exists in distortion: it only provides emotional effect by virtue of its approximation. Rather than wallow in the fact that disease had carnivalized his body, Bakhtin takes up the issue of disease for its associative effects. Ridicule through the invocation of disease could be therapeutic with respect to disease; one could actually laugh in the face of death. There can be no doubt that osteomyelitis changed Bakhtin's body image even before his right leg was removed: even if you can forget someone else's pain, you cannot forget your own (I will return to the pertinence of pain in the conclusion). Bakhtin made this body image the ground for a life-affirming embrace of the popular and the festive in the social construction of everyday life. For some this may sound like an obvious compensation for the hardships and downright gloominess of Bakhtin's life, but this, I think, misses the point. The body image and the phantom limb which marks its reconstitution are both grotesque images of a chthonian potential, if not reality – the after-images of a struggle with mortality that many aspects of contemporary culture now insistently desensitize, as if the active liminality of the flesh is a ruse of technology. This is where Bakhtin's experience of prosthesis must be read against the grain of normative notions of the cyborganic self. The body image is not just a zone of personal restoration, even if the ideology of the whole, the complete, the autonomous body remains hegemonic in particularly Western concepts of selfhood. Indeed, what the latter attempts to mystify through personification, the grotesque displaces through socialization. For Bakhtin, the 'material bodily principle' (Bakhtin, 1984: 19) is embodied by a people, those whose renewal can only occur collectively. It is this principle of sociality that needs to be constantly reconnected to cyborganic critique. Of course, there is no simple formula for the socialization implied here. Bakhtin himself too often subjected the principle to typification – as in his by now infamous reference to the 'senile, pregnant hags' of the Kerch terracotta collection – an image that Mary Russo (1986, 1994) has quite rightly challenged and reaccentuated in provocative ways. It is no coincidence that engendering has not only challenged the sexism of Bakhtin's world-view, but the grotesque itself rearticulates the feminist imperative in deconstructing the 'man-made' interface of the cyborg as a wholly male *Übermensch*. In this sense, the grotesque of the body electric is an anxious zone of engagement about imaging the social not as a site in which the normative defines the aberration (as patriarchies have often deigned to mark off the feminine), but as a contestatory space. This understanding is why corporeal feminism has provided some of the most provocative critiques of socialized bodies, including cyborgs. The dismembered body in pain is the *mise-en-scène* of a social paroxysm about what counts as equally human.

Beginning with his discourse on the value of the human body in history (when his osteomyelitis was already acute) and culminating in his extraordinary work on Rabelais (when, as we have noted, Bakhtin enters the world of the abject amputee), Bakhtin explores in detail the process of grotesquery and the imperative coordinates of the Other. The discourse of the body itself allows a topographic approach to the inner workings of the I/Other nexus. But we must keep in mind that all this talk of body image and phantom limb, crucial elements of grotesque epistemology, is not a paean to metaphoricity, as if the volatile body is *only* a discursive effect or an aesthetic exuberance for monstrosity: the political space traced by grotesquery is one in which the social, the psychic, and the discursive vectors of power are enmeshed in a determinate, and overdetermined, materiality. Here we may begin to specify dialogism somewhat differently from the social space of the utterance. If we interpret the dialogic as centrifugal interactivity, then the grotesque as transgressive dialogizes both the interpersonal and the intrapersonal. The erupting surfaces of the human body are signs of its unstable or porous existence (as Grosz notes, the 'detachable, separable parts of the body . . . retain something of the cathexis and value of a body part even when they are separated from the body' (Grosz, 1994: 81)), but they are also the manifestation of the relations between its inner and outer 'selves'. The divisions of the Self, its exclusions and its denials, are the social imprimatur of how it gets articulated, put together, outwardly *and* inwardly. They are representations not only of social determination but social ambivalence. Indeed, our excitement with the prospect of cyborganic politics has much to do with the ambivalence it entails, with the Janus-faced propensity of interconnectivity. As Russo (1994) astutely points out, the grotesque has a crucial role in the discourse of risk-taking: the error or aberration is a realm of possibility (certainly, this is one way we might understand the pathos and deep irony of Shelley's 'monster', as a literal embodiment of the risk of creation). As such, grotesque performances are those that challenge the normative by invoking not only the lower bodily stratum, but an array of practices that foreground and oppose the disciplinary zeal of social hierarchies. We know that modes of socialization create aberration and that the body tenaciously fights the *surveiller/punir* system of domination that Foucault explores. What is less understood, however, is the ambivalence inscribed in opposition by the mode of the excessive in grotesquery itself. The revolting body is not *necessarily* the body of revolt.

This, I believe, is a salutary reminder to the doyens of excess, particularly those who celebrate the liberatory prospect of augmentation. The ambivalence of the cyborg is also a question about whether the 'replaceable you' is always already a 'disposable you'. What has often been over-enthusiasti-cally dubbed 'progress' in the twentieth century has meant a plethora of prosthetic body parts where alternative modes of socialization might have told a different story (again, the replaceable parts that substitute for the limbs ripped off by landmines do not challenge the culture of violence symbolized by the landmines, but compensate it, appease it). The cyborg was conceived by the military–industrial complex as a more competent killing machine (precisely the symptom most celebrated in its cultural projections – *The Terminator*, *Robocop*, and to some extent, *Aliens*). Indi-vidual societies may now breathe a sigh of relief that mutually assured destruction (MAD) did not come to pass. The problem remains that domi-nant forms of cyborg possibility recode the irrationality of progress as an ineluctable discourse of increased efficiency. The intervention of the grotesque does not end this cycle of apoplexy, but it does raise the stakes in cyborganic critique by continually questioning the logic of body formation, production, and reproduction. For every duplication as sameness, grotes-query offers duplication as difference and disjunction. The grotesque cyborg is one that refuses its own discourse of perfectability and the ideal-ism of transcendence by coming to terms with and questioning the material limits on 'existence' (just as Baty recognizes the sham of cyborg socializa-tion in *Blade Runner* – androids are pre-programmed to expire, just like medicine, food, and almost every electrical appliance you could care to name). When Haraway uses the oft-quoted formulation 'I'd rather be a cyborg than a goddess', she articulates, in a profound way, the logic of discrepant cyborganics. The grotesque of the body electric is the place where the normative is undone and undoes itself; it is also the place where the power to make is also the power to make otherwise.

I began with Bakhtin's leg as a way to link grotesquery to the cyborganic and I want to close by noting the power of pain in formulating oppositional critique. Why? Bakhtin, I would argue, does not take his mind off the pain of his osteomyelitis by writing; rather, the pain of his degenerative disease is written into his formulation of the grotesque. In Elaine Scarry's brilliant analysis, *The Body in Pain* (1985), pain itself is explored as a manifest limi-nality, one that conjures both aversion (pain is something one fights) and a double-sense of self and external agency (the body fighting itself and being disciplined from without). Significantly, the sense of pain has no external object, a fact that leads Scarry into a recondite critique of its contrastive apoetheosis, imagination (which always has objects, even when imaginary objects, as its projected correlative). In his early work on the aesthetic, Bakhtin has learned the lesson of his body's inconstancy, but turns this into a theory of externality, or exotopy and outsidedness. Reading Scarry's analysis, one begins to see the logic of pain for Bakhtin's own theorization. Bakhtin notes:

> When I project myself into another's suffering, I experience it precisely as *his* suffering – in the category of the *other*, and my reaction to it is not a cry of pain,

but a word of consolation or an act of assistance. Referring what I have experienced to the *other* is an obligatory condition for a productive projection into the other and cognition of the other, both ethically and aesthetically. Aesthetic activity proper actually begins at the point when we *return* into ourselves, when we *return* to our own place outside the suffering person, and start to form and consummate the material we derived from projecting ourselves into the other and experiencing him from within himself. (Bakhtin, 1990: 26; original emphasis)

In the thrall of pain, Bakhtin realizes that pure identification with the Other is a fiction (no one can fully experience his pain), and that the aesthetic begins with an axiological understanding of the Other as separable, and formatively so, in the production of aesthetic meaning. Pain, ironically, becomes the way to explain the conditions of the object-filled world of I/Other relations, the cognitive flux of the imagination. The aspect of negation crucial to pain is also constitutive of popular festive imagery in the book on Rabelais. It is not that Bakhtin's bodily pain gets externalized in the extensive treatment of the carnivalizing body politics of others. I would say, however, that it is not a coincidence that the degenerative body (the body in pain, the decaying, dying body) is overreached by the becoming body (the body in a life-affirming festive mode, the restorative *and* revolutionary body in the marketplace of the popular). Pain is the absent presence in the odd occurrence of dismemberment in Bakhtin's lists. And pain, of course, with no objective correlative, exists in the phantom limb that would otherwise deny its possibility: 'The object that has been destroyed remains in the world but in a new form of being in time and space; it becomes the "other side" of the new object that has taken its place' (Bakhtin, 1984: 410). And thus, I would suggest, even in the heady world of clean, chrome prosthesis, in the bright lights of the cyborg for technoscience, we should look for the 'other side' of augmentation: the grotesque in the evidence of Bakhtin's leg.

Notes

1 Strictly speaking, the 'body electric' is not cyborgian but, since Bradbury's short story, it has come to be interpreted as such. 'I sing the body electric' is borrowed from Whitman, whose exuberance for mesmerism included the notion that electricity might cure ailments of various kinds. In a strange way, the cyborg is moving back through history to this mode of understanding.

2 Reference provided in personal correspondence with Galin Tihanov of Jesus College, Oxford. The pain associated with Bakhtin's osteomyelitis should not be underestimated. In his later years Bakhtin was taking painkillers by the handful.

3 Of course, this chapter does not answer such a question. I would suggest, however, that there are elements to our bodily imperfections that define our agency in relation to capital. One does not have to be a latter-day Luddite to see that machines replace humans on the basis of more than simple efficiency in output, but because humans have an endearing weakness: they challenge structures of oppression.

4 Obviously, I do not endorse Bakhtin's theorization *tout court*, not only because of some of the dubious engendering of the grotesque he deploys, but also because he is impatient with the uncanny, with the psychic aspects of grotesquery (again, these might be read as a symptom

of his own condition). For more on this aspect of the grotesque, see Wolfgang Kayser, *The Grotesque in Art and Literature* (1963). For a feminist critique of Bakhtinian grotesque that combines and transforms concepts of the grotesque body and the uncanny, see Mary Russo, *The Female Grotesque* (1994). For a detailed if somewhat dry un-festive exegesis on the grotesque, see Bernard McElroy, *Fiction of the Modern Grotesque* (1989).

5 This fact is noted by Donna Haraway in her cogent introduction to Chris Hables Gray, (ed.) *The Cyborg Handbook* (1995). This is easily the most comprehensive collection on cyborganic phenomena to date, although other useful material will be noted below. The 'white rat' as cyborg is a staple of science fiction – see, for instance, the films *Cyborg* and *Blade Runner* where the term aptly describes authority's conception of cyborganic being.

6 I will not attempt to summarize all the points that Haraway advances, although I am particularly interested in their ironic mode. Avid readers of Haraway know that there are pertinent differences in the versions of her manifesto – some conditioned by her exchanges with Sandra Harding over the status of science for feminism, others overdetermined by the changed circumstances of the socialist–feminist project in the years following Haraway's initial statement in 1985. See, Donna Haraway, 'A manifesto for cyborgs: science, technology, and socialist feminism in the 1980s' (1985: 65–107); edited and reprinted as 'A manifesto for cyborgs: science, technology, and socialist feminism in the late twentieth century', in Donna Haraway (1991).

7 These and other details of Bakhtin's health have been provided for me by Nikolai Panjkov in personal correspondence. Panjkov has been extremely helpful in clarifying some of the mystery of Bakhtin's ailments. Much of this material is now available in Russian in the journal, *Dialog/Karnaval/Kronotop*, including Bakhtin's conversations with V. Duvakin and excerpts from his letters to Kagan and Pinsky. Presumably it will also form part of the *Collected Works*, which David Shepherd at the Bakhtin Centre in Sheffield, UK, is arranging to have translated.

8 Again, these details emerge in correspondence with Panjkov. We know what happened to Bakhtin's leg. It would be interesting to discover the fate of his prosthesis. Tihanov commented to me that he has not yet seen a photograph of Bakhtin from the waist down after the amputation that clearly shows the results of his surgery. But of course, in my argument, in the realm of the Other one never sees the phantom limb anyway.

References

Bakhtin, Mikhail M. (1984) *Rabelais and His World*. Trans. Hélène Iswolsky. Foreword by Krystyna Pomorska. Bloomington, IN: Indiana University Press.

Bakhtin, Mikhail M. (1990) *Art and Answerability: Early Philosophical Essays by M.M. Bakhtin*. Eds M. Holquist and V. Liapunov. Trans. and notes V. Liapunov. Austin, TX: University of Texas Press.

Clark, Katerina and Holquist, Michael (1984) *Mikhail Bakhtin*. Cambridge, MA: Harvard University Press.

Gray, Chris Hables (ed.) (1995) *The Cyborg Handbook*. London: Routledge.

Grosz, Elizabeth (1994) *Volatile Bodies: Toward a Corporeal Feminism*. Bloomington, IN: Indiana University Press.

Haraway, Donna (1985) 'A manifesto for cyborgs: science, technology, and socialist feminism in the 1980s', *Socialist Review*, 80: 65–107.

Haraway, Donna (1991) *Simians, Cyborgs, and Women: the Reinvention of Nature*. New York: Routledge.

Holquist, Michael (1990) 'Introduction' to Mikhail M. Bakhtin, *Art and Answerability: Early Philosophical Essays by M.M. Bakhtin*. Eds M. Holquist and V. Liapunov. Trans. and notes V. Liapunov. Austin, TX: University of Texas Press. pp. ix–xlix.

Kayser, Wolfgang (1963) *The Grotesque in Art and Literature*. Trans. Ulrich Weisstein. Bloomington, IN: Indiana University Press.

McElroy, Bernard (1989) *Fiction of the Modern Grotesque*. London: Macmillan.

Russo, Mary (1986) 'Female grotesques: carnival and theory', in Teresa de Lauretis (ed.), *Feminist Studies/Critical Studies*. Bloomington, IN: Indiana University Press. pp. 213–39.

Russo, Mary (1994) *The Female Grotesque*. London: Routledge.

Scarry, Elaine (1985) *The Body in Pain: The Making and Unmaking of the World*. Oxford: Oxford University Press.

7

BAKHTIN'S DIALOGICAL BODY POLITICS

Hwa Yol Jung

Body am I entirely, and nothing else; and soul is only a word for something about the body.

– Friedrich Nietzsche[1]

Prologue

In Western modernity, it was Descartes who fastens a metaphysical clamp on the interpretive art of the body which I call carnal hermeneutics. The regime of the Cartesian *cogito*, which represents the *habitus* of the modern mind, valorizes the canonical institution of the mind's I (eye) which is at once disembodied, monologic, and ocularcentric. It is the mind transcendentalized from, rather than immanentized in, the body. As it is the act of the mind as 'thinking substance' (*res cogitans*), the *cogito* is inherently monologic because it is always and necessarily *ego cogito* (the 'I think') – the epitome of an 'invisible man' in complete isolation from others, both other minds and other bodies. As a thinking substance, the mind is independent of the body (*res extensa*); it needs nothing more than itself to exist. Once the self (ipseity) and the other (alterity) are viewed as disembodied substances, two self-contained entities, monologism – or even solipsism *in extremis* – is inevitable. For Descartes, moreover, the mind as *cogito* erected the privatized, insulated, and echoless chamber of 'clear and distinct ideas', of disembodied spectacles. The Cartesian metaphysics whose epicentre is the *cogito* may be identified with the hegemony of vision, for example, panoptic metaphysics: as the product of the sovereign gaze of *kosmotheoros*, whose single glance can assuredly scan the entire universe, it identifies my (corporeal) being-in-the-world with what I think of it.

The 'enlightened', Cartesian logocentric tradition of Western modernity, which despises and manhandles the body as a philosophical pariah or 'untouchable', has been seriously questioned, challenged, and deconstructed by Nietzsche and his twentieth-century genealogists. One of the most prominent genealogists of Nietzsche, of his carnal hermeneutics, is the inimitable literary 'charismocrat', Bakhtin. Only recently, however, have we begun to explore Bakhtin as a *bona fide* social and political thinker. The main purpose of this chapter is to explore the way in which Bakhtin's dialogical body politics subverts and interrupts the monologism of main-stream Western modernity at the crossroads of postmodernity and *éctiture féminine*. They intersect one another as inscriptions of the body inasmuch as postmodernity is the subversion of modernity on the one hand and *écriture féminine* scandalizes the 'phallacy' of 'malestream' thought on the other (see Aronowitz, 1994: 142; Gardiner, 1992: 3–4).

The (Kin) Aesthetic Harmonics of Social Existence

> Aesthetics is born as a discourse of the body.
>
> – Terry Eagleton[2]

At the time when I was immersed in the carnal phenomenology of Maurice Merleau-Ponty, the discovery of Bakhtin's dialogical body politics, for me, could be likened to Nietzsche's feeling of unbound joy when he unearthed Dostoevsky's 'underground man'. Bakhtin is a Slavic Tantrist (Clark and Holquist, 1984: 87) or, perhaps better, a Nietzschean 'Bodysattva' – to alter slightly the Buddhist term *Bodhisattva*, that is, the 'Enlightened One' who, by way of the body, is capable of 'awakening' the harmonics of the world. Interestingly, *Bodhisattva* is a conjugal word of *Bodhi* and *Sattva*, of truth and existence. So *Bodysattva* may be read as the body's truth as the way of existence. The body is, for Bakhtin, connected to everything we do and think, without exemption. His Slavic Tantrism is deeply rooted in, and stems from, the kenoticism of Russian Orthodoxy that reveres all matters for their spiritual potentials. Thus the body as the material subject and condition of human existence, too, must be revered for its spiritual potential.

The body matters, it matters deeply. *But for the body, politics itself would be still-born and brain-dead*. The visible body is the true soulmate of the invisible mind. Indeed, *I am my body*. This body of mine is two-dimensional. Its visible dimension is called the flesh, while its invisible dimension the soul. They are, as it were, a double helix. As the mind and the body are reversible phenomena, there is the mind in body and there is also the body in mind: to use James Joyce's invertible ambigrammatical expression ('Greekjew is Jewgreek'), the mind/body *is* the body/mind.

The 'aesthetic' (*aisthesis*) is pre-eminently a carnal affair, it *is* kinaes-thetic. It is *not* – to couch it in Nietzsche's expression – a discourse of 'a "beautiful soul" in a misbegotten corpse' (see Arifuku, 1991: 221). It is born of the discourse of the body as the kinaesthetic site of performance(s) which is at once theatrical, literary, psychoanalytical, and ethical.[3] Thus the body as a (kin)aesthetic phenomenon 'speaks' many languages: it 'speaks' the language of both silence and gesture. In the first place, from the standpoint of embodiment, the opposite of speech is not writing but silence. Not only is silence the karma of the body, but also 'the embodiment of silence is action' (Dauenhauer, 1980: 111). Norman O. Brown speaks of silence as the body's language. For silence is nothing but the word activated and become flesh. 'To recover the world of silence . . .', he asserts, 'is to recover the human body. . . . The true meanings of words are bodily meanings, carnal knowledge; and the bodily meanings are the unspoken meanings. What is always speaking silently is the body' (Brown, 1966: 265). Silence is indeed a (kin)aesthetic art. To modify his formula slightly: 'silence is the (m)other tongue' (Brown, 1966: 265). After the fashion of Susan Sontag (1969: 32), it may be said that silence as the body's language is not the 'incineration', but a cure for the 'pollution' of language. In the second place, gesture is both 'mute speech' and 'corporeal writing'. Gesture is a kinetic art of corporeal performance. According to the American literary critic R.P. Blackmur, it *is* indigenous to language; and 'if you cut it out you cut roots and get a sapless and gradually a rotting if indeed not petrifying language' (1952: 4). Samuel Beckett – the playwright who has an uncanny way of economizing words and relishing the language of silence – is incontrovertible when he says that in gesture as language the spoken and the written are one and the same: performance *is* composition (1929: 11).

By *inhabiting* the world by way of the body, we have access to 'the performative magic of the social' (Bourdieu, 1990: 57). As the body is the initial insertion of the self into the world of others, other bodies, the social or intersubjective is always already *intercorporeal*. To be human is to be interhuman, and to be interhuman is first to be intercorporeal. Interestingly, the English forms *am* and *is* have evolved anagrammatically from the Sanskrit *asmi*, 'to breathe' (Jaynes, 1976: 51). In the beginning, breath (or cry as a corporeal event) and being have, as it were, the same mother: *to be is to breathe* (or to cry). Rodin's *La Cathédrale* (1908) – the sculptural masterpiece that depicts two right (rite) hands tenderly coming together – surpasses all other artistic renditions in sanctifying kinaesthetically the embodied reciprocity or piety of humanity, that is, in affirming and certifying the sacrament of human co-existence. Thus the body speaks the sacramental language of social existence and its harmonics. Here Nietzsche's insight is immensely helpful inasmuch as he challenges and transgresses the speculative and specular conundrum of *theoria* and attempts to replace it with *aisthesis*. By replacing *theoria* with *aisthesis*, Nietzsche means to invert Platonism, which seeks eternal ideas radiated from the 'mind's eye'. Nietzsche's body politics is an upsurge in opposition to the long-established and continuing tradition of all that theoretic speculation has implied and entailed since the time of Plato. In *The Birth of Tragedy* (1967), the young Nietzsche valorizes music as the aesthetic incorporation of all performing arts – perhaps in the ancient Greek sense of *mousike* that includes oral poetry, dance, drama, and music – as the consummate aesthetic: 'it is only as an *aesthetic phenomenon* that existence and the world are eternally *justified*' and that 'only music, placed beside the world, can give us an idea of what is meant by the justification of the world as an aesthetic phenomenon' (Nietzsche, 1967: 52, 141). For Nietzsche, in short, the world is 'measured' (in the musical sense of *metron*) by the aesthetic of music whose primary condition of being is to *attune* ourselves to the world both human and non-human in producing the *harmonics* of relationships.

Sociality is inconceivable without bodies-in-relation (that is, inter-corporeality). The body is the living site of sociality, it actively places us in the world with other people and other things. The phenomenologist Erwin W. Straus (1966: 211) argues for the 'privileged status' of the body for the existential condition of the human as being-in-the-world. The body is directly related to other bodies. The mind, too, is a *relatum* because of the body which populates itself in the world of other people (*Mitwelt*) and other things (*Umwelt*). Embodiment is truly an intertwinement or chiasm of 'body *in* the mind' and 'mind *in* the body'. As the term *in* is ecstatic, not static like an object in the world, embodiment is an active mode of being-in-the-world. Only because we are embodied beings, we are irreducibly and inalienably social and thus ethical.

For Bakhtin, society as embodied or intercorporeal is neither a collection of invisible minds nor a seriality of visible objects. The body is not an object among other objects in the world. Rather, it is an active subject, an event-making agent: as I live my body, I exist as my body, as my flesh. For Bakhtin as for the existential phenomenologist Maurice Merleau-Ponty – to use the suggestive expression of Clark and Holquist (1984: 175) – '*the body answers the world by authoring it*' (added emphasis). Bakhtin understands well the originally Nietzschean idea of *initium*, which signifies the human potential to embark on and inscribe something new in the face of history. The notion of the lived body or the embodied self as *initium* thus rejects the Scylla of egocentricity on the one hand and the Charybdis of anonymity on the other. Both egocentricity and anonymity misunderstand the true nature of the social or dialogical: they bring death to the social (cf. Merleau-Ponty, 1970: 40 and Gardiner, this volume). In this vein, Merleau-Ponty (1973: 205) contended that in Sartre's thought there is no 'intersubjectivity' but only 'a plurality of subjects' who are held together by 'the hopeless heroism of the I' and in which the Other is seen by the I as pure negativity. Similarly, Bakhtin – for whom hell is *not* other people – opposes Freudian 'psycholo-gism' or ego-psychology because in Freudianism there is the irreconcilable antagonism between the demands of the ego's instinct or desire (pleasure principle) and the restrictions of civilization (reality principle). In compar-ing Freud with Bakhtin, Clark and Holquist remark: 'In Freud, self is suppressed in the service of the social; in Bakhtin, self is precisely a func-tion of the social. In Freud, the more of the other, the less of the self; in Bakhtin, the more of the other, the more of the self' (1984: 206). Bakhtin's genealogy of the social opposes the idea of both '*I* own meaning' (egocen-tricity) and '*no one* owns meaning' (anonymity) and opts for the 'middle way' or dialogical principle: '*we* own meaning'.[4] In the 'we', in the fulgura-tion of social existence, the self and the other are active co-producers of meaning. Thus the social is never simply 'given' (*dan*) but always 'conceived' or 'posited' (*zadan*). 'Language', Bakhtin writes, 'is not a neutral medium that passes free and easily into the private property of the speaker's intentions; it is populated – overpopulated – with the intentions of others' (1981: 294).

The Logos of Heterotopia: The Dialogics of Difference

> To be alone is no longer to be.
>
> – Tzvetan Todorov[5]

> The solution to the problem of identity: Get lost.
>
> – Norman O. Brown[6]

To be (fully) human *is* to be interhuman. Not unlike Rodin's sculpture *La Cathédrale* (1908) or the rite of towering two hands, Jackson Pollock's painting *Cathedral* (1947), with labyrinthine lines with uncountable intersections, sanctifies an interwoven web of relationships. Relation, subjectivity, and difference are intimately related and complementary but never oppositional terms. Difference is a distinct mark of the social or interhuman. But for difference, there would be no sociality. In sum, 'interbeing' or 'interdividuality' is heterotopic.

What identity is to modernity, difference is to postmodernity. Difference is indeed the cradle of the postmodern deconstruction of modernity. In other words, there is the difference between the dialectics of identity and the dialogics of difference(s): dialogics privileges difference, while dialectics advantages identity. Hegel's dialectics of identity point to the monologism of modernity. The dialectical succession of *Aufhebungen* – to use Bakhtin's language – 'finalizes' itself in the *identity* of identity and difference. Gianni Vattimo (1993: 160) judiciously concludes that the Hegelian dialectics consummates the long metaphysical tradition in Western philosophy. Bakhtin insists that there is the difference between 'dialectics' and 'dialogue' (or dialogics): 'Take a dialogue and remove the voices (the partitioning of voices), remove the intonations (emotional and individualizing ones), carve out abstract concepts and judgments from living words and responses, cram everything into one abstract consciousness – and that's how you get dialectics' (Bakhtin, 1986: 147). For him, therefore, the dialectics of identity *are* abstract and speculative 'theoretism': one is folded into the other. Hegel's logocentric identity between the 'real' and the 'rational' is also repudiated by Lyotard (1988: 179): Auschwitz is 'real' but not 'rational'. On the other hand, Bakhtin's dialogics of difference – very much like the Sinitic logic of *yin* and *yang* – finds no final foreclosure or is 'unfinalizable'.[7] Hegel's 'theoretism' and Marx's 'ideologism' are equally dogmatic because they foreclose history as a movement, as an open future. The open-ended dialogics of difference foster the idea that a multiplicity of differences finds no ending. Speaking of Dostoevsky, who is his philosophical protagonist, Bakhtin writes in unequivocal and forceful terms:

> . . . at the center of Dostoevsky's artistic worlds must lie dialogue, and dialogue not as a means but as an end itself. *Dialogue here is not the threshold to action, it is the action itself.* It is not a means for revealing, for bringing to the surface the already ready-made character of a person; no, in dialogue a person not only shows himself outwardly, but he becomes for the first time that which he is – and, we repeat, not only for others but for himself as well. *To be means to communicate dialogically. When dialogue ends, everything ends.* Thus dialogue, by its very essence, cannot and must not come to an end. At the level of his religious-utopian

world-view Dostoevsky carries dialogue into eternity, conceiving of it as eternal co-rejoicing, co-admiration, con-cord. At the level of the novel, it is presented as the unfinalizability of dialogue, although originally as dialogue's vicious circle. (Bakhtin, 1984a: 252; added emphasis; cf. Bakhtin, 1986: 170)

Heidegger's *Differenz* as *Unterschied* strengthens Bakhtin's dialogics of difference(s) as a postmodern alternative to the dialectics of identity. *Unterschied* combines 'difference' (*Differenz*) with the 'between' (*Unter*). It connects, preserves, and promotes difference and the relational. Difference as dif/ference is capable of conserving the principle of complementarity in interhuman relationships. Nancy Julia Chodorow (1980) brings her psychoanalytical insight to the clarification of differentiation which is central to the health, security, and promotion of a relational self. Differentiation even provides the basis of both spontaneity and autonomy. She judiciously contends that 'we are all to some degree incorporations and extensions of others. . . . *Differentiation is not distinctness and separateness, but a particular way of being connected to others*. This connection to others, based on early incorporations, in turn enables us to feel that empathy and confidence that are basic to the recognition of the other as a self [and, I might add, of the self as an Other]' (Chodorow, 1980: 10–11; original emphasis).

There is a holy alliance between Bakhtin's dialogics of difference(s) and gynocentric feminism that subverts Hegel's dialectics of identity, including his logocentric resistance to the body. As Judith P. Butler puts it, Hegel's subject 'wants to know itself, but wants to find within the confines of this self the entirety of the external world; indeed its desire is to discover the entire domain of alterity as a *reflection* of itself, not merely to incorporate the world but to externalize and enhance the borders of its very self' (1987: ix–x; original emphasis). To sum up, Hegel's dialectics of identity 'manhandles' (Ferguson, 1993: 55) the feminine dialogics of difference: as Thomas Laqueur elegantly puts it, '*man* is the measure of all things, and woman does not exist as an ontologically distinct category' (1990: 62; original emphasis).

Luce Irigaray wants to recognize the dialogics of (feminine) difference as *an ontologically distinct category*. She means to unveil and unmask the 'phallacy' of identity. As human sexuality is nothing but human relationships turned into intimate carnal contact, sexual difference is for Irigaray (1995) a substrate of radical alterity, of the otherness of the Other. But this feminine substrate is not just a fig-leaf hiding difference. Her feminist philosophy of sexual difference is indeed the 'subversion of identity' – *subversion* in the etymological sense of 'overturning' (*vertere*) and 'displacing' from 'below' or 'underground' (*sub*): it means to subvert the 'malestream' domination and oppression of modern identity. She contends that without difference, the very notion of subjectivity itself becomes undermined while without radical alterity, intersubjectivity becomes suspect. For its name sake, intersubjectivity is the meeting of two subjectivities with distinction wherein each subjectivity is different because it is unique. Irigaray vigorously contends that the issue of women's liberation has reached 'beyond simply a quest for equality between the sexes' (1995: 11). The solution to men's exploitation of women must come only by way of the dialogics of sexual difference. 'Equality between men and women', Irigaray insists, 'cannot be achieved without a *theory of gender as sexed* and a rewriting of the rights and obligations of each sex, *qua different*, in social rights and obligations' (1993: 13; original emphasis). It is a matter of social justice, she maintains, to give cultural values to female sexuality and genealogy for the sake of balancing out the power of one sex over the other. In sum, Irigaray intimates the dialogical model of the *two* rather than the monological mode of the *one* – one is man and the other is woman who is 'an autonomous and different subject' (*je* or I) (1993: 48). The model of 'equality' without the dialogics of sexual difference in which man and woman become homogenized is a singular model of subjectivity which, as Irigaray points out, has been historically masculine and hierarchical – man on top and woman at bottom in patriarchy. Against privileging a universal model valid for all men and all women, Irigaray advocates the paradigmatic model of two autonomous and different subjectivities in order to ensure and promote inter/subjectivity – that is, to facilitate their co-habitation and dialogue. By so doing, Irigaray transverses gendered parochialism on the one hand and genderless universalism on the other.

The Telos of Heterotopia: The Ethics of Difference

> To see the face is to speak of the world. Transcendence is not an optics, but the first ethical gesture.
>
> – Emmanuel Levinas[8]

> Freeplay [*jeu*] is the disruption of presence.
>
> – Jacques Derrida[9]

Ludwig Feuerbach's Copernican discovery of 'Thou' is a breakthrough in ethics and sociopolitical thought. Heterotopia is primarily an ethical notion and conversely what is ethical is heterotopic. Heterotopia demands the *primacy of the Other*, of alterity over the self.

(i) The 'we' decentres the embodied self. As dialogue is the interplay of speaking and answering (responding), speaking without the response is monological. Thus the primacy of the response dictates the happening of a dialogue. In other words, heteronomy is the soul of dialogue. In the language of Bakhtin's dialogism, therefore, the matter of 'addressivity' is the regulative idea of dialogue and the logosphere. The anticipated presence of the response gives dialogue and the logosphere the assured sense of pragmaticity. Speaking of the internal dialogism of the word, Bakhtin asserts:

> every word is directed toward an *answer* and cannot escape the profound influence of the answering word that anticipates. . . . Primacy belongs to the response, as the activating principle: it creates the ground for understanding, it prepares the ground for an active and engaged understanding. Understanding comes to fruition only in the response. Understanding and response are dialectically merged and mutually condition each other; one is impossible without the other. (Bakhtin, 1981: 280–2; original emphasis)[10]

Bakhtin's dialogical principle is quintessentially a linguistic principle with an ethical overtone. The anatomy of his 'translinguistics' (*metalingvistika*) is unmistakably the heart of his seminal contribution to carnal hermeneutics as social discourse. In it the utterance is a molecular segment, and the word is an atomic unit, of the dialogue. It dialogizes mind and body: the uttered word becomes flesh. Because it is conceived as verbal acts, embodied acts that are concerned with pragmatic rather than theoretic results, Bakhtin's translinguistics may be defined as performative utterances or a parley of perform-ances. Language is never a 'prison house', but an 'ecosystem', precisely because it is defined in terms of utterance as a happening of social praxis. Utterance as performance is a boundless ecology of relationships both communicative and grammatological. More importantly, in the grammato-logical trilogy of the author, the text, and the reader, the reader precedes in importance the author in the understanding of the text.

Moreover, Bakhtin's translinguistics is a nexus of doing things with words with others or in the co-presence of others. Here, it – his Slavic Tantrism, for that matter – cannot escape from but must confront Freud's psychoanalysis with its psychologism notwithstanding. In this regard, Shoshana Felman (1983) evokes the psychoanalytical sense of corporeality or the carnal dimen-sion of language when she views speech (*parole*) as 'corporeal promise' (*promesse corporelle*), which beckons a conjugal relationship between Austin's philosophy of language as speech acts and Freudian/Lacanian psychotherapeutic discourse as the 'talking cure'. The originality of Jacques Lacan, according to Felman (1987), lies in his discovery of an 'irreducibly dialogic' structure in psychotherapeutic discourse and knowledge: structured like language, the unconscious is the discourse of the Other. Speaking of his psychoanalytic theory, Felman stresses the fact that the 'true thrust' of the psychoanalytic dialogue between the therapist and the client as 'talking bodies' is illocutionary: 'fundamentally, the dialogic psychoanalytic discourse is *not so much informative as it is performative*' (Felman, 1987: 118–19; added emphasis), and thus is necessarily ethical as well.

(ii)   We would be remiss if we failed to recognize an affinity between the structural requirement of 'answerability' ('response-ability') in Bakhtin's dialogical principle and Emmanuel Levinas's ethics of proximity, which privileges the face and epitomizes human co-presence or interhuman pres-ence in terms of the structural primacy of the Other (*l'autrui*). The face is, according to Ludwig Wittgenstein (1980: 23e), 'the soul of the body'. It is the most expressive surface of the body and its performance. Thus it domi-nates our social encounters. Like the body itself, the face is language because it is expressive flexion; its rhetoric, too, is transitory pictogrammes.

The ethics of proximity as an embodied phenomenon is characteristic of Levinas's phenomenology of the face (*visage*), which is an ethic of the 'I' (ipseity) who is capable of facing (responding to) the other as 'you' (alter-ity). The face-to-face with the other may be called an 'interface'. The face is indeed an ethic, a human ethic: 'The epiphany of the face is ethical' (Levinas, 1969: 199). As the face speaks (in silence), speaks uniquely from and for each individual, it is a *de facto* ethical discourse. As such, it is an ethical hermeneutic of the body or the human as embodied. In Levinas's social ontology, which accents the primacy of the ethical, subjectivity comes into being as 'heteronomic': 'It is my inescapable and incontrovertible answerability to the other that makes me an individual "I"' (Levinas and Kearney, 1986: 27). Thus the notion of responsibility or answerability that coincides with the ethical is, first and foremost, the confirmation of the 'I' with the face as its most basic modus. Levinas writes, therefore, that responsibility is 'the essential, primary and fundamental structure of subjectivity. For I describe subjectivity in ethical terms. Ethics, here, does not supplement a preceding existential base; the very node of the subjective is knotted in ethics understood as responsibility' (Levinas, 1982: 95). In truth, responsibility is a heterocentric imperative. Because each individual is unique or 'singular' and thus different, his or her responsibility is, for Levinas, 'non-transferable' or irreplaceable. In the final analysis, *alterity is the ethical site of responsibility if not the site of the ethical itself* because ethics involves doing the good not for oneself but only and always for others. Heteronomy elevates the singular Other to the altar of interhuman relationships.

As an enfleshed ethic of proximity, care – always tender – not only has a touch of feminine difference but also belongs to a feminine genealogy. It is also a feminine response to and resolution for egocentrism (Cartesian or otherwise) and Anglo-Saxon liberalism as 'rights talk'. The ethic of care is a momentous turn in ethics itself. As it refers to that social or, more specifically, consociational process which is active, ongoing, and unfinished, the ethic of care is the prototype or archetype of responsibility as heteronomic. It is not pre-moral but fully moral. In the academic discourse of the American feminist movement, Carol Gilligan's pioneering work *In a Different Voice* (1982) birthed the ethic of care as the privileged marker of feminine difference. As opposed to Lawrence Kohlberg's 'theoretic' and 'monologic' focus on abstract rights and formal rules for the development of moral conduct, she centres her ethical concern on the 'performative' and 'dialogic' basis of relationships and responsibility. Care is heteronomic, a relational ethic *for* others, while rights are self-centred. Indeed, the ethic of care has a distinctly feminine face, it is uniquely a feminine and embodied ethic.

(iii) *Jouissance* is engendered by corporeal feminism, by 'gynesis' – to appropriate the neologism of Alice A. Jardine (1985) which signifies the feminine genesis of things and the valorization of the feminine. As carnal enjoyment, or ecstasy, it is not a feminine mystique but truly a Tantric idea.[11]

Jouissance is a carnal affair and has a thousand faces. Carnival is a species of them. Carnival which is, for its Latin name sake (*carne/vale*), an incarnation of the festive body as a 'Freude/an' affair. The body's exteriority as 'ecstasy' is manifested in the carnivalesque that is characteristic of humans as *homo ludens*, whose body politics is unavoidably ethical as well as aesthetic, cultural, and political. Harvey Cox (1969: 82) is unerring when he proposes that the carnivalesque imagination is indispensable to the survival and periodic rejuvenation of human civilization, including its political institutions. He contends, however, that when it becomes a pawn of ideology or a particular political programme, it loses its critical edge and creative *punch* and becomes shrivelled into a caged bird, toothless tiger, or – to use Bakhtin's metaphor – 'a fish in an aquarium'.

The carnivalesque is the most radical aspect of the dialogics of difference because it serves as a *non-violent technique of social transformation* by the maximal display of the body. It is festive politics that is a communal celebration of festive bodies whose space is filled always with the extravagant display of colourful vestemes and lavish gustemes. As Michel Jeanneret puts it, 'it is as if stylistic invention and the subversive power of comedy defy censure and liberate repressed desire. Through the magic of language, the rights of the body and its impulses are restored, abundance replaces austerity, and pleasures which are normally covert or repressed can be indulged' (1991: 9). In depicting the Renaissance which is the most carnivalesque period of European history, Pieter Bruegel often painted the festive scenes of the carnivalesque as a ludic parley of people, as a gluttonous feast, and a specular pageantry. The power of Bakhtin's dialogics lies in the interpretive and transformative power of the carnivalesque.

The most distinguishing marker of carnival is that it means to be subversive or metamorphic from the ground up and intends to preserve and perpetuate intersubjective dialogue at the same time. As it is heresiarchal, carnivalization breaks up and 'reverses' the colourless and prosaic monopoly of the established order of power. It dismantles the hierarchical by freely and irreverently blending – in the language of Bakhtin – 'the profane and the sacred, the lower and the higher, the spiritual and the material'(1984b: 285–6). According to the philosophic playwright Luigi Pirandello, the Latin *humor* designates 'a physical substance in the form of fluid, liquid, humidity, or moisture' (1974: 2), and humans are said to have four 'humors' – blood, bile, phlegm, and melancholy. And the humorist sees the world not exactly in the nude but in 'shirt sleeves'. For Pirandello, the principium of humor lies in edifying 'the feeling of the opposite' (*negativa*) in what we do and think. By splitting every affirmation into a negation, humor triggers and engenders the 'spontaneous birth' (*ingegno*) of things. To put it more politically, humor as *negativa* uncloaks, unmasks, or exposes the 'dirty bottom' of officialdom and the established regime.

Bakhtin's work on Rabelais establishes a set of protocols for the carnivalesque, including gastronomy and gustemes. He discovers the interlocking link between the two basic human activities: eating and speaking. He speculates that 'the origins of language itself may lie in the sharing of food as a primal expression of culture over nature, establishing a connection between digestion and dialogue' (see Clark and Holquist, 1984: 301). Indeed, symposium is a feast of words: language goes on holiday at table talk. To quote Jeanneret again, 'It is after all the same organ the tongue, which savours words and delights in foods' (1991: 2). It took the personal experience of 'lean times' for Bakhtin to discover the phenomenology of dietetics as a celebration: '[m]an's encounter with the world in the act of eating is joyful, triumphant; he triumphs over the world, devours it without being devoured himself' (see Clark and Holquist, 1984: 301).

Leszek Kolakowski judiciously observes that throughout the ages there is an incurable antagonism between 'a philosophy that perpetuates the absolute' and 'a philosophy that questions accepted absolutes' (1968: 33). In other words, the antagonism between the 'priestly' and the 'jesterly' are the two most general forms of intellectual culture at any given period of time in history. The former attempts to guard the absolute at any cost, while the latter is motivated by its distrust of the absolute or a stabilized system and wishes to deconstruct it. Carnival is the 'jesterly' play of difference aiming for the creation of an alternative or reversible world order. As a ludic form of subversion, it is playfully, that is, non-violently, subversive as it intends both to deconstruct a 'real' world and to reconstruct a 'possible' world at the same time. Clowning dethrones the stable and established hierarchy of all kinds. In the Bruegelian and Rabelaisian themes of Bakhtin's body politics, to carnivalize the world is to dialogize it: in it carnivalization and dialogization go hand in hand. As a protest against the monological 'misrule' of officialdom, carnivalesque life transgresses and transforms the canonical order of truth and the official order of reality. As Bakhtin himself writes, it

is past millennia's way of sensing the world as one great communal performance. This sense of the world, liberating one from fear, bringing one person maximally close to another (everything is drawn into the zone of free familiar contact), with its joy at change and its joyful relativity, is opposed to that one-sided and gloomy official seriousness which is dogmatic and hostile to evolution and change, which seeks to absolutize a given condition of existence or a given social order. From precisely that sort of seriousness did the carnival sense of the world liberate man. But there is not a grain of nihilism in it, nor a grain of empty frivolity or vulgar bohemian individualism. (Bakhtin, 1984b: 160)

The carnivalesque is in brief a celebration of dialogue and community; it liberates people and brings them together and induces them to participate in communal living. Here it would be remiss if we were not to come to terms, provisionally if not conclusively, with the perceptive commentary on carnival proffered by Terry Eagleton:

Carnival is so vivaciously celebrated that the necessary political criticism is almost too obvious to make. Carnival, after all, is a *licensed* affair in every sense, a permissible rupture of hegemony, a contained popular blow-off as disturbing and relatively ineffectual as a revolutionary work of art. As Shakespeare's Olivia remarks, there is no slander in an allowed fool. (Eagleton, 1981: 148; original emphasis)

Eagleton, however, is only half right. Even as a licensed occurrence, carnival is a two-sided weapon: one side is permission or authorization, and the other side is action unconstrained by law or accepted rules. It is then 'licentious' in every sense, indeed: it is, in other words, capable of transgressing or reversing the repressive *status quo* by playing out fully what Arthur Rimbaud called the aesthetic 'licentiousness' (*dérèglement*) of all the senses.

Umberto Eco (1984: 3), too, attempts to falsify what he calls 'the hyper-Bachtinian [*sic*] ideology of carnival' as *actual* liberation. Not unlike Eagleton, he contends that carnival is only 'an *authorized* transgression' because what it parodies must already be recognized as 'rules and rituals' (Eco, 1984: 6). Thus it is not an instance of real transgression but represents the existence of the rule and an example of lawful reinforcement rather than an instance of real transgression. In essence, carnival is 'only an instrument of social control and can never be a form of social criticism' (see Eco, 1984: 7). However, Eco sees what he calls 'humour' as 'a form of social criticism': there is a possibility of transgression in humour rather than in carnival. When Eco regards carnivalization as an act of 'revolution', he fails to acknowledge the difference between the destructive 'seriousness' of revolution and the non-frivolous 'playfulness' of carnival: as Mao Zedong used to say, 'revolution is not a dinner party'. Both Eagleton and Eco, in the final analysis, fail to recognize the idea that *l'esprit de corps* of carnival lies in a beckoning of non-violent resistance for change by choosing the median between reticent submission and violent killing. It is committed to practise the politics of restraint based on the sacrament of heteronomy or the unelivinable Other, which is the 'compassionate' soul of dialogue. In the politics of restraint, out of reverence for the sanctimonious presence of the Other (both human and non-human), the freedom to resist and rebel, too, is never absolute or autonomous, but always and necessarily relational (cf. White, 1993: 135-59 and Gardiner, 1993: 37).

Unlike revolution, which is both a violent form of subversion and 'the price to be paid for the abolition of differences' (see Ozouf, 1988: 12), carnival in and for the preservation of dialogue is the playful body in rebellion. As Bakhtin (1986: 134–5) insists, the distinguishing mark of violence is that *it knows no laughter* – that is, no 'Gogolian [laughing] laugh' that is joyful and festive but not frivolous, satirical, cynical, and negative. In both intention and result, subversion by violence brings death to dialogue whose epiphany is the singular Other. For it, there is no alternative because it intends to exterminate the opposition. As all prejudices and violence ensuing from them are the inevitable consequence of the intolerance of difference, there exists a radical distinction between the violence of intolerance and the laughter of tolerance. Carnival is not, although it may lead to, carnage. Nor is it all playful or ludic (see Caillois, 1979). It is, however, an antidote to violence as well as domination (political or sexual) both of which deny a genuine dialogue or reciprocity. This claims neither that the carnivalesque monopolizes non-violence nor that carnivalesque moments are absent from violence (see Le Roy Ladurie, 1979: 229ff.). The political anatomy of the carnivalesque points to a genuine alternative to getting fixed on violence as – to use the famed expression of Karl von Clausewitz – the normal continuation of politics by other means.

Non-violence is not merely a reaction to violence, but it asserts itself as the alternative to the making of history with the intent to preserve and perpetuate intersubjective dialogue in humanity. Thus carnival's empowerment of non-violence decisively takes the side of Albert Camus's (1956) 'rebel' or 'man in revolt', who renunciates calculated violence and eventually the totalitarian outcome of dialectical violence that ends what Bakhtin calls dialogue. For rebellion is a 'protest against death' as well as against tyranny, brutality, terror, and servitude (see Outram, 1989: 106–23). The true rebel is the one who senses and cultivates his or her allegiance to dialogue and human solidarity with no intention of obliterating the Other. His or her rebellion or non-violent subversion stands tall 'midway' between silence and murder in refusing to accept being what he or she is. The rebel willingly acknowledges the dialogical interplay between the ethical principle of culpability and the epistemological principle of fallibility, whereas the revolutionary thrives on the monological absoluteness of inculpability and infallibility, however noble or ignoble his or her cause may be. Epistemological dogmatism and moral absolutism have no place in carnivalesque life because they contradict the essence of Bakhtin's dialogical principle that always recognizes the ever-present, porous moment and zone of ambiguity that resides and persists between complete doubt and absolute certainty.

Epilogue

> If we keep on speaking the same language together, we're going to reproduce the same history.
>
> – Luce Irigaray[12]

Mikhail Bakhtin has come of age as a social and political thinker. Recently, Mark Poster (1993) speculated that the great traditions of Western political thought are exhausted: liberalism and Marxism as two competing ideologies 'no longer serve as effective frameworks to make political experience intelligible and no longer function as spurs to the Enlightenment project of emancipation, to the extent that the project may still coherently organize political thought and action' (1993: 1–2). Bakhtin is a Maitreyan 'Bodysattva' whose dialogical body politics would fill a gaping chasm in the alleged inefficacy of contemporary social and political philosophy.

Heterotopia is the keyword that characterizes Bakhtin's thought for which *the body really matters*. As it is wedded to everything we do and think, the body speaks the language of social existence. To be social is first to be intercorporeal. Only by way of the 'aesthetic' (*aisthesis*) can we say that the body and the world are made out of the same material. Body politics liberates us from the epistemocratic regime of the Cartesian *cogito* and from Hegel's dialectical 'theoretism'. Michel Foucault and Jürgen Habermas, who are two master architects of contemporary social and political philosophy, may very well be faulted for turning deaf ears to the body as *active agent*. On the one hand, Foucault's philosophical contribution lies in his profound genealogical insights into the institutional practices of the medical, incarcerated, and sexual body as ubiquitous 'power relations'. On the other hand, Habermas acknowledges no importance of the body, subjective or objective, and thus undermines his own theory of communicative action. He knows of no 'communicative body' and remains a logocentrist who means to *replace* subject-centred reason with reason translated into communicative action.

The pinnacle of Bakhtin's heterotopia or dialogical body politics is the primacy of the singular Other in all relationships. Difference begets relationships but it does not abort them. It is this heterocentric idea that prompts Hans-Georg Gadamer (see Grondin, 1994: 124) to say that the heart of (dialogical) hermeneutics is the possibility that the Other might be right. In the same vein, Catherine Clément (1994: 201) intimates that the Tantric philosopher privileges the Other as the altar of *jouissance* by suspending his own to 'the cry of the Other'. Bakhtin's embodied heterotopia, like Levinas's heteronomy, Irigaray's dialogical 'ethics of sexual difference', and Gilligan's embodied ethic of care, culminates in his 'architectonics' of responsibility. It is indeed a breakthrough in social and political philosophy in that it radicalizes further the Copernican discovery by Ludwig Feuerbach of 'Thou' in two ways. In the first place, Bakhtin incorporates the ethical by making it stand on its feet rather than on its head. In the second place, it activates the carnivalesque side of his Slavic Tantrism by making it the moral equivalent of and a *pharmakon* for violence. Carnivalesque performance, likened to chemotherapy, is not meant to be panacea for all politics. It anaesthetizes the historical inevitability of violence (war or 'blood rites' in particular) as the normal continuation of politics by other means. Contrary to the conventional wisdom of politics as violence, Bakhtin's heresthetic politics guarantees the rite of passage to the 'civilizing' process of what he calls the 'architectonics' of responsibility which privileges the singular Other over the Self by affirming heteronomy embedded in the principium of difference.[13]

In conclusion, non-violence is the 'compassionate' playmate of the carnivalesque. Bakhtin's ethico-heresthetic politics of difference, which transcends Nietzsche's pure aestheticism precisely because of its heresiarchal ethics of responsibility, deconstructs the 'theoretic' dialectics of identity. It seeds a lotus flower – to use the metaphor of Tantric Buddhism – in an attempt to wean us from the vicious and labyrinthine circle of violence and destruction (see Outram, 1989: 164). 'Perhaps', Nietzsche declares, 'even if nothing else today has any future, our *laughter* may yet have a future' (1966: 150). The ludic element of Bakhtin's embodied heterotopia teaches us a vital lesson that the intellectual, too, is a compassionate 'heretic' who is eternally suspicious of and perpetually irritating to mainstream politics and believes in politics as the Havelian art of the impossible.

Notes

1 Nietzsche (1959: 146).

2 Eagleton (1990: 13).

3 Eagleton (1990: 13) advances the thesis that the aesthetic is born of the discourse of the body and *aisthesis* is a revolt against the tyranny of *theoria*. Brooks, too, speaks of an 'esthetics of narrative embodiment' or the 'somatization of story' in that 'the body is a key sign in narrative and a central nexus of narrative meanings' (1993: 25).

4 Vygotsky's (1962) developmental theory of thought and language is noteworthy here in which, on the one hand, there is the inseparability of thought and affectivity and, on the other, there is no sharp division between the inner and the outer since they are two moments of one process. For a discussion concerning Vygotsky and Bakhtin, see Wertsch (1991: 46–66).

5 Todorov (1990: 89).

6 Brown (1973: 76).

7 Bakhtin's dialogics is most close to the Chinese transformative logic of *yin* and *yang*. Jullien (1992) describes the latter as *la propension* (*shi*) *de la réalité* which is dynamically continuous and alternating with no final foreclosure.

8 Levinas (1969: 174).

9 Derrida (1972: 263).

10 Bakhtin focused his attention on the question of 'answerability' or 'response-ability' in his early philosophical works (1990, 1993).

11 It is worth mentioning the recent fascinating study of women in Tantric Buddhism, of *yogini-tantra*, by Miranda Shaw entitled Passionate Enlightenment (1994). In the first place, Tantric Buddhism eulogizes the body or flesh as an 'abode of bliss' by embrcing sexual desire and pleasure for liberation or enlightenment. In the second place, it is a gynocentric view of Tantrism where women represent the idea of blissful intimacy as a path to enlightenment.

12 Irigaray (1985: 205).

13 The archetype of ethico-aesthetic politics is traceable to Balinese *negara* or 'theatre state' in the nineteenth century where, as Geertz puts it, 'big fish [do not] eat little fish' and 'the rags of virtue [do not] mask the engines of privilege' (1980: 123). See Bristol, who writes that '[c]arnival is put into operation as resistance to any tendency to absolutize authority, and to the disruptive radicalizations of social life proposed and implemented by powerful ruling elites' (1985: 213).

References

Arifuku, Kōgaku (1991) 'The problem of the body in Nietzsche and Dōgen', in Graham Parkes (ed.), *Nietzsche and Asian Thought*. Chicago: University of Chicago Press. pp. 214–25.

Aronowitz, Stanley (1994) *Dead Artists, Live Theories, and Other Cultural Problems*. New York: Routledge.

Bakhtin, Mikhail M. (1981) *The Dialogic Imagination: Four Essays by M.M. Bakhtin*. Ed. M. Holquist. Trans. C. Emerson and M. Holquist. Austin, TX: University of Texas Press.

Bakhtin, Mikhail M. (1984a) *Problems of Dostoevsky's Poetics*. Ed. and Trans. C. Emerson. Minneapolis, MN: University of Minnesota Press.

Bakhtin, Mikhail M. (1984b) *Rabelais and His World*. Trans. Hélène Iswolsky. Foreword by Krystyna Pomorska. Bloomington, IN: Indiana University Press.

Bakhtin, Mikhail M. (1986) *Speech Genres and Other Late Essays*. Eds C. Emerson and M. Holquist. Trans. V.W. McGee. Austin, TX: University of Texas Press.

Bakhtin, Mikhail M. (1990) *Art and Answerability: Early Philosophical Essays by M.M. Bakhtin*. Eds M. Holquist and V. Liapunov. Trans. and notes V. Liapunov. Austin, TX: University of Texas Press.

Bakhtin, Mikhail (1993) *Toward a Philosophy of the Act*. Eds M. Holquist and V. Liapunov. Trans. and notes V. Liapunov. Austin, TX: University of Texas Press.

Beckett, Samuel (1929) 'Dante ... Bruno. Vico .. Joyce', in Samuel Beckett et al., *Our Exagmination Round His Factification for Incamination of Work in Progress*. Paris: Shakespeare. pp. 3–22.

Blackmur, R.P. (1952) *Language as Gesture*. New York: Harcourt, Brace.

Bourdieu, Pierre (1990) *The Logic of Practice*. Trans. Richard Nice. Stanford, CA: Stanford University Press.

Bristol, Michael D. (1985) *Carnival and Theater*. New York: Methuen.

Brooks, Peter (1993) *Body Work*. Cambridge, MA: Harvard University Press.

Brown, Norman O. (1966) *Love's Body*. New York: Alfred A. Knopf.

Brown, Norman O. (1973) *Closing Time*. New York: Random House.

Butler, Judith P. (1987) *Subjects of Desire*. New York: Columbia University Press.

Caillois, Roger (1979) *Man, Play, and Games*. Trans. Meyer Barash. New York: Schocken Books.

Camus, Albert (1956) *The Rebel*. Trans. Anthony Bower. New York: Alfred A. Knopf.

Chodorow, Nancy Julia (1980) 'Gender, relation, and difference in psychoanalytic perspective', in Hester Eisenstein and Alice Jardine (eds.), *The Future of Difference*. Boston, MA: G.K. Hall. pp. 3–19.

Clark, Katerina and Holquist, Michael (1984) *Mikhail Bakhtin*. Cambridge, MA: Harvard University Press.

Clément, Catherine (1994) *Syncope*. Trans. Sally O'Driscoll and Deirdre M. Mahoney. Minneapolis, MN: University of Minnesota Press.

Cox, Harvey (1969) *The Feast of Fools*. Cambridge, MA: Harvard University Press.

Dauenhauer, Bernard P. (1980) *Silence*. Bloomington, IN: Indiana University Press.

Derrida, Jacques (1972) 'Structure, sign, and play in the discourse of the human sciences', in Richard Macksey and Eugenio Donato (eds), *The Structuralist Controversy: The Languages of Criticism and the Sciences of Man*. Baltimore, MD: Johns Hopkins University Press. pp. 247–72.

Eagleton, Terry (1981) *Walter Benjamin or Towards a Revolutionary Criticism*. London: Verso.

Eagleton, Terry (1990) *The Ideology of the Aesthetic*. Oxford: Basil Blackwell.

Eco, Umberto (1984) 'The frames of comic "Freedom"', in Thomas A. Sebeok (ed.), *Carnival!* Berlin: Mouton. pp. 1–9.

Felman, Shoshana (1983) *The Literary Speech Act*. Trans. Catherine Porter. Ithaca, NY: Cornell University Press.

Felman, Shoshana (1987) *Jacques Lacan and the Adventure of Insights*. Cambridge, MA: Harvard University Press.

Ferguson, Kathy E. (1993) *The Man Question*. Berkeley, CA: University of California Press.

Gardiner, Michael (1992) *The Dialogics of Critique: M.M. Bakhtin and the Theory of Ideology*. New York: Routledge.

Gardiner, Michael (1993) 'Bakhtin's carnival: utopia as critique', in David Shepherd (ed.), *Bakhtin: Carnival and Other Subjects*. Amsterdam: Rodopi. pp. 20–47.

Geertz, Clifford (1980) *Negara: The Theatre State in Nineteenth-century Bali*. Princeton, NJ: Princeton University Press.

Gilligan, Carol (1982) *In a Different Voice*. Cambridge, MA: Harvard University Press.

Grondin, Jean (1994) *Introduction to Philosophical Hermeneutics*. Trans. Joel Weinsheimer. New Haven, CT: Yale University Press.

Irigaray, Luce (1985) *This Sex Which Is Not One*. Trans. Catherine Porter. Ithaca, NY: Cornell University Press.

Irigaray, Luce (1993) *Je, Tu, Nous*. Trans. Alison Martin. New York: Routledge.

Irigaray, Luce (1995) 'The question of the other', in Lynne Huffer (ed.), *Another Look, Another Woman*. Trans. Noah Guynn. *Yale French Studies*, no. 87. New Haven, CT: Yale University Press. pp. 7–19.

Jardine, Alice A. (1985) *Gynesis*. Ithaca, NY: Cornell University Press.

Jaynes, Julian (1976) *The Origin of Consciousness in the Breakdown of the Bicameral Mind*. Boston, MA: Houghton Mifflin.

Jeanneret, Michel (1991) *A Feast of Words*. Trans. Jeremy Whitely and Emma Hughes. Chicago: University of Chicago Press.

Jullien, François (1992) *La Propension des Choses*. Paris: Seuil.
Kolakowski, Leszek (1968) *Toward a Marxist Humanism*. Trans. Jane Ziekonko Peel. New York: Grove Press.
Laqueur, Thomas (1990) *Making Sex: Body and Gender from the Greeks to Freud*. Cambridge, MA: Harvard University Press.
Le Roy Ladurie, Emmanuel (1979) *Carnival in Romans*. Trans. Mary Feeney. New York: George Braziller.
Levinas, Emmanuel (1969) *Totality and Infinity*. Trans. Alphonso Lingis. Pittsburgh, PA: Duquesne University Press.
Levinas, Emmanuel (1982) *Ethics and Infinity*. Trans. Richard A. Cohen. Pittsburgh, PA: Duquesne University Press.
Levinas, Emmanuel and Kearney, Richard (1986) 'Dialogue with Emmanuel Levinas', in Richard A. Cohen (ed.), *Face to Face with Levinas*. Albany, NY: State University of New York Press. pp. 13–33.
Lyotard, Jean-François (1988) *The Differend*. Trans. Georges Van Den Abbeele. Minneapolis, MN: University of Minnesota Press.
Merleau-Ponty, Maurice (1970) *Themes from the Lectures at the Collège de France, 1952–1960*. Trans. John O'Neill. Evanston, IL: Northwestern University Press.
Merleau-Ponty, Maurice (1973) *Adventures of the Dialectic*. Trans. Joseph Bien. Evanston, IL: Northwestern University Press.
Nietzsche, Friedrich (1959) *The Portable Nietzsche*. Ed. and trans. Walter Kaufman. New York: Penguin Books.
Nietzsche, Friedrich (1966) *Beyond Good and Evil*. Tr. Walter Kaufman. New York: Random House.
Nietzsche, Friedrich (1967) *The Birth of Tragedy*. Trans. Walter Kaufman. New York: Random House.
Outram, Dorinda (1989) *The Body and the French Revolution*. New Haven, CT: Yale University Press.
Ozouf, Mona (1988) *Festivals and the French Revolution*. Trans. Alan Sheridan. Cambridge, MA: Harvard University Press.
Pirandello, Luigi (1974) *On Humor*. Trans. Antonio Illiano and Daniel P. Testa. Chapel Hill, NC: University of North Carolina Press.
Poster, Mark (1993) 'Introduction', in Mark Poster (ed.), *Politics, Theory, and Contemporary Culture*. New York: Columbia University Press. pp. 1–12.
Shaw, Miranda (1994) *Passionate Enlightenment*. Princeton, NJ: Princeton University Press.
Sontag, Susan (1969) *Styles of Radical Will*. New York: Farrar, Straus and Giroux.
Straus, Erwin W. (1966) *Phenomenological Psychology*. New York: Basic Books.
Todorov, Tzvetan (1990) *Genres in Discourse*. Trans. Catherine Porter. New York: Cambridge University Press.
Vattimo, Gianni (1993) *The Adventure of Difference*. Trans. Cyrian Blamires. Baltimore, MD: Johns Hopkins University Press.
Vygotsky, Lev Semenovich (1962) *Thought and Language*. Trans. Eugenia Haufmann and Gertrude Vakar. Cambridge, MA: The MIT Press.
Wertsch, James V. (1991) *Voices of the Mind*. Cambridge, MA: Harvard University Press.
White, Allon (1993) *Carnival, Hysteria, and Writing*. Oxford: Clarendon Press.
Wittgenstein, Ludwig (1980) *Culture and Value*. Ed. G.H. von Wright. Trans. Peter Winch. Chicago: University of Chicago Press.

8

KNOWING THE SUBALTERN: BAKHTIN, CARNIVAL, AND THE OTHER VOICE OF THE HUMAN SCIENCES

Michael Bernard-Donals

> After turning the pieces of the puzzle around and around many times and shuffling them this way and that, I see they fit. They outline a more or less coherent story, as long as one sticks strictly to anecdote and does not begin pondering what Fray Luis de Leon called 'the inherent hidden principle of things'. . . . Where I find it impossible to follow . . . is what makes me think of it continually and weave and unweave it a thousand times; it is what has impelled me to put it into writing in the hope that if I do so, it will cease to haunt me.
>
> – Mario Vargas-Llosa[1]

> Let us stress in this the prophetic picture of complete destruction of the established hierarchy, social, political, domestic. It is a picture of utter catastrophe threatening the world. . . . [And yet this same destruction] also prepared a new, scientific knowledge of this world, which was not susceptible of free, experimental, and materialistic knowledge as long as it was alienated from man by fear and piousness and penetrated by the hierarchic principle. The popular conquest of the world . . . destroyed and suspended all alienation; it drew the world closer to man, to his body, permitted him to touch and test every object, examine it from all sides, enter into it, turn it inside out, compare it to every phenomenon.
>
> – Mikhail Bakhtin[2]

In the 1980s, Gayatri Spivak made current in mainstream literary and cultural studies the term 'subaltern', referring to those subjects which occupy a position so marginal and whose voice is so fragmented in relation to a dominant culture and language that they are potentially forever silenced and spoken for by that dominant culture. Since then, the post-colonial branch of the cultural studies movement has been concerned with finding a way to give voice to the position of the subaltern because the subaltern's silence – or, to use Homi Bhabha's (1990) phrase somewhat out of context, the non-sense of liminality – proves to be the anomaly, the stutter, in the coherent narrative of a dominant culture's story. And it is the liminal voice that proves so compelling, and so potentially liberatory, to writers who find that they nevertheless cannot speak or write it.

The impossible contradiction of writing what cannot be written concerns me here, because it seems to me that Mikhail Bakhtin, in writing the manuscript that would eventually become *Rabelais and His World* (1984b), is attempting to provide a glimpse of that very same contradiction. How is it, he asks, that those on the margins of a culture, by speaking the unspeakable and performing the unperformable, can nevertheless symbolically transgress – and potentially rupture – that culture's formally instituted laws and paradigms? What forms would such a transgression take? One that runs against the grain of any formal quality that would give shape to our attempts to categorize them? Bakhtin's notion of carnival and subversion – with its attention focused on the micro-politics of sanctioned and undermining cultural forms, licit and illicit language, spoken and unspoken (but performed) utterance – can contribute in productive ways to the postcolonial debate over whether or not the subaltern has a voice and what shape that voice may take.

This chapter will speculate about ways to 'hear' the voice of the subaltern by plotting the coordinates of the questions about subalternity on a Bakhtinian chart. Specifically, I want to map how material circumstances prevent a subject from having a voice but nevertheless grant a licence for activity. It is activity that, because it goes unrecognized by the cultural body that would sanction it, forces those who misrecognize it to rearrange radically their way of seeing and interpreting that very cultural body. It is the possibility of a radical transformation of the ways a culture sees and understands the relations among its subjects that is the central contribution of a Bakhtinian notion of carnival to cultural studies and postcolonial theory.

Voice and the Subaltern

Saul Zuratas, the central and yet oddly absent main character of Vargas-Llosa's *El Hablador* (translated, incorrectly to my ear, as *The Storyteller* rather than 'the talker'), is remembered by the novel's narrator as highly unusual in both appearance and in his desire to know a culture not his own. 'Slang words and popular catch phrases appeared in every sentence he uttered, making it seem as though he were clowning even in his most personal conversations' (Vargas-Llosa, 1989: 9). This clownish man is nicknamed 'mascarita' for the strawberry-coloured birthmark that covers one side of his face and for the absurdly red, wiry hair that stands on end at the top of his head, and he is, in every sense of the word, an outsider: he is from a smallish Peruvian town, the son of a convert to Judaism and in pursuit of a doctorate in anthropology that he will never finish. The narrator recounts mascarita's fascination with Kafka, with left politics, and with a group of native people from the Peruvian jungle uplands, the Machiguenga. Zuratas eventually disappears – it is said that he has gone on aliyah to Israel – and the narrator recalls a photograph taken in the Amazon forest of a Machiguenga storyteller, *un hablador*. This is a memory that is not a memory, for the narrator has neither seen the Machiguenga nor can he believe the possibility made real in the photographic image: Zuratas has himself *become* a Machiguenga *hablador*.

This possibility, however, is not the conundrum of the novel, nor is it the vexing problem of post-colonial studies. Those working with literatures and cultures outside of the Western tradition are certainly concerned with trying to name the particularities of those cultures, to understand the relation between one's culture, a culture that most often has been complicit in the marginalization of the indigenous one, and that 'other culture'. But what one leaves Vargas-Llosa's novel with is not the sense that Zuratas has or has not become the Machiguenga storyteller from the photograph, or that mascarita has found a way to investigate one culture from the perspective of another in a satisfactory way; rather, one gets the sense that the narrator has made it all up to satisfy the haunting sense in his own mind that something has been lost, that Zuratas must be spoken for, and that the Machiguenga, those with whom Zuratas had been most fascinated and almost obsessed, would provide him his voice, all through the narrator's pen.

Whose voice is it that we hear in the alternating sections of the novel, some of which are told in the voice of the Western-educated narrator but some of which are told in the rhythms and – so we are led to believe – through the eyes of a Machiguenga storyteller? What I will be arguing in this chapter is that it is the voice of the first-world speaker – who in *El Hablador* is modelled after Vargas-Llosa himself: Western-educated, a member of the monied classes, a speaker of the language, in this case academy Spanish – but that the palpability of that voice should not necessarily be equated with the subaltern's voicelessness. For, what you see in Zuratas, mascarita, the grotesque, and what you see in the Machiguenga, the people who walk but who can only be heard through the language of anthropology (and of fiction) is the carnivalization and subversion – the limit and the excess – of the language of the West, of the novelist, and of mimetic representation itself.

In her essay, 'Can the subaltern speak?' (1994), Gayatri Spivak answers her own question and says no, 'the subaltern cannot speak', because even an *ad hoc* attempt to speak in terms unsanctioned by those in control of state apparatuses – men, the wealthy or governing elite, members of class society – will necessarily be reintegrated into the narrative of culture only in terms of those sanctioned languages. What interests Spivak here are cases, first, like those of the narrator and of Zuratas before his disappearance, in which the marginal or subaltern voice is spoken for, and cases, secondly, like those of the Machiguenga, whose voice can only be listened for but never completely understood. In the first case, invoked by people like Sara Suleri (1992), Mae Henderson (1990), Kwame Anthony Appiah (1991) and, by implication, Tim Brennan (1990), first-world intellectuals see the subaltern collectively as those subject positions that fall outside the purview of the rule of law and economy and politics as representing a limit to both system and law. What lies beyond those limits is seen as a transgression, a site potentially free of the management and interpellation of the law. The problem is that in trying to recuperate the emancipatory potential of such locations, the lived experience of those who occupy such positions 'serves as fodder for the continuation of another's epistemology' (Suleri, 1992: 765). The subaltern becomes spoken for.

Spivak is interested, also, in the second case in which the subaltern, 'subsistence farmers, unorganized peasant labor, the tribals and the communities of zero workers on the street or in the countryside' (1994: 84), cannot be heard at all, in which she can be considered only the silence circumscribed by the voices of an interpretable text. This is what Homi Bhabha has called, in a different context, the articulation of colonial non-sense, 'the momentous, if momentary, extinction of the recognizable object of culture in the disturbed artifice of its signification, at the edge of experi-ence' (Bhabha, 1990: 206). It is the stuttering, uncanny recognition of the photograph of a Machiguenga storyteller that leads the narrator of *El Hablador* to tell us about the clownish Mascarita, and wonder about the trajectory of the Machiguenga people who had allowed a white photo-grapher to get that close. In this case, Spivak tells us, we listen for the subal-tern but know that we will not hear, but we will nevertheless recognize something in the text-surrounded blankness; but as she warns us by invok-ing Derrida, such a search for the Other of history seems 'to hide the relent-less recognition of the Other by assimilation' (Spivak, 1994: 89) to that very text. It really is only a momentary, affective understanding, if we can call it understanding at all. In this case the margin is always on the inside, it invades and corrupts the language of the first-world intellectual and of the rule of law, but its effect is disruptive, and it is, as some like Appiah have complained, far too textual to be noticed for very long in the face of poverty and lawlessness and exploitation and the rise of cultural forms that the intel-lectual doesn't notice because he can't read them (Appiah, 1991: 356–7).

Spivak gestures to a third alternative, of 'speaking to' rather than for the subaltern, not to represent her politically or represent her mimetically but to begin to articulate what renders her voice disruptive and momentarily visible. But there are two problems with that gesture that I want to move beyond here. First, it is only a gesture. Post-colonial studies have told us that 'the inaccessible blankness circumscribed by an interpretable text is what a postcolonial critic of imperialism would like to see developed within the European enclosure as *the* place of the production of theory' (Spivak, 1994: 89), and Appiah has suggested that we should be paying attention to forms not of novelistic production but to indigenous, hybrid 'all-consuming visions of [a] less-anxious creativity', works that are there not *for* a consumer or viewer but because 'someone cared for its solidity; it is there because it will take us further than our feet will take us' (Appiah, 1991: 357), further than traditional (that is to say, Western) reading will take us. Despite these gestures, however, most of the work since these essays were written in the late 1980s have been focused on Western art, Western literature, Western assimilation and refractions of non-Western cultural production, and even the work focused on non-Western texts has been done through western theoretical lenses – the text that surrounds Spivak's 'blankness' rather than the otherness, the blankness itself. Secondly, given the language of the Western intellectual and the invisibility of the position of the subaltern subject, what is heard beyond the limit of the sanctioned voice is always already assimilated by that voice.

If we take Spivak at her word, however, we would have to say that the subaltern voice is far from momentary, is far more sustained, than these data suggest, and is potentially just as visible in first-world texts as it is in those cultural forms whose formal nature intellectuals cannot begin to see. Appiah's example of the Yoruba figure, *Man with a Bicycle*, presents one alternative to the subsumption of the subaltern to Western idioms. That figure – of an African man holding the handles of a bicycle while walking alongside it – prompted James Baldwin, who was a member of a panel choosing pieces to be included for a 1987 show on African art at New York's Center for African Art, to say:

> This is something. This has got to be contemporary. He's really going to town! It's very jaunty, very authoritative. His errand might prove to be impossible. . . . He is challenging something – or something has challenged him. He's grounded in immediate reality by the bicycle. . . . He's apparently a very proud and silent man. He's dressed sort of polyglot. Nothing looks like it fits him too well. (cited in Appiah, 1991: 339)

The figure up-ends discussions of what is authentic and what is kitsch, what is national and what is transnational, because – suggests Appiah – of its immediacy. And its immediacy is what strikes Baldwin enough to remark upon the piece's jauntiness and upon the harlequinesque figure of the man – adorned, very clearly, with what is meant to be more or less traditional Yoruba headdress, but walking alongside one of those sturdy three-speed bicycles that have less to do with Yoruba tradition than they do with twentieth-century African and Asian urban transportation, and wearing clothes that just don't seem to fit. *Man with a Bicycle* does not mark the beginning of agency that is also its negation (the creation of a work that can only be consumed by the viewer). Instead, it marks the insertion of an agency that requires an entirely new set of criteria with which to understand why this work has the effect that it does, and what the material conditions of such an effect are that circumscribe this new activity. The same effect can be seen in *El Hablador*: as the sections written in the voice of the *hablador* accumulate, they become less confusing because the reader can pick up on the narrative devices indigenous to the text. But at the same time, as these sections accumulate, it becomes clear that the character, Saul Zuratas, and the storyteller are beginning to merge, and by the end of the novel it matters less who the speaker of these sections is than it matters how the Western narrator of the entirety of the novel/story has managed to provide the section with its presence and its effect. And its effect is similar to the one *Man with a Bicycle* had on James Baldwin. It forces a recognition of challenge, subversion, and an urgent need to resituate the position of the reader's subjectivity because standard language or interpretive tools or intellectual categories are being jammed by the dissonance – the subaltern voice – in the work itself.

Voice and Carnival

It is just this dissonance that Bakhtin talks about in his book on Rabelais and carnival. The question I want to answer in this section and the next one is how the forced reorientation of the subjectivity of the reader on confronting works like *El Hablador* (and *Man with a Bicycle*) can be made more than an affective jolt and into something like an understanding that nevertheless recognizes the radical otherness of the work itself. And I want to answer it by noting that it is just this transition, from bodily play to discursive knowledge, from laughter and the overturning of sense to recognition and ethical activity, that is implicit in Bakhtin's tract on carnival, a fact valuable for cultural studies. What remains to be done is to find a way to make the effects of those intrusions more than simply palpable but understandable.

Bakhtin is interested in the way Rabelais's images 'have a certain un-destroyable nonofficial nature; . . . These images are opposed to all that is finished and polished' (1984b: 3). One way to understand this passage is formally: what Bakhtin concerns himself with here, and in the chapters that follow on the carnivalesque, is the rough-hewn character of the images and the stories themselves. But unfinishedness more importantly has to do with the open-endedness of discourse, of the impossibility of naming once and for all the other in a discourse, and of having spoken the final word, of finishing a conversation or story. This is the sense that is most closely related to notions of subalternity, and which can help us to understand the vexing problem of a novel like *El Hablador* or a work like *Man with a Bicycle*, because unfinishedness is related to the more or less unstated (or rather, Bakhtin's less than adequately theorized) understanding of social change through discursive exchange.

When, in his discussion of remnants of the grotesque during the Renaissance, Bakhtin uses the term *interior infinite*, he is referring to what he calls the 'important discovery' of a subjectivity that has 'depth, complexity, and inexhaustible resources' (1984b: 44). A speaker gets a sense of this complexity when she attempts to address herself to someone. In order for someone to speak, she must construct for herself a set of characteristics that 'fix' the other person, to give her a name with which to 'know' her. She must also try to name herself, so that she is able to sense how she might be understood for that other. But neither name nor story fixes the subject, because the person creating the name cannot occupy the place of the other, and in fact cannot fully understand the complexities of her own location either. The result is what Bakhtin called an 'excess of vision', an excess that is linked, in *El Hablador*, to 'what Fray Luis de Leon called "the inherent principle of things"' (Vargas-Llosa, 1989: 241), the result of an attempt to write a coherent story that conscientiously ignores those pieces of the puzzle that simply do not fit.

It's what does not fit in any act of naming or speaking that leads Spivak away from being sanguine about the possibilities for the subaltern voice to be included in what Ken Bruffee, in the context of writing instruction, has called the 'conversation of [hu]man kind' (1984: 635). Even in the books on the connection between ideology and language, Bakhtin's interlocutors, Medvedev and Voloshinov, have a difficult time theorizing *how* 'every ideological structure [and language is the ideological structure *par excellence*] refracts the generating socioeconomic reality, and does so in its own way' (Bakhtin and Medvedev, 1985: 16), in part because at this point in their understanding of language they were hard pressed to see how the failure adequately to name did anything but impede agency. But if, as Bakhtin in the Rabelais book suggests, the act of speaking produces an excess or unspeakable (perhaps unspoken) sign, then the act of speaking is *unfinished* in the sense that the marginal or marginalized or ambient sign can itself be perhaps not heard but certainly reintegrated into the subsequent utterance. But because it is not part of the 'official version' of the utterance, it is very much potentially destabilizing of it in measurable ways. It isn't just that a carnival discourse, the unofficial and unsanctioned undermining of official language, is potentially disruptive and always unfinished because of its excessive nature. Language itself, even in its official version, excludes and marginalizes aspects of being that return to haunt that official version both politically and aesthetically. Carnival acts as a wedge that potentially opens up a space in which we are apt to catch a glimpse of excess.

The forum in which we do the work of investigating just this carnival aspect of any utterance is the panoply of lived life. In *Rabelais*, Bakhtin goes so far as to suggest that there is what he calls a 'two-world condition' in lived life. Bakhtin here is speaking specifically about the medieval and early Renaissance world of Western and Central Europe, in which individuals 'built a second world and a second life outside of officialdom, a world in which all medieval people participated more or less' (1984b: 6). This condition is the result of a centripetal, sanctioning cultural force that consolidated class and state and that rewarded adherence to ecclesiastical and to other official forms. The more important point is that lived life includes not only what we speak and name, but also what we cannot speak (or refuse to speak). Lived life returns in some other form that is nevertheless recognizable as another 'distinct portion of itself'. Bakhtin even goes so far as to suggest that, as carnivals and feasts became less the province of everyday life and more something to be set aside for revelry by landowners, these feasts came more and more to be associated with 'crisis time', 'moments of death and revival, of change and renewal', 'of breaking points in the cycle of nature or in the life of society and man' [sic] (1984b: 9). Recognizing the crisis associated with carnival and with the excessive and unspoken is important if we want to reconsider the possibility of recognizing and understanding the subaltern. It is important because it forces us to be aware of the critical and disruptive potential in everyday events, like the death of a family member or, as in the case of the Yoruba figure so noticed by James Baldwin, the creation of a work that refracts the material conditions of the mundane act of walking to or from work in contemporary Nigeria. The series of events that leads Saul Zuratas to disappear and to 'reappear' to the narrator of *El Hablador* as an insider/outsider in Machiguenga culture as a storyteller is the encroachment upon that culture by members of a university department of language and anthropology in which Zuratas was, for a short while, a student. This would certainly qualify, I should think, for members of the Machiguenga, as crisis time. What is important to notice is just how that crisis is met: not by revolution or by flight into the forest, as narrated by the voice of either Zuratas or any individual Machiguenga, but by the palpable disruption and up-ending of the everyday, humdrum narrative of a storyteller, who himself has as his calling the continuation of the narrative of the 'people who walk' (but who have no direct, unmediated voice), a narrative that turns out to be that of the Western narrator. How else do you explain the third section of the book putatively narrated by a storyteller on the encroachment of the Viracochas, the whites? It is that section that is intruded upon by Kafka, in which the storyteller was 'changed into an insect. . . . A Buzz-buzz bug, perhaps. A Gregor-Tasurinchi. I was lying on my back' (Vargas-Llosa, 1989: 203). It is intruded upon by the voice of the storyteller's parrot calling the storyteller's name, 'Mas-ca-ri-ta, Mas-ca-ri-ta, Mas-ca-ri-ta . . .' (1989: 234). Crisis time here is met with a narrative of the everyday – of life and death, of bad spells cast and men and women in love – but it is a narrative that is so up-ended that the name of the narrator and the name of the storyteller become so confused as to become unhitched from the generic constraints of novel or even conception. What you hear is not the voice of the subaltern at the critical juncture of crisis, but the voice of the narrator disrupted by the unspoken presence of the unseen and inaccessible subaltern centre of the book itself. This is no political revolution, but a discursive crisis rendered visible and susceptible to analysis if we are only attentive to the circumstances of lived life that create it.

The disruption of the voice of the narrator in *El Hablador*, as both mundane and revolutionary – the 'two-world condition' – assumes a view of history that is non-linear, and (at least in Bakhtin's view) cyclical. In trying to name the everyday events of a lived life from the perspective of historical time – as in the Renaissance when 'grotesque images . . . become the means for the artistic and ideological expression of a mighty awareness of history and of historic change' (Bakhtin, 1984b: 25) – those named images nevertheless 'preserve their peculiar nature, entirely different from ready-made, completed being' (1984b: 25) and historical time. The effect of the marginal/everyday upon history is rupture, what Bhabha recognizes as aporia, ellipsis, the dislocation of the grotesque, or perhaps marginal, certainly subaltern ('not possessing one's own hegemonic position' from which to speak) (see Bhabha, 1994: 52–60; quote from 59). This rupture expresses itself (at least, suggests Bakhtin, in popular festive forms of the carnivalesque) in the erasure of the line between past and future, the possible and the impossible. 'The author of the "[prophetic] riddle"' of events of dread and wonder also foretells the 'complete destruction of the established hierarchy, social, political, and domestic' (Bakhtin, 1984b: 237) and, I would add, generic/discursive. If such a crisis time is anything like Benjamin's 'blasting the moment out of the continuum of history', in which the figural Angelus Novus moves forward through time with his back to the future and with his eyes on the disaster of the present blowing him backward (Benjamin, 1969: 262, 257–8), then we have a way to understand not the language or voice of the subaltern but the circumstances of crisis that increase the likelihood of an 'authorial exchange' whose anxious attempts to name the other provide radical excess, and the character of prophecy and the future in the present through which the language of that other might be expressed or through which it may have an effect.

Such an effect uncannily rings in a reader's future in a way that forces her to reconsider the name of (aspects of) the other in herself. Finally, Bakhtin is interested in the potential for parody, laughter and debasement in the carnival exchange to lead to what he calls 'freedom'. Inasmuch as freedom is necessarily elusive as a state of being, it nevertheless has effects that can be measured in certain instances, instances that potentially change human ethical activity from that point forward. This, I think, is the kind of freedom Bakhtin has in mind when he ascribes to carnival a peculiar logic of the 'inside out' (*à l'envers*), of the 'turnabout', of a continual shifting 'from top to bottom, from front to rear' which is 'frank and free, permitting no distance between those who came in contact with each other and liberating from norms of etiquette and decency imposed at other times' (1984b: 11, 10). The laughter that comes of inversion has an 'indissoluble and essential relation to freedom' from sanction, from the law, and from conventional notions of the Divine (1984b: 89). If we go back to the Dostoevsky book (1984a, 185ff.), the laughter evoked through the parodic exchange in carnival comes from a feeling of ambivalence about the utterances themselves and which takes precedence, which is the 'serious' word and which is meant to undercut or destabilize it. Bakhtin suggests that parody is meant to 'regenerate'.

What is regenerated is one's sense of self, one's understanding of how she has a place in lived life, in history, a sense drawn 'from the outside world. It is the ideological interpretation of one's social recognizance and tenability by rights, and of the objective security and tenability provided by the whole social order, of one's individual livelihood' (Voloshinov, 1986: 89). The ambivalence evoked by reorienting one's own language to another's language also in part reorients the material with which one constructs a self in the first place. Laughter, in the instance of parody, can be seen as a physical manifestation of an irruption of excess into a discourse characterized by the orderliness of its naming of a self and an object of discussion, and it marks a certain freedom to the extent that it provides a way out of the univocity of that name. In *El Hablador* the storyteller's parrot mimics Zuratas's nickname, 'Mas-ca-ri-ta, Mas-ca-ri-ta', and it makes the position of the reader ambivalent. That parroted name levels two discourses, one utterable and one unutterable, one recognizable in the language of the Western novelist, and one unrecognizable (the language of the storyteller) except in the way that it invades the narrator's language. The name becomes, in Bakhtin's terms, untenable, freed to show the reader just how adroitly it manages to, in Baldwin's terms, go to town.

Ideology and the Subject

What we have learned is that Bakhtin's understanding of the carnival is connected to an historical time that is not linear but, in Benjamin's terms, shot through with *other* time. Such an understanding resituates not just the carnivalized subject, the clown or the rogue, but the speaking subject. Like Bakhtin, Bhabha suggests in the essays that comprise *The Location of Culture* (1994) that the identification by that subject of an imagined, named place and time locate her both centrally as a 'citizen' but also (by dint of what she cannot say) as a stranger to those aspects of nation and culture that are not and cannot be named. The state, the location of utterance, is an originary point of *difference*, a difference that is irrepressible and yet which announces the weight of the historical *gran récits* by the ruptures which cannot help but be seen in that larger narrative. It is this originary point that Spivak would like to see as the beginning of a post-colonial intervention.

She begins, much as Bakhtin does, by asking about what is omitted from the (colonial) master narrative. Spivak's question is as much about the language that cannot be spoken as it is about the *conditions about which* can be spoken, and in this she has in mind, I think, those subjects so marginalized as to be unclassifiable in terms of the ideologies that define 'citizen-subjects', like members of the Machiguenga tribe, or those who, like Mascarita, are demographically and culturally unnameable (a Jew by choice in a Christian country who believes in the magic of the native cultures). Spivak suggests that such a question draws our attention to the weight of those national narratives, and the sense that such a narrative 'takes on its own impetus as it were, so that one begins to see *reality* as non-narrated' (Spivak, 1990: 19). In part, suggests Spivak, the work of the post-colonial critic is to be attentive to the momentum of such narratives so as to suggest the points at which those narratives seem to be stories of *forgetting* their connection to the real, the conditions that bore them. Inasmuch as each narrative, and particularly each colonial narrative, names not the materiality of the state but the momentum gathered by the story itself as it works itself up into a seamless garment that says over and over again 'I am I', Spivak's method is in part to put pressure on those narratives by looking for places where the utterance works too hard, where it seems not to be saying 'I am I' but rather 'Don't look at that which isn't me'. The places to look for such ruptures in the narrative are 'on the other side' of such attempts to forge identity (Spivak, 1990: 28), not necessarily in the originary point of utterance as though it were a point-in-space, but in an effect of some unseen or unperceived cause: the formation of a subject prior to its insertion into the narrative of identification, of the 'I', of univocal voice.

If we put this back into the terms of Bakhtin's writing on carnival (or on authorship, or on parody), the location or point of origin is the moment of *impossibility of speech*. It is the location in time and space at which the speaker recognizes that she cannot predict or understand the voice of the other, and that, paradoxically, she cannot see herself as the other does. At that moment she *misspeaks*, says the wrong thing, says what she does not mean and thereby produces a word, an effect, that disturbs the context of the situation while at the same time (re)constructs it. If we push this far enough, every utterance, every word, is potentially parodic because every utterance is directed at what we think our interlocutor – or what we ourselves, if we were able to say our name, our 'I' – might say.

A subject defined by its otherness and its connection to the necessity for self-(mis-)identification is in many ways consistent with Spivak's reformulations of Marxist theory, which more clearly articulate the position of the 'uninterpellated' subject. In her work on the literature of India, agency is both active and constrained, both radically textual (in that we speak and are spoken as subjects) and entirely material. The constraints upon agency are the result of a convergence of effects (political and social) that tend to situate or place individuals in material and social relation.

As Spivak puts it, we should act as if we 'cannot consider all other subjects, and that [we] should look at [our] own subjective investment in the narrative that is being produced.... [T]he western theoretical establishment should take a moratorium on producing a global solution.... Try to behave as if you are part of the margin, try to unlearn your privilege.... [I]t is an invitation for the investigating subject to see that the projects are produced within a much larger textuality' (Spivak, 1990: 29, 30). The classical (or, perhaps, ham-handed vulgar) Marxist tradition sees class as an analytical tool with which we can understand individuals' relations to one another given the material and discursive constraints of ideology. Spivak's reformulation insists on a two-way relation: individual subjects interpellated ideologically by their relations to others, but interpellation itself is affected by the naming and misnaming, remembering and forgetting, narrating and untelling. Like Bakhtin, Spivak wants to make room for what is left out by trying to identify moments in which what is left out makes its way from the margin to the centre, not as text but as effect on text. But what Spivak leaves untheorized – like Kwame Anthony Appiah, in his otherwise accurate description of the production of 'otherness-as-commodity' in Western assumptions about African art – is just what 'unlearning privilege' or 'behaving as if we were on the margin' looks like.

This is because, according to Spivak, it isn't possible. As I've tried to suggest all along, what's especially odd about the subaltern in this view is that it's a position occupied by identifiable human subjects but that it is clearly inaccessible by other human subjects that do not occupy those positions. For her, the term subaltern is 'truly situational' (1990: 141). Part of the problem here is that Spivak (and her interlocutors in the Subaltern Studies Group, including Ranjit Guha) takes the term from Gramsci. Hegemony is exerted upon those subjects who 'share an interest' and who participate in a culture dominated by a number of complex ideological forces. But those subjects who do not share the interests valorized by those defining the tasks of the state or its culture are left out, and so do not have access to the political and cultural arena. 'The subaltern really had no access to those narratives of nationalism, those narratives of internationalism, nationalism, secularism'; the subaltern is non-narrativizable, and so the only political or discursive position it can occupy is as 'a non-narrativizable subject of opposition' (Spivak, 1990: 142, 145). This is why, Spivak suggests, there can be no subaltern position in the first world, and certainly not in the United States: every interest is so completely brought under the narrative of class and is so completely involved in an economy that proliferates images for pleasure (1990: 143–4) that the possibility of the subaltern is coopted and reintegrated into that economy. What you get is either the narrative of pleasure and class or silence, with silence occasionally erupting into the narrative of nation or transnational economy, but which is subsequently coopted by that narrative (see the concluding section of 'Can the subaltern speak?').

Bakhtin, fortunately, tells another story. While his notion of the subject is similar to Spivak's, and while his understanding of the voice on the margins whose tendency it is to disrupt wider historical or linear narratives of nation and class is similar to Spivak's, his ideas about the palpability and the effect of the radical subaltern voice is not. *Rabelais and His World*, along with the material on monologism/dialogism and on language as material, suggests that the tendency to see language and class as intransigent and monolithic, is unavoidable. (We can't 'talk our way out of' class or out of a paradigmatic way of understanding self or world.) But at the same time, there exists what might be called a 'subaltern effect' or 'Otherness effect' inherent in language itself. Such an effect marks the boundaries of class and of understanding but it also exceeds it, like the excess of vision required in the utterance of one's name, like the excess of narrative that could be said to result in the composition of the narrator's story that forms the heart of *El Hablador*.

The subaltern effect is visible in the space occupied by work like *Man with a Bicycle*, created by 'those who will not see themselves as Other' (Appiah, 1991: 356), because the anxiety of non-coincidence is nothing to become anxious about. It is the effect that 'renders [voice] more material, closer to man [sic] and his body, more understandable, and lighter' (Bakhtin, 1984b: 380). It is visible in the space where, 'despite unimaginable poverty; despite wars, malnutrition, disease, and political instability, . . . cultural productivity grows apace: popular literatures, oral narrative and poetry, dance drama, music and visual art all thrive' (Appiah, 1991: 356). And, in first-world cultures, it is visible in the parrot that cries 'Mas-ca-ri-ta, Mas-ca-ri-ta', and haunts the peripheral vision not of a narrator in Florence but a novelist and politician from Peru exiled in Spain.

Conclusion

This is what we have learned from Bakhtin: because language itself is the always unfinished creation of a subject in the midst of the verbal and ideological material through which we mediate lived life, and because the act of utterance entails both saying that which you didn't intend and the potentially liberatory excess that comes with the act of misremembering and misnaming your self and your interlocutor and your location, every act of speech is an act of otherness, of exteriority, or marginalization and cooptation by the centre. Learning this entails understanding the fragility of what we say, and the fragility of the location – not really a location at all, but an aporia between myself and the 'I' – from which we say it. Spivak is right: there is no subaltern in the first world. But she is also wrong: there is a subaltern effect even in the most monologic of utterances. Spivak is also right to suggest that we are most likely to be aware of the effect of the subaltern where the pressure of colonization and exploitation are exerted on a national or cultural language. But Bakhtin suggests that such pressure – of domination and exploitation, silence and exile, misuse and cooptation – exists in the language of a Peruvian novelist as it does in the language of the Indian intellectual. How, then, do we most actively engage this subaltern effect?

We do so by paying close attention to the location of utterance. As Bhabha (1990, 1994) has suggested of the margins that now exist in the heterogeneity of the cosmopolitan city centre, and as Bakhtin has suggested of fools, peasants and idiots in the marketplace, it is by first investigating the location of marginal culture that we begin to match the characteristics of the liminal, the carnival, and the subaltern with the effects that they have not just on those locations but upon the investigator. Here I will be relying on Satya Mohanty's essay, 'Epilogue', but I have in mind also the work of Bakhtin: '[O]ur location is an objective feature of the world in which we live, the world as it is constituted precisely by various "positions" of power and powerlessness. As such, our location is causally significant; it shapes our experiences and our ways of knowing' (Mohanty, 1995: 110).

Neither Mohanty nor Spivak want to reduce an attentiveness to position to an attempt to try to place ourselves in the position of the other, and in so doing ask whether those others have anything valuable to tell us. To do so would be to ask, like the narrator of *El Hablador* does of Saul Zuratas before he disappears, whether 'polygamy, animism, head shrinking, and witch doctoring with tobacco brews represent a superior form of culture' (Vargas-Llosa, 1989: 24). It would amount to simply a different form of colonialism. And there is some serious doubt, suggests Mohanty, whether even the most radical anti-foundational position can be useful to a cultural studies project which tries to take seriously the possibility that there are other ways of knowing, voices which we may not be able to hear, precisely *because* of the values we hold or the paradigms within which we work.

Mohanty suggests, like Bakhtin, that we act 'as if' we were able to know something about the position of the other – as in a speaking situation – and treat our knowledge 'as if' it was objective, knowing full well that it nevertheless is mediated by our own inextricable position in the historical *gran récit*. The 'subaltern effect' that is simply part and parcel of our predicament as subjects cut across by discursive and ideological material lures us into thinking of the other as the other-to-be-named, while at the same time it frees us to be able to think of the other as the other-who-cannot-be-spoken. It allows us to suggest that, while we may not be able to hear the voice of the subaltern, there are portions of a world that both the subaltern and we share in common.

Important to such a programme is the need to approach this tension in an 'open-ended way: thus, a basic question to ask about particular disagreements is whether – and to what extent – they refer to the same things, the same features of the world' (Mohanty, 1995: 114). To put it the way Roy Bhaskar does, to say of two radically disparate understandings – the licit and the illicit, historical time and 'crisis time', one's location and the statement that names that location – that they produce a clash or a stutter is to presuppose 'that there is something – a domain of real objects or relations existing and acting independently of their (conflicting) descriptions – over which they clash. Hence incommensurable theories must share a part world in common' (Bhaskar, 1989: 19). Mohanty and Bhaskar both suggest, in part, that the position of the subaltern is not directly accessible, any more than the utterance of the pronominal 'I' locates the position of the subject; and that contextualizing the subaltern in terms of the larger cultural or historical narrative that by coercion or by sheer entropy, or what Bakhtin would call centripetality, coopts it and more or less swallows it whole is simply unavoidable. But both also suggest that we learn significantly about those very subaltern positions (or, in Bakhtin's terms, those clowns, peasants, dunces, fools) by dint of their effect upon broader cultural narratives; and both suggest that those positions provide a *more* accurate sense of the nature and characteristics of broad cultural narratives because they are quite apparently the positions most affected by them. Spivak's concern, mirrored by Appiah's, that women and third-world artists and thinkers become 'otherness machines' (Spivak, 1990: 356), prized because they represent those who cannot be spoken form, is at least partly mitigated here: in the words of Sandra Harding, it is the third-world intellectual, the woman who has worked in oppressive conditions in the north of India,

> the outsider within, the marginal person now located at the center, the person who is committed to two agendas that are themselves at least partially in conflict – the liberal feminist, socialist feminist, Sandinista feminist, Islamic feminist, or

feminist scientist – who has generated feminist sciences and new knowledges. (Harding, 1992: 455)

Knowledge created under these kinds of dissonant conditions, from this multiplicity of locations, is superior to what we might think of as 'objective' knowledge because it not only mirrors, apropos Bakhtin, the conditions under which we all speak, but also because it requires

> the strong objectivity that can take the subject as well as the object of knowledge to be a necessary object of critical, causal-scientific!-social explanations. . . . Understanding ourselves and the world around us requires understanding what others think of us and our beliefs and actions, not just what we think of ourselves and them. (Harding, 1992: 460, 461)

This, I take it, is what Bakhtin may have meant when he says, in *Rabelais and His World*, that the reduction, the excess, the incommensurable 'prepared a new, scientific knowledge of this world' which 'destroyed all alienation; it drew the world closer to man, to his body, permitted him to touch and test every object, examine it from all sides, enter into it, turn it inside out, compare it to every phenomenon' (1984b: 381). We may not be able to name the subaltern, the marginal, we may not occupy the positions of pieceworkers in factories in Malaysia, and we may not know for certain the significance of the stories that justify the nomadism of a particular Peruvian people, but by being attentive to the effects of those positions upon the narratives and the economies of the national or the transnational or the intellectual, and by understanding that those positions mark the boundaries, the limits, of objectivity and of what we take to be the coherence of a culture, the subaltern may be seen to have more than simply a transitory existence, and that his story, though told through the pen of either a Gayatri Spivak or a Mario Vargas-Llosa, might nevertheless mark the position of writing, of telling, itself.

Notes

1 Vargas-Llosa (1989: 241, 244).
2 Bakhtin (1984b: 237, 381).

References

Appiah, Kwame Anthony (1991) 'Is the post- in postmodernism the post- in postcolonial?', *Critical Inquiry*, 17: 336–57.
Bakhtin, Mikhail M. (1984a) *Problems of Dostoevsky's Poetics*. Ed. and trans. C. Emerson. Minneapolis, MN: University of Minnesota Press.
Bakhtin, Mikhail M. (1984b) *Rabelais and His World*. Trans. Hélène Iswolsky. Foreword by Krystyna Pomorska. Bloomington, IN: Indiana University Press.
Bakhtin, Mikhail M. and Medvedev, P.N. (1985) *The Formal Method in Literary Scholarship: A Critical Introduction to Sociological Poetics*. Trans. Albert J. Wehrle. Cambridge, MA: Harvard University Press.
Benjamin, Walter (1969) *Illuminations: Essays and Reflections*. Ed. H. Arendt. Trans. H. Zohn. New York: Schocken Books.

Bhabha, Homi (1990) 'Articulating the archaic: notes on colonial nonsense', in Peter Collier and Helga Geyer-Ryan (eds), *Literary Theory Today*. Ithaca, NY: Cornell University Press. pp. 203–18.

Bhabha, Homi (1994) *The Location of Culture*. New York: Routledge.

Bhaskar, Roy (1989) *Reclaiming Reality: A Critical Introduction to Contemporary Philosophy*. London: Verso.

Brennan, Timothy (1990) 'The national longing for form', in Homi Bhabha (ed.), *Nation and Narration*. New York: Routledge. pp. 44–70.

Bruffee, Ken (1984) 'Collaborative learning and the "conversation of mankind"', *College English*, 46: 635–52.

Harding, Sandra (1992) 'Rethinking standpoint epistemology: what is "strong objectivism"', *Centennial Review*, 36 (3): 437–70.

Henderson, Mae Gwendolyn (1990) 'Speaking in tongues: dialogics, dialectics and the black woman writer's literary tradition', in Henry Louis Gates, Jr (ed.), *Reading Black, Reading Feminist: a Critical Anthology*. New York: Meridian. pp. 116–42.

Mohanty, Satya P. (1995) 'Epilogue. Colonial legacies, multicultural futures: relativism, objectivity, and the challenge of otherness', *PMLA* 110 (1): 108–18.

Spivak, Gayatri Chakravorty (1990) *The Post-Colonial Critic: Interviews, Strategies, Dialogues*. Ed. Sarah Harasym. New York: Routledge.

Spivak, Gayatri Chakravorty (1994) 'Can the subaltern speak?', in Patrick Williams and Laura Chrisman (eds), *Colonial Discourse and Post-Colonial Theory*. New York: Columbia University Press. pp. 66–111.

Suleri, Sara (1992) 'Woman skin deep: feminism and the postcolonial condition', *Critical Inquiry*, 18: 756–69.

Vargas-Llosa, Mario (1989) *The Storyteller*. Trans. Helen Lane. New York: Penguin.

Voloshinov, V.N. (1986) *Marxism and the Philosophy of Language*. Trans. L. Matejka and I.R. Titunik. Cambridge, MA: Harvard University Press.

PART III

CONVERSATIONS

9

'THE INCOMPARABLE MONSTER OF SOLIPSISM': BAKHTIN AND MERLEAU-PONTY

Michael Gardiner

> Not only do we have a right to assert that others exist, but I should be inclined to contend that existence can be attributed only to others, and in virtue of their otherness, and that I cannot think of myself as existing except in so far as I conceive of myself as not being the others: and so as other than them. I would go so far as to say that it is of the essence of the Other that he exists. I cannot think of him as other without thinking of him as existing. Doubt only arises when his otherness is, so to say, expunged from my mind. (Marcel, 1949: 104)

The respective intellectual projects of Mikhail Bakhtin and the French existential phenomenologist Maurice Merleau-Ponty display a number of remarkable affinities, in terms of their basic assumptions, overarching thematic preoccupations, and critical strategies, as has been noted in brief elsewhere (Holquist, 1990: xxxv; Jung, 1990: 95). What I wish to argue in this chapter is that, considered together, these two figures have much to offer to post-Cartesian human sciences, particularly with respect to overcoming the solipsistic tendencies of modernist accounts of selfhood, identity, knowledge, and so forth. Such theories, it will be argued here, are irrevocably tainted by what David Michael Levin calls a 'deep narcissism'. By succumbing to the fantasy of 'total self-determination, total self-grounding', the monadistic subject of modernity refuses to recognize otherness, and interprets the world as a projection of its own cognitive faculties. This situation has, Levin remarks, precipitated 'an affective and epistemological abyss between self and others. No sense of community can join together what has been separated by this abyss' (Levin, 1991: 56, 59). In contesting such an egocentric subjectivism and the threat to genuine sociality that it entails, Bakhtin and Merleau-Ponty seek to reverse this alienation between self and other, and between body and world, in order to uphold the Utopian possibility of an 'ideal community of embodied subjects' (Merleau-Ponty, 1970: 82). As such, they argue that it is only by jettisoning the stubborn residue of Cartesianism that remains mired in Western thought and adopting a more 'dialogical' world-view that we can grasp the intrinsically open, interactive nature of bodies and selves as they co-exist within a shared life-world. Bakhtin and Merleau-Ponty therefore endeavour to dislodge the egological, narcissistic subject from the pinnacle of Western metaphysics. Yet there is no deconstruction of the subject as such in their writings: the self remains an active, engaged agent, the initiator of a series of ongoing projects, and not simply an *effect* of external power-relations or modes of signification, as many postmodernists have suggested (Burkitt, 1994; Gardiner, 1996a). In what follows, I shall concentrate on two major questions. First, precisely how do Bakhtin and Merleau-Ponty characterize the challenge of solipsism, and why do they view the Cartesian self (the archetypal subject of modernity) as such a serious threat to the dialogical values they espouse? Secondly, what concrete alternative to this egocentric hyper-rationalism do they advance? By juxtaposing the writings of Bakhtin and Merleau-Ponty in this manner, I seek to reveal a striking convergence of themes and problematics that will, it is hoped, serve as an impetus to further inquiry and discussion.

The Challenge of Solipsism

The enigmatic title of this chapter – the 'incomparable monster of solipsism' – is chosen from a lecture on the philosophy of nature delivered by Merleau-Ponty during his tenure at the Collège de France in the 1950s. In referring to solipsism as an 'incomparable monster', he was not indulging in empty phrase-mongering or rhetorical hyperbole. Throughout his career, Merleau-Ponty railed against what he variously called 'high-altitude thinking', Cartesian dualism, and objectivism. This 'philosophy of reflection' is rooted in the belief that the production of knowledge involves a solitary subject contemplating an external world consisting of discrete facts, which is then 'possessed' in thought via a sovereign act of cognition. The capacity for abstract, rational thought is considered to be the highest and most admirable human faculty, a view Merleau-Ponty refers to as 'psychism'. In the philosophy of reflection, the subject that grasps the world in a purely cognitive manner is, in effect, a disembodied observer. Since the epistemic truths generated by this transcendental ego are timeless and universal, the actual situation within which any given thinker is located is inconsequential. The egological self 'makes itself "indifferent", pure "knower", in order to grasp all things without remainder – to spread all things out before itself – and to "objectify" and gain intellectual possession of them' (Merleau-Ponty, 1964a: 162). Accordingly, the world lies prostrate before this omniscient subject's purview, like the captured booty and slaves paraded triumphantly before a victorious warrior-potentate. What this philosophy attempts to achieve is a kind of magical transcription: to substitute a rigorous and irrefutable system of crystalline logic and conceptual rigour in the place of a complex, multi-valent, and ambiguous reality. This transcription is designed to establish absolute lucidity and certainty where there was once obfuscation, to 'take out an insurance against doubt', as Merleau-Ponty puts it, although the premium to be paid for such clarity is 'more onerous than the loss for which it is to indemnify us' (1968: 36). Such an overwhelming desire for epistemological certitude and logical coherence is, for many theorists, the *locus classicus* of modernity (de Certeau, 1984; Ferguson, 1989). The transcription of the world into a pure, 'algorithmic' language and the use of idealized representations and formalist theories of knowledge as surrogates for the concrete world is something that disturbed Merleau-Ponty greatly; at one point, he likened it to 'a nightmare, from which there is no awakening' (1964b: 160). Not only is the body alien to this psychical subject: other selves are equally mysterious entities that can have no authentically dialogical relationship *vis-à-vis* the rational *cogito*. The external world presents itself as a collection of inert facts that is wholly Other, and which becomes a *threat* to my sovereignty unless I can master it and transform it into something I can use. Consequently, in the modern context we tend to relate to others and to the world instrumentally. The logical *terminus* of such an attitude is the rapacious and domineering orientation of modern scientific and technological rationalism, or what Merleau-Ponty calls a 'new prometheanism' (1970: 103).

Mikhail Bakhtin develops a remarkably similar diagnosis of the solipsistic and pathological tendencies of modernity, particularly in his earliest, phenomenological writings. His position here is that although the history of Western thought has been periodically marked by perspectives that have rejected the validity of bodily, lived experience in favour of abstruse theoretical constructions – Platonism being the archetypal example – modern forms of thought have most systematically detached what he terms 'Being-as-event' from abstract cognition, in order to privilege the latter. Hence, 'discursive theoretical thinking' functions to denigrate the sensuous and tangible character of the lived event, perpetrating a 'fundamental split between the content or sense of a given act/activity and the historical actuality of its being' (Bakhtin, 1993: 2). Once alienated from the lifeworld, grand theoretical systems acquire a proxy life and operate according to their own internal laws, which bypass the experiential world of practical consciousness and action. This has palpable sociopolitical consequences: under the regime of modernity, flesh-and-blood individuals have become subordinated to the immutable laws of history, mind, or the unconscious, with the result that we cease to be present in the world as 'individually and answerably active human beings' (1993: 7). Such a necessitarian logic is reflected in the unabashedly utilitarian character of modern science and technology, in which any activity is justified by reference to the internal criterion of the conceptual paradigm and the overriding goal of technical efficacy and control. Parenthetically, this also demonstrates his pronounced hostility to nomothetic social science and abstract, idealist philosophy. Echoing the Frankfurt School's concept of 'instrumental reason', Bakhtin asserts that technology, 'When divorced from the once-occurrent unity of life and surrendered to the will of the law immanent to its development, is frightening; it may from time to time irrupt into this once-occurrent unity as an irresponsibly destructive and terrifying force' (1993: 7). Hence, the logic of Bakhtin's rejection of the rigid fact/value distinction and mechanistic determinism of modern scientific positivism recapitulates Merleau-Ponty's own position. Both clearly repudiate what Merleau-Ponty calls the 'bad dialectic', as exemplified by Hegel's notion of an immanent rationality in history operating 'behind the backs' of real human subjects, and jointly embrace a 'dialectic without synthesis' that does not terminate in perfection, completion, and so on.

For Bakhtin, the central imperative of modernity is, therefore, its attempt to transcend our situatedness in concrete time/space by recourse to what Heidegger called the 'technological world-picture' (see Simpson, 1995). This yearning for transcendence allows us to abrogate the difficult existential and moral demands that everyday life places upon each of us as incarnate subjects. 'As disembodied spirit, I lose my compellent, ought-to-be relationship to the world, I lose the actuality of the world' (Bakhtin, 1993: 47). The quest to live such a 'non-incarnated fortuitous life' can only result in a ghostly, illusory existence separated from the world, an 'indifferent Being not rooted in anything' (1993: 43). This privileging of the cognitive, disincarnate subject results in a pronounced tendency to equate the self as such with egocentric, subjective mental processes, what Bakhtin calls 'psychic being'.

In his earliest writings, the blanket term he applies to this phenomenon is 'theoretism'. This refers to the rationalist project of subordinating the 'living and in principle non-merging participants of the event' to a formalized, metaphysical system projected by a hypostatized consciousness, which devalues or expunges any experience or viewpoint that it cannot fully assimilate. Such a 'transcendent-logical transcription' inevitably suppresses the 'eventness' of embodied social existence, and encourages a 'blind faith in "technical" systems and laws, unfolding according to their own immanent logic' (Morson and Emerson, 1989: 9). In essence, Bakhtin strongly validates Merleau-Ponty's belief that there is a terrible price to be paid for the epistemic certitude sought by scientific rationalism. The sociocultural conditions of modernity have encouraged us to privilege a purely cognitive relation to the other and our environment (what Bakhtin refers to as 'epistemologism'), which in turn reinforces a strictly utilitarian attitude towards the world. Abstract, dispassionate contemplation from afar supplants our active and incarnated participation in a shared horizon of value and meaning. Bakhtin insists that a properly ethical and 'emotional-volitional' relation to the other and the acceptance of genuine responsibility requires the presence of a 'loving and value-positing consciousness', and not a disinterested, objectifying gaze. Torn out of this living and interactive context connecting self, other and world, the subject succumbs to the gravitational pull of solipsism; it thereby 'loses the ground of its being and becomes vacuous, arrogant; it degenerates and dies' (Bakhtin, 1990: 274).

Embodiment and the 'Jointing of Being'

I have sought to demonstrate that Merleau-Ponty and Bakhtin diagnose the central ethical, epistemological and ontological pitfalls of modernity in strikingly similar terms. To begin with Merleau-Ponty, how does he respond to the challenge of a solipsistic idealism? In *Signs*, he celebrates the demise of 'high-altitude thinking', and declares that 'the philosophy of God-like survey was only an episode' (Merleau-Ponty, 1964a: 14). Its lengthy reign has ended; accordingly, we must develop alternative perspectives that will enable us to 'plunge into the world instead of surveying it[,] descend toward it such as it is instead of working its way back up toward a prior possibility of thinking it – which would impose upon the world in advance the conditions for our control over it' (1968: 38–9). To accomplish this, he adumbrates an 'interrogative' philosophy that jettisons the epistemological fetish of modern thought and re-establishes our perceptual and bodily connection to the world. In *The Phenomenology of Perception* (1962) and related works of the 1940s, Merleau-Ponty was concerned primarily with mapping the various manifestations of embodiment in terms of the relation between perceiving subject and perceived world, comprising such phenomena as sensory experience and expressivity, spatiality and motility, affect and temporality. Here, the precise character of alterity was not a topic that concerned Merleau-Ponty unduly (Dillon, 1988: 85). However, his growing appreciation of the work of such pioneering structuralists as Lévi-Strauss, Lacan and Saussure, each of whom sought to 'decentre' the Cartesian subject, prompted a 'linguistic turn' in his own thinking and brought in its wake an increasing emphasis on the self/other relation, especially as mediated by language (Schmidt, 1985: 11). In his subsequent writings, such themes as historicity, symbolic and aesthetic expression, intersubjectivity and intercorporeality are foregrounded, culminating in what is arguably his most provocative (though unfinished) work, *The Visible and the Invisible* (1968).

In *The Visible and the Invisible* and related essays, Merleau-Ponty refuses to see the world as a collection of static, self-contained things, or acquiesce to the notion that our relation to the world is a contemplative and purely cognitive affair. This confuses reified concepts and beliefs with our environment as it actually exists, as it develops in time/space and is experienced and actively transformed by reflexive, incarnated subjects. For Merleau-Ponty, the world is always in a state of Heraclitean flux, birth and death, transformation and 'becoming' – but in an unpredetermined manner lacking any sort of overarching Hegelian *telos*. The lived world, unlike the idealized world projected by a disengaged consciousness, is unfinished, pregnant with new potentialities and vibrant, pulsating energies. This applies equally to human beings: 'the perceiving subject undergoes continued birth; at each instant it is something new. Every incarnated subject is like an open note-book in which we do not yet know what will be written' (Merleau-Ponty, 1964b: 6). To evoke one of Merleau-Ponty's most provocative notions, we are part of the 'flesh of the world'. Our world is not a tableau of inert objects and things that we apprehend passively, but a living and complexly inter-acting medium in which we as body-subjects are enmeshed. My body 'is made of the same flesh as the world (it is a perceived), and moreover [this] flesh of my body is shared by the world, the world *reflects* it, encroaches upon it and it encroaches upon the world'. World and body therefore exist 'in a relation of transgression or of overlapping' (1968: 248). But they overlap in a most peculiar way. Rather than imperiously survey the world around me from an Olympian height, my senses reach out to the world, respond to it, actively engage with it, shape and configure it – just as the world, at the same time, reaches into the depths of my sensory being. As such, the human perceptual system is not a quasi-mechanical apparatus that exists only to facilitate representational thinking, to produce reified 'concepts' or 'ideas'; rather, it is radically intertwined with the world itself.

Furthermore, my bodily and perceptual introjection into the world makes possible a *self*-perception, a mode of reflexivity that is not merely cognitive but corporeal, what Merleau-Ponty refers to as *reversibility*. As I experience the world around me, I am simultaneously an entity in the world: the seer is also the seen, I can touch myself touching, and hear myself speaking. If this supposition is correct, our traditionally dualistic ways of understanding the relation between self and world must be abandoned, and it compels us to engage in an 'ontological rehabilitation of the sensible'. However, the world is not experienced by me alone, and therefore any project of 'onto-logical rehabilitation' must also address what Husserl called the 'problem of other people'. My point of view is not the only possible opening on to the sensible milieux that constitutes the flesh of the world. We must supplement our openness on to the world with a 'second openness' – that of other selves. For Merleau-Ponty, the world is presented to me in a 'deformed' manner; that is, my perspective is skewed by the precise situation that we occupy at a particular point in time/space, by the idiosyncracies of our personal psychosocial development and the broader historical context of my exist-ence. Insofar as we are 'thrown' into a universe lacking intrinsic significance – that is, the world does not consist solely of unalterable 'things-in-them-selves' – the task that faces each of us is to make the world meaningful, to realize, in an architectonic sense, coherent patterns out of the flux of the world as it is presented to us in raw experiential form. The world, in short, 'is something to be constructed' (Merleau-Ponty, 1982–83: 39). We are 'condemned' to make continual value-judgements and generate novel meanings, to go beyond the structures and situations we inherit in order to create new ones. Indeed, this is precisely how Merleau-Ponty defines freedom: as the appropriation of a '*de facto* situation by endowing it with a figurative meaning beyond its real one' (1962: 172). Yet the accomplishment of this project is necessarily a partial and unfinished one. Reality presents itself to each body-subject as a world of gaps and invisibilities, lacunae and blind-spots; it is mediated by our concrete particularity, the unique aperture through which we open on to the universe. Although the world constitutes a coherent totality (albeit 'structured in difference'), there is no possibility that a given subject can comprehend this world *qua* totality, insofar as we only have access to the existentially and physically delimited horizon within which we perceive, act and think. We can never 'possess' the totality of the world through a purely intellectual grasp of our environment; thus, our knowledge of the experiential world is always constrained and one-sided. To assume otherwise would be to lapse into the myth of the self-constituting, egological subject, in which, as Horkheimer puts it, 'the sole *raison d'être* of the world lies in affording a field of activity for the transcendental self, [where] the relationship between the ego and nature is one of tyranny' (Horkheimer, 1992: 108).

The conclusion Merleau-Ponty draws is that no two individuals will experience the world in precisely the same way. Perception must be 'understood as a reference to a whole which can be grasped, in principle, only through certain of its parts or aspects. The perceived thing is not an ideal unity in the possession of the intellect, like a geometrical notion' (Merleau-Ponty, 1964b: 16). One might be tempted to conclude that Merleau-Ponty recapitulates Nietzsche's argument regarding perspectivalism. But this would be erroneous. Although both thinkers insist that our access to the world is mediated by our body, and that our situatedness in concrete time/space makes each of our perceptual openings on to the world singular and irreplaceable, the crux of Nietzsche's argument is that the world is qualitatively different for each observer because it is constituted through the interpretative strategies brought to bear on the world by every subject. For Merleau-Ponty, by contrast, the decisive issue is this: although the meaning of the world for each of us is constructed from the vantage-point of our uniquely embodied viewpoint, and hence irreducibly pluralistic, we continue to inhabit the same world – that is, we are *co-participants* in a universe that ultimately transcends any particularistic perspective (McCreary, 1995). As such, the world is best comprehended as 'a totality open to a horizon of an indefinite number of perspectival views which blend with one another [and] which define the object in question' (Merleau-Ponty, 1964b: 16). Such an emphasis on intersubjective 'blending', this intertwining and overlapping through which we participate *collectively* in the apprehension and construction of a shared sociocultural and physical environment, implies that the world has the ontological status of an 'in-itself-for-others', and not simply an 'in-itself-for-us'. Although my placement in the world is not shared identically by another person, this is no barrier to a reciprocal, mutually enriching relationship between self, other and world. The body-subject thereby constitutes the 'vehicle of a relation to Being in which third parties, witnesses can intervene' (Merleau-Ponty, 1968: 62). In entering into the totality of the world in concert with others, I gain access to a more complete perspective on the world. I cannot literally see behind my back, but it is 'seen' nonetheless, by the generalized vision of Being that is part of the sensible world. But more than this: in the encounter with another self, I have access to an external viewpoint through which I am able to visualize myself as a meaningful whole, a Gestalt. Relying on an idiosyncratic reading of Lacan, Merleau-Ponty suggests that we can escape the prison-house of solipsism, but only through an apprehension of ourselves in the 'mirror' of the other, a vantage-point that enables us to evaluate our own existence and consummate a coherent self-image. This explains his comment that 'we are never our own light to ourselves' (1968: 47). Equally, however, there is no overarching fusion or coincidence between self and other in such an encounter, no 'arbitrary intrusion of a miraculous power transporting me into the space of another person' (1982–83: 44). Metaphorically, self and other could be said to constitute concentric circles that *nearly* overlap, but that never completely usurp each other's unique situation in concrete time/space, although there always remains the potential for mutual recognition and 'communicative transivity' between a multiplicity of body-subjects.

In arguing that, as embodied subjects, we are radically intertwined with the world, Merleau-Ponty also reminds us that we are bound up with the dynamic cycles and processes of growth and change, birth and death, that are characteristic of nature as a whole. In making this claim, he seeks to counter the supposition that nature is mere dead matter, with no connection to our own incarnated lives (Langer, 1990; Russon, 1994). The 'blind productivity' of modern technoscience is indicative of an attitude of absolute detachment from and indifference to nature, which reduces it to the status of what Heidegger called a 'standing-reserve' (1977: 298) – that is, a domain that exists only for the exclusive use of human beings and their abstract technical designs. 'Technology and science range before us energies which are no longer *within* the framework of the world but are capable of destroying it', asserts Merleau-Ponty. 'They provide us with means of exploration which, even before having been used, awaken the old desire and the old fear of meeting the absolute Other' (1970: 103). Insofar as our minds are incarnate and our bodies necessarily partake of the physical and biological processes characteristic of the natural world, there is an overlapping of spirit and matter, subject and object, nature and culture. As Merleau-Ponty suggests in 'Eye and mind', because embodied subjects are in reality 'dense, rent, open beings', we can say that there 'is no break in the circuit; it is impossible to say that nature ends here and that man [*sic*, and *passim*] or expression starts here' (1964b: 188–9). A scientific mode of thinking that imperiously surveys the world and which objectifies and dominates nature must be supplanted by a philosophy that understands the world as a dynamic, living organism 'pregnant' with a myriad of potentialities. By refusing to sever the 'organic bonds' that link us immutably to external nature, we can come to the realization that we are part of an 'eternal body', a generalized flesh that can never expire. Evoking Bergson, Merleau-Ponty argues that our body reaches out to the stars and is co-extensive with the universe as a whole, thereby constituting a 'primordial *We*'. As he writes: 'There is a kinship between the being of the earth and that of my body. This kinship extends to others, who appear to me as other bodies, to animals whom I understand as variants of my embodiment, and finally even to terrestrial bodies' (Merleau-Ponty, 1970: 122–3).

From his earliest writings, Bakhtin likewise argues that the impoverishing dualism of Cartesian rationalism can only be combated by a repudiation of the abstractions of idealist philosophy, so as to grasp the nature of the concrete deed or 'act' as it constitutes the essential 'value-centre' for human existence. Like Merleau-Ponty, he asserts that the self is a dynamic, embodied and creative entity that strives to attribute meaning and value to the world. Each of us is cast into an external world of brute factuality, consisting of objects and events that confront us and demand a response. In reacting to this pure 'givenness', the inherited meanings and structures of the world, we are impelled to sculpt the discrete elements of this environment into coherent and meaningful wholes (Pechey, 1993). We are forced to make certain choices and value-judgements with respect to our Being-in-the-world, to transform this proffered givenness into a coherent 'world-for-me'. In making the world a meaningful place, the subject actively engages with and alters its lived environment; and, in so doing, continuously transforms itself. This is an ongoing process: the self is continually 'reauthored' as its life and circumstances change, and hence is 'unfinalizable'. What Bakhtin is striving to outline here is a phenomenology of what he terms 'practical doing', one that focuses on our incarnated activities within a lifeworld that exists 'prior' to the more rarefied operations of abstract cognition. If we manage to participate directly in the 'actual eventness of the once occurrent act', we can enter 'into communion with the actual, historical event of Being' (Bakhtin, 1993: 1, 6). Furthermore, only if we think and act in such a 'participative' fashion can we be wholly responsible or 'answerable' for our actions, in the sense that we are reflexively conscious of the existential meaning of our acts and their implications, ethical or otherwise. Being-as-event must therefore be lived through, and not passively comprehended from afar. Hence, the impoverishing and necessitarian mode of thought perpetuated by modernity, which overlooks the inherently value-laden and embodied character of human life, can only be combated by a repudiation of theoretical abstraction pursued as an end to itself, so as to grasp the concrete deed as the axiological centre around which human existence revolves. Answerability demands the presence of an incarnated and participative subject. In challenging the logic of high-altitude thinking, Bakhtin argues, first, that there is no possibility of surmounting our 'unique place in once-occurrent Being'; and secondly, that theoretical cognition is only one aspect of a wider 'practical reason'. Abstract philosophical or aesthetic contemplation *as such* can never gain entry into this universe of lived Being; it requires 'actual communion' with the concrete actions I perform, with the 'reversibility' that is inscribed in my living corporeality. Hence, both Merleau-Ponty and Bakhtin strongly contest what Emmanuel Levinas characterizes as the 'primacy of intellectual objectivism, which is affirmed in science, taken as the model of all intelligibility, but also in Western philosophy, from which that science emerges' (Levinas, 1994: 22). The penchant for abstract theory and the objectification of the world on the part of the modernist paradigm represents a retreat from lived experience, a symptom of alienation that is registered in a pervasive desire to transcend '*this* world, [which] is seen, heard, touched, and thought' (Bakhtin, 1993: 57). Indeed, for Bakhtin this attempt to escape the ontological rootedness of our lived existence by recourse to abstruse theories or sociopolitical dogmas is tantamount to finding an 'alibi' in Being.

In *Toward a Philosophy of the Act* (1993), Bakhtin stresses the nature of the situated and embodied character of lived existence and its consequences for ethics, aesthetics, and ontology. He has relatively little to say at this point about intersubjectivity and intercorporeality. However, in the concluding segment of this work, Bakhtin does suggest that a genuine moral philosophy cannot be formulated outside the 'contraposition' of self and other. Any attempt to answer the solicitation of the world must be sensitized to the fact that I and other commingle in the ongoing event of Being, that we are equal participants in a shared lifeworld, yet remain uniquely incarnated. Although this insight is not sufficiently elucidated here, in the later essay 'Author and hero in aesthetic activity' the I/other relation becomes Bakhtin's central *leit-motiv*. Here, he reminds us that life is always directed towards the 'yet-to-be'; as such, Being is properly understood as an 'open process of axiological accomplishment' (1990: 129). Yet in engaging with the world as embodied beings, our ability to attribute meaning and significance solely through our own thoughts, deeds and perceptions is subject to certain limitations, particularly with respect to the 'authoring' of our own selfhood. As such, he places singular emphasis on the phenomenon of 'transgredience' – that which transcends or lies outside our immediate subjective existence and cognitive activity, and which necessarily partakes of 'otherness'. Bakhtin's central argument is that just as we are impelled to attribute meaning to the object-world around us, we need to envisage *ourselves* as coherent and meaningful entities. But from our own vantage-point (the 'I-for-myself'), we are manifestly incapable of envisioning our outward appearance, and of comprehending our location within the 'plastic-pictorial world' (that is, the lived environment of objects, events, and other selves). To be able to conceptualize ourselves as cohesive meaningful wholes, which is fundamental to the process of individuation and self-understanding, we require an additional, external perspective. Hence, the other exists in a relation of externality or 'exotopy' *vis-à-vis* ourselves, in a manner that transcends, or is 'transgredient' with respect to, our own perceptual and existential horizon. Looking 'through the screen of the other's soul', Bakhtin writes, 'I vivify my exterior and make it part of the plastic-pictorial world' (1990: 30–1).

We can only exist, to evoke a visual metaphor that Merleau-Ponty also uses, through the 'borrowed axiological light of *otherness*' (Bakhtin, 1990:

134). Since each of us occupies a unique time/space, we can see and experience things others cannot, within our sphere of self-activity. The reverse is equally true, in that the other can visualize and apprehend things that we are unable to. Hence, the other has a 'surplus of seeing' with regard to ourselves, and vice versa, a scenario that corresponds directly to what Merleau-Ponty calls the 'reversibility of perspectives'. Bakhtin insists that this co-participation cannot occur solely through the medium of 'cognitive discursive thought' – again, this would be to succumb to the error of epistemologism. Genuinely participative thinking and acting requires an engaged, embodied relation to the other and the world at large. Otherwise, the intrinsically affective and moral character of the self/other encounter is fatally undermined. Our capacity for abstract cognition and representational thinking is incapable of grasping the incarnate linkage between myself and another within the fabric of everyday social life, cannot comprehend our 'organic wovenness' in a shared social and natural world: 'only the other human being is experienced by me as connatural with the outside world and thus can be woven into that world and rendered concordant with it' (Bakhtin, 1990: 40).

This stance starkly reveals the deleterious consequences of a subjectivistic idealism. Solipsism, Bakhtin remarks, might be a compelling argument if I were the only sentient creature in the world. But inasmuch as we always confront and dialogically engage with other persons within the lifeworld, it would be 'incomprehensible to place the entire world (including myself) in the consciousness of *another* human being who is so manifestly himself a mere particle of the macrocosm' (1990: 39). Moreover, insofar as values are present or embodied in all human actions and experiences, moral or ethical considerations must be rooted in the common lifeworld, in tangible, everyday circumstances. Accordingly, both Bakhtin and Merleau-Ponty explicitly reject the possibility of an absolutist ethical system along Kantian lines, mainly because such systems rely on overgeneralizing and spuriously universalistic principles. By contrast, for both thinkers the ability to recognize the other's words and gestures as analogous to my own, as part of the same lifeworld and structure of perceptual experience, is ultimately what makes a viable intersubjective ethics possible (see Gardiner, 1996b). 'True morality does not consist in following exterior rules or in respecting objective values', Merleau-Ponty asserts (in terms that are strikingly Bakhtinian), but rather 'of establishing that communication with others and with ourselves' (Merleau-Ponty, 1964c: 40).

Yet, at the same time, Bakhtin is adamant that this commingling of self and other within the lifeworld does not erase their 'radical difference', inasmuch as outsidedness or exotopy must be successfully maintained in any genuinely dialogic encounter. Another's existence can only be enriched by me, and vice versa, 'only insofar as I step outside it, actively clothe it in externally valid bodiliness, and surround it with values that are transgredient' (Bakhtin, 1990: 70). This is an important point that is amplified in Bakhtin's later writings, particularly after his own 'linguistic turn' of the late

1920s. Through the dialogical encounter the integrity of difference is always maintained, but in a manner that does not preclude the possibility of solidarity or consensus. In 'From notes made in 1970–1', he asserts that while rhetoric as mastered by the Sophists was primarily concerned with securing victory over an opponent, genuine dialogue (in the Socratic sense) reaches out to the other, invites the other to engage in the co-pursuit of truth. Through dialogue, 'one can reach solutions to questions that are capable of temporal solutions, but not to ultimate questions' (Bakhtin, 1986: 152). A dogmatic monologism precludes the possibility of authentic dialogue or consensus; yet Bakhtin would equally reject a postmodernist relativism, because it assumes a priori the incommensurability of viewpoints, a position that renders dialogue unnecessary or superfluous. For Bakhtin, *à la* Merleau-Ponty, there is no convincing reason why a 'unified truth' cannot be expressed through a plurality of overlapping perspectives and viewpoints, rather than through the monocular perspective of a disembodied observer. When 'one and the same object is contemplated from different points of a unique space by several different persons', he suggests, it 'occupies different places and is differentially presented within the architectonic whole constituted by the field of vision of these different persons observing it' (1993: 63).

Hence, from his earliest writings it is clear that Bakhtin is concerned with the dialogical character of human embodiment, what Hwa Jol Jung (1990) astutely terms a 'carnal hermeneutics'. For Bakhtin, the architectonic value of my incarnated self can only be affirmed in and through my relation to a concrete other: 'the body is not something self-sufficient: it needs the *other*, needs his recognition and form-giving activity' (1990: 51). Yet his early phenomenological work construes intercarnality primarily in terms of the overlapping of visual fields (the 'surplus of vision'). In much of Bakhtin's subsequent work of the 1920s and early 1930s, the earlier preoccupation with bodily experience and intercarnality tends to recede, and linguistic and auditory metaphors are increasingly foregrounded (Gardiner, 1998). However, in his writings on Rabelais and Renaissance popular culture, he returns once again to the theme of embodiment, most notably in *Rabelais and His World* but also in the essay 'Forms of time and of the chronotope in the novel' and elsewhere. This development is anticipated in a highly compressed discussion contained in 'Author and hero in aesthetic activity' (included in *Art and Answerability*) concerning the succession of different 'body canons' that have appeared during European history. Here, Bakhtin suggests that there has, at periodic intervals, been a strong emphasis placed on an introspective subjectivism at the expense of an embodied dialogism. Some of the more obvious examples of the former include Platonism and medieval theology, wherein the body is construed as an entity isolated from the world and of secondary importance to 'spirit' or 'mind'. Although the main figures of the Renaissance – especially Montaigne and Erasmus – successfully rehabilitated the body, with their stress on passions, feelings, sensuous pleasures, and the inherent value of external nature, this sensibility was overturned by the seventeenth-century counter-Renaissance and the Enlightenment. With the rise to predominance of a mechanistic cosmology, itself precipitated by the consolidation of capitalism and the rapidly centralizing nation state's need to contain dissent during a period of intense religious conflict, the body was interpreted as analogous to a machine, a mere physiochemical container for the rational *cogito*. Accordingly, there has been a strong tendency since the early modern period to view human beings as primarily cognitive or rational subjects – an ethos that functioned to reduce each actual body to an abstract, universal 'rationality' held to be characteristic of the human race as a species (Toulmin, 1990).

This insight became a central theme of Bakhtin's work of the late 1930s and 1940s. In his essay on the chronotope, for instance, he celebrates Rabelais's novel *Gargantua and Pantagruel* because it epitomizes the epochal transformation that occurred during the Renaissance in terms of how people viewed their bodies and their relationship to the material world. Rabelais managed to portray human events and activities 'under the open sky', in real, interactive contexts. It was precisely this emphasis on the concrete and the sensuous that was rejected by the feudal theocracy, which renounced the body and its pleasures so as to achieve spiritual transcendence in the realm of an imaginary afterlife. Medieval scholasticism, in other words, developed a system of abstract concepts and ideals, and substituted this for the living connections between people, things and organic processes. Rabelais is such an important figure for Bakhtin precisely because he challenged decisively the 'theoretism' of medieval ideology; as such, Rabelais plays roughly the same role of culture hero as does Montaigne in Merleau-Ponty's work. Rabelais's project, writes Bakhtin, represents an attempt to create a 'spatially and temporally adequate world able to provide a new chronotope for a new, whole and harmonious man, and for new forms of human communication' (Bakhtin, 1981: 168). In Rabelais's 'new picture of the world', there is no trace of a mind/body or spirit/matter dualism of the sort promulgated by the 'other-worldly idealism' of feudal theology, and later reflected in the philosophy of Descartes and Leibniz. By integrating the human body into its spatio-temporal and natural milieux, Rabelais was able to confront the medieval tendency to construe the flesh as an inevitably corrupt and polluted substance, an idea that has served to maintain an 'immeasurable abyss' between body and world.

In *Rabelais and His World* (1984b), Bakhtin continues in this vein, suggesting that the body as depicted in *Gargantua and Pantagruel* is not an autonomous, individuated entity. Rather, it is in a very real sense a collective body, the 'body of the human race as a whole', which is inextricably intertwined with all of the myriad processes of change and development characteristic of the natural world. The 'grotesque body' supersedes its boundaries, particularly those parts of the body which directly interact with the external world: the nose, the mouth, the anus, and the sexual organs (Roderick, 1995). The Rabelaisian body is open, unfinished; its connection with the universe is revealed because it transgresses its own limits by assimilating the material world and by merging with other beings, objects and animals. Bakhtin argues that the material bodily principle 'is opposed to severance from the material and bodily roots of the world; it makes no pretence to renunciation of the earthly, or independence from the earth and body' (1984a: 19). Echoing Merleau-Ponty's idea of the 'eternal body', he suggests that death can only threaten the solitary, egocentric individual, not the organic collectivity; as such, the physical demise of a particular organism is only a transitory moment in an overarching cosmic cycle encompassing continuous birth, growth, death and rebirth. Inasmuch as the grotesque body represents a 'collective historical life of the social whole', there are no private, solipsistic worlds in the carnival chronotope. The material bodily principle implies that all individuals co-participate in a shared physical milieux; they eat, drink, procreate, live and die within the same lived space and the 'immanent unity of time'. It was only with the emergence of class society and bourgeois individualism that this organic and immanent unity of time/space was shattered, a development that was encouraged by the philosophical idealism of the post-Renaissance period. 'Consciousness' became synonymous with the radically interiorized *cogito*, an abstract, inward-looking form of intellection that eschewed any contact with everyday, sensuous reality and which severed cognition from the body and nature.

Bakhtin's interpretation of Rabelais and carnival culture implies that a radicalized understanding of our own embodiment and our material connection to the external environment can play an important role in overcoming the mind/world dualism of Western thought (Bell, 1994; Gardiner, 1993). If Cartesianism facilitates an absolute schism between nature and culture, mind and body, self and other, the carnivalesque heals this split, by fostering a new dialogical paradigm that overcomes the solipsistic and anthropocentric tendencies of modernity. Hence, both Bakhtin and Merleau-Ponty view the natural world as *processual*, as bound up in a constant, non-teleological mode of 'becoming'. Insofar as mind, body and nature are not separate but overlapping and intertwined, the human being is palpably not an 'acosmic subject' (Merleau-Ponty, 1962: 441). According to this perspective, nature ceases to be viewed as mere raw material, as pure 'object', but as a partner in this overarching developmental process in which we are inextricably embedded. The 'whole of nature', writes Merleau-Ponty, 'is the setting for our own life, our interlocutor in a sort of dialogue' (1962: 50).

Conclusion

In this chapter I have argued that both Bakhtin and Merleau-Ponty characterize the 'monster of solipsism' as a central impediment to the cultivation of dialogical relations between self, other and world, and, *inter alia*, the realization of authentic human sociality and community. The egological subjectivism promoted by Cartesian-inspired philosophies is, to use an evocative metaphor of Bakhtin's, a poor medium for a 'plurality of unmerged consciousnesses to blossom' (1984a: 26). As such, Bakhtin and Merleau-Ponty privilege a philosophy of co-existence over a philosophy of consciousness, one that insists that our selfhood is constituted dialogically and that our relation to others is inherently *ethical*. 'The *cogito* is false only in that it removes itself and shatters our inherence in the world', asserts Merleau-Ponty. 'The only way to do away with it is to fulfill it, to show that it is eminently contained in interpersonal relations' (1964c: 133). *In nuce*, both thinkers underscore and valorize continual transformation, ambiguity and interaction, as opposed to the modernist predilection for order, stasis, symmetry, and predictability (Bauman, 1992), in which the self is understood as an unfinalizable 'open notebook'. Such a perspective underscores the centrality of the living connection between our embodied selves and a world of other 'body-subjects', objects, and organic processes. In highlighting what Nick Crossley usefully terms a 'corporeal intertwining' (1996: 174), Bakhtin and Merleau-Ponty would concur strongly with Husserl's observation that 'Nature, the body, and also, interwoven with the body, the soul are constituted all together with a reciprocal relationship with each other' (cited in Merleau-Ponty, 1964a: 177). Yet, at the same time, our particularity is not dissolved into an anonymous social mass: there is no Habermasian *telos* in communicative and bodily interaction necessarily leading to some sort of agreement or harmonization of desires and activities (although, of course, 'local' and pragmatic forms of intersubjective assent are always possible). Rather, this transivity promotes a decentring, a heightened awareness of the presence of the other in ourselves (and vice versa), but in a manner that preserves the 'radical difference' between self and other. 'We should', writes Merleau-Ponty, 'return to this idea of proximity through distance, of intuition as auscultation or palpation in depth, of a view which is a view of self, a torsion of self upon self, and which calls "coincidence" in question' (1968: 128). In striving to think through the ramifications of the cardinal principle of 'unity-in-diversity' – rather than making a fetish of pure 'difference' as such – their approach is in many respects at odds with postmodernist theorists who regard Nietzsche as an iconic precursor. As we stand on the threshold of the *fin-de-millennium*, it would seem that the respective, overlapping projects of Bakhtin and Merleau-Ponty provide us with richer soil than do many modernist and postmodernist theories for fostering a new intersubjective paradigm, one that respects the ubiquity of social difference, yet does not circumscribe or negate our 'will to dialogue'.

References

Bakhtin, Mikhail M. (1981) *The Dialogic Imagination: Four Essays by M.M. Bakhtin*. Ed. M. Holquist. Trans. C. Emerson and M. Holquist. Austin, TX: University of Texas Press.
Bakhtin, Mikhail (1984a) *Problems of Dostoevsky's Poetics*. Ed. and trans. C. Emerson. Manchester: Manchester University Press.

Bakhtin, Mikhail (1984b) *Rabelais and His World*. Trans. Hélène Iswolsky. Foreword by Krystyna Pomorska. Bloomington, IN: Indiana University Press.

Bakhtin, Mikhail M. (1986) *Speech Genres and Other Late Essays*. Eds. C. Emerson and M. Holquist. Trans. V.W. McGee. Austin, TX: University of Texas Press.

Bakhtin, Mikhail M. (1990) *Art and Answerability: Early Philosophical Essays by M.M. Bakhtin*. Eds M. Holquist and V. Liapunov. Trans. and notes V. Liapunov. Austin, TX: University of Texas Press.

Bakhtin, Mikhail M. (1993) *Toward a Philosophy of the Act*. Ed. M. Holquist. Trans. and notes V. Liapunov. Austin, TX: University of Texas Press.

Bauman, Zygmunt (1992) *Intimations of Postmodernity*. London and New York: Routledge.

Bell, Michael (1994) 'Deep fecology: Mikhail Bakhtin and the call of nature', *Capitalism, Nature, Socialism*, 5 (4): 65–84.

Burkitt, Ian (1994) 'The shifting concept of the self', *History of the Human Sciences*, 7 (2): 7–28.

Certeau, Michel de (1984) *The Practice of Everyday Life*. Berkeley, CA, and Los Angeles, CA: University of California Press.

Crossley, Nick (1996) *Intersubjectivity: The Fabric of Social Becoming*. London: Sage.

Dillon, M.C. (1988) *Merleau-Ponty's Ontology*. Bloomington, IN: Indiana University Press.

Ferguson, Harvie (1989) *The Science of Pleasure: Cosmos and Psyche in the Bourgeois World View*. London: Routledge.

Gardiner, Michael (1993) 'Ecology and carnival: traces of a "green" social theory in the writings of M.M. Bakhtin', *Theory and Society*, 22 (6): 765–812.

Gardiner, Michael (1996a) 'Foucault, ethics and dialogue', *History of the Human Sciences*, 9 (3): 27–46.

Gardiner, Michael (1996b) 'Alterity and ethics: a dialogical perspective', *Theory, Culture and Society*, 13 (2): 121–44.

Gardiner, Michael (1998) 'Bakhtin and the metaphorics of perception', in Barry Sandywell and Ian Heywood (eds), *Interpreting Visual Culture: Studies in the Hermeneutics of Vision*. London and New York: Routledge.

Heidegger, Martin (1977) *Martin Heidegger: Basic Writings*. Ed. David Farrell Krell. San Francisco: Harper San Francisco.

Holquist, Michael (1990) 'Introduction: the architectonics of answerability', in M.M. Bakhtin, *Art and Answerability: Early Philosophical Essays by M.M. Bakhtin*. Eds Michael Holquist and V. Liapunov. Trans. and notes V. Liapunov. Austin, TX: University of Texas Press.

Horkheimer, Max (1992) *Eclipse of Reason*. New York: Continuum.

Jung, Hwa Jol (1990) 'Mikhail Bakhtin's body politic: a phenomenological dialogics', *Man and World*, 23: 85–99.

Langer, Monika (1990) 'Merleau-Ponty and deep ecology', in Galen A. Johnson and Michael B. Smith (eds), *Ontology and Alterity in Merleau-Ponty*. Evanston, IL: Northwestern University Press.

Levin, David Michael (1991) 'Visions of narcissism: intersubjectivity and the reversals of reflection', in Martin Dillon (ed.), *Merleau-Ponty Vivant*. Albany, NY: SUNY Press.

Levinas, Emmanuel (1994) *Outside the Subject*. Stanford, CA: Stanford University Press.

Marcel, Gabriel (1949) *Being and Having*. London: Dacre Press.

McCreary, Mark (1995) 'Merleau-Ponty and Nietzsche: perspectivism in review', *Metaphysical Review*, 2 (3): 1–11.

Merleau-Ponty, Maurice (1962) *Phenomenology of Perception*. London: Routledge & Kegan Paul.

Merleau-Ponty, Maurice (1964a) *Signs*. Evanston, IL: Northwestern University Press.

Merleau-Ponty, Maurice (1964b) *The Primacy of Perception*. Ed. James M. Edie. Evanston, IL: Northwestern University Press.

Merleau-Ponty, Maurice (1964c) *Sense and Non-Sense*. Evanston, IL: Northwestern University Press.

Merleau-Ponty, Maurice (1968) *The Visible and the Invisible*. Ed. Claude Lefort. Evanston, IL: Northwestern University Press.

Merleau-Ponty, Maurice (1970) *Themes from the Lectures at the Collège de France 1952–1960*. Evanston, IL: Northwestern University Press.

Merleau-Ponty, Maurice (1982–3) 'The experience of others (1951–1952)', *Review of Existential Psychology and Psychiatry*, 28 (1–3): 33–63.

Morson, Gary Saul and Emerson, Caryl (1989) 'Introduction: rethinking Bakhtin', in Gary Saul Morson and Caryl Emerson (eds), *Rethinking Bakhtin: Extensions and Challenges*. Evanston, IL: Northwestern University Press.

Pechey, Graham (1993) 'Eternity and modernity: Bakhtin and the epistemological sublime', *Theoria*, 81 (82): 61–85.

Roderick, Ian (1995) 'The politics of Mikhail M. Bakhtin's carni-phallic body', *Social Semiotics*, 5 (1): 119–42.

Russon, John (1994) 'Embodiment and responsibility: Merleau-Ponty and the ontology of nature', *Man and World*, 27: 291–308.

Schmidt, James (1985) *Maurice Merleau-Ponty: Between Phenomenology and Structuralism*. London: Macmillan.

Simpson, Lorenzo C. (1995) *Technology, Time and the Conversations of Modernity*. London and New York: Routledge.

Toulmin, Stephen (1990). *Cosmopolis: The Hidden Agenda of Modernity*. Chicago: University of Chicago Press.

10

BAKHTIN AND MANNHEIM: AN INTRODUCTORY DIALOGUE

Raymond A. Morrow

> For in the ideological horizon of any epoch and any social group there is
> not one, but several mutually contradictory truths, not one but several
> diverging ideological paths. . . . Such is the dialectic of real life.
>   – Mikhail Bakhtin and P.N. Medvedev[1]

> No one social stratum, no one class is the bearer of the total movement;
> nor is it legitimate to assess this global process merely in terms of the
> contributions of one class . . . the harmony of the whole can be grasped
> only by taking into account the whole contrapuntal pattern of all the
> voices.
>
> – Karl Mannheim[2]

There is no basis for assuming that there were mutual influences between
Karl Mannheim (1893–1947), the Hungarian philosopher and sociologist
who worked in Weimar Germany until his exile to England in the 1930s, and
Mikhail Bakhtin (1895–1975), the philosopher and cultural theorist who was
the leader of the 'Bakhtin circle' in the Soviet Union in the 1920s. But this
chapter introduces the thesis of a *simultaneous* and *independent* elaboration
in the 1920s of a sociology of culture based on a theory of the historical,
interactive and linguistic foundations of knowledge. Surprisingly, the nature
and extent of this convergence between Bakhtin and Mannheim has not
been heretofore acknowledged, let alone addressed. Further, these earlier
developments shed new light on origins of contemporary currents in social
theory variously referred to as 'anti-foundationalist', 'poststructuralist', and
'postmodern'. Most recently, the Bakhtin circle has been described 'as an
attempt to abort the structuralist stage in order to achieve a stand that we
would readily associate with our own poststructuralism. The broad outlines
of this strategy can be discerned now' (Godzich, 1985: x). Similarly, it has
been argued that in calling the 'absolute Reason' of the Enlightenment into
question, Mannheim 'lays the groundwork for an anti-foundational social
science even though it is not entirely realized in his own work' (Hekman,
1986: 79). This chapter will explore these retrospectively evident affinities
through a very selective comparison of aspects of Bakhtin's and
Mannheim's conceptions of knowledge, language and culture.

Problems in the reception of both authors have deflected attention from
possibilities of comparison. On the one hand, the primarily literary

reception of Bakhtin has led to a focus on his work as a form of literary criticism, hence marginalizing questions relating to a theory of ideology and knowledge. Of course, the disputed status of the authorship of texts in the Bakhtin circle contributes to these difficulties. Those stressing his literary and phenomenological side find it convenient to ignore the more 'Marxist' works associated with the Bakhtin circle. The point of departure for the purposes at hand can be found in Gardiner's (1992) attempt to reconstruct Bakhtin in terms of the theory of ideology critique and critical hermeneutics, as well as Bernard-Donals (1994) interpretation of Bakhtin as caught 'between phenomenology and Marxism'. On the other hand, the reception of Mannheim within positivist sociology long obscured the hermeneutic foundations of Mannheim's work (Simonds, 1978), and Frankfurt School and neo-Marxist interpretations dogmatically rejected it as relativistic and undermining classical ideology critique (Jay, 1974).

On the basis of a superficial *sociologistic* reading of Mannheim and a narrow *phenomenological* reading of Bakhtin, it would be easy to construe their projects as diametrically opposed because of three fundamental differences: first, the absence of a theory of language, dialogue and verbal discourse in Mannheim, especially as culminating in Bakhtin's conception of the carnivalesque; secondly, Mannheim's strong sociological structuralism and methodological use of formalist art theory of styles as opposed to Bakhtin's resistance to sociological reductionism and formalism of all kinds in the name of the primacy of living speech; thirdly, a substantive focus on a theory of literature (based on the novel) as opposed to Mannheim's focus on organized political ideologies as genres of political discourse.

But clues to a deeper convergence are evident in Bakhtin's suggestion that Dostoevsky's characters were indeed talking representations of ideological standpoints – 'the characters are ideologists' (Bakhtin, 1986: 116); or 'that Dostoevsky offers, in artistic form, something like a sociology of consciousness . . . and thus offers material that is valuable for the sociologist as well' (Bakhtin, 1984b: 32). As a youthful admirer of Dostoevsky, Mannheim would have instantly recognized the intellectual kinship of Bakhtin's approach to his own sociology of knowledge. Hence the *apparent* differences of tone and approach may be understood better as more reflective of very different discursive opponents and social contexts. Analysing such deeper affinities requires more general metatheoretical categories for getting beyond the classic splits between the ideographic and nomothetic in the human sciences, as well as formulations of critical hermeneutics that neglect the methodological problematic of historical-structural analysis in the sense of a generalizing, but non-positivist social science (for example, Morrow (with Brown), 1994). It will be argued that Mannheim and Bakhtin *share* essential elements of such a metatheory and a related theory of culture. Accordingly, it can be argued that *Mannheim has an explicit theory of the social subject and implicit theory of language* that calls for something like Bakhtin's metalinguistics, and that *Bakhtin has an implicit theory of society and ideology* that calls for something like Mannheim's strategy of historical-structural societal analysis and general theory of interpretation and ideology. The focus of the following discussion will be on identifying these convergent themes, though a thorough evaluation or further development of these issues cannot be taken up here.

The overall career trajectory of both authors was very similar and can be divided into four parallel periods: early writings (1918–24) strongly influenced by neo-Kantian philosophy and phenomenology (Bakhtin, 1990, 1993; Mannheim, 1971: 8–58); the formulation of a social theory of knowledge based on a critical engagement with Marxist theory in the late 1920s (Bakhtin, 1984b; Bakhtin and Medvedev, 1985; Mannheim, 1936, 1952; Voloshinov, 1986); various extensions and new departures based on this framework in the 1930s and 1940s (Bakhtin, 1981, 1984a; Mannheim, 1953, 1956); and a final phase marked by wider recognition and attempts to extend these insights into new areas (Bakhtin, 1986; Mannheim, 1940). Space limitations preclude a closer analysis of the intellectual and biographical basis of these historical affinities. Instead, it is necessary to focus on a systematic frame of comparison based on reconstructions of Bakhtin's conception of metalinguistics.

Working in a rather different intellectual milieu than Mannheim, Bakhtin's metatheory originates in a historical, hermeneutic critique of the linguistic structuralism associated with Ferdinand de Saussure, as well as Czech and Russian formalism (Bakhtin and Medvedev, 1985). The outcome he variously described as 'metalinguistics' (sometimes translated as 'translinguistics') or a 'sociological poetics'. This overall strategy has been summarized by Morson and Emerson in terms of three global concepts: *prosaics* (a term not used by Bakhtin), *unfinalizability* and *dialogue* (1990: 15ff.). As we shall see, Mannheim's sociology of knowledge was grounded in three parallel assumptions that can be described in terms of the foundations of culture in *everyday life*, a critique of *totality*, and valorization of competing perspectives as the basis of *truth-generative social processes*. The primary difference in these two strategies is that Bakhtin's empirical focus was on a 'sociological poetics' based on the speech genre of the *novel* as opposed to Mannheim's concern with a 'sociology of knowledge' based on the genre of modern *political ideologies*. In effect, for Mannheim political ideologies assume the privileged function of Bakhtin's novels as exemplars of modern communicative forms through which are expressed emergent types of social identity, conflict, and utopian vision.

Metatheoretical Perspectives

Phenomenological Foundations

Morson and Emerson define their use of the term *prosaics* (a term coined by them) as follows:

> Prosaics encompasses two related, but distinct, concepts. First, as opposed to 'poetics', prosaics designates a theory of literature that privileges prose in general

and the novel in particular over the poetic genres. Prosaics in the second sense is far broader than a theory of literature: it is a form of thinking that resumes the importance of the everyday, the ordinary, the 'prosaic'. (Morson and Emerson, 1990: 15)

Prosaics in this second, phenomenological, sense has been shared by a range of novelists and philosophers such as Wittgenstein. In the case of Bakhtin, however, this metatheoretical position is developed in the context of a critique of literary formalism based on the artificiality of poetic language. Instead, Bakhtin privileges the language of the polyphonic novel because it captures the phenomenology of everyday life left out of the formalizations of linguistics. As we will see, prosaics in this second sense was broadly shared by Mannheim.

But what about prosaics in the first sense, as a theory of literature? As Morson and Emerson argue, 'Prosaics in the first sense – a serious, comprehensive theory of literature that privileges prose and the novel – is, so far as we know, Bakhtin's unique and original creation' (Morson and Emerson, 1990: 16). Yet it is also possible to imagine analogous forms of 'prosaics' in other cultural fields than literature or verbal art. Whereas Bakhtin's prosaics in this first sense is directed towards the idealizations of *verbal art* based on the models of poetry based in structuralist linguistics, Mannheim can be credited with a prosaics of *historical knowledge* which, while not altogether unique in the same sense, involved a parallel rejection of the idealizations of scientific knowledge based on the ahistorical formalisms of the natural sciences. In the process, the 'prose' of historical knowledge as a form of discourse is privileged as a peculiarly modern form of self-reflection. This question will be taken up in the final section.

But the initial issue here is Mannheim's prosaics in the form of his understanding of the phenomenological foundations of the human sciences, a point missed by those who see his focus on organized ideologies as somehow at odds with an understanding of their relation to everyday life (Berger and Luckmann, 1967). In his early work he referred to Dilthey's crucial conception that 'socio-genetic consideration of cultural formations is actually a mere extension and consistent sustaining of an attitude which belongs to the "everyday experience of life", that it cannot and should not depart from this basis without the greatest care' (Mannheim, 1982: 75). Hence, an important problem for cultural sociology should be to investigate 'pre-scientific learning from experience' or 'situated knowledge' (1982: 76). For this reason, he continues, proponents of quantitative modes of thinking fail to see that in 'real life' people continue naively to 'employ methods of knowing incomprehensible to the official logic . . . the special capacity of the concrete, prescientific practical actor consists in perspectivistically bringing the facts given into an order relevant to himself and to his own situation, by means of the category "situation"' (1982: 158). Even in his later writings on ideology, he reiterates again and again the premise that the emergence of consciousness can only be understood in relation to lived-experience – '*mit dem lebendigen Leben*' – (Mannheim, 1970: 409).

For Mannheim, social scientific positivism could be traced to a failure to differentiate clearly two qualitatively different forms of knowledge (natural scientific and historical), and the tendency to impose the abstract logic of the former on the latter. Though he uses the somewhat unfortunate term 'conjunctive knowledge' to contrast historical knowledge with the formalism of natural science, he also speaks of it as 'existential knowledge' which is viewed as the outcome of an ongoing, interactive process of communication: '*I* become different and the *Other* becomes different, at every moment; and our conjunction becomes different thereby, since it is constantly being created anew by self-correction and mutual orientation' (1982: 193).

Unfinalizability and Essential Perspectivity

Bakhtin's concept of unfinalizability corresponds broadly to a critique of totalizing thinking as incapable of understanding the variety and openness of social life: 'The term appears frequently in his works and in many different contexts. It designates a complex of values central to his thinking: innovation, "surprisingness", the genuinely new, openness, potentiality, freedom, creativity' (Morson and Emerson, 1990: 37). Bakhtin's point of departure is thus a rejection of what he calls the 'theoretism' dominant in Western philosophy. By this he refers to the tendency to reduce events to rules and structures (as in semiotics or Marxist dialectics): 'As Bakhtin puts it in his early writings, theoretism thinks away the "eventness" of events, which becomes secondary rather than primary' (Morson and Emerson, 1990: 50). But it should be stressed that the principle of unfinalizability should *not* be taken as a total rejection of structuralist-type methods in cultural analysis, as opposed to their totalizing and essentializing abuses; otherwise Bakhtin's affirmation of the social conditioning of knowledge – despite his rejection of simplistic Soviet Marxist accounts of it – becomes incomprehensible. It is in this context that we can also understood his flexible use of narrative analysis in the study of the novel and focus on historical genre theory generally.

Mannheim develops a similar critique of totalizing and reductionist modes of inquiry, whether in the form of Hegelian (or Marxist) teleology or positivist nomothetic laws. The basis of Mannheim's historicism is a critique of Hegel's totalizing identity theory that monologically unified subject and object; instead, Mannheim proposes a historicist stance that recognizes something like the principle of what Bakhtin calls 'unfinalizability': 'It follows, however, that in the nature of the case, no single concept can be adequate to a spiritual reality (as, for example, the *polis*), since every spiritual reality, in the course of history, changes its spiritual being' (1982: 228). The relativizing, historicist point of departure of Mannheim's theory of the human sciences is thus the notion of the '*essential perspectivity*' that limits all historical knowledge: 'This inevitable perspectivity thus resides in the fact that particular historical contents can only become visible, in particular aspects, from particular life centers that occur within this history itself' (1982: 274).

Mannheim also develops a critique of sociological positivism. In particular he uses Lukácsian language to analyse the effects of extreme formalization which 'undertakes an alienation of the object, but also presupposes just such "estrangement"' (1982: 185–6): 'Generalizing and formalizing are, in our opinion, valid "technical" procedures and also have their uses in sociology . . . for *concrete thought*, however – for the thinking of the concrete – they can serve merely as a springboard. Does, in fact, formalization not always lead to distortion, if we look at it from the viewpoint of the concrete?' (Mannheim, 1952: 159).

Both authors are acutely aware of the way in which their conception of the historicity and openness of thought and language exposed them to charges of relativism. Both consistently rejected this charge as stemming from a false opposition between dogmatism and relativism. As Bakhtin warns: 'The polyphonic approach has nothing in common with relativism (or with dogmatism). But it should be noted that both relativism and dogmatism equally exclude all argumentation, all authentic dialogue, by making it either unnecessary (relativism) or impossible (dogmatism)' (Bakhtin, 1984b: 69). As a consequence, it is possible to envision a dialogical conception of truth: 'It is quite possible to imagine and postulate a unified truth that requires a plurality of consciousness, one that in principle cannot be fitted within the bounds of a single consciousness, one that is, so to speak, by its very nature *full of event potential* [*sobytiina*] and is born at a point of contact among various consciousnesses' (1984b: 81).

Mannheim terms his parallel position 'relationism': 'This first non-evaluative insight into history does not inevitably lead to relativism, but rather to relationism. Knowledge, as seen in the light of the total conception of ideology, is by no means an illusory experience. . . . Knowledge arising out of our experience in actual life situations, though not absolute, is knowledge none the less' (Mannheim, 1936: 85–6).

Language, Texts and Dialogue

The notion of what can be termed *truth-generative processes* helps focus attention on the ways in which Bakhtin and Mannheim share a concern with understanding the social construction of knowledge as an historical and interactive process. From this perspective it becomes possible to compare Bakhtin's dialogical metalinguistics with Mannheim's perspectival critical hermeneutics in terms of three basic themes: first, linguistic foundations in a non-formalist, historical sociolinguistics based on a creative conception of language; secondly, a social and communicative theory of texts and discourse based on the study of genres and styles; and thirdly, a preoccupation with the implications of the multiplicity of voices and standpoints competing for truth claims as presented, respectively, in novels and political ideologies.

Language

The shared foundation of cultural analysis for Bakhtin and Mannheim is an interactionist theory of language based on the primacy of the utterance as a unit of analysis. The starting-point of Bakhtin's metalinguistics is thus a form of stylistics that opposes linguistic formalism by focusing on a dialogical understanding of whole utterances: 'After all, our thought itself – philosophical, scientific, and artistic – is born and shaped in the process of interaction and struggle with others' thought, and this cannot but be reflected in the forms that verbally express our thought as well' (Bakhtin, 1986: 92). Bakhtin's unifying concept of dialogue is thus formulated in response to traditional stylistics as informed by 'abstractly linguistic categories': 'Stylistics must be based not only, and even *not as much*, on linguistics as on *metalinguistics*, which studies the word not in a system of language and not in a "text" excised from dialogic interaction, but precisely within the sphere of dialogic interaction itself, that is, in that sphere where discourse lives an authentic life' (Bakhtin, 1984b: 202).

For a number of reasons, Mannheim does not develop his theory of culture with reference to theories of language and linguistics, at least outside the tradition of classical hermeneutics (Dilthey). We must assume that he had some knowledge of contemporary linguistics, especially the formalism criticized by the Bakhtin circle, but found it irrelevant for his purposes. Instead, he drew indirectly upon stylistic analysis in painting and developed his own theory of ideological discourse and interpretation. Nevertheless, it is clear that his conception of stylistics involved a metalinguistics in Bakhtin's sense, and that it also developed out of a critique of formalism, but in this case that found in art history (rather than Russian literary formalism).

Mannheim's earliest writings acknowledge the centrality of language given his conception of 'conjunctive' (existential) knowledge: 'Language brings articulation and fixation into the stream of conjunctive experience. It brings commonly experienced stretches into relief, fixes them, and suspends the universal flow. . . . Knowledge remains perspectivistic, bound to a particular experiential space' (Mannheim, 1982: 200–1). Further, his stylistic and interpretive theory is based on what Bakhtin later termed speech genres, given Mannheim's early distinction between the fragmentary 'sentence' and the 'utterance', which he describes as 'the specific totality of the sentence': 'That is precisely the miracle of living speech: that it always places each word in a unique context and that it can bestow an individual meaning to each word from the specific totality of the sentence and, even more, from the undercurrent of the communication flowing from its rhythm and the stream of association' (1982: 197). Summarizing this conception, Mannheim speaks in implicitly dialogical terms of the 'responding object' of communication:

> In our analysis, which was a genealogy of meaning and, as such, altogether disregarded the problem of historical origins, we constructed an experiential

community by first positing a single individual, whom we brought into existential relationship to a *vis-à-vis* in order to depict his conjunction with this *vis-à-vis* (which at first was a thing) within a transitory segment of his existence. Then we posited a 'responding' object, which was at the same time also a subject, in place of the lifeless *vis-à-vis* and then had a conjunctive experiential space emerge from this constellation. This conjunctive experiential space we still filled with perspectivistic experiences, shaped by the moment and constantly changing in the flow of shared life. (Mannheim, 1982: 204–5)

As well he is aware that the 'miracle of living speech' derives from its audience, and the difference between 'reading' and 'listening' as phenomenological experiences. Using the example of the difference between *reading* and *listening* to a revolutionary speech, he concludes that in reading 'we grasp the words more or less exclusively in the general meanings, which are all that is accessible to us, and not in their unique reference to the experiential complex which was experienced in common and which continues to vibrate in all of the listeners at the time of the living address' (1982: 198). In short, he is acutely aware of the creative functions of language as part of social practice as evidenced in how historical concepts 'have a function as concepts for the furtherance of life, and this signifies not only an apprehension of reality but also its transformation'. Marx is credited with a 'magnificent' formulation of this point in saying, '"Philosophers have only interpreted the world in different ways; the point is to change it" ('Theses on Feuerbach'). Every concept possesses this transformative impulse at all times in the conjunctive space of life and experience' (1982: 199).

Discourse and Texts

Bakhtin and Mannheim's theory of discourse can thus be compared in terms of: (i) 'a form of stylistic analysis based on the utterance and speech genres; (ii) theories of textual interpretation concerned with the interplay of the extrinsic and intrinsic; and (iii) a particular focus on the dialogical relations within and between narratives.

Stylistics and Speech Genres

For Bakhtin, the more general framework developed for cultural analysis is based on a theory of 'speech genres'. The problem of speech genres is elaborated as part of a polemic against linguistic reductionism and is based on privileging the complete 'utterance' or discourse as the unit of analysis, rather than the individual sentence: 'All three of these aspects – thematic content, style, and compositional structure – are inseparably linked to the *whole* of the utterance and are equally determined by the specific nature of the particular sphere of communication' (Bakhtin, 1986: 60; original emphasis). Though he does not propose a taxonomy of such speech genres, Bakhtin does make a fundamental distinction between relatively simple *primary* speech genres grounded in everyday life and *secondary* (complex) genres – 'novels, dramas, all kinds of scientific research, major genres of commentary, and so forth' which 'arise in more complex and comparatively highly developed and organized cultural communication (primarily written) genres that is artistic, scientific, sociopolitical, and so on' (1986: 62). In short, 'Utterances and their types, that is, *speech genres, are the drive belts from the history of society to the history of language*' (Bakhtin, 1986: 64; added emphasis).

The methodological foundation of Mannheim's sociology of culture is a form of *stylistic analysis* developed specifically for complex ideological discursive systems. He attributes to Lukács the insight that ' "style" is at once an aesthetic and a sociological category' (Mannheim, 1982: 86), but relies primarily upon art history to illustrate the methodological aspects of his argument. In this context he develops a critique of traditional art history which is parallel to Bakhtin and Medvedev's (1985) critique of linguistic formalism. It is of particular significance that the Bakhtin circle was much more sympathetic to the type of formalist art history that is Mannheim's point of departure, focusing their attack on Russian literary formalism which had abandoned analysing the interplay between form and content, as well as between ideology and form. As a consequence, this type of 'European formalism not only did not deny content, did not make content a conditional and detachable element of the work, but, on the contrary, strove to attribute deepening ideological meaning to form itself' (Bakhtin and Medvedev, 1985: 49).

And it was from this same European formalism based in art history that Mannheim derived a strategy of formal analysis of styles, but he coupled this intrinsic analysis with an extrinsic (sociological) aspect that he felt was implicit in the practice of art historians (1982: 86). As he argues, any classification of formal features inevitably departs from the 'level of immanence' because 'we encounter works which do not exhibit any of the external identifying features, or do so only in part, and which nevertheless reveal, as is commonly said, the "Gothic spirit" ' (1982: 86). Accordingly, as he later concludes, the sociology of knowledge must make this genetic aspect a central part of investigation in a way that was neglected by art historians such as Alois Riegl (Mannheim, 1952: 78).

Further, such inquiry also includes what Bakhtin would call intertextuality: 'The seemingly incredible fact that someone can create something that not even he can wholly understand can be explained in light of our recent reflections by recalling that a work always takes up out of the historical community and retains numerous moments, motifs and elements, as well as, most importantly, deep inclinations towards purposes deemed proper to works' (Mannheim, 1982: 240).

Theories of Interpretation

The Bakhtin circle took the problematic of a theory of textual interpretation as a foundational question, even though it was never fully developed: 'A dialectical conception of the "intrinsic" and the "extrinsic" of literature and extraliterary reality (ideological and otherwise) is an obligatory condition for a formulation of a genuine Marxist literary history' (Bakhtin and Medvedev, 1985: 155). This problematic was taken up occasionally by Bakhtin in various ways, but the pressures of Soviet orthodoxy precluded full engagement with forms of inquiry that would challenge Soviet Marxism's conception of sociology as the basis of the 'extrinsic' moment of the contextualization of texts. Partly as a consequence, Bakhtin was more at home at the intrinsic pole of literary analysis, even though his approach remained resolutely sociological in focusing on intertextual issues and making allusions to explaining the history of genres. Nevertheless, this dialogical relation between texts precludes the reduction of the creative text to causal explanation: 'Any truly creative text is always to some extent a free revelation of the personality, not predetermined by empirical necessity. Therefore, it (in its free nucleus) admits neither of causal explanation nor of scientific prediction' (Bakhtin, 1986: 106–7).

In contrast, Mannheim was especially innovative in attempting to develop an analysis of intrinsic versus extrinsic textual interpretation. Though he lacked a developed theory of language, his theory of textual interpretation is in effect a sociolinguistic construct. He develops a theory of interpretive understanding built around a distinction between 'immanent' and 'genetic' interpretations (Mannheim, 1971: 116–31). In this respect, his contribution advances beyond Bakhtin by outlining the basis for forms of genetic meaning interpretation that are social psychological and sociological but *not* reductionist in reifying meaning through causal analysis. What is most distinctive in Mannheim – and this differentiated him from Bakhtin – is his effort to develop a *non-causal, interpretive theory* of social contextualization that is most fully exemplified in the complete text of his study of conservatism (Mannheim, 1986).

His point of departure is parallel to the refractive conception of a base-superstructure model cautiously embraced by Bakhtin in his more materialist moments (Voloshinov, 1986). As Mannheim stresses, the point is not to accept or reject the base-superstructure model *per se*, so much as to develop it in a non-reductionist direction that takes into account the cultural bases of the economic: '. . . whatever reservations one may have about certain kinds of applications of "historical materialism", it is just this correlation between base and superstructure which has become the inescapable foundation of every modern sociology of culture' (1982: 177), even in the work of authors such as Max and Alfred Weber, as well as Scheler (1982: 282, note 21). The crucial step that Mannheim takes in revising this formulation is his insistence that the 'material' base and economic life were themselves spiritual-cultural phenomena – *that material life is cultural life*: 'it is this *mental* element which makes *economy* out of mere drive-satisfaction' (1952: 163).

Accordingly, Mannheim develops a preliminary classification of forms of interpretation based on the general distinction between viewing cultural phenomena 'intrinsically', hence as they present themselves, as ideas, and 'extrinsically' with reference to external meaning contexts, of which the most extreme form is 'causal explanation', a positivistic form which Mannheim (like Bakhtin) rejects as the basis for cultural sociology.

Dialogical Relations

In opposing traditional linguistics, Bakhtin argues that language must be defined at the outset in interactionist, communicative terms: 'Any understanding is imbued with response and necessarily elicits it in one form or another: the listener becomes the speaker' (Bakhtin, 1986: 68). In other words, all utterances are part of an unending 'chain' of responses (later described as intertextuality), even in the case of complex, secondary genres in the arts and sciences.

Though Mannheim does not develop an explicit theory of dialogue in Bakhtin's sense, he does introduce a number of considerations that reflect the dialogical implications of his overall approach. Aspects of this have already been touched upon in his interactionist conceptions of language and its creative possibilities. But his whole conception of historically analysing the formation and dynamics of ideological complexes is based on an intertextual analysis of the historical development of thought. As well, his attention to competition and democratization as cultural processes results in a number of *dialogical* insights.

Mannheim's discussion of *competition* as a social process, for example, begins with the distinction between existentially-determined and natural scientific thought, and notes that his discussion refers to the former. Further, he rejects that he is proposing a reductionist argument because he views competition as merely a 'co-determinant' of cultural phenomena (along with generations, etc.) that is much more general than its specific economic form in capitalism. In the case of thought, however, the goal of competition takes on a specific form: 'It appears that the different parties are all competing for the possession of the correct social diagnosis (*Sicht*), or at least for the prestige which goes with the possession of this correct diagnosis' (Mannheim, 1952: 196). The notion of competition as a cultural phenomenon, in short, forces us to revise the more familiar Mannheimian notion of the perspectival character of truth and the rivalry among forms of thought and culture in a dialogical direction. From this latter position, thought is not merely perspectival, it is related through processes of mutual constitution through which opponents enter into dialogue: 'We will not pursue this line of thought farther, however, but will merely point out that in the socially differentiated thought process, even the opponent is ultimately forced to adopt those categories and forms of thought which are most appropriate for orientation in a given type of world order' (1952: 222).

At the same time, the general cultural process of what Mannheim calls *democratization* introduces the possibility of communicative relations that begin to break down social hierarchies. In his later work he analyses hierarchical social distanciation in communicative terms as three fundamental dyadic relations: the 'I-object relationship' characteristic of manipulative actions; the 'I-thou relationship' involving existential relations; and the 'I-myself' relationship' linked to self-identity. These relations are viewed in terms that border on dialogical language. It is argued, in fact, that the over-coming of 'I-object' relations based on hierarchy is part of a general process of cultural democratization culminating in the more extensive formation of 'I-thou' relations. As a consequence, 'creating a basis for purely existential relationships is the greatest potential achievement of democracy' (Mannheim, 1956: 242). Further, the basis for the I-myself relation is ulti-mately viewed as *others*: 'for a man can become a "person" *for himself* only to the extent that he is a "person" for others and others are "persons" for him ... in such a way that he can become a person for others and be addressed as such on numerous occasions before he can see himself as a person' (1956: 244). Mannheim explicitly links the process of democratiza-tion to the valorization of 'free discussion', hence dialogue: 'There is only one step from the Kantian consciousness-in-general to a characteristic feature of modern, democratic society: its faith in the all-healing virtue of free discussion', a possibility that is traced back to Socratic dialogue (1956: 191–2).

To summarize, methodologically speaking, the convergent focus of Bakhtin and Mannheim's theory of discourse was thus threefold: (i) a struc-tural (but non-formalist) theory of stylistics suitable for the historical analy-sis of the depth narrative structure, respectively of the novel and political ideologies; (ii) a non-reductionist theory of interpretation designed to comprehend the relationships between intrinsic and extrinsic analysis of texts understood as discourses; and (iii) a conception of the dialogical competition and conflict between perspectives as the basis of a theory of knowledge and moral-ethical conception of democratic openness. Now we can turn to some of the implications of the novel and political ideologies as paradigmatic cases for discourse analysis.

The Novel versus Ideology as Speech Genres

Perhaps the most striking contrast between Mannheim and Bakhtin is their respective focus on opposite types of speech genre: monological ideologies as opposed to the novel as a polyphonic discourse. There are several key themes of Bakhtin's theory of the novel and Mannheim's theory of ideology that are suggestive for the purposes of comparison at hand: (i) a respective stress on the uniqueness of the novel and ideology in representing modern forms of human experience; (ii) the contrast between polyphonic novel and monological ideologies as, respectively, the highest and most problematic expressions of these possibilities; and (iii) the contrast between the carnival-esque as a pervasive novelistic strategy that carries with it utopian impulses of resistance and critique, as opposed to the more sober interplay between ideological and utopian thought in politics and social science.

The Speech Genres of Modernity

For Bakhtin, the novel as a genre provides the key to understanding modernity: 'The novel has become the leading hero in the drama of literary development in our time precisely because it best of all reflects the tendencies of a new world still in the making; it is, after all, the only genre born of this new world and in total affinity with it' (1981: 7). Though Bakhtin also traces the pre-history of the novel, he does so in order ultimately to proclaim the uniqueness of the modern novel culminating in the Renaissance novels of Rabelais and Cervantes which 'play such a titanic role in the formulation of a new literary and linguistic consciousness' (Bakhtin, 1981: 80).

For Mannheim, modern political ideologies serve a parallel function as a privileged discourse for understanding modernity:[3] 'From a sociological point of view the decisive fact of modern times, in contrast with the situation during the Middle Ages, is that this monopoly . . . which was held by the priestly caste is broken, and . . . a free intelligentsia has arisen' (1936: 11). Further prerequisites were the ensuing emergence of epistemological, psychological and sociological perspectives that culminate in a relativizing of thought in terms of its historical construction. The final outcome was the self-conscious exploration of the ideological and utopian dimensions of thought. Whereas ideologies arise from conflicts between groups, 'The concept of *utopian* thinking reflects the opposite discovery of political struggle, namely that certain oppressed groups are intellectually so strongly interested in the destruction and transformation of a given condition of society that they unwittingly see only those elements in the situation which tend to negate it' (1936: 40).

Polyphonic versus Monological Narratives

Bakhtin's concept of the polyphonic novel provides a useful point of departure for comparison with political ideologies: 'The polyphonic work has several distinct and irreducible centers. It follows that the work's unity cannot be monological, because monologism achieves unity by incorporating all elements of the work into a single design governed by a single ultimate semantic authority' (Morson and Emerson, 1990: 254).

By contrast, it would initially appear that political ideologies constitute an essentially *monological* genre based on a 'single design', an assumption echoed in Mannheim's contention, based on his structuralist stylistic analysis, that every ideological complex has a depth structure that constitutes its historical identity. As such political ideologies would appear to provide inhospitable terrain for exploring the dialogical character of creative thought and expression. This focus on relatively monological forms of organized discourse is part of the reason that commentators gloss over his broader understanding of everyday life (that is, his phenomenological and anti-finalizing points of departure), let alone his disclosure of the dialogical features of ideological competition. Above all, however, Mannheim was preoccupied with a dialogical analysis of ideologies, a theme culminating in his rejection of the Hegelian Marxist conception of history and the notion of a privileged class: 'the harmony of the whole can be grasped only by taking into account the whole contrapuntal pattern of all the voices' (1952: 125).

The further development of Mannheim's early metalinguistic approach was largely shaped by his concern with the stylistic and sociogentic analysis of 'genres' of modern ideologies as utterances or discourses. But despite this focus on differentiating genres of ideologies, Mannheim was also concerned with analysing their underlying unity in a non-formalizable manner, much like Bakhtin's general theory of the novel as a modern cultural form. Similarly, Mannheim often employs the metaphor of counterpoint, speaking of the 'contrapuntal interplay' of cultural forms (for example, 1982: 130). Above all, his strategy argued that all ideologies struggle against monologization as part of the process of sustaining their dynamic development in competition with one another, a process within which anti-dialogical self-closure becomes self-destructive.

The Carnivalesque versus Social Science

In one key respect the focus on the novel as opposed to political ideologies produced distinctively different outcomes. Though Mannheim's approach situated the formation of, and competition between, ideological complexes in the struggles of everyday life, he remained fully within the dominant tradition of viewing ideology critique in cognitive terms as a process of argumentation and disputation. Though he recognized that such confrontations between perspectives were inevitably accompanied by emotional and valuational responses, he only saw one possible strategy for facilitating such political dialogue: a relatively autonomous political science that might inform social protagonists. In other words, 'while we believe that interests and purposes cannot be taught, the investigation and communication, however, of the structural relationship between judgment and point of view, between the social process and the development of interest, is possible' (1936: 163). In effect, Mannheim provided a sophisticated rationale for the institutionalization of the social sciences as a strategy for mediating the conflict between ideologies, a suggestion that elicited the scorn of the Frankfurt School in its early revolutionary phase.

In contrast, the literary focus of Bakhtin's work drew attention to a very different dialogical strategy: the carnival and the carnivalization of literature. Above all, the carnival experience 'has worked out an entire language of symbolic concretely sensuous forms. . . . This language cannot be translated in any full or adequate way into a verbal language, and much less into a language of abstract concepts, but it is amenable to a certain transposition into a language of artistic images that has something in common with its concretely sensuous nature; that is, it can be transposed into the language of literature' (Bakhtin, 1984b: 122). Carnival life is created with a series of transformative potentials deriving from its capacity to suspend ordinary life and relations of power (culminating in the 'mock crowning and subsequent decrowning of the carnival king') through a breaking down of social distance, the construction of new forms of interpersonal relations, redefinitions between high and low culture, and processes of profanation that reconnect people with their bodies and nature (1984b: 123).

What would be the equivalent for the 'carnivalization' of ideologies in Mannheim's sense? On the one hand, he is sceptical of utopian revolutionary thought in characterizing the notion of 'dialectical transformation' as the rationalization of the irrational (1936: 132). Utopian thought is defined as 'situationally transcendent ideas' that challenge the *status quo* in ways that effectively 'succeed through counteractivity in transforming the existing historical reality into one more accord with their own conceptions' (1936: 195–6). By this practical criterion, Bakhtin's notion of carnivalization remains problematic to the extent that mock crowning and decrowning leaves existing power relations unchanged. On the other hand, Mannheim did discuss at one point a general process of cultural democratization that involved the gradual breakdown in social distance in a manner that is reminiscent of Bakhtin's account of the carnivalization of literature.

Conclusion: Dialogue and the Sociology of Knowledge

The conclusion of this preliminary dialogue is that, read together, Mannheim and Bakhtin provide important insights of both historical and contemporary significance. What are some of the possibilities that follow from appreciating the dialogical relations between these two theories of culture?

With respect to Mannheim, Bakhtin above all provides the fully developed critical metalinguistics (theory of dialogue, language, speech genres, etc.) only hinted at in Mannheim's early work and repeated in muted form in his later appreciation of American pragmatism.[4] Much of this is specific to questions of the novel and literature, but other aspects could profitably be applied to enriching or going beyond Mannheim's analysis of ideologies and culture.

Secondly, with concepts such as polyphony and heteroglossia, Bakhtin provides important resources for thinking about new ideological forms and formations. Mannheim's analyses of ideologies were in effect structuralist analyses of ideological monologues, but one of the most distinctive features of his analysis was a focus on the relative lack of closure within standpoints as well as their contrapuntal interplay over time. Though the focus is more structuralist, as Morson and Emerson suggest, 'Bakhtin would probably concede that in monologic works, the structuralist analysis is correct. But he maintains that in polyphonic works the same device performs a radically different function. Specifically it allows the work to achieve not closure by anticlosure but genuine *lack* of closure' (1990: 253–4; original emphasis).

Thirdly, the notion of the carnivalesque in the novel introduces the possibility of forms of dialogue that draw upon the comic, ironic and parodic capacities of language. Mannheim's focus on ideologies led him to stress the more sober aspects of intellectual dialogue, even though the long history of political cartoons and satire might have alerted him to comparable genres of ideological discourse.

As for the dialogical implications for Bakhtin, Mannheim's strategy first opened up the possibility of a generalized form of ideology analysis impossible under the politicized circumstances of working in the Soviet Union. Though this stance has long contributed to Mannheim's dismissal as a 'relativist' on the part of Western Marxists, in the current 'postmodernist' climate circumstances have changed dramatically since something like relational theories of ideologies *de facto* dominate academic discourse.

More fundamentally, Mannheim provides some clues for rethinking Bakhtin's relationship to sociology and Marxism. In literary discussions the terms 'sociological' and 'Marxist' are used and contrasted rather casually and without adequate specification. For example, Morson and Emerson argue that though 'Bakhtin's early writings were emphatically *not* sociological' those of the '1930s and 1940s . . . were deeply sociological. . . . Bakhtin appears to have responded with theories of language and literature that were sociological without being Marxist' (1990: 118–19). Such terminology polarizes 'sociological' and 'Marxist' in a simplistic manner rejected by contemporary critical social theory. As Gardiner effectively demonstrates, Bakhtin's metalinguistics can best be read as a form of critical hermeneutics – hence part of the extended tradition of critical theory that includes Mannheim (see, for example, Gardiner, 1992: 99ff.) – but this does not resolve the question of his theory of society. The most fundamental issue at stake is a dialogue *within* critical hermeneutics, that is, between those who side with Gadamer in defending a strong anti-structuralism, and those who would follow Mannheim, Habermas, Bourdieu and others in defending a stronger explanatory form of historical structuralism (Morrow (with Brown), 1994; Morrow and Torres, 1995).

The most fundamental problem is that *Bakhtin has a negative answer to this problem*, that is, a critique of Marxist and sociological reductionism, without resolving the tension between interpretation (*Verstehen*) and a form of explanation (*Erklären*) that does not take the classical nomothetic form. This ambiguous stance in turn opened the way for a polarization of interpretations between the *phenomenological* Bakhtin primarily concerned with the carnivalesque and polyphony, and a *Marxist* preoccupied with a materialist theory of ideology. As Bakhtin himself agonizes inconclusively in a late fragmentary comment: 'The problem of the limits of causal explanation. The most important thing is to avoid severance from the text (even if it is only potential, imagined, or inferred)' (1986: 106). In surprising ways Mannheim introduced complementary questions of enduring significance for addressing just this and related questions.

Notes

An earlier draft of this chapter was presented to a session organized by Greg Nielsen and Jean-François Côté at the Annual Meetings of the Canadian Association of Sociology and Anthropology, Montreal, University of Quebec at Montreal (4–7 June 1995).

1 Bakhtin and Medvedev (1985: 19–20).

2 Mannheim (1952: 125).

3 The links between literature, ideology and the origins of sociology have been extensively explored, for example, Lepenies (1988).

4 Alvin Gouldner should be given credit for having drawn attention to the need for a socio-linguistic re-interpretation of Mannheim's theory in terms of a 'grammar of ideology' (Gouldner, 1976) prior to the Bakhtin reception in the West.

References

Bakhtin, Mikhail M. (1981) *The Dialogic Imagination: Four Essays by M.M. Bakhtin*. Ed. M. Holquist. Trans. C. Emerson and M. Holquist. Austin, TX: University of Texas Press.

Bakhtin, Mikhail M. (1984a) *Rabelais and His World*. Trans. Hélène Iswolsky. Foreword by Krystyna Pomorska. Bloomington, IN: University of Indiana Press.

Bakhtin, Mikhail M. (1984b) *Problems of Dostoevsky's Poetics*. Ed. and trans. C. Emerson. Minneapolis, MN: University of Minnesota Press.

Bakhtin, Mikhail M. (1986) *Speech Genres and Other Late Essays*. Eds C. Emerson and M. Holquist. Trans. V.W. McGee. Austin, TX: University of Texas Press.

Bakhtin, Mikhail M. (1990) *Art and Answerability: Early Philosophical Essays by M.M. Bakhtin*. Eds M. Holquist and V. Liapunov. Trans. and notes V. Liapunov. Austin, TX: University of Texas Press.

Bakhtin, Mikhail M. (1993) *Toward a Philosophy of the Act*. Ed. M. Holquist. Trans. and notes V. Liapunov. Austin, TX: University of Texas Press.

Bakhtin, M.M. and Medvedev, P.N. (1985) *The Formal Method in Literary Scholarship: A Critical Introduction to Sociological Poetics*. Trans. Albert J. Wehrle. Cambridge, MA and London: Harvard University Press.

Berger, Peter and Luckmann, Thomas (1967) *The Social Construction of Reality*. Garden City, NY: Doubleday Anchor.

Bernard-Donals, Michael P. (1994) *Mikhail Bakhtin: Between Phenomenology and Marxism*. Cambridge: Cambridge University Press.

Gardiner, Michael (1992) *The Dialogics of Critique: M.M. Bakhtin and the Theory of Ideology*. London and New York: Routledge.

Godzich, Wlad (1985) 'Forward', in M.M. Bakhtin and P.N. Medvedev, *The Formal Method in Literary Scholarship: A Critical Introduction to Sociological Poetics*. Trans. Albert J. Wehrle. Cambridge, MA and London: Harvard University Press. pp. vii–xiv.

Gouldner, Alvin W. (1976) *The Dialectic of Ideology and Technology: The Origins, Grammar, and Future of Ideology*. New York: Seabury Press.

Hekman, Susan J. (1986) *Hermeneutics and the Sociology of Knowledge*. Notre Dame, IN and London: University of Notre Dame Press.

Jay, Martin (1974) 'The Frankfurt critique of Mannheim', *Telos*, 20: 72–89.

Lepenies, Wolf (1988) *Between Literature and Science: The Rise of Sociology*. Trans. R.J. Hollingdale. Cambridge: Cambridge University Press.

Mannheim, Karl (1936) *Ideology and Utopia*. Trans. Edward Shils. New York: Harcourt, Brace.

Mannheim, Karl (1940) *Man and Society in the Age of Reconstruction: Studies in Modern Social Structure*. Trans. Edward Shils. New York: Harcourt, Brace & World.

Mannheim, Karl (1952) *Essays on the Sociology of Knowledge*. Ed. P. Kecskemeti. London: Routledge & Kegan Paul.

Mannheim, Karl (1953) *Essays on Sociology and Social Psychology*. London: Routledge & Kegan Paul.

Mannheim, Karl (1956) *Essays on the Sociology of Culture*. Trans. Ernest Mannheim and Paul Kecskemeti. London: Routledge & Kegan Paul.

Mannheim, Karl (1970) *Wissenssoziologie: Auswahl aus dem Werk*. Trans. Kurt H. Wolff. Neuwied and Berlin: Luchterhand.

Mannheim, Karl (1971) *From Karl Mannheim*. Trans. Kurt H. Wolff. New York: Oxford University Press.

Mannheim, Karl (1975) 'Letters to Lukács', *New Hungarian Quarterly*, 16 (57): 93–105.

Mannheim, Karl (1982) *Structures of Thinking*. Trans. David Kettler, Volker Meja and Nico Stehr. London, Boston, MA: Routledge & Kegan Paul.

Mannheim, Karl (1986) *Conservatism*. Trans. David Kettler, Volker Meja and Nico Stehr. London and New York: Routledge & Kegan Paul.

Morrow, Raymond A. (with D.D. Brown) (1994) *Critical Theory and Methodology*. Newbury Park, CA and London: Sage.

Morrow, Raymond A. and Torres, Carlos A. (1995) *Social Theory and Education: A Critique of Theories of Social and Cultural Reproduction*. Albany, NY: State University of New York Press.

Morson, Gary Saul and Emerson, Caryl (1990) *Mikhail Bakhtin: Creation of a Prosaics*. Stanford, CA: Stanford University Press.

Ricœur, Paul (1986) *Lectures on Ideology and Utopia*. Trans. George H. Taylor. New York: Columbia University Press.

Simonds, A.P. (1978) *Karl Mannheim's Sociology of Knowledge*. Oxford: Oxford University Press.

Voloshinov, V.N. (1986) *Marxism and the Philosophy of Language*. Trans. L. Matejka and I.R. Titunik. Cambridge, MA: Harvard University Press.

11

THE DEATH AND REBIRTH OF THE AUTHOR: THE BAKHTIN CIRCLE AND BOURDIEU ON INDIVIDUALITY, LANGUAGE AND REVOLUTION

Ian Burkitt

The announcement of the 'death of the author' has been made repeatedly in the social sciences for well over a decade, first with the advent of post-structuralism and then with the rise in popularity of postmodern analyses. This announcement heralds a significant development in the human sciences in that it bolsters the move against individualism, against the idea of the individual as a point of origin for discourses and text. Instead of the individual being placed at the centre of the analysis and seen as the well spring of all original points of view, statements, discourses, and as the fount of all knowledge, now the individual is displaced in favour of the text: he or she is no longer the author of text, but its very construct and vehicle. Texts predate any given individual. As Althusser once said of ideologies, they lie in wait of the person before her or his birth and, in learning these pregiven texts or discourses, her or his subjectivity is called out or constructed. We are all, then, the subjects of texts, placed within them from birth onwards and, whenever we speak, we can only say what the various discourses in our culture allow us to say. As individuals we are not the authors of text, but can only give voice to the discourses that surround us, and our existence, therefore, is of little interest to the social scientist except, perhaps, as a nodal point in the interstice of competing or overlapping discourses.

By now this is a familiar story and, in its recounting, there is a danger of turning it into a caricature. However, there is little doubt that poststructural and postmodernist theories take for granted that the author is dead and that discourses and texts are the main focus of interest. This position, though, is not satisfactory for everyone, and for those who find it wanting, there is much to be welcomed in the rise of interest in the works of Mikhail Bakhtin. For in Bakhtin, we find the possibility of the rebirth of the author, but not the author as of old: that is, it is not a question of reviving the old impression of the author as a unique point of origin, the sole author of texts which are his alone. In Bakhtin, the author is no more a point of origin than she or he is in Derrida, except that, for Bakhtin, the author is not killed off but recast as a speaker within a context, one who utilizes appropriate sets of speech genres.

What I want to concentrate on in this chapter, then, can be divided into two connected parts. The first is the way that Bakhtin's work allows us to reintroduce a notion of the author, one who produces various utterances that embody *both* an individual perspective and also a sense of collective experience. This occurs because authors are part of the network of social relations and communication, and in producing an utterance they draw from the collectively recognized speech genres which constitute a relatively standard form of expression. However, authors are active in various contexts, which have a degree of uniqueness within them and allow authors to produce distinctive utterances. The individuality of the author is, from a Bakhtinian perspective, of some importance, but only in that his or her utterances flow from the situation and not from some pregiven inner essence of individuality. Furthermore, all utterances are a link in a chain of other utterances, so that all speech echoes with the voices of others. There is no such thing as an individual voice given in isolation. The second part of the chapter draws out the consequences of the rebirth of the author for oppositional or radical discourses, tracing the origins of these to the author's position in relations of power, and viewing language as a major instrument of social struggles. Radical or heretical discourses are therefore authored within a network of social relations, as are established world-views and beliefs. In elaborating what I believe to be two central themes of Bakhtin's perspective, I also draw heavily on the work of Pierre Bourdieu, which for me is a highly productive point of comparison. I hope to illustrate that by utilizing the work of both the Bakhtin circle[1] and Bourdieu, one can develop a more practical and embodied understanding of language in opposition to the more purely textual analyses of structuralists, poststructuralists and postmodernists.[2]

Speech Genres, Practical Contexts and the Author

What Bakhtin refers to as 'speech genres' are equivalent to the term 'discourse' in contemporary social science literature, in that speech genres are given sets of statements involving positions, world-views, ideologies, and linguistic styles which usually find their expression in certain practices in the everyday world. However, in most discourse analysis, emphasis is placed on the discourse itself and how this structures practices, whereas for Bakhtin speech genres always occur in the flow of human activity, so that language is not privileged over action, nor vice versa. While language is not necessarily given the organizing role, it is clear that speech genres are always the necessary accompaniment to human activity. Also, for Bakhtin, the author is not simply a construct of the a priori discourse, a position within its already structured frame, but a person within networks of communicative relationships who brings speech genres to life through his or her utterances.

> All the diverse areas of human activity involve the use of language. Quite understandably, the nature and form of this use are just as diverse as are the areas of human activity. . . . Language is realized in the form of concrete utterances (oral and written) by participants in the various areas of human activity. . . . Each separate utterance is individual, of course, but each sphere in which language is used develops its own *relatively stable types* of these utterances. These we may call *speech genres*. (Bakhtin, 1986: 60)

These genres are not limiting because the possibility of their diversification is boundless: the reason for this is that the scope of human activity is inexhaustible and thus speech genres will multiply as the horizons of social relations and activities expand. Discourses cannot be said to position individuals as such, but rather, *individuals actively use speech genres to orient themselves in their relationships and interactions*. Also, speech genres are heterogeneous in that each different sphere of human activity will have its own repertoire of speech genres. This could be the military command barked out on the parade ground, the technical language of limited scope used in scientific or business reports, the everyday chit chat between people in the street or workplace, a political debate in a bar, or the words of love between two lovers. Different speech genres have different degrees of flexibility, of latitudes for creativity and novelty, but most allow for some innovation. This would certainly be true of the more 'unofficial', informal speech genres involved in everyday life which are relatively open and have a more fluid structure.

Indeed, there is great similarity between Bakhtin's notion of the fluid structure of certain speech genres and Bourdieu's (1977, 1990a) idea of generative schemes or structures found in social practices. By generative structure, Bourdieu means a recursive pattern in social practices produced through the socially instilled dispositions of agents that can be seen in abstract terms as a 'structure', but which, in practice, subtly changes in each practical context of activity. So a generative structure is a form of action or speech that has a structure within it, but one that is remodelled in each act or speech act. As Michael Gardiner notes in his chapter in this volume, drawing links between Bakhtin and Merleau-Ponty, life is seen as directed towards the yet-to-be, and social action is a structured yet open process which requires accomplishment.

This means that the author has some importance for both Bakhtin and Bourdieu, for while the author is not a point of unique origin for a speech genre, nevertheless all such genres are realized only in the utterances of participants in human activity. The emphasis for Bakhtin is not placed on the individual author, but on the speaker who is enmeshed in relations of communication with others and in what Shotter (1993) would call 'joint activity'. Bakhtin's focus is not, therefore, on the individual author, but on the way that many speakers realize speech genres in the context of their everyday relationships and interactions. Texts are always contextualized in the concrete situations that agents find themselves in and utterances are composed by the way the person uses speech genres to give expression to their social positioning. As Vygotsky claims, in comments that parallel Bakhtin's position, 'oral speech is regulated by the dynamics of the situation. It flows entirely from the situation in accordance with th[e] type of situational-motivational and situational-conditioning process' (1987: 203). So, we find in Vygotsky a similar idea, that speech is not the direct expression of the author but flows from the situation the person is in and, to give expression to that situation, the person draws upon wider social meanings (or speech genres) for their concrete utterances. In any utterance there is, then, a triangulation of speech genres, the concrete social situations in which they are realized as utterances and, finally, the persons located in situations who use the speech genres to form utterances.

In this approach the text is not bled of all human and non-discursive aspects, as it is in the work of many poststructuralists and postmodernists. Instead of this, as much concentration is given to persons in relations of communication and the various contexts in which they act, as is given to the speech genres themselves. Bakhtin's work therefore fits in with the style of thinking being developed by Gergen (1994), which aims to escape 'the prison of the text' that results from a purely linguistic analysis and, instead, moves away from analysis of text to that of communication. I would like to suggest that making such a move has two important consequences. First, it allows us to envisage language and, more particularly, speech, as a concrete relational and active process, one which is open and generative in its structure. Secondly, it allows us to reintroduce some notion of the author, albeit one that is based on a decentred identity, where the author is only to be thought of as located in a network of relations and speech genres and is not a point of origin for these things. As Bakhtin himself claims, language is not about individual expression but about communication, which is a relational process wherein people take turns as both speakers and listeners. The alternation of these roles is not that between active speaker and passive listener, but rather both positions are active ones. A listener is just as active in the process of communication as the speaker, and each utterance made by the participants is a link in a complex chain of other utterances. This is what Bakhtin means when he says that language is about communication, that the utterance of one person is a response to the utterance of another, the speech flowing from the situation and not from the individual. But once more, it is not the structure of language or text that fully determines this active process; rather, it is activity itself as much as the speech genres which govern the form of utterances. As Gardiner says, 'from a Bakhtinian point of view, therefore, language is best understood as praxis, as a continual performance or "lived event"' (1992: 191).

The author belongs to a dialogue and to various speech genres, but his or her own individuality marks the utterance. By individuality, Bakhtin is not referring to something internal and given to the self, but to the biography of an individual who has a social and historical location. A person will always bring something of his or her own biography and socially formed self into a dialogue with others and this individuality will characterize his or her utterances. The utterance is always both a response to the utterance of others and an attempt to provoke a certain response from others, yet it is also the utterance of a particular person. Even the complexly structured and specialized works of scientific and artistic genres are also part of a dialogue with other such works, and the individuality of the author is manifest in 'his style, his world view, and in all aspects of the design of his work. This imprint of individuality marking the work also creates special internal boundaries that distinguish this work from other works connected with it in the overall process of speech communication in that particular cultural sphere' (Bakhtin, 1986: 75). So even in the confines of a scientific report there is room for the individuality of the author to show through. Bakhtin claims that in very standard speech genres, such as official or technical languages, there is little scope for the expression of what he calls our 'speech will', or the mark of our own individuality: this may be apparent only in the choice of genre and, in some cases, in the expressive intonation that the individual gives the utterance. This is also the means by which people are often able to express humour, by taking a standard or expected remark and infusing it with an opposite or ironic intonation. Here, individuality is not in the words that are spoken but in the *way* in which they are spoken. Either way, Bakhtin is interested in the author for the very reason that they are able, by various means, to bring the standard words and phrases of certain speech genres to life through their performance.

In terms of the more creative speech genres, Bakhtin believes that while these may be open to greater degrees of creativity on the part of the author, the genres must be fully mastered in order to be manipulated in a relatively innovative way. As he says,

> The better our command of genres, the more freely we employ them, the more fully and clearly we reveal our own individuality in them (where this is possible and necessary), the more flexibly and precisely we reflect the unrepeatable situation of communication – in a word, the more perfectly we implement our free speech plan. (Bakhtin, 1986: 80)

All this is highly reminiscent of Bourdieu's notion of strategies within social action and the way that individuals employ these in the everyday world. For Bourdieu, everyday actors are like sport's persons playing a game, in that, although the players have learned the strategies of the game, they are not necessarily aware of their knowledge of such strategies while they are playing it. Their various actions and reactions seem to appear almost spontaneously, as if by instinct, and yet the finest players – those capable of the greatest innovations – are always the most highly trained, possessing the greatest mastery of their game. Bourdieu thinks that a similar process occurs in social action, in that those individuals who are the most skilled social actors are also those with the greatest mastery of the various strategies employed in human activity within particular cultures. The most skilled, those with the greatest mastery, are also those most capable of surprise. Thus,

> [strategy] is the product of the practical sense as the feel for the game, for a particular, historically determined game – a feel which is acquired in childhood, by taking part in social activities. . . . The good player, who is so to speak the game incarnate, does at every moment what the game requires. That presupposes a permanent capacity for invention, indispensable if one is to be able to adapt to indefinitely varied and never completely identical situations. (Bourdieu, 1990b: 62–3)

Bakhtin argues a similar thing in terms of the speech genres employed in social activity, in that the more a particular genre is in our command the more skillfully we can use it. We can bend this tool for our own purposes to reflect precisely the speech situation and thus our own individual position within it, or, to paraphrase Bakhtin, the more precisely we are able to implement our own individual speech plan. By the term 'speech plan' he means that which the speaker wishes to say in his or her whole utterance; not just in individual words or sentences but in the entire contribution of the individual to the dialogue. This is also referred to as the speaker's 'speech will', which encapsulates the idea of something one wishes to say. Again, though, individual speech plans and wills are not the direct expression of a person but of the speech situation. And the means individuals must use to form their utterances are the speech genres themselves, which are not individual but collective phenomena. Yet despite this notion of the mediated nature of every utterance – and that the individual does not author the speech genres – the structural aspect of language, that which makes possible the form and plan of each utterance, is never separated in Bakhtin's work from the practical use of language, its sole function as a means of communication. This is the problem that exists in many forms of poststructuralism and postmodernism – from Foucault to Derrida – where discourses and texts are separated from their central role in the process of communication. This gives to many forms of structural, poststructural and postmodern analyses their anti-humanist feel, that the structural aspects of language, or the positioning and constructing aspect of discourse, is the only important feature, in which case the communicative function of language is lost. In contrast to this Bakhtin stresses the way in which language is a communicative device which is actually *used* by people. In this way he belongs solidly to the tradition of Russian linguists, semiologists, philosophers and psychologists who gravitated around Vygotsky and, taking their cue from Marx, saw language as a tool used in human practice. The notion of language as practice is the key to understanding Bakhtin's ideas.

Bakhtin also talks of the 'sense' of the utterance, of how each utterance is a link in a chain of speech communication and we only make sense of it in that context. However, in his work, and that of the Bakhtin circle more generally, there is also an understanding of language as a sensuous form of practice.[3] There is not only an analysis of the way people use speech genres to make sense of another's utterance, but an understanding that, in its very use, speech has a sensuous quality. When we use speech we are guided by its 'feel', by an apparently intuitive sense of whether the speech is right for the situation we are in. Like Bourdieu's notion of strategy and a feel for the game, we have all learned to be intuitive speakers with a feel for our language(s) and the ability to use them with varying degrees of appropriateness in specific situations. We may not necessarily have even to think about this use in any conscious sense of the term 'thought', for our utterances may be produced relatively unconsciously, flowing from the reservoir of speech that is around us rather than inside us. Writing also has this sensuous quality, not only in that, like speech, it is an active, embodied process, but that the writing flows from the various genres that the author is engaged with or utilizing. This is perhaps the reason why many authors and composers tend to refer to themselves as the vehicles of what they have written rather than as the sole originators. Speech and writing has a sensuous quality, then, that often outstrips the author's conscious comprehension.

For Bakhtin, there is also an expressive aspect in speech that refers to the speaker's emotional evaluation of the content of his or her utterance. The evaluative attitude determines the form and composition of the utterance and, once again, intonation is all important here. That is because the words and speech genres themselves have no emotion contained in them: the only emotion they can possess is that infused into them by the speaker in the utterance. All language is neutral until it is turned into a means of expression by the speaker. However, we need not see emotion as purely individual, but can conceptualize it as emerging from the situation as a way of acting and speaking appropriate for that context (Burkitt, 1997). Thus, as Wittgenstein (1958) claims, joy is not a thing that exists inside people, but is a way of speaking and acting joyfully in a condition of life that gives a person joy. This reflects Bakhtin's view that the words themselves contain no emotion, for it is the way in which they are spoken, the way they are acted out, that gives the utterance its emotional content. Intonation is just one way of communicating emotion through language so that utterances can take on their emotional colouring. Expressive intonation does not exist in the system of language, then, but like the emotion itself it belongs to the utterance – to the socially lived event of emotional expression.

As with Wittgenstein's analysis of emotion words, these only take on their meaning in the act, in the practice of the emotional context. For Bakhtin,

emotion, evaluation, and expression are foreign to the word of language and are born only in the process of its live usage in a concrete utterance. The meaning of a word in itself (unrelated to actual reality) is, as we have already said, out of the range of emotion. There are words that specifically designate emotions and evaluations: 'joy', 'sorrow', 'wonderful', 'cheerful', 'sad', and so forth. But these meanings are just as neutral as are all the others. They acquire their expressive colouring only in the utterance, and this colouring is independent of their meaning taken individually and abstractly. For example: 'Any joy is now only bitterness to me'. Here the word 'joy' is given an expressive intonation that resists its own meaning, as it were. (Bakhtin, 1986: 87)

Thus, emotional colouring and expressive intonations are another way in which the author's individuality comes through in the lived practice of linguistic communication. However, authors are not just located in every-day communicative relations and interactions which form a level playing field where all speakers are equal. The contexts from which the utterances of individuals flow are located in a hierarchy of social class and power relations, and the speech of every person is marked by this. While the Bakhtin circle argue that language does not in itself carry any ideological content – being as neutral in respect of ideology as it is with emotion – ideology is nevertheless expressed in language through its use by competing social groups and classes. Language always comes into play in the social struggles between various groups and crystallizes these conflicts, providing one of the means through which certain groups or individuals can become dominant and others can challenge that dominance. The individual, then, can become a revolutionary, authoring heretical discourses that oppose the ideological hegemony of established social groups; but he or she can only produce oppositional utterances in a social context where new speech genres emerge within the ferment of social struggles.

Power, Ideology and Revolution

As Bakhtin understands it, there is a differentiation of speech genres and styles according to class structure. Voloshinov puts this slightly differently, in that class position gives to language a different accent, by which he means not only a different dialect or form of expressive intonation, but a different emphasis and, in some cases, a different world-view. Language itself is neutral when it comes to ideology, but the utterances of authors from within different class positions gives language its ideological accents. Anthony Giddens claims that to study ideology 'is to examine how structures of signi-fication are mobilized to legitimate the sectional interests of hegemonic groups' (1979: 188). Here, the structure of signification is clearly seen as neutral, but it is the way this is mobilized or used that could be said to be ideological. The difference between this and the Bakhtin circle is that ideology is not just about the legitimization of hegemonic interests, but is more to do with the expression of different world-views through the same struc-ture of signification.

> Class does not coincide with the sign community, *i.e.*, with the community which is the totality of users of the same set of signs for ideological communication. Thus various different classes will use one and the same language. As a result, differ-ently oriented accents intersect in every ideological sign. Sign becomes an arena of the class struggle. (Voloshinov, 1986: 23)

In this, Voloshinov identifies two different types of ideology, established and behavioural ideology. Established ideology tends to belong to power-ful social groups and to the bureaucracy, whereas behavioural ideology belongs to the world of the everyday actor, that is, the great mass of people and their own popular forms of culture. Of course, established and behavioural ideologies are not separate things, for established ideology only grows out of behavioural ideology, becoming the more formalized ideology of the group.

> The established ideological systems of social ethics, science, art, and religion are crystallizations of behavioural ideology, and these crystallizations, in turn, exert a powerful influence back upon behavioural ideology, normally setting its tone. At the same time, however, these already formalized ideological products constantly maintain the most vital organic contact with behavioural ideology and draw sustenance from it; otherwise, without that contact, they would be dead, just as any literary work or cognitive idea is dead without living, evaluative perception of it. (Voloshinov, 1986: 91)

Thus established ideology must be capable of being incorporated into the world-view of everyday agents and turned into a lived event: that is, a perspective that has meaning and relevance in the various contexts in which people act. Like speech genres – which are also an aspect of established ideology – these things must be potentially usable in practice or easily assimilated into the actor's world-view for them to have meaning or relevance. But as they become part of the lived events of everyday life and acted out in practice as behavioural ideologies, the established ways of understanding become subtly changed in the process. However, established ideologies are not only associated with the ruling class, but can become part of what Bourdieu calls the 'heretical discourses' of the dominated, and as such form the language and ideologies of opposition movements and parties. So established ideology is not just the ideology of ruling groups, but is the meaningful ideology of all those who possess a publicly recognized and accepted discourse or speech genre. In everyday life people draw upon these genres to try to express their own individual situations: they are authors, but only become so by drawing from the speech genres and ideologies circulating around them.

In contrast to the notion of established ideology, Voloshinov uses the term behavioural ideology

> for the whole aggregate of life experiences and the outward expressions directly connected with it. Behavioural ideology is that atmosphere of unsystemized and unfixed inner and outer speech which endows our every instance of behaviour and action and our every 'conscious' state with meaning . . . [its] content is ideological through and through, determined not by individual . . . factors, but by factors of a purely sociological character. (Voloshinov, 1986: 91)

Much lived experience, then, may have relevance to only a small number of people so that, although it is still sociological in character, it cannot be expressed through the established forms of ideology. Such experience may go without being articulated and remain only vaguely in the awareness of certain individuals, close to what Freudians would think of as the unconscious psychical realm, or what Voloshinov calls 'unofficial consciousness' (Shotter and Billig, this volume; Voloshinov, 1976). This is the most fluid and dimly perceived aspect of behavioural ideology, which is constituted by all those accidental and undeveloped experiences that happen to us all. The

more clear strata of behavioural ideology are more directly linked to ideological systems and so are more creative and serious in terms of their contribution to a culture.

> Compared to an established ideology, [behavioural ideology is] a great deal more
> mobile and sensitive: they convey changes in the socio-economic basis more
> quickly and vividly. Here, precisely, is where those creative energies build up
> through whose agency partial or radical restructuring of ideological systems
> comes about. Newly emerging social forces find ideological expression and take
> shape first in these upper strata of behavioural ideology before they can succeed
> in dominating the arena of some organized, official ideology. Of course, in the
> process of this struggle, in the process of their gradual infiltration into ideologi-
> cal organizations (the press, literature, and science), these new currents in behav-
> ioural ideology, no matter how revolutionary they may be, undergo the influence
> of the established ideological systems and, to some extent, incorporate forms,
> ideological practices, and approaches already in stock. (Voloshinov, 1986: 92)

So established ideology is always drawn upon and put into practice
through behavioural ideology, and this is how established ideas come to be
renewed and reinvigorated. Yet behavioural ideology – in which there is to
be found many new and unformed ideas, along with ideas that oppose existing, accepted ideologies – is never completely separate from established
ideology and this 'official' doctrine always infiltrates and shapes the 'unofficial' doctrine in various ways. Indeed, Voloshinov's idea of behavioural
and established ideology is similar to, although much more developed than,
Bourdieu's notion of official and unofficial language. Established ideology
is that which is accepted within society as the 'correct' way to proceed, and
this may involve explicit codification of language and practices in the way
that Bourdieu describes it (1990b). On the other hand, behavioural ideology refers to the everyday language and practice of a group, which may
include repressed practices out of which various heretical discourses can
emerge. This occurs because, for Voloshinov, social relations between individuals and between groups are always discursive relations.

In a sense, as in Mannheim (1936), a social ideology governs all our
discursive productions and inner thoughts, but for Voloshinov this by no
means forms an a priori framework that cannot be changed. Everyday
discursive practices put the wider ideology into daily use within particular
situations, subtly altering it in the process. And while established ideology
reflects the dominant tendencies in culture and society, behavioural ideology can also be formed within groups which are in opposition to the established order. Like Bourdieu, Voloshinov understands language, and
symbolic productions in general, to always be infused with power relations.
In this respect the two thinkers have in common a fascination with the
notion of 'accent' and 'dialect', which refers not only to a particular regional
dialect placed upon a common language, but a subtle reformation of dominant cultural ideas within particular groups. Bourdieu links dialect to power
relations by claiming that,

> the linguistic differences between people from different regions cease to be
> incommensurable particularisms. Measured de facto against the single standard

of the 'common' language, they are found wanting and cast into the outer dark-
ness of *regionalisms*, the 'corrupt expressions and mispronunciations' which
schoolmasters decry. Reduced to the status of quaint or vulgar jargons, in either
case unsuitable for formal occasions, popular uses of the official language undergo
a systematic devaluation. (Bourdieu, 1991: 53–4)

These regional dialects are devalued because they betray differences in
the status hierarchy of society, constituted by differences in class, region,
gender, religion, race and ethnicity. A dialect can instantly reveal any of
these things and place one instantly in the socially ordered strata of differences. Language is always tied to power because, for both Bakhtin and
Bourdieu, the production of an official language is bound up with the
centralization of the nation state, through which the official or legitimate
language becomes bureaucratically regulated. With the centralization of the
nation state, the conditions are created for the production and enforcement
of a unified national language and the regional dialects and accents suffer
as a consequence. State institutions, in particular schools and educational
establishments, become the means of transmitting and enforcing the official
codes. Grammarians and linguists are the academics employed in the
process of codification of the official language as rules and laws, abstracting
the principles of the language as a basic, inviolable code. All breaches or
violations of the code are then seen as mistakes. As Bourdieu claims, once
a particular language has 'impose[d] itself as the only legitimate one, the
linguistic market has to be unified and the different dialects (of class, region
or ethnic group) have to be measured practically against the legitimate
language or usage' (1991: 45). Apart from this codification, languages only
exist in their practical state, as behavioural ideology, but aspects of this –
along with the speech genres, meanings and ethics it embodies – become
the official language and thus are turned into established ideology. What
Bourdieu and Voloshinov would agree on, then, is that linguists like Saussure who study linguistic codes partly abstracted from their performance,
do not see 'the relationship between the structured system of sociologically
pertinent linguistic differences and the equally structured systems of social
differences' (Bourdieu, 1991: 54). They do not see the connection between
language, power and social structure.

   This leads to another aspect that linguists do not often study which is the
link between established discourses and ideologies, on the one hand, and
the socio-economic conditions they reflect and refract, on the other. Again,
in poststructural and postmodern discourses this way of seeing things has
become highly unfashionable, reminiscent as it is of Marxist sociological
analysis. Yet Voloshinov and Bourdieu put a different spin on this, for they
are not claiming that language and ideology are simply a superstructure to
an economic base, but that language, discourse and ideology are an integral
part of social differences and struggles, whether people realize this or not.
Indeed, this lends a more sociological character to the understanding of
social opposition and resistance. Since Foucault, the notion of resistance has
been a central one in social analysis, and yet this concept was one that

Foucault had great difficulty in grounding. At times it appeared that resistance to authority and established ideas was to be thought of as an individual act of will and, indeed in some of his writings, Foucault gives to resistance a biological foundation in terms of the recalcitrance of the human organism towards efforts to discipline it (Foucault, 1980). In his later writings, Foucault sought the bases of resistance in local knowledges which oppose themselves to the more global discourses that aim to govern the population. But still, Foucault could not explain how these local knowledges arose, given that his corpus of works had tended to foster the view of knowledge as the prime medium of power and domination. Unlike Voloshinov and Bourdieu, he never sought the social basis for the formation of local knowledges and did not develop a practical view of the production and reproduction of language.[4]

Socio-economic conditions can be linked to speech genres, ideologies, and official languages in other ways, particularly in terms of the ownership of various forms of capital which allows for the official publication of specific styles and therefore their formalization. Bourdieu says that,

> it is necessary to distinguish between the capital necessary for the simple production of more or less legitimate ordinary speech, on the one hand, and the capital of instruments of expression (presupposing appropriation of the resources deposited in objectified form in libraries – books, and in particular in the 'classics', grammars and dictionaries) which is needed to produce a written discourse worthy of being published, that is to say, made official, on the other. This production of instruments of production, such as rhetorical devices, genres, legitimate styles and manners and, more generally, all the formulations destined to be 'authoritative' and to be cited as examples of 'good usage', confers on those who engage in it a power over language and thereby over the ordinary users of language, as well as over their capital. (Bourdieu, 1991: 58)

In this way, publication tends to make things official, but in order to achieve this one must have access to the means of publication and also to the speech genres and styles considered worthy of publication. However, this need not disqualify disadvantaged groups, as various ideologies can be published as tracts or pamphlets which can then form official languages or speech genres. These may be constituted from those aspects of behavioural ideology that everyone has sensed, but done so only fleetingly: the author then becomes the person who picks up on these collective experiences and is able to give them a public voice, making them official as objectified statements. From this standpoint,

> An author in the proper sense of the word is someone who makes public things which everyone felt in a confused sort of way; someone who possesses a special capacity, that of publishing the implicit, the tacit; someone who performs a real task of creation. A certain number of acts become official as soon as they are public, published. . . . Publication is the act of officialization *par excellence*. The official is what can and must be made public, displayed, proclaimed, before everyone's eyes, in front of everyone, as opposed to what is unofficial, or even secret and shameful. (Bourdieu, 1990b: 81–2)

Here, once again, we witness the rebirth of the notion of the author. An author is not, as we said earlier, the sole originator of an utterance, a discourse, or a belief system. However, he or she does bring into existence a text or discourse which makes public what many already knew or sensed, but had not yet spoken. The author utters in coherent words and sentences what others had felt but not been able to say. Perhaps using the styles or forms of established ideologies, the author is one who speaks and therefore makes objective the behavioural ideologies that had previously been only implicitly known. By giving behavioural ideology form, in a way that everyone can understand, the author makes *real* what many had only subjectively and fleetingly sensed. The author, then, plays the important part in social struggles of publishing and objectifying behavioural ideology, thereby creating heretical discourses which can become the focal point of opposition to established belief systems and the social hierarchy. Authors can be conservative figures, endlessly reproducing established ideologies and speech genres, but they are also in a position to take up the mantle of the revolutionary. Although, seemingly, the product of an individual creative spirit, a new or heretical discourse is the property of the social group from which it stems, and the revolutionary author is only she or he who uttered what was tacitly already there into an explicitly codified existence.

The views which authors succeed in publishing can then become formalized as part of the accepted outlook of a group or class, part of their established ideology. Furthermore, these published aspects of experience, of behavioural ideology, can become formalized to the extent that they become part of the official culture of a national group. For example, in the popular culture revolution of the 1960s in America and Britain, forms of popular music that had their roots in the Afro-American experience – which had until then been regarded as belonging to certain marginalized racial groups, or at least as working-class or blue-collar forms of culture and, as such, unofficial – became part of the official or established culture as the appeal of rock and rhythm and blues was extended to the white middle class through groups such as the Beatles and the Rolling Stones. In this process, aspects of the behavioural ideology of a group became formalized by being taken into the realms of established culture, and the established culture itself became more informalized, with a relaxation of strictly formal manners and styles of expression. This could be seen in Britain where greater tolerance began to be shown towards regional dialects and accents (the Beatles themselves had marked Liverpool accents that made them unmistakably from the poorer north of Britain). Suddenly, more regional dialects were to be heard in the media and, with them, a wider variety of language, forms of expression and, what had been up until then, unofficial attitudes and opinions. All of these now became expressed and, by implication, formalized through the established media. This is an example of what Voloshinov means by the dynamic interchange between established and behavioural ideology and how, in this process, the formalized codes can become more informal through a mixing with the unofficial.

This displays the plurality of world-views and social struggles within the symbolic order, or what Bakhtin calls the heteroglossia of language. As he claims,

> Language – like the living concrete environment in which the consciousness of the verbal artist lives – is never unitary. It is unitary only as an abstract grammatical system of normative forms, taken in isolation from the concrete, ideological conceptualization that fill it, and in isolation from the uninterrupted process of historical becoming that is characteristic of all living language. Actual social life and historical becoming create within an abstractly unitary national language a multitude of concrete worlds, a multitude of bounded verbal-ideological and social belief systems; within these various systems (identical in the abstract) are elements of language filled with various semantic and axiological content and each with its own different sound. (Bakhtin, 1981: 288)

While there is only one national language as a formal, abstract code, the ideological content within it is as varied and as heteroglot as the social groups and associations within the population. The various world-views and social belief systems that these groups create are different constructions of reality, but each one is created from a sociohistorical position within the relations of society. This plurality of world-views provides the basis for the different ideological positions in society and the heteroglossia of language itself.

> Thus at any given moment of its historical existence, language is heteroglot from top to bottom: it represents the co-existence of socio-ideological contradictions between the present and the past, between differing epochs of the past, between different socio-ideological groups in the present, between tendencies, schools, circles and so forth, all given a bodily form. These 'languages' of heteroglossia intersect each other in a variety of ways, forming new socially typifying 'languages'. (Bakhtin, 1981: 291)

This leads into Bakhtin's almost anarchistic belief in the power of carnival to shatter this appearance of unity within diversity, of the false impression of stability created by established and official ideologies. As such, carnival subverts the authoritative view of things and reveals the heteroglossia at the centre of language and sociohistorical relations. As Gardiner says,

> In the typical carnival image we find the 'pathos of shifts and changes, of death and renewal', an 'all-annihilating and all-renewing' force worked out in special carnival time which celebrates the 'joyful relativity' of all hierarchical, authoritarian structures. As such, all genuine carnival images are profoundly dualistic, and contain within themselves 'both poles of change and crisis': birth with death, youth and old age, and praise with abuse. Such symbolic strategies are designed to facilitate the 'violation of the usual and the generally accepted', which David Carroll (1983: 80) characterizes as a 'momentary, "aesthetic" break with the structures, laws, and dogmatically imposed "truths" which determine the place of "the people" under normal conditions'. (Gardiner, 1992: 46–7)

Carnival, then, creates conditions of fluidity and ambiguity that elevates change and becoming – all the conditions of behavioural ideology and heteroglossia – over the stable and the fixed, which are the very conditions favoured by the authorities with their established ideologies. To say that this is an anarchist position is not to suggest that Bakhtin favours the perpetually disruptive or the continually chaotic, but that, like many anarchists, he recognizes the importance of the everyday conditions that form a cauldron out of which the various ideologies arise. Without the conditions of heteroglossia and behavioural ideology, no language and culture could survive, for they would never become the basis of lived events and take on meaning. They would die in their icy formality and the straitjacket of their own codified nature. Heteroglossia and behavioural ideology provide the conditions in which even the formalized aspects of language and ideology can take on life. However, with the notion of carnival there emerges in Bakhtin's work not simply the prospect of the continual renewal of a culture, which we have talked of up until now, but of the overthrow of the established authorized view of the world and with it the collapse of social hierarchy and authority. Herein lies the possibility of revolution and the existence of revolutionary authors.

Bakhtin, of course, is not saying that revolution is achieved through actual, specific carnivals, but is using the carnival as a metaphor to unveil the social processes that would come into play in the overthrow of established authority. On carnivals and feast days, especially in the Middle Ages, a folk culture would be displayed which was often in direct opposition to that of church and state. Gardiner says that,

> Carnival effectively broke down the formalities of hierarchy and the inherited differences between different social classes, ages and castes, replacing established traditions and canons with a 'free and familiar' social interaction based on the principles of mutual cooperation, solidarity and equality. (Gardiner, 1992: 52)

While popular culture always has this potential for revolution, it is clear that, even in the Middle Ages when popular culture was more radical than today, there had to be an objective crisis in the social structure before these popular forms could come to the fore. Even then, as Bakhtin shows in his book on Rabelais (1984), the influence of radical forms of popular culture are short-lived, their effects on literature and poetry in the early Renaissance period were soon overshadowed by the rise of the centralized and rationalized nation state, headed by the aristocracy. Furthermore, the social order of the Middle Ages was not brought to an end by carnival alone, but by other influences on the power structure and by the socio-economic conditions of the times.

Thus, Bakhtin's approach can often lack a properly developed theory of the institutional frameworks of power and the way that these become ingrained in the actions and bodily dispositions of agents. Power is not so much expressed by agents in the acceptance of an orthodox view which needs to be turned upside down by carnival, as in the pre-discursive doxa of accepted ways of carrying on that forms the everyday habitus. The problem, then, is not simply one of challenging the consciously accepted established ideology with a radical or heretical discourse, but, as Bourdieu makes clear, there must also be a corresponding objective social crisis which calls into question many of the accepted and tacit modes of institutionalized activities and incorporated bodily dispositions.

Politics begins, strictly speaking, with the denunciation of this tacit contract of adherence to the established order which defines the original doxa . . . the heretical break with the established order, and with the dispositions and representations engendered by it among the agents moulded according to its structures, itself presupposes a conjuncture of critical discourse and objective crisis, capable of disrupting the close correspondence between the incorporated structures and the objective structures which produce them, and of instituting a kind of practical *épochè*, a suspension of the initial adherence to the established order. (Bourdieu, 1991: 127–8)

Only in times of social crisis, then, when the entire network of social relations is disrupted, do critical voices really sound out loud and gain the potential to lay down the foundation for a new order. In this way, Bourdieu's perspective adds another dimension to that of the Bakhtin circle, for it is made clear that heretical discourses and carnival are not enough, on their own, to bring about social revolution. A critical discourse does not instantly and directly transform the social structure of which it is part, and this accounts for the feeling of frustration experienced by many social critics who know just how hard it is to try to persuade others that the world needs changing. Revolution can only occur through an alignment of critical discourses with objective crises, in which the view of a new social order takes on meaning and sense – as well as becoming a real possibility – for everyday actors.

Conclusion

It is appropriate that the work of Bakhtin should emphasize so powerfully the theme of death and renewal, for it has been my argument here that consideration of the works of the Bakhtin circle and Bourdieu allows us to build upon the theme of the death and rebirth of the author. The author may well have died as an isolated individual who creates novel expressions that emanate from the core of his or her own unique being, but for the Bakhtin circle and Bourdieu, the author can be said to be reborn as a social being whose utterances give expression to the social context of his or her activity, as well as to his or her own historically and culturally constituted biography, and that this is achieved by the author utilizing the speech genres common in the linguistic and social community.

These genres, along with the author who uses them to give form to his or her utterances, are also part of the power relations within social groups, which are expressed through the speech genres as accents and ideologies. The interplay of the different accents, and of established and behavioural ideology, make possible the utterances of socially situated persons which are marked by the power relations between classes, races, ethnicities, genders and religions. Ideologies are not false beliefs, but express the social situation of their author, and it is this location and context that appears in the utterance as *both* a mark of individuality *and* an expression of verbal-ideological and social belief systems. Within these contexts, the author can play the role not only of the conservative – giving utterance to ideologies that are already established – but of the revolutionary, who gives linguistic shape to the formless behavioural ideology that has not yet crystallized into an objectified heretical discourse. We are, then, the authors of history, but we can only act as such collectively – dialogically – for language is a form of social praxis and could not become a lived event in any other way.

Notes

1 I refer here to the Bakhtin circle following Gardiner's (1992) use of the term to indicate the group of linguists working around Bakhtin himself who drew upon many of his ideas. In this piece, the term is used to point out the similarities with the writings of Voloshinov, and to avoid the controversy sparked by Clark and Holquist (1984), who have argued that Bakhtin was really the author of the books published under the name of V.N. Voloshinov. The controversy is avoided here because it is not at all central to my arguments.

2 The parallels between Bakhtin, Voloshinov and Bourdieu are brought out by the latter who mainly sees the similarity in terms of the opposition between the more practical approach to language and the structural one. For Bourdieu, the structural linguist, such as Saussure, is interested more in the codified system of language, whereas those who view language as praxis are more concerned with linguistic performance and the practical, sociological contexts in which this occurs (see Bourdieu, 1990a: 17, 31, 32).

3 See the chapters by Gardiner and Jung in this volume about how sensuous, embodied human interconnectedness is the basis for Bakhtin's ideas on language and communication.

4 Not only did Foucault lack a practical and communicative theory of language, but this approach spilled over into his analysis of ethics, which was concerned with the relationship of seemingly isolated individuals to systems of codes, dictums and precepts (Foucault, 1986). He never considered that the ethical relationship might be a relationship between social beings, as in a dialogical understanding of ethics (Gardiner, 1996).

References

Bakhtin, Mikhail M. (1981) *The Dialogic Imagination: Four Essays by M.M. Bakhtin*. Ed. M. Holquist. Trans. C. Emerson and M. Holquist. Austin, TX: University of Texas Press.

Bakhtin, Mikhail M. (1984) *Rabelais and His World*. Trans. Hélène Iswolsky. Foreword by Krystyna Pomorska. Bloomington, IN: University of Indiana Press.

Bakhtin, Mikhail M. (1986) *Speech Genres and Other Late Essays*. Eds C. Emerson and M. Holquist. Trans. V.W. McGee. Austin, TX: University of Texas Press.

Bourdieu, Pierre (1977) *Outline of a Theory of Practice*. Cambridge: Cambridge University Press.

Bourdieu, Pierre (1990a) *The Logic of Practice*. Cambridge: Polity Press.

Bourdieu, Pierre (1990b) *In Other Words: Essays Towards a Reflexive Sociology*. Cambridge: Polity Press.

Bourdieu, Pierre (1991) *Language and Symbolic Power*. Cambridge: Polity Press.

Burkitt, Ian (1997) 'Social relations and emotions', *Sociology*, 31 (1): 37–55.

Carroll, David (1983) 'The alterity of discourse: form, history, the question of the political in M.M. Bakhtin', *Diacritics*, 13 (2): 65–83.

Clark, K. and Holquist, M. (1984) *Mikhail Bakhtin*. Cambridge, MA: Harvard University Press.

Foucault, Michel (1980) *Power/Knowledge*. Brighton: Harvester Press.

Foucault, Michel (1986) *The Use of Pleasure: The History of Sexuality*, Vol. 2. London: Viking Penguin.

Gardiner, Michael (1992) *The Dialogics of Critique: M.M. Bakhtin and the Theory of Ideology*. London: Routledge.

Gardiner, Michael (1996) 'Alterity and ethics: a dialogical perspective', *Theory, Culture & Society*, 13 (2): 121–43.

Gergen, Kenneth J. (1994) *Realities and Relationships: Soundings in Social Construction*. Cambridge, MA: Harvard University Press.

Giddens, Anthony (1979) *Central Problems in Social Theory: Action, Structure and Contradiction in Social Analysis*. London: Macmillan.

Mannheim, Karl (1936) *Ideology and Utopia*. Trans. Edward Shils. New York: Harcourt, Brace & World.

Shotter, John (1993) *Conversational Realities: Constructing Life Through Language*. London: Sage.

Voloshinov, V.N. (1976) *Freudianism: a Marxist Critique*. Eds I.R. Titunik and N. Bruss. New York: Academic Press.

Voloshinov, V.N. (1986) *Marxism and the Philosophy of Language*. Trans. L. Matejka and I.R. Titunik. Cambridge, MA: Harvard University Press.

Vygotsky, L.S. (1987) *The Collected Works of L.S. Vygotsky*, Vol. 1. New York: Plenum Press.

Wittgenstein, Ludwig (1958) *Philosophical Investigations*. Oxford: Blackwell.

PART IV

ETHICS AND EVERYDAY LIVES

12

BAKHTINIAN PERSPECTIVES ON 'EVERYDAY LIFE' SOCIOLOGY

Courtney Bender

Most American sociologists employing Bakhtin's theories draw on his discussions of language and discourse (DiMaggio, 1997; Higginbotham, 1993; Steinberg, 1993). To date, however, few have noted how Bakhtin's theories of dialogue and heteroglossia depend on his understanding of everyday life that he developed early in his career (Gardiner, 1996; Shields, 1996) and sustained throughout, even as he turned his focus to literary topics (Morson and Emerson, 1990). Bakhtin's earliest existing work, *Toward a Philosophy of the Act* (1993) is apparently the introduction to a lost essay devoted to the ethics of the act written between 1919 and 1924. In it, Bakhtin outlines a theory that locates ethical actions within everyday events, situating the ethical moment as ongoing in events, rather than given (1993: 56). He emphasizes the role of the 'self', seeing selves as 'answerable' or responsible for their actions. Bakhtin's understanding of everyday life and focus on microsociological aspects of social interaction appears on its face to share some basic elements with phenomenological and interaction-ist perspectives largely taken for granted in American 'everyday life sociology' (Adler et al., 1987). Nevertheless, when placed in comparative dialogue, Bakhtin's notions expose the limits of the mainstream traditions' accounts of the constitution of everyday life and suggest alternative perspectives that overcome some of their elisions.

Toward a Philosophy of the Act is directed against descriptions of every-day life found in neo-Kantian transcendentalism (drawing meaning and justification for life events in a priori moments) and Bergsonian *durée* (life passing without accruing meaning and understanding). Bakhtin worried that these theories lent philosophical weight to the burgeoning powers of modern bureaucracies. Such theories, Bakhtin wrote, strip individuals of their unique positions within everyday life, making them 'pretenders' who speak with alibis rather than from their own unique, responsible positions.

Bakhtin grounds his notions of ethical responsibility and a unique self in 'participatory thinking' that occurs *within* lived experience, or what he terms 'once-occurrent Being' (Bakhtin, 1993: 2). These themes of the self's unique positioning and the location of ethical truth within prosaic acts undergird the essay and appear in all of Bakhtin's work on the novel and literary subjects, including heteroglossia and polyphony in both literary and non-literary speech genres (see, for instance, Bakhtin, 1981: 293–7; 1984: 101ff.; 1986: 60–102).

In the following pages I compare Bakhtin's perspective on everyday life with classical Schutzian and Meadian definitions. Bakhtin shares some emphases with phenomenology and pragmatism (he had certainly read both Husserl and William James) as each emphasizes the importance of prosaic acts and analyses agency within them as intersubjectively negotiated. Unlike Bakhtin, however, phenomenologists and interactionists seldom analyse or understand events in terms of what makes them creative, singular or contingent, turning instead to the repeated and habitual aspects that can be studied across events. In overlooking the particular contingencies that make up any particular interaction, the mainstream discussions of everyday life neglect the very aspects that Bakhtin finds most important in understanding an act's relation to other acts, ethics, and history. Bakhtin understands the self as uniquely developed and engaged in relations to others within unique events. As a result, theory does not collapse under the weight of institutionalized structures and rules which, once postulated, turn attention away from the messiness that we observe and bear in mind throughout everyday life. As such, Bakhtin moves us towards a theory that takes into account the contingencies that are constitutive of everyday, ethical action.

Bakhtin is neither the first nor the only social thinker to emphasize that the everyday sphere is not merely habitual and repetitive. In fact, some have emphasized the redemptive aspects of everyday life, either as a space for constructing 'tactics' against dominant orders, or as a space where more systematic resistance can gain force (de Certeau, 1984; Gardiner, 1995; Lefevbre, 1991; Scott, 1985). While Bakhtin shares with these thinkers a sense that everyday acts are the locations of ethical acts, his general sense is that everyday life is too disorganized, contingent, and messy to develop particular challenges to any social order. Bakhtin's unrelenting emphasis on acts as unique and unrepeatable combination of selves, perspectives, and ideas keeps him from imagining everyday life as a space of opposition (Bender, 1997; Morson and Emerson, 1990).

**Phenomenology and the Social Construction of Reality:
Distinguishing Meaning from Everyday Life**

Berger and Luckmann (1966; Berger, 1967) state that social interactions filter the infinite meanings that are possible in brute, chaotic reality into a finite set of frames that we can manage. According to Berger and Luck-mann, we only experience life through its social constructions, even though meaning is always constructed in acts and institutions that change over time through social interactions. In this world, symbols are constructed and agreed upon in interactions; these symbols limit the complexity of life and organize it in institutions. Institutions, in this sense, are not only the large categories of the state, market, public sphere and so on, but are also the myriad established, repeated activities that we take for granted. Actors constantly use these symbols and are thus embedded in a dialectical flux between creating and created meaning.

Meaning is highly pragmatic and efficient in our everyday lives, Berger and Luckmann argue. The everyday is an undifferentiated, monolithic 'here and now' in which social actors assume that others around them operate with the same meanings and goals. Everyday life is the space of habitual-ized action, where meanings are 'embedded as routines in [a] general stock of knowledge, taken for granted by him' and which furthermore free 'the individual from the burden of "all those decisions"' (1966: 53). This every-day knowledge is socially constructed and reconstructed through objectified and institutionalized habits. As such, everyday life is practical and instru-mental and we willingly suspend doubt within it in order to get through it. We bracket questions about what our acts mean, and other questions that require reflection about the assumptions of everyday living, and we save them for other times. 'Since everyday life is dominated by the pragmatic motive', Berger and Luckmann say, 'recipe knowledge, that is, knowledge limited to pragmatic competence in routine performances, occupies a prominent place in the social stock of knowledge' (1966: 42).

This description of everyday life has been extremely influential in Ameri-can sociology, strengthening social constructionist views that ground much of the discipline. Its foundation in Alfred Schutz's work takes everyday life to be our 'paramount reality'. Schutz compares the ways we apprehend people to the way we apprehend inanimate objects. When pragmatic think-ing is extended in the habitual world of everyday life, the specific conscious-ness of other individuals is given, much as we consider objects we encounter as already given. Just as we assume that every fountain pen functions in the same way and base our acts according to that assumption, so I assume that every consciousness is like my own. That is, our standpoints or positions are fundamentally interchangeable (that I could be in another's place) and our worlds, or our 'meaning systems' are also interchangeable (Schutz and Luckmann, 1973: 59–60). Without denying the fact that each individual modifies the same socialized space and is unique, phenomenologists contend that within everyday reality, our relationships hinge on the prag-matic assumptions of similarity (1973: 61). This assumption of similarity and shared meaning are required for communication.

Phenomenologists suggest that life is separated between everyday life (structured by habits) and 'provinces of meaning' where we reflect on every-day life. In a word, everyday life is not a moral sphere at all: instead, religion and other 'meaning' systems that stand outside everyday life provide every-day life with meaning (Wuthnow, 1992: 30). Everyday life is only ascribed meaning as we move into and out of other spheres of life; those other spheres of meaning never enter into our paramount reality (Schutz and Luckmann, 1973: 22–4). Religion and other principle-laden systems of meaning are compartmentalized and we move from everyday reality into them, and back again. We take Kierkegaardian leaps between these finite systems because they cannot be reduced to another, and Schutz writes, 'only when we experi-ence a specific shock that bursts the limits of that which is for us a momen-tarily "real," finite province of meaning, must we transfer (or "wish" to) the accent of reality to another province of meaning' (Schutz and Luckmann, 1973: 25; cf. Durkheim, 1995: 54). As the spheres are logically distinct, any interaction between them would show us that our meanings are mere constructions and this fact would cause our faith in them to falter.

Leaping from one province of meaning to another is important, Schutz believes, because it forces individuals to look at paramount reality as more than the pragmatic here and now. Yet while Schutz emphasizes this as a possibility, Berger and Luckmann strongly state that our excursions out of everyday life hardly affect everyday life interactions within particular spheres, as in the following case:

> For instance, as a businessman I know that it pays to be inconsiderate of others. I may laugh at a joke in which this maxim leads to failure, I may be moved by an actor or a preacher extolling the virtues of consideration, and I may concede in a philosophical mood that all social relations should be governed by the Golden Rule. Having laughed, having been moved and having philosophized, I return to the 'serious' world of business, once more recognize the logic of its maxims, and act accordingly. Only when my maxims fail to 'deliver the goods' in the world to which they are intended to apply are they likely to become problematic to me 'in earnest'. (Berger and Luckmann, 1966: 44)

Provinces of meaning provide us with meaning and order when we need to escape from the banality of everyday life or crave the comfort of ordered systems of meaning. Berger, Schutz and Luckmann establish the sense that we make assumptions and objectify others in order to get through the nitty-gritty of our life. Yet this 'getting through' sets thought and responsibility, oddly enough, *outside* 'paramount reality'. The interpretive frame provided here only allows us to act and think within finite frames of non-overlapping meaning. The ethical moment is embedded within institutions, rather than in particular responses to concrete situations.

Schutz, Berger and Luckmann therefore separate the ethical moment from everyday acts. Bakhtin addresses and criticizes a similar separation in *Toward a Philosophy of the Act* and proposes an alternative to this schizo-phrenic self who shuttles back and forth between meaningful thoughts and non-meaningful acts. Bakhtin argues that the ethical, religious, and meaningful are constituent and present in each act. Before considering his proposal at greater length, let us turn to consider issues articulated in inter-actionism.

Pragmatism and Interactionism: The Problem of Shared Meaning

George Herbert Mead and his interpreters developed an interactionist model of the self and of everyday life. Mead's perspective, as Blumer notes, is centred on the belief that 'human groups or society exists in action and must be seen in terms of action. This picture of society as action must be the starting point' (1969: 6). As in pragmatism, society is constantly recreated in intersubjective communication about actions and objects. This emphasis on constant recreation points to a significant difference between Schutz's phenomenology and American pragmatic tradition, since for interactionists, meaning is embedded in the act. Bakhtin shares this sense with the interactionists, for as Michael Holquist writes in the forward to *Toward a Philosophy of the Act*, '[f]or Bakhtin, the unity of an act and its account, a deed and its meaning, if you will, is something that is never a priori, but which must always and everywhere be *achieved*. The act is a deed, and not a mere happening (as in "one damned thing after another")' (Holquist, 1993: xii).

However, Mead states that we interact on a symbolic level, understanding one another's meanings through shared gestures and signs. We respond to others' actions and we create meaning in their actions and response. There is a 'triadic' nature to meaning, which comprises a speaker and respondent, and the situation or act in itself. This understanding is similar to Bakhtin's perspective (as we will see) except in one crucial regard. According to the interactionists, the symbols we use to communicate meaning hold the *same* meaning for both individuals in an interaction. Blumer suggests that if there is a misunderstanding along the path of the 'triadic nature of meaning' then 'communication is ineffective, interaction is impeded, and the formation of joint action is blocked' (1969: 9). Communication in acts is possible *only* to the extent that there is sufficient congruence, so that individuals can see themselves taking on the role of another and understand that position. In this theory, individuals have many roles, and our places in them are necessarily transmutable. Thus, 'to indicate to another what he is to do, one has to make the indication from the standpoint of that other' (Blumer, 1969: 9).

The notion that one can (and must) take on the standpoint of another in order to communicate is central to Mead's description and discussion of the two-part self. The self gains consciousness, Mead says, in conversations with itself, thus giving it a social (though highly cognitive) foundation (Mead, 1962: 173). While this 'I' continues in internal conversations with itself and with memory of the past, the 'me' is the externally social self that is constituted through the 'organized set of attitudes of others which one himself assumes'. That is, the 'me' is a set of roles; this is the self that others experience. The 'I' remains the potential yet historically continuous part of the self and we do not experience it as such, but only as it provides a 'novel element' in acts that make each self specific and untranslatable. While the 'me' is role-taking, the 'I' provides something in addition to what the role calls for, an individual mark. Acts have no certainty until they are completed. Mead writes, 'There is a moral necessity but no mechanical necessity for the act . . . [without its] two phases there could be no conscious responsibility, and there would be nothing novel in experience' (1962: 179).

It is important to note that, for Mead, the 'me' and the 'I' are both directed towards the 'generalized other' which Mead describes as the society or community. Unlike a real flesh and bone 'other', the generalized other is an abstraction that represents the rules of the game or the given rules of society. Through testing the rules of childhood games, individuals learn how to respond to abstract rules that govern behaviour. These behavioural patterns are articulated in general terms so that individuals can participate in the shared meaning of community or society by taking on any role in the game, becoming in essence, anyone (Mead, 1962: 152ff.). The ability to cognitively become *anyone* (the interchangeability of roles developed through shared relationships to the generalized other) is the linchpin of Mead's understanding of human communication. As roles are considerably easier to analyse than the interior relationship between I and me, most interactionists bracket the creative role of the I, focusing instead on individuals developing through 'organizing individual attitudes of others into the organized social or group attitudes, and by thus becoming an individual reflection of the general systematic pattern of social or group behavior in which it and the others are all involved' (1962: 158).

In an interactionist perspective, we are socialized by taking on roles in which our actions are determined to a large degree by the a priori social understanding of those roles. Acts from this standpoint appear routine, as they also appear to be in Berger and Luckmann's phenomenology. In the moment of everyday life, Blumer says, action is mainly 'repetitive and stable' because we have clear ideas of what a situation will entail in the ways that we and others are expected to act in it. In these settings we 'share common and pre-established meanings of what is to be expected in the action of the participants' (Blumer, 1969: 17). Even though meaning is found and formed in concrete interactions, interactionism invariably focuses on the role of the community or society. The potentially liberating view of individuals negotiating meaning in concrete acts is undercut in the theory of the generalized other that establishes that meaning between individuals is 'shared' a priori of interactions.

Toward a Philosophy of the Act: Participative Thinking and Answerable Acts

Interactionism and phenomenology both begin as theories based on the intersubjective, microsociological construction of acts and of social life. Both begin with theories of the act and the individual, and as such making their theories' scope of evaluation quite different enterprises from the kind of sociology concerned with changing market structures, ideological formulations of social movements, grand theories of the state and the like. Both theories, however, eventually come to express the 'self' as embedded in institutionalized spheres that continue to exist regardless of the people who work, live, and move within them. Their latent juxtapositions of self and society contribute to the collapse of the self and its acts. Ironically, in these theories of everyday life no *particular* individual ever has to exist. Anyone else in that position would do just as well. We take on roles and we move through the pragmatic world using actions that entail assumed outcomes. In the end, these theories tell us more about structures than they do about the individuals who live in them. Bakhtin's early work can be brought into this impasse, and reinvigorate both theories by positing acting agents who do not share meaning with unreplaceable others and whose ethical actions are constituted in particular, unique acts.

The position Bakhtin articulates in *Toward a Philosophy of the Act* grew from his concern that individuals in modern society feel no responsibility for their own lives or actions. Bakhtin pins his critique on neo-Kantians and Russian Formalists, both of whom draw a distinction between unethical, prosaic everyday life and the ethical, cultural and rational realms by privileging theoretical or aesthetic thinking over prosaic, participatory thinking. Privileging the abstract essentially leads away from responsibility and ethical action instead of towards it. Bakhtin then attempts to reconcile prosaic life (bound to our physical bodies) and cognitive or theoretical thinking (free to move as it pleases) in a concept of the answerable act, where ethical responsibility arises out of the actualization of both the repeated and the unique in specific social events.

Bakhtin finds both aesthetic and theoretical thinking problematic precisely because they abstract what they imagine to be 'important' from actual events located within real time and space, and gain life of their own within this abstract realm of thinking. Philosophies employing aesthetic intuition or theoretical thinking divide the content of an act (its product) from the act itself (or its actual historical performance). While formal moments of thinking do no harm in and of themselves, theoretical thinking often attempts to 'pass itself off as the whole world', and in doing so, the 'truth' of acts are erased (Bakhtin, 1993: 8). Bakhtin therefore argues that while the content of an act is important, it is important only as individuals take responsibility for that content within the act itself, and 'sign' their acts.

Both theoretical and aesthetic thinking limit the degrees to which individuals act responsibly because they locate the most important aspects of an act outside the responsible self participating in the event itself. This is a grave failing, as it allows individuals to displace their unique responsibilities either through appealing to a categorical 'good' posited by theoretical thinking, or by merging with the 'other' posited in aesthetic thinking. Bakhtin's ethical self, in contrast, participates in events from a particular position that is hers or his alone, and cannot be replaced with any other position or anyone else's moral imperative.

In contrast, theoretical thinking is divorced from its boundedness within real life and posits an 'every man' that exists potentially and that is far from a unique participating and acting being. In a similar fashion, aesthetic thinking draws the subject away from its own position by melding with and becoming inseparable with an other. Leaving behind one's own established position is at best a chimera that presupposes 'my own uniqueness and the uniqueness of my place constitute an inessential moment that has no influence on the character of the essence of the world's being' (Bakhtin, 1993: 15). Bakhtin contrasts aesthetic empathy which gives away one's own position with active empathizing, where 'I do not lose myself completely, nor my unique place outside it, even for a moment'. This is the beginning of an ethical moment, where 'It is I who empathize actively into the object: empathizing is my act, and only that constitutes its productiveness' (1993: 15). In this critique, Bakhtin begins an argument that we cannot share meaning with others, and that, furthermore, the 'ethical act' is grounded in an awareness of difference. This perspective is quite different from that put forward by Berger and Luckmann and Mead, who each suggest that an assumption of shared meaning is *necessary* for communication.

Bakhtin suggests both that everyday life is participative and that the ethical moment of an act occurs uniquely within the act itself. The truth of an act is not accessible outside the act itself, in which the unique self plays a crucial part. 'Once-occurrent uniqueness or singularity cannot be thought of, it can only be experienced or lived through. . . . This [subject] cannot be determined in the categories of non-participant theoretical consciousness – it can be determined only in the categories of . . . an actually performed act' (1993: 13). Participative thinking emphasizes that I can only understand theoretical ideas and other people within specific actions that exist in relation to myself.

While this appears obvious, putting it into practice in theories of everyday life has proved more difficult. As we have seen, the participative qualities of action are easily denigrated in theories that suggest a separation of the objective, repeatable components of an act (its products) from its subjective, seemingly contingent aspects. Such a split defines what is repeatable as important and the specific contexts in which it is found as relatively less so. The message is divorced from its medium and ethical component of an act is understood as part of the act's content or product, or as a role that individuals take on in given social contexts.

In defining acts as 'answerable' or 'responsible', Bakhtin seeks to integrate the 'subjective' side of an act with its 'formal' aspects yet without falling into relativism (1993: 71). Rather than seeing acts as only defined by their product (that is, being systematic, logical, or categorically correct) acts are also constituted by the locations in which they happen, as individuals are embedded in specific horizons that modify pure thinking. As an individual acts

> . . . he sees clearly *these* individual, unique persons whom he loves, *this* sky and *this* earth and *these* trees . . . and the time; and what is also given to him simultaneously is the value, the actually and concretely affirmed value of these persons

and these objects ... and he understands the ought of his performed act, that is, *not* the abstract law of his act, but the actual, concrete ought conditioned by his unique place in the given context of the ongoing event. (Bakhtin, 1993: 30)

The truth of an event, Bakhtin says, comes about in the relationship of understanding from a particular perspective and the obligation of acting from that position. This truth is easily articulated within the act and it can be described precisely because it is related to the concrete and common surroundings that comprise the event. Truth in participatory action is not, however, the *product* of the act or its transcript. Transcripts, Bakhtin argues, emphasize content at the expense of an event's tone (Bakhtin, 1990). An act's truth is based on individually socialized, given unique bodies that stand in unique relations to the natural world and to other people. Our 'non-substitutable' positions carry over into our acts; they can be neither replicated by us nor enacted by anyone else. It is this specificity that makes acts uniquely answerable. Bakhtin writes, 'there are as many different worlds of the event as there are individual centers of answerability, *i.e.*, unique participative (unindifferent) selves. If the "face" of an event is determined from the unique place of a participative self, then there are as many different "faces" as there are different unique places' (1993: 45). Bakhtin does not view a world apart from the specific, responsible relationships that constitute it. 'All these abstract categories are here constituent moments of a certain living, concrete and palpable (intuitable) once-occurrent whole – an event' (1993: 32).

The unique answerability of our acts is expressed only in acts, making the 'tone' or emotional cast that we give to acts also important aspects of an act's truth. 'Everything that I have to do with is given to me in an emotional-volitional tone, for everything is given to me as a constituent moment of the event in which I am participating' (Bakhtin, 1993: 33). Tone orients action, reflects the uniqueness of an event, and provides it its immediate and ongoing truth. The tone of an act is firmly lodged within the act itself. It does not descend into an act, but comes into being with relation to the act's product/content, that is, its author's specific horizon and face. It is, Bakhtin says, the moment where the Kantian ought enters an act. Tone is connected to 'being true to' or being 'faithful' to an act in relation to the horizon of the actor, and is always active. Tone is 'not the content of an obligation ... but my signature below it – the fact that at one time I acknowledged or undersigned the given acknowledgment' (1993: 38).

Bakhtin's emphasis on the specificity of acts that constitute social life highlights his career-long disdain of institutions. Although he does not deny their existence, they have *no* place in his theory of the act. Bakhtin concentrates solely on individuals making meaning and existing without alibis or roles that take over their unique positions. He is very critical of modern selves who rush to bracket individual answerability by taking on the voice or authority of someone other than ourselves. Using a voice or affecting a position that downplays our unique position (as when we speak for every one, or the Party, or the Church) allows people to speak from an alibi, and diminishes the ethical content and oughtness of the act itself (1993: 40–2). 'A life lived on the tacit basis of my alibi in Being falls away into indifferent Being that is not rooted in anything' (1993: 43). As everyone occupies a unique place in being, we are each ultimately accorded a non-alibi of being with individual responsibility. We must answer for our own acts by taking into account our unique place in the spatial and temporal moment, our relationships with other people and objects, and the content or product of an act (even though this 'content' is only as one more moment of the act). This architectonic of the act orients the answerable act, which is 'precisely that act which is performed on the basis of an acknowledgment of my obligative uniqueness' (1993: 42).

Toward a Philosophy of the Act focuses much attention on the unique locations of individuals and their acts. This attention, nevertheless, should not lead to the mistaken notion that the self is complete or even possible as a construction outside concrete relations with other people. 'Answerability' invokes the necessity of a dialogue between two people who come into an event (in Bakhtin's view) with specific horizons of meaning, and who then act to answer others' actions. Although Bakhtin's understanding of dialogue would blossom later in his career, this early articulation of the self suggests the things to come. Bakhtin's notion of the self comprises three relational parts, the 'I, the other, and I-for-the-other' (1993: 54). The I-for-myself is a constantly unique person and a unified whole, but is not articulated in the relationship between the I-for-the-other and the other-for-me – it is always potential and undifferentiated. Unlike Mead's 'I', it is not directed towards social situations, but is always hidden and potential.

The I-for-the-other and the other-for-me are always specific constructions occurring in unique acts. They are always partial, incomplete, and unfinalized. According to Bakhtin, when I interact with another person I do not see all of him or her, but only the parts that are contingent on the act's specificity. That person, within that particular action, is the other-for-me. Likewise, that part of the I that is actualized as a concrete I-for-the-other is always just one I, one that the other sees, reacts to and answers. It is within the specific relation between these partial selves in an event that answerability is constructed. Using the example of love, Bakhtin states that 'the other's love of me sounds emotionally in an entirely different way to me – in my own personal context – than the same love of me sounds to him, and it obligates him and me to entirely different things. Yet there is no contradiction here' (1993: 46).

Bakhtin's perspective provides fresh insight into the gap between the macro-societal world and the finite, micro-societal specificity of individual life. If everything is experienced in the act itself, then there is, perhaps, no reason to continue articulating a split between individual and society. Both self and society are constituted in acts. As Bakhtin muses,

> The impelling inspiration of my small life and the boundless world is that of my participative (unindifferent) non-alibi in Being; this is an answerable expansion of the context of actually acknowledged values from my own unique place. But

insofar as I am detached from that unique place, a split arises between the possible boundless world of cognition and the very small world of values that have
been acknowledged by me. (Bakhtin, 1993: 50)

Acts tie the boundless world with the small life, tying together culture and
individuals in local, understandable (and responsible) acts.

From Everyday Life Sociology to a Prosaic Sociology

Toward a Philosophy of the Act provides a wealth of new material that
speaks to the taken-for-granted notions of socially constructed worlds and
institutions and to sociologists' methods for studying everyday life. Yet how
can we study social life populated with these partial selves? Although the
answers to that question will be left for another day, it bears noting what a
'prosaic sociology' would *not* look like.

Bakhtin is highly critical of the separation of theoretical thinking and
everyday action. While his argument was launched particularly against neo-
Kantians, it can be extended to engage a similar separation that appears in
the phenomenological distinction between ethical reflection and repetitive,
habitual action. Phenomenology compartmentalizes meaning in spheres or
sets of knowledge that do not interact. If they were to interact, the
constructed nature of reality would become evident and society would
falter. The force of the phenomenologists' argument and its contrast to
Bakhtin's is evident in its understandings of doubt. Schutz and Luckmann
see doubt as a harmful aspect of living were it to enter into every part of
life. If doubt enters into individuals' actions within everyday reality, it para-
lyses individuals, and makes them incapable of making decisions or
knowing what to do next. Rather, they state, individuals fall into rote action
and do not think (nor are they required to think) about each act. They doubt
only in spheres that are bracketed off from everyday life: '[i]n theoretical
thinking, I can make doubt a methodological principle. In the world of
everyday life, I am interested, in contrast, in being able to orient myself in
action in routine ways' (Schutz and Luckmann, 1973: 14–15).

In contrast, Bakhtin situates doubt as a constant moment of intersubjective truth. The many different faces and perspectives that constitute an act
present the individual with a variety of options and agents that he or she
may have to answer. This multiplicity throws the truth of any one way of
acting into question, and resolves it only in acts' resolution. Thus, 'we recognize doubt as a distinctive value. It is precisely doubt that forms the basis of
our life as effective deed-performing, and it does so without coming into
contradiction with theoretical cognition' (Bakhtin, 1993: 45). That is, doubt
is not an activity that rises in reflection in spheres of meaning, but rather is
a constitutive part of acting. It is a creative moment that helps craft the
outcome and tone of concrete acts.

Berger and Luckmann's example of the businessman (given in a section
above) who uses different judgements in a serial fashion throughout life,

denotes the phenomenological view that we come to hold multiple perspectives, but only serially and disparately. In contrast, Bakhtin's focus on participatory thinking emphasizes how we grasp and take into account multiple perspectives as we engage lived experience. In a later essay, Bakhtin notes that it is nearly impossible not to see our own multiple meaning systems, or abstract values, through the eyes of other values that we enact on a daily basis. He ridicules the idea that anyone lives like the illiterate peasant who,

> . . . naively immersed in an unmoving and for him unshakable everyday world; prayed to God in one language, sang songs in another, spoke to his family in a third, and when he began to dictate petitions to the local authorities through a scribe, he tried speaking yet a fourth language. (Bakhtin, 1981: 295–6)

From a Bakhtinian perspective such a person could not exist. Each event coordinates a spatial and temporal and externally relational aspect and also an internal relationship to many types of meaning. Where Berger and others understand meaning systems (such as religion) as providing a singular framework that orients individuals in a dimension outside everyday space and time, Bakhtin views the everyday coordinates of life as the concrete framework that accords a 'once-occurrent unity of Being'.

It would be debilitating to live in a closed environment where an individual 'rests assured in the inviolability of his own language'; no one would learn anything in such a setting (Bakhtin, 1981: 295). Our different languages are in dialogue with each other within acts. The variability and specificity of everyday life always makes participatory thinking, answerable action, a necessity, as Morson and Emerson state:

> since all people participate in many different groups and master diverse social languages, and since all institutions draw diverse members who interact with multiple outsiders, this kind of amalgamation is always taking place. And as it does, speech genres, words, and syntactic structures come to be differentially intoned and to change. (Morson and Emerson, 1990: 342)

Two issues separate symbolic interactionist and Bakhtinian interpretations of everyday life. Bakhtin focuses on the uniqueness and the unrepeatability of humans and their actions, wherein acts are uniquely answerable. This stands in contrast with symbolic interactionist definitions of action that are oriented towards rules and that depend on the assumption that the meaning of an event is shared among actors. The differences between Bakhtin and the interactionists therefore hinge on their notions of the self. Bakhtin's 'self' is always directed towards an actual, living and concrete other, whereas the interactionist self develops through relation to an abstract, generalized other. Emerson contrasts the differences in Mead's two-part model of the self and Bakhtin's three-part self, noting that 'Bakhtin's otherness is intensely personalist: his scenarios of the self are chamber scenes in which the other is not necessarily "organized" at all' (Emerson, 1993: 6). In contrast to the interactionist self that develops through gaming and 'learning the rules', Bakhtin's consciousness arises concretely 'wrapped around another' (Bakhtin, 1986: 138). Bakhtin's self learns to respond to *many* others, and learns *many* different ways of inter-acting (as he will come to say, each person learns multiple speech genres (Bakhtin, 1986)) that encompass the other-for-myself and the I-for-another. Mastering answerability entails finding the right tone and content to present in many situations, as well as mastery of understanding one's own relation-ship to others and their relationships to the self. Bakhtin's self has 'me's specific to concrete situations; they develop only in contact with others-for-myself (and not through contact with a *general* other). In positing a model of the self that situates a potential self in relation to multiple, disorganized others, Bakhtin posits a self that is radically multiple and unique in the world when compared to the self portrayed by symbolic interactionists, whose self ossifies in roles and in communities.

Without a generalized other, or a commonly shared 'world-view' (as the phenomenologists put it) Bakhtin's self goes through life without a community – at least as it is typically defined by sociologists. Communities are almost always defined as groups that *share* a set of values, concerns and knowledge: one thinks of a community of welders, a church community, a neighbourhood community. Present-day models of community make assumptions that no one can adequately test, namely that any group of people actually *does* share values and goals. Bakhtin's view of acts as locations where specific individuals interact while not sharing definitions of the situation, or only partially share meaning, not only breaks from socio-logical tautologies of the shared communities of meaning, but it also demonstrates an alternative understanding of social interaction. This alternative is *centred* on the assumption that dialogue is not only possible, but perhaps enlivened when people do not share meaning. What we share is not as interesting as what we do not share. We cannot learn or progress from shared meaning; we only learn by encountering new ideas and acting them out in intersubjective acts.

Despite their initial grounding in the manifestations of everyday life, neither phenomenology nor interactionism is ultimately interested in indi-viduals' acts in everyday situations. Mead and the interactionists concen-trate on the relation of individuals to a generalized other who learn socialized behaviour that can be articulated with reference to many situ-ations, and on the transmutation of meaning. Likewise, phenomenologists focus on what is objective and repeatable, allowing the contingencies and emotional aspects of acts to escape without notice. Neither provides an understanding of how people make decisions in varied, unique, contingent contexts. Neither makes individual, unique people encountered throughout daily life necessary to their definitions of intersubjectivity. Rather, each depends on the codification of intersubjective moments in social insti-tutions. This is the greatest failing of everyday life sociology as we know it: our everyday life, which is fraught with meaning, decisions, moral and emotional valuation, that world we experience as physical, mental, emotional and social bodies, is stripped of its variability, tonality, and its oughtness, and is left a repetitive, habitual plane.

Bakhtin provides us with a vantage to the world that 'is seen, heard, touched, and thought, a world permeated in its entirety with the emotional-volitional tones of the affirmed validity of values' (1993: 56). Such a turn is essential to the interpretation of everyday life as a moral, creative plane that is recognizable to us both as people who live in the world and as people who write about it.

Note

I wish to thank Caryl Emerson, Robert Wuthnow, Paul DiMaggio and the editors of this volume for thoughtful readings, comments, and encouragement on earlier drafts of this chapter.

References

Adler, Patricia, Adler, Peter and Fontana, Andrea (1987) 'Everyday life sociology', *Annual Review of Sociology*, 13: 217–35.

Bakhtin, Mikhail M. (1981) *The Dialogic Imagination: Four Essays by M.M. Bakhtin*. Ed. M. Holquist. Trans. C. Emerson and M. Holquist. Austin, TX: University of Texas Press.

Bakhtin, Mikhail M. (1984) *Problems of Dostoevsky's Poetics*. Ed. and trans. C. Emerson. Minneapolis, MN: University of Minnesota Press.

Bakhtin, Mikhail M. (1986) *Speech Genres and Other Late Essays*. Eds. C. Emerson and M. Holquist. Trans. V.W. McGee. Austin, TX: University of Texas Press.

Bakhtin, Mikhail M. (1990) *Art and Answerability: Early Philosophical Essays by M.M. Bakhtin*. Eds. M. Holquist and V. Liapunov. Trans. and notes V. Liapunov. Austin, TX: University of Texas Press.

Bakhtin, Mikhail M. (1993) *Toward a Philosophy of the Act*. Ed. M. Holquist. Trans. and notes V. Liapunov. Austin, TX: University of Texas Press.

Bender, Courtney (1997) 'Kitchen work: the everyday practice of religion, cooking, and caring for people with AIDS', PhD dissertation, Princeton University, Princeton, NJ.

Berger, Peter (1967) *The Sacred Canopy*. Garden City, NY: Doubleday.

Berger, Peter and Luckmann, Thomas (1966) *The Social Construction of Reality*. Garden City, NY: Doubleday.

Blumer, Herbert (1969) *Symbolic Interactionism: Perspective and Method*. Berkeley, CA: University of California Press.

de Certeau, Michel (1984) *The Practice of Everyday Life*. Berkeley, CA: University of California Press.

DiMaggio, Paul (1997) 'Culture and cognition', *Annual Review of Sociology*, 23: 263–87.

Durkheim, Emile (1995) *The Elementary Forms of Religious Life*. New York: Free Press.

Emerson, Caryl (1993) 'American philosophers, Bakhtinian perspectives: William James, George Herbert Mead, John Dewey and Mikhail Bakhtin on a philosophy of the act'. Paper presented at the Transnational Institute, Moscow.

Gardiner, Michael (1995) 'Utopia and everyday life in French social thought', *Utopian Studies*, 6 (2): 90–123.

Gardiner, Michael (1996) 'Alterity and ethics: a dialogical perspective', *Theory, Culture & Society*, 13 (2): 121–43.

Higginbotham, Evelyn Brooks (1993) *Righteous Discontent: The Women's Movement in the Black Baptist Church 1880–1920*. Cambridge, MA: Harvard University Press.

Holquist, Michael (1993) 'Introduction', in M.M. Bakhtin, *Toward a Philosophy of the Act*. Ed. M. Holquist. Trans. and notes V. Liapunov. Austin, TX: University of Texas Press.

Lefevbre, Henri (1991) *Critique of Everyday Life*. London: Verso.

Mead, George Herbert (1962) *Mind, Self and Society*. Chicago: University of Chicago Press.

Morson, Gary Saul and Emerson, Caryl (1990) *Mikhail Bakhtin: Creation of a Prosaics*. Stanford, CA: Stanford University Press.

Schutz, Alfred and Luckmann, Thomas (1973) *The Structures of the Life-World*. Evanston, IL: Northwestern University Press.

Scott, James C. (1985) *Weapons of the Weak: Everyday Forms of Peasant Resistance*. New Haven, CT: Yale University Press.

Shields, Rob (1996) 'Meeting or mis-meeting? The dialogical challenge to *verstehen*', *British Journal of Sociology*, 47 (2): 275–94.

Steinberg, Marc W. (1993) 'Rethinking ideology: a dialogue with Fine and Sandstrom from a dialogic perspective', *Sociological Theory*, 11 (3): 314–20.

Wuthnow, Robert (1992) *Rediscovering the Sacred: Perspectives on Religion in Contemporary Society*. Grand Rapids, MI: Eerdmans.

13

THE SHOCK OF THE OLD: MIKHAIL BAKHTIN'S CONTRIBUTIONS TO THE THEORY OF TIME AND ALTERITY

Barry Sandywell

> The word does not enter the utterance from a dictionary, but from life, from utterance to utterance.
>
> – Mikhail Bakhtin and P.N. Medvedev[1]

The following chapter has several objectives.[2] Its primary aim is to support a reading of Mikhail Bakhtin's later writings as indicating a profound departure from conventional ways of thinking in the human sciences; a related aim is to suggest that a full appreciation of this reorientation depends upon an understanding of Bakhtin's dialogism as an ethics of alterity (or *heterology*); a third objective is to argue that the 'philosophical anthropological' horizon of Bakhtin's thought can be seen most graphically in his exploration of the theme of temporal alterity articulated in his analysis of *speech genres* and the associated theory of the *chronotopic organization of meaning*. I conclude that the full implications of this hermeneutics of alterity were not fully realized, and that a part of the explanation for this lies in the limiting 'philosophy of consciousness' which restricted Bakhtin's conception of the dialogical realm. Given the limited space of this short chapter, I will concentrate primarily on the problem of establishing *theoretical* links between alterity, time, and speech genres, leaving empirical explorations of specific chronotopes for a separate essay.

The Dialogical Principle

> I live in a world of others' words.
>
> – Mikhail Bakhtin[3]

It is generally recognized today that the work of the Russian thinker Mikhail Bakhtin (1895–1975) provides an important basis for the criticism of forms of inquiry which derive their inspiration from a subject-centred, monological conception of reality. As Bakhtin's texts enter the 'great time' of critical evaluation we can see that the disparate themes of his life-work converge upon the task of deconstructing forms of discourse that have licensed monological conceptions of reality.[4] In this chapter I will argue that Bakhtin's project derived from an *ethical* vision of *heteroglossia* (*raznorechie*). Put most simply, the idea of heteroglossia holds that every culture exhibits the material and temporal traces of '*another's speech in another's language*' (Bakhtin, 1981: 324; original emphasis). Heteroglossia reflects the fundamental other-languagedness or 'double-voicedness' of human experience. This is the sense in which the dialogized *utterance* (*vyskazyvanie*) can be regarded as the paradigm case of an unfinalizable historical event, displaying the simultaneous constitution and transgression of boundaries relating self to the other in the medium of historical time. From this perspective every act of communication is articulated within a parasitical arena of multiple voices where limits are simultaneously constituted and subverted. The central philosophical task of Bakhtin's metalinguistics is thus to integrate the situated freedom to transform existing structures with a recognition of the embeddedness of human activities in pre-existent space–time frameworks.[5]

In contemporary critical theory Bakhtin is known primarily for theorizing the concept of language-in-use (*slovo*) as an unfinalizable dialogical process and 'applying' this model to the carnivalesque language of folk humour in the later Middle Ages. But this reading of Bakhtin fails to appreciate how the 'unfinalizability' of speech reflects the *multi-temporalized* texture of social existence, or more specifically how the heteroglot nature of language reflects the *heterotemporality* of social existence. In fact to speak of 'existence' or 'being' (*bytie*) in this context is to reference a diverse spectrum of temporal relationships between speech, text, ideological milieu, addressees, styles of utterance, and social structures. Where life is 'by its very nature dialogic' (1984b: 293) human existence has to be understood as situated in the fractured intersections and liminal boundaries of temporalized self/other relations. Bakhtin, in fact, frequently invokes dialogue as a synonym for 'life' and its repression as an allegory of death.

The concept of temporal alterity can be introduced by the claim that human life-in-the-world is an irreducible historical process. It follows that all human activity is event-like and therefore relationally open to future possibilities of meaning and sociation. This vision of creative alterity is arguably Bakhtin's major contribution to philosophical hermeneutics. But I wish to propose that Bakhtin advanced the even stronger claim that the temporal agonism of self/other relations is a *constitutive condition of all experience*. To exist as a reflexive agent presupposes dialogical projects of meaning situated in moral contexts of verbally articulated space and time. It follows that every act of communication arises from a background of past dialogical encounters and ideological struggles. In place of a closed and monological epistemology Bakhtin formulates a historicized vision of reality endlessly refigured from 'open-ended' relational processes of communicative interaction. The logosphere of human culture, for Bakhtin, incorporates an unfinalizable dialectic between the conflicting impulses of unity (closure, monologue, authoritative discourse) and alterity (openness, dialogue, carnivalesque humour, dissemination). On the one hand, human action is unintelligible when separated from the quest for unified significance – the desire for coherent meaning and transcontextual identity which Bakhtin occasionally describes as an 'orientation toward unity' in the life of language and culture (for example, 1981: 274–5; cf. Voloshinov, 1986: 74). Yet on the other hand, these unities are invariably 'imposed' constructions that are subverted by the open-ended processes of difference and alterity. Indeed, the basic media of verbal synthesis – human embodiment, performative speech, and interpretive dialogue – function to destabilize the dream of totalization. Bakhtin presents this conflict as an interminable struggle between the *centripetal* and *centrifugal* processes of meaning. The former refer to 'the forces that serve to unify the verbal-ideological world' (1981: 270); the latter consist of processes which disturb the ideal of a stable, unitary discourse. The term 'centrifugal' symbolizes the heteroglossial forces which destabilize established cultural meanings and hierarchies – the *carnivalesque* aspects of experience.

Yet every enterprise of verbal regulation and domination is fated to be undermined by the subversive irruption of heteroglossial speech. Bakhtin isolated two important sources of heteroglossial discourse in European history in the underground culture of the carnivalesque and in the emergence of 'novelistic prose' in the polyphonic fictions of Grimmelshausen, Cervantes, Rabelais, Fielding, Smollett, Sterne, Goethe and others: 'Carnival was the true feast of time, the feast of becoming, change, and renewal. It was hostile to all that was immortalized and completed' (1984a: 10). In fact the heteroglossial novel assumed some of the functions of carnival as a central medium of modern consciousness. The conflict between identity and difference is allegorized as a mythical 'contest' – analogous to the Empedoclean agonism of *Love* and *Hate* or the Freudian struggle between *Eros* and *Thanatos* – 'a contradiction-ridden, tension-filled unity of two embattled tendencies in the life of language' (1981: 272). Expressed more theoretically: all human activities are situated in the normative realms of text-mediated communication; each utterance that is cognitively 'directed toward its object, enters a dialogically agitated and tension-filled environment of alien words, value judgments and accents' (1981: 276). The interweaving themes of textual inscription and ethical indebtedness are thus folded into the idea of the 'unfinalizability' of every project of meaning: on the one hand, there can be no 'last word' in human experience, but on the other hand, nothing is 'absolutely dead: every meaning will have its homecoming festival' (1986: 170).

Time and Alterity

> Every entry into the sphere of meanings is accomplished only through the gates of the chronotope.
>
> – Mikhail Bakhtin[6]

These general reflections can be condensed in the thesis that temporal alterity is a constitutive condition of individual and collective identity: without temporality, no alterity; without alterity, no difference; without difference, no meaning; without meaning, no world. The dialogues of everyday life are embedded in larger contexts of signifying praxis inscribed with the traces of past acts of significant address. Indeed, from the perspective of dialogism we *are* our conversations. In his last writings Bakhtin framed the theme of the *infinite* 'dialogue of languages' by means of the chronotope of 'great time', expressing a communality of the remote past and future which relates the everyday experience of the present to the 'distant' reflexivities of past voices and anonymous semantic configurations (1986: 169–70). This 'interanimation of languages' (1981: 51, 67–8, 296) is what binds the unfinished past to the open-ended present, the world of predecessors to the world of contemporaries.[7]

The 'double-voiced' dialectic of simultaneously *addressing the past* and *being addressed by the past* provides the *leitmotif* for Bakhtin's discussion of the 'unfinalizable' presence of traces of the past in the present: 'every word is directed toward an *answer* and cannot escape the profound influence of the answering word that it anticipates' (1981: 280; original emphasis). In other words the internal dialogization of discourse presupposes the reflexive temporalities of the past as a condition for present acts of interpretation. This is why internal dialogization 'is present to a greater or lesser extent in all realms of the life of the word' (1981: 284). In the 'strong' dialogical framework every human activity necessarily involves *agonistic processes* of communication through polemical acts of symbolic exchange. Every form of exchange between self and other presupposes heteroglossial time as its concrete medium. In this respect the 'past' can be likened to a palimpsest of contexts providing the setting for contemporary speech acts – including the history of speech conventions and achieved textual forms, the congealed time of inherited *speech genres*, the 'long-durational' time of national languages and cultures. Even the other person who first speaks to me in the shared time of face-to-face interaction is necessarily a voice resonant with echoes from the past:

> 'Everything that pertains to me enters my consciousness, beginning with my name, from the external world through the mouths of others (my mother, and so forth), with their intonation, in their emotional and value-assigning tonality. I realize myself initially through others: from them I receive words, forms, and tonalities for the formation of my initial idea of myself. (Bakhtin, 1986: 138)

The other precedes the individual chronotopes of self-experience (the *I-for-myself*): 'Just as the body is formed initially in the mother's womb (body), a person's consciousness awakens wrapped in another's consciousness. Only later does one begin to be subsumed by neutral words and categories, that is, one is defined as a person irrespective of *I* and *other*' (1986: 138; original emphasis).

The voices of alterity are theorized as both an *ontological* gift and an *axiological* invitation to meaning. By abandoning the myth of Adamic naming (or its epistemological equivalent in the clear and distinct speech of the *cogito*), we see that there can be no 'first' or 'last' word, no absolutely self-standing ground of discourse and no self-evident 'origin' of meaning. The gift of meaning is always already textually mediated by past layers of symbolic exchange. Hence, to recover the meaning of past action and events is to activate the semantic possibilities of inscribed praxis by striving to realize the promise of past signification. But the creation of other modes of understanding can only be realized through my responses to the questions and solicitations of the voices of the past. The hermeneutical task is not to recover past texts 'as they were originally intended' or to merge with an alien past, but rather to reanimate the claims of congealed significance in a creative dialogue with the past: '*Creative understanding* does not renounce itself, its own place in time, its own culture. . . . In order to understand, it is immensely important for the person who understands to be *located outside* the object of his or her creative understanding – in time, in space, in culture' (1986: 7; original emphasis). To understand we must learn to see from the perspective of the other: 'It is only in the eyes of *another* culture that foreign culture reveals itself fully and profoundly (but not maximally fully, because there will be cultures that see and understand even more)' (1986: 7; original emphasis). The genesis of new questions and the disclosure of other forms of understanding presupposes the possibility of novel dialogical encounters: 'Such a dialogic encounter of two cultures does not result in merging or mixing. Each retains its own unity and *open* totality, but they are mutually enriched' (1986: 7; original emphasis). Responsive speech discloses the world as an unfinished project (*zadanie*) of meaning saturated with references to past acts of significance.

This brings us to a crucial point in the argument. We have seen that heteroglossia and alterity are categories of axiological response (see 1986: 94). It follows that every attempt to articulate a 'new' meaning already carries within it references to a dense network of past ideological struggles. Thus the most mundane act of saying something to an interlocutor is already a deeply historicized act of communication mediated by pregiven conditions of expression, semiotic conventions, and other ideological and material circumstances. Said otherwise, the unfolding temporality of living utterance is a process in which an unfinalizable past 'lingers on' in the present, prefiguring possible shapes of the future: 'there are immense, boundless masses of forgotten contextual meanings. . . . Nothing is absolutely dead . . .' (1986: 170; cf. 1986: 139, 121–2). Where 'coming-to-be' (*stanovlenie*) takes precedence over 'being' (*bytie*) the category of time becomes a placeholder for acts of possible interpretation, a field of transformations in which the world is made to signify in different ways. We can therefore no longer view the remote contexts of the past as a passive background of signification; the past is shot through with the alterities and reflexivities of unfinished and partially realized projects of meaning. The past, in effect, is a virtual realm of transgressive occasions. Indeed, in many of Bakhtin's later texts, the reflexive solicitations of the past are viewed as the most active source in the dialogical constitution of meaning. Here 'the old' is not a frozen structure of past events but a fabric of active difference that motivates future semantic transformations. Moreover, each strong act of interpretive revision reflexively alters the past and changes the conditions for further interpretation.

In Bakhtin's metalinguistics talk is the basic 'unit' of cultural life. But speech is itself only possible because the chain of utterances implicates a continuum of genres ranging from the simplest form of face-to-face utterances – the single word reply to a question – to elaborate forms of official discourse, ideologies, and stylized literary codes (1986: 62–3, 98–9). Every form of utterance projects a responsive other, an addressee or communicative recipient ('Anything that does not answer a question is devoid of sense for us' (1986: 145)). Bakhtin makes the principle of *addressivity* a defining feature of generic expression: 'Each speech genre in each area of speech communication has its own typical conception of the addressee, and this defines it as a genre' (1986: 95; cf. 97–100). The other as *addressee*, moreover, is an historical variable influenced by a range of social, political, and cultural displacements. Hence 'the historical study of changes in these concepts [of the addressee] would be an interesting and important task' (1986: 98). *Addressivity* is thus 'a constitutive feature of the utterance; without it the utterance does not and cannot exist' (1986: 99). And in this context 'the other' includes not only the world of contemporary addressees but also the open totality of voices which continue to speak to the present. In a somewhat paradoxical vein, we can say that the addressee situated in the *there and then* is the fundamental occasion which motivates my speech in the *here and now*. For example, the spatial and temporal 'distance' between addressor and addressee might function as a creative source of ambivalence, misinterpretation, and semantic change. The realm of past texts may induce shock and surprise within the established canons of contemporary discourse. To understand the other we need to be prepared for the *shock of the old*.

The Historicity of Speech Genres

> Dialogue and dialectics. Take a dialogue and remove the voices . . . remove the intonations . . . carve out abstract concepts and judgments from living words and responses, cram everything into one abstract consciousness – and that's how you get dialectics.
>
> – Mikhail Bakhtin[8]

In what sense can we conceptualize time in dialogical terms? As self-conscious agents we experience the passage of time 'from the inside' – for example, in choosing courses of action. This intimacy with time is close to what the phenomenologist Alfred Schutz calls the 'community of time', experienced most immediately in the phenomenon of acting and 'growing older' together (Schutz, 1964: 109–10). Schutz describes this co-presence as a form in which a 'simultaneity' of two streams of consciousness is realized. The 'We-relation' provides a temporal framework for social encounters based upon the face-to-face co-presence of individuals in the *hic et nunc* of concerted activity. In other words, consociality based upon temporal and spatial *presence* is made the paradigm of social interaction (Schutz, 1964: 23). The repetition of everyday face-to-face encounters is routinized into stable interactional formats transcending the sphere of face-to-face interaction in the form of normative rituals and relationships which then appear to agents as autonomous and independent structures. This reification of social action facilitates the 'disembedding' of social relations from their immediate context and their displacement through space and time. For example, the temporal and spatial coordination of ongoing dialogical life is premised upon a framework of trust sustained by the mutual commitment of participants to the 'same' locus of spatiotemporal referents, the same archive of background knowledge, indexical particulars, and topical 'relevances'. Contemporaries are assumed to be able to tell the same stories and utilize artfully the same 'stock of knowledge' in interpreting the course and consequences of practical activities. In other words, the temporal order of the We-relation sustains a common system of references and shared experience.[9]

Like Schutz, Bakhtin is also concerned to relate consciousness, intersubjectivity, and trust (1986: 97). But in the light of Bakhtin's heteroglossial principle it is evident that signifying practices cannot be adequately described as hermetically enclosed 'units' within a consensual communality of culture. Unlike the discrete, bounded 'We-experiences' of the phenomenologist, the dialogic realm is striated by forms of semiotic praxis drawn from past agonistic relations and ideological structures. The link between micro-textual and macro-societal discourses lies in Bakhtin's theory of *chronotopes*. One clue to how this perspective might be carried further can be found in Bakhtin's emphasis upon the time-binding and time-transcending character of narrative transactions; only the dialectic between retroactive and proactive temporality involved in the day-to-day negotiation of meaning can open up the past to the present 'liberating antiquity from the captivity of time' (1986: 5–6). In this sense our 'access' to the past is only possible by virtue of polemical practices of reading, narration, and interpretive retrieval. The concept of pastness is transformed from a realm of finalized objects or 'horizons' into a dialogic arena of active reinscription. The past becomes an index for a range of possible chronotopical relations elicited by the speech genres of particular traditions and cultures. From this point of view, every human activity in the 'now' is indebted to the reflexivities of the past.

The parallel between temporal multiplicity and the historicity of space–time schemata has been touched upon throughout this chapter. These two themes come together in the theory of *speech genres*. The seminal idea here is that our access to reality is mediated by the chronotopic repertoires of particular speech communities. In fact Bakhtin claims that there is not 'a single new phenomenon (phonetic, lexical, or grammatical) that can enter the system of language without having traversed the long and complicated path of generic-stylistic testing and modification' (1986: 65). This is the point where the concern for *meaning* interfaces with a theory of society and history. Speech genres 'are the drive belts from the history of society to the history of language' (1986: 65). But what does Bakhtin include in the concept of 'speech' or 'utterance'?

Dialogism stresses the performative, rhetorical, and expressive aspects of language use *in specific historical settings and communities*. A number of constitutive features of language as utterance (*slovo*) can be distinguished. The first feature lies in the 'real' delimitation of utterances in the turn-taking sequences of conversational interaction. The conventions of sequential talk are viewed as the source of the 'real unity' of the utterance as a basic unit of communication: 'The utterance is not a convention, but a real unit, clearly delimited by the change of speaking subjects, which ends by relinquishing the floor to the other, as if with a silent dixi, perceived by the listeners (as a sign) that the speaker has finished' (1986: 71–2). A second aspect of discourse is what Bakhtin calls the *finalization* of the utterance, the 'boundedness' of expressions ('When hearing or reading, we clearly sense the end of the utterance, as if we hear the speaker's concluding *dixi*. This finalization is specific and is determined by special criteria. The first and foremost criterion for the finalization of the utterance is the *possibility of responding to it*, or more precisely and broadly, of assuming a responsive attitude toward it' (1986: 76; original emphasis)). The integrity of the utterance is constituted by social norms governing response (for example, by conventions defining the 'semantic exhaustiveness of the theme', 'the speaker's plan or speech will', and 'typical compositional and generic forms of finalization' (1986: 76–7)). The third feature of the utterance is its orientation to the speaker and to other participants – the utterance is referentially directed to the other as a form of address (1986: 84–6; 'the expressive aspect is a constitutive feature of the utterance' (1986: 90)).

The concept of *utterance* also includes the congealed 'products' or material deposits of past acts of dialogue – the artifacts, practices, common-sense, philosophical doctrines, written texts, and institutions that make up the operative contexts of a living culture. Many of these traces are sedimented as 'texts' in which the living dialogic tonalities and intonational features of their original contexts have been effaced and lost. Thus the realm of writing is depicted as the fossilized remainder of once-living activities of verbal creativity. To borrow a Marxist idiom, the ideological codes constituting speech genres appear as the congealed forms of vital speech.[10] To reactivate such congealed formations – what Bakhtin elsewhere calls the 'deep currents of culture' (1986: 3) – is to reanimate the voices of the past through an active process of disengagement and self-reflection.[11]

Against this background the question of time can now be reformulated in terms of the semiotic organization and creative functions of speech genres. Simply expressed, genres provide the deep structures which schematize reality, developing 'a complex system of means and methods for the conscious control and finalization of reality' (Bakhtin and Medvedev, 1991: 133). Generic creativity is in turn shaped by the ideological practices of finalization as these function in particular societies, traditions, and cultures. We can therefore relate different forms of experience, social interests, and 'world-views' to dominant chronotopes: 'Each genre is only able to control certain definite aspects of reality. Each genre possesses definite principles of selection, definite forms for seeing and conceptualizing reality, and a definite scope and depth of penetration' (Bakhtin and Medvedev, 1991: 131). Speech genres 'organize our speech in almost the same way as grammatical (syntactical) forms do. We learn to cast our speech in generic forms and, when hearing others' speech, we guess its genre from the very first words; we predict a certain length . . . and a certain compositional structure; we foresee the end; that is, from the very beginning we have a sense of the speech whole, which is only later differentiated during the speech process' (Bakhtin, 1986: 79). 'Genres (of literature and speech) throughout the centuries of their life accumulate forms of seeing and interpreting particular aspects of the world' (1986: 5). Thus generic forms both constrain and facilitate communication through the mediating offices of their specific chronotopes. In ontological terms the chronotope functions as 'the primary means for materializing time in space' (1981: 250).

This led to Bakhtin's programme for a sociological poetics of genres centred upon the chronotopic conventions of verbal discourse. For Bakhtin, 'a genuine poetics of genre can only be a sociology of genre' (Bakhtin and Medvedev, 1991: 135). It also proscribes every ahistorical approach to literary and cultural analysis:

> Trying to understand and explain a work solely in terms of the conditions of its epoch alone, solely in terms of the conditions of the most immediate time, will never enable us to penetrate into its semantic depths. Enclosure within the epoch also makes it impossible to understand the work's future life in subsequent centuries. . . . Works break through the boundaries of their own time, they live in centuries, in *great time* and frequently (with great works, always) their lives there are more intense and fuller than are their lives within their own time. (1986: 4; original emphasis; cf. 1986: 167–8)

For example, one of the criterial features of canonical works of art lies in their function of mediating the great time of literary tradition. Unlike the more circumscribed functions of everyday communication, the 'great artwork' crystallizes questions and problems of an ultimate character; and in this sense 'a work gains in significance, that is, it enters *great time*' (1986: 4). The texts of earlier writers are liberated from the captivity of their original lifeworlds by later acts of critical reading ('and literary scholarship is called upon to assist in this liberation' (1986: 5)). The artwork is a medium of self-reflection which articulates past, present and future significance (1986: 151).

To summarize, I have argued that Bakhtin's heterology commends a dialogized conception of cultural creation as a process of communicative struggle between self and other. Implicit in this conception is a privileging of verbal discourse under the sign of the heteroglossial principle. The discovery of chronotopicity leads to the idea of reactivating the reflexivities of past signification, embedded in configurations of space–time relations. We then see that 'alterity' is shorthand for a vast domain of temporal forms, the 'layering of meaning upon meaning', the different 'times' (or space–times) inscribed in the semantic worlds of everyday language (1986: 121). I have also suggested that dialogical heterology presupposes a strong sense of the unredeemed possibilities of past experience.

Temporal Polyphony

> Time is always endowed with meaning. Imaginary time is significant time and the time of signification. This manifests itself in the significance of the scansions imposed on calendar time (recurrence of privileged points: feasts, rituals, anniversaries, etc.), in the instauration of essentially imaginary bounds or limit-points for time as a whole, and in the imaginary significance with which time as a whole is vested by each society.
>
> – Cornelius Castoriadis[12]

The concept of speech genre allows us to frame the problem of time in the language of heteroglossia, polyphonic unfinalizability, semantic potential, and similar textual tropes. 'Time' can now be viewed as a dialogically mediated construction that is inseparable from a society's general communicative and interactional strategies. Bakhtin's theory of time can be defined by contrasting it to three other concepts of temporality – the objective, phenomenological, and social-constructionist paradigms. From an objective or realist standpoint, time is simply the 'fourth dimension' of world experience, a realm of real temporal passage into which the stream of history continuously pours. Time is imagined as a path leading from the past into the present – or perhaps, in a less linear model, as a series of forking paths, routes, or branching lines. But we can also view time phenomenologically in terms of the concrete *experiences* of temporal consciousness. This is the idea of time as *duration* in the work of Henri Bergson and the 'lived temporality' explored by Edmund Husserl where experienced time is described as an intentional 'syntheses' of retentional and protentional horizons (for example, the interdependence of recollection and anticipation in the biographical experience of human beings in the lifeworld).[13]

The phenomenological analysis of the temporality of the *Lebenswelt* (see Luckmann, 1991: 155–9; Schutz, 1967a) leads directly to the problem of narrative discourse and the multiple 'times' of other forms of life. This is best seen in the passage from biographical time to historical time, from 'my' place 'in the here and now' to the multiple temporalities of historical lifeworlds. To this extent we can speak of time as an historical 'creation' and examine the construction of temporality as a socially organized phenomenon. Bakhtin also depicts the literary chronotope of biographical time – one sub-species of the biographical novel – as time that 'cannot but be included in the longer process of historical, but embryonically historical, time' (1986: 18). This is exemplified in the experience of generations which 'already provides an entry into historical duration'. And yet 'the biographical novel itself does not yet know true historical time' (1986: 18). For the latter we need a richer concept of *historicity*, of the way in which agents experience history in both subjective and objective terms, of history as a 'realm' of existence unique to human beings (see Luckmann, 1991: 151–66).

The problem of time can also be approached in social-constructionist terms. This is where Bakhtin's theory of chronotopes proves seminal. We have suggested that speech genres can be viewed as social frameworks of meaning mediating biographical and historical experience. Thus the narratives that I use to map the course of my life are drawn from historical rhetorics which are in principle available to others in representing their own 'location' in space and time. Typically these chronotopes of identity are embedded in the collective narratives of powerful institutions and organizations. To borrow Schutz's expression, they form part of the stock of narrative knowledge available to agents in everyday life. The formation, institutionalization, and transmission of such imaginary chronotopes in different societies constitutes an important topic in the sociology of knowledge.[14]

From a constructionist perspective we can extend Bakhtin's definition of the *chronotope* – a concept that was initially developed for the analysis of the space–time categories in literary texts – to include practices and systems which span the whole field of social activities (customs, law, religion, mythology, ritual, science, and so on). From this perspective, the historical variability and cultural functions of different spatiotemporal grids form central themes in a reflexive sociology, leading to critical explorations of social chronotopes informing the imaginary systems of whole societies and civilizations.[15] One important task for this type of research would be to explore the social construction of different concepts of time and subjectivity as social-historical variables by analysing the different modes of alterity institutionalized by different economies of time.[16] By generalizing Bakhtin's theory in this way we can generate a fourth perspective on time, a paradigm which approaches temporality in terms of a society's dominant imaginary chronotopes. This might be called the paradigm of *dialogical inscription*. Bakhtin, for example, frequently refers to the importance of cultural inscriptions as instances of materialized dialogue:

> These are visible vestiges of man's creativity, traces of his hands and his mind: cities, streets, buildings, artworks, technology, social organization, and so on. . . . The work of the seeing eye joins here with the most complex thought processes. But regardless of how profound these cognitive processes may be, how saturated with the broadest generalizations, they are never ultimately broken off from the work of the eye, from concrete sensory signs and the living figurative word. (Bakhtin, 1986: 25)

This approach to time and alterity commends a conception of the world as a *general social text*. Inscriptive technologies – writing systems, art forms, electronic transcription, and so on – are central to the construction of different forms of temporal consciousness (for example, the contrast between preliterate societies and civilizations with writing).[17] Societies create space–time relations *in* and *as* sociotextual inscriptions across the whole range of cultural practices. Temporal frames are constituted in the same heteroglossial processes that create the diverse universes of symbolic activity. We might hypothesize that different chronotopes produce different *symbolic forms* of dialogical life and experience, and with these forms different modes of *historicity and self-reflection*. In other words, social chronotopes organize the world in space–time grammars; and this 'timing' can be understood as the social-imaginary work of inscriptions or, if this be taken generically, of *textual practices*. Temporality, in other words, emerges as an *effect* of the social processes of meaning inscription or *semiopraxis*. Thus we can say that the more differentiated the domain of chronotopicity, the more complex are the semiotic repertoires available to individuals and communities. Selfhood emerges within the matrices of semiopraxis made possible by particular chronotopic configurations. Conversely, the abstractness, one-sidedness, or impersonality of chronotopic repertoires (in monologic regimes, for example) leads to corresponding abstract, partial, or objectified forms of experience. Here there is a dialectical relationship between forms of self-hood and chronotopic schemes of cultural self-reflection.

These semantic possibilities are especially significant for artworks that are fabricated from temporal and dialogic contexts. The discourse of the polyphonic novel is Bakhtin's paradigm case. A consciousness that changes and develops presupposes a view of time as a mutable and plural field of possibilities; furthermore, the discovery of *characters* subject to mutational shifts in circumstance and fortune introduces new forms of time to the existing temporal frames (for example, characters in literature who change their style of being, attitudes, fundamental relation to others; characters who 'learn' from their experience). The *Bildungsroman* introduces a chronotopicity in which the dialogue between self and world assumes a real-historical character. Here both sides of the dialogue – subject and world – are reciprocally related and mutable. The world posited by this chronotope is no longer 'an immobile orientation point for developing man' (Bakhtin, 1986: 23). With the appearance of Gargantua and Pantagruel, Simplicissimus, and Wilhelm Meister the chronotope of self-world appears. The self now 'emerges *along with the world* and he reflects the historical emergence of the world itself' (1986: 23; original emphasis).

It is only with the modern heteroglossial novel that the self and world begin to open towards the historical past and the historical future. The polyphonic novel proscribes all 'closure' and 'finalization' by deconstructing the time–space systems of monologic forms and embracing the revolutionary experiment with historical becoming. The modern novel is a polyphonic genre which explicitly recognizes the heteroglossia of meaning and the existence of alternative and multiple temporalities. This is another sense in which moderns live in a reflexive and mediated world (1981: 366–7). Indeed, for Bakhtin the term 'novel' is almost a synonym for verbal reflexivity. There is an elective affinity between the novel and modernity (1981: 4–5, 7–8). The novel is the modern site for *generic* reflexivity, the parodic self-questioning of the dominant verbal styles and ideologies which pervade modern life:

... the novel gets on poorly with other genres. There can be no talk of a harmony deriving from mutual limitation and complementarities. The novel parodies other genres (precisely in their role as genres); it exposes the conventionality of their forms and their language; it squeezes out some genres and incorporates others into its own peculiar structure, reformulating and re-accentuating them. (Bakhtin, 1981: 5; cf. 1981: 10–11)

Bakhtin theorizes the novel as *the* auto-critical genre whose very principle is unending development through self-parody (1981: 412).[18]

The theme of *becoming* returns us to Bakhtin's discussion of the 'novel-ization' of modern experience and the emergence of 'great time'. By contrast to the chronotopes of pre-modern, oral culture, the polyphonic time-consciousness of modernity leads to the discovery of real historical time and to a productive dialogue with alterity in the medium of 'great time'. Great time is the temporal equivalent of 'polyglossia' at the level of cultural traditions, the polyphonic intersection of time-lines in every cultural artifact and discourse, the time of collective, national, and civiliza-tional processes, the time of 'human emergence and development' (1986: 11). The polyphonic novel which valorizes the present enables modern consciousness to comprehend 'great time' as the historicity of culture itself with its own rhythms and relatively autonomous forms of development. Its temporal coordinates include dialogic relationships that span centuries and even millennia ('of peoples, nations, and cultures' (1986: 167)). It discloses the 'we' that integrates all previous societies in the history of the species: 'a complex unity of all humanity, all human cultures (a complex unity of human culture), and a complex unity of human literature' (1986: 167). The 'polyglot We' of great time includes anonymous others who reach back into the sources of cultural creativity and possible interlocutors solicited by future acts of interpretation. In Western European culture it refers to a canonical tradition of creative genres from Homer and Plato down to those in the present who still respond to the 'reflexive' call of the dialogical past. Such canonical texts function as bridges across time, media of interlocution which bind the present to the past (see 'Response to a Question from the *Novy Mir* Editorial Staff', in 1986: 4; cf. 1986: 151, 170).

Conclusion: Towards a Hermeneutics of Alterity

In this schematic, exploratory chapter I have suggested that Bakhtin's heterology leads directly to a theory of multiple temporalities in which forms of time, alterity, and meaning merge together to constitute the imaginary matrix of social experience. Bakhtin's dialogism celebrates the multi-temporality of human existence, stressing the contingent interplay of past, present, and future forms of life correlated with different speech genres and cultural traditions. In place of the idea of a single time or 'history', we have to consider the reality of an intersecting series of 'space–times' ('histories'). As Castoriadis has observed in a related context, 'time is essentially linked to the emergence of alterity. Time is this emergence as such – whilst space is "only" its necessary concomitant. Time is creation and destruction – that means, time is being in its substantive determinations' (Castoriadis, 1991: 61–2).[19]

To develop this perspective into a framework of further research we need to overcome some of the limitations inherent in Bakhtin's dialogism. I will conclude by sketching a general strategy which such a critique might take. First, it is apparent that not all conversations with the past are possible or even conceivable; despite the all-embracing characterization of modern culture as implicitly polyphonic, many forms of dialogic encounter have been excluded by the dominant institutions of contemporary society. Bakhtin tends to abstract dialogic relations from concrete forms of domination, power, and authority. And despite his own rejection of monologism, Bakhtin says relatively little about the material and ideological repression of alternative forms of communication and, relatedly, almost nothing about the subversion of present organizations of meaning by marginalized forms of experience. We suspect that a lingering respect for the logic of identity may have led Bakhtin to underestimate the importance of his own discoveries for a more general theory of alterity and difference.

Secondly, Bakhtin tends to confine dialogue to the realms of concrete speech, modelling language upon a personal image of the voice as an expressive consciousness. Correspondingly, he underplays his own discovery of the heteroglossial nature of sociocultural textuality. His dialogism is primarily oriented to the canonical spheres of 'verbal' art and this prevented Bakhtin from theorizing heteroglossia as a general paradigm for all social and cultural formations. This may also account for Bakhtin's lack of interest in exploring the larger social and political forces that have rationalized language and culture on a civilizational and global scale.

Thirdly, Bakhtin retained an 'auratic' conception of tradition as an unbroken continuum of cultural creativity, organized into an idealized dialogue of canonical texts. To avoid this reification of canonical time we need to develop an account of power relations in explaining how institutions control and repress the subversive voices of the past. To advance in this direction we should understand the conversation with the past in political and adversarial terms (for example, by foregrounding the struggle of repressed forms against patterns of authoritative speech and dominant ideologies). This perspective needs to incorporate both the constraining alterities of traditions and the ways in which the past problematizes, contests, and occasionally subverts the institutions of the present. While Bakhtin's theory of chronotopes helpfully foregrounds the material constraints upon cultural conversation and understanding, the key 'elements' of his hermeneutics are left like the *disjecta membra* of a theory of meaning: *embodiment* (material relations, artifacts, constraints); the *ideological chronotopes of dominant discourse*; the multiple *social contexts* of communication.

The later Bakhtin – for example, in *Speech Genres and Other Late Essays* (1986) – recognizes but does not explicitly explore the deeper dimensions of reflexivity his own theorizing implicitly invokes. For example, the notion of 'great time' elides a range of difficult problems associated with the theory of multiple temporality, especially with respect to understanding the appearance of subversive alterities and the struggle between different orders of meaning. Without a more radical social analysis of time we have little hope of understanding the repressed yet still latent reflexivities and utopian possibilities of past experience.

Finally, and perhaps in a more sociological vein, we should also consider such little-noticed 'long-durational' processes as the evolution of linguistic communities and traditions, the development of schools of thought, sciences and disciplines, the imperceptible sedimentation of everyday beliefs, 'mentalities', and related institutional processes of collective memory. These diachronic phenomena are, of course, connected with complex spatiotemporal structures and institutional realities. For example, the invention of chronotopes that organize and extend the workings of the state megamachine, chronotopes which resist or struggle against such 'civil' incorporation (nomadism, the chronotopicity of resistance, rebellion, and revolution), the 'enlightened' space–time of linear 'progress', 'development', teleological fulfilment (Judaic-Christian chronotopes of beginnings and endings), the struggles to impose state time upon earlier magic, folkloric and traditional space–time systems, the concrete vicissitudes of cross-civilizational space–time relationships, the fusion of theocentric chronotopes and more secular systems of space–time differentiation, and so on. Future theory and research needs to consider the social-imaginary time schemas of whole civilizations and the critical conjunctures where civilizations take it upon themselves to 'colonize' other societies (with their own indigenous time-frames defining the intelligibility of events, changes, and developments articulated in these societies. In this respect the emergence of what has been called 'world-time' and 'hybridization' will become central to a critical theory of great time.[20]

Notes

1 Bakhtin and Medvedev (1991: 122).

2 My thanks to Michael Gardiner for comments on an earlier, and much longer, version of this chapter.

3 Bakhtin (1986: 143).

4 Important resources for this re-evaluation include the following: Clark and Holquist (1984); Dentith (1995); Gardiner (1992, 1996); Holquist (1986, 1989, 1990); Morson (1981); Morson and Emerson (1989); Patterson (1988); Pechey (1993); Stallybrass and White (1986); and Todorov (1984).

5 Bakhtin's mature reflections on this theme can be found in his essay 'The Problem of Speech Genres', in Bakhtin (1986: 60–102).

6 Bakhtin (1981: 258).

7 For the theme of 'great time' [*bol'shoe vremia*] or the 'great time of culture' [*bol'shoe vremia kul'tury*] see Bakhtin, 'Response to a Question from the *Novy Mir* Editorial Staff', in Bakhtin (1986: 1–9, 151, 169, 170). For a profound meditation on the theme, see Pechey's lyrical essay (1993).

8 Bakhtin (1986: 147).

9 For these themes, see Schutz (1967b) and Schutz and Luckmann (1973); for an overview, see Luckmann (1991: 151–66).

10 See Bakhtin on 'reification' (1986: 162, 168); 'thinglike environments' (1986: 164); 'word-mummies' (1986: 168); 'congealed world views' (1986: 165–6). See the 'cadavers' imagery of 'monumentalized' language in Voloshinov (1986: 71).

11 Today a range of genealogical strategies have been developed to pursue this kind of semantic reactivation. See Sandywell (1996: Vol. 1, ch. 10) for a survey of different approaches to the 'archaeology' of signifying praxis.

12 Castoriadis (1991: 50).

13 Husserl (1964); Schutz (1967b); cf. Merleau-Ponty (1962).

14 For example, the existence of multiple time-frames as normative chronotopes (the variable ways in which societies and cultures construct imaginary grids of space–time in order to typify prescribed patterns of activities and practices); the effects of social change, industrialization, capitalist work systems, and the like upon the modern culture of time; the institutional construction of timetables, coordinated activities, planning schedules, and so on. For the standardization of time zones and the rationalization of global time, see Kern (1983) and Schivelbusch (1986). Schivelbusch's work on the coming of the railway system is subtitled 'The Industrialization of Time and Space in the Nineteenth Century'.

15 Consider the impact of technological changes upon the perception of time, temporal experience, and different understandings of history. For the emergence of historical consciousness in the modern era, see Breisach (1994). See Bakhtin (1986: 121); cf. Castoriadis (1991: 51–3); Sandywell (1996: Vol. 1).

16 See Castoriadis (1991: 41). For example, the variant concepts of time in the history of theoretical science from the Aristotelian and Ptolemaic time-frame, the abstract substantial time-frame of Galilean–Newtonian science, to the Einsteinian schema of time–space in relativity theory and modern particle physics. In the light of relativity physics when looking at the stars at night today, we now know that we are not staring into space but into time. For the space–time-frames in contemporary physics, see Smoot and Davidson (1993).

17 Bakhtin remained silent about the relationships between new modes of inscription, technology, and social chronotopes. Thus we find only scattered remarks about the wider political and cultural impact of changes in 'reflexive technologies' (oral discourse, alphabetization, scripts, print technology, and so on). Yet his own dialogical perspective lends itself to further development in the direction of a theory of *technopoiesis*. For the development of this concept, see Sandywell (1996: Vol. 1, Introduction).

18 For the novel as an 'antigeneric' genre, see Terras (1991: 519) and, more specifically, Jones (1990). For the appearance of 'open-characters' in the biographical novel and, more especially, the modern *Bildungsroman*; see Bakhtin (1986: 16–25, 21–5); cf. Bakhtin (1981: 342ff.).

19 'Multiplicity of being is an irreducible, primary datum. It is a given. But what is also given is that multiplicity exists as difference on the one hand, as otherness on the other hand. Insofar as difference is a dimension of being, there is identity, pesistence, repetition. Insofar as otherness is a dimension of being, there is creation and destruction of forms. And indeed, otherness entails difference' (Castoriadis, 1991: 63).

20 I am thinking of the distinction between the *histoire des événéments* and *histoire des conjonctures* made by the Annales' historians. The concept of long-duration and conjunctural history includes the time of great crises, wars, revolutions, turning points, which often entail collective death and extermination of whole societies and civilizations. The emphasis upon conjunctural encounters and conflicts precipitated by the contact between different societies and civilizations leads to the concept of *global time* – the non-synchronic 'intersection' of the space–time systems of whole societies and civilizations. See Eberhard (1965); Mann (1988); Paz (1985).

References

Bakhtin, Mikhail M. (1981) *The Dialogic Imagination: Four Essays by M.M. Bakhtin*. Ed. M. Holquist. Trans. C. Emerson and M. Holquist. Austin, TX: University of Texas Press.

Bakhtin, Mikhail M. (1984a) *Rabelais and His World*. Trans. Hélène Iswolsky. Foreword by Krystyna Pomorska. Bloomington, IN.: Indiana University Press.

Bakhtin, Mikhail M. (1984b) *Problems of Dostoevsky's Poetics*. Ed. and trans. C. Emerson. Minneapolis, MN: University of Minnesota Press.

Bakhtin, Mikhail M. (1986) *Speech Genres and Other Late Essays*. Eds C. Emerson and M. Holquist. Trans. V.W. McGee. Austin: University of Texas Press.

Bakhtin, Mikhail M. (1990) *Art and Answerability: Early Philosophical Essays by M.M. Bakhtin*. Eds. M. Holquist and V. Liapunov. Trans. and notes V. Liapunov. Austin, TX: University of Texas Press.

Bakhtin, Mikhail M. (1993) *Toward a Philosophy of the Act*. Ed. M. Holquist. Trans. and notes V. Liapunov. Austin, TX: Texas University Press.

Bakhtin, Mikhail M. and Medvedev, Pavel N. (1991) *The Formal Method in Literary Scholarship: A Critical Introduction to Sociological Poetics*. Baltimore, MD and London: Johns Hopkins University Press.

Bender, John and Wellbery, David E. (eds) (1991) *Chronotypes: The Construction of Time*. Stanford, CA: Stanford University Press.

Breisach, Ernst (1994) *Historiography: Ancient, Medieval, and Modern* (2nd edn). Chicago: University of Chicago Press.

Castoriadis, Cornelius (1984) *Crossroads in the Labyrinth*. Brighton: Harvester Press.

Castoriadis, Cornelius (1987) *The Imaginary Institution of Society*. Cambridge: Polity Press.

Castoriadis, Cornelius (1991) 'Time and creation', in John Bender and David E. Wellbery (eds), *Chronotypes: The Construction of Time*. Stanford, CA: Stanford University Press. pp. 38–64.

Clark, Katerina and Holquist, Michael (1984) *Mikhail Bakhtin*. Cambridge, MA: MIT Press.

Dentith, Simon (ed.) (1995) *Bakhtinian Thought: An Introductory Reader*. London: Routledge.

Eberhard, W. (1965) *Conquerors and Rulers*. Leiden: Brill.

Gardiner, Michael (1992) *The Dialogics of Critique: M.M. Bakhtin and the Theory of Ideology*. New York and London: Routledge.

Gardiner, Michael (1996) 'Alterity and ethics: a dialogical perspective', *Theory, Culture and Society*, 13 (2): 121–43.

Hirschkop, Ken and Shepherd, David (eds) (1989) *Bakhtin and Cultural Theory*. Manchester: Manchester University Press.

Holquist, Michael (1986) 'Introduction', in M.M. Bakhtin, *Speech Genres and Other Late Essays*. Eds C. Emerson and M. Holquist. Trans. V.W. McGee. Austin, TX: University of Texas Press. pp. ix–xxiii.

Holquist, Michael (1989) 'Bakhtin and the body', *Critical Studies*, 1 (2): 19–42

Holquist, Michael (1990) *Dialogism: Bakhtin and His World*. London: Routledge.

Husserl, Edmund (1964) *The Phenomenology of Internal Time Consciousness*. Bloomington, IN: Indiana University Press.

Jones, Malcom V. (1990) *Dostoevsky after Bakhtin: Readings in Dostoevsky's Fantastic Realism*. Cambridge and New York: Cambridge University Press.

Kern, Stephen (1983) *The Culture of Time and Space, 1880–1918*. Cambridge, MA: Harvard University Press.

Luckmann, Thomas (1991) 'The constitution of human life in time', in John Bender and David E. Wellbery (eds), *Chronotypes: The Construction of Time*. Stanford, CA: Stanford University Press. pp. 151–66.

Mann, Michael (1988) *States, War and Capitalism: Studies in Political Sociology*. Oxford: Basil Blackwell.

Merleau-Ponty, Maurice (1962) *Phenomenology of Perception*. London: Routledge & Kegan Paul.

Morson, Gary S. (1981) *Bakhtin: Essays and Dialogues on His Work*. Chicago and London: University of Chicago Press.

Morson, Gary S. and Emerson, Caryl (eds.) (1989) *Rethinking Bakhtin: Extensions and Challenges*. Evanston, IL: Northwestern University Press.

Patterson, David (1988) *Literature and Spirit: Essays on Bakhtin and His Contemporaries*. Lexington, KY: The University Press of Kentucky.

Paz, Octavio (1985) *One Earth, Four or Five Worlds: Reflections on Contemporary History*. Manchester: Carcanet.

Pechey, Graham (1993) 'Eternity and modernity: Bakhtin and the epistemological sublime', *Theoria*, 81 (82): 61–85.

Sandywell, Barry (1996) *Logological Investigations* (3 vols). London: Routledge.

Schivelbusch, Wolfgang (1986) *The Railway Journey: The Industrialization of Time and Space in the Nineteenth Century*. Leamington Spa, Hamburg and New York: Berg.

Schutz, Alfred (1964) *Collected Papers* (vol. 2). The Hague: Martinus Nijhoff.

Schutz, Alfred (1967a) *Collected Papers* (vol. 1). The Hague: Martinus Nijhoff.

Schutz, Alfred (1967b) *The Phenomenology of the Social World*. Evanston, IL: Northwestern University Press.

Schutz, Alfred and Luckmann, Thomas (1973) *The Structures of the Life-World*. Evanston, IL: Northwestern University Press.

Smoot, George and Davidson, Keay (1993) *Wrinkles in Time: The Imprint of Creation*. London: Little, Brown.

Stallybrass, Peter and White, Allon (1986) *The Politics and Poetics of Transgression*. London: Methuen.

Terras, Victor (1991) *A History of Russian Literature*. New Haven, CT: Yale University Press.

Todorov, Tzvetan (1984) *Mikhail Bakhtin: The Dialogical Principle*. Minneapolis, MN: University of Minnesota Press; Manchester: Manchester University Press.

Voloshinov, V.N. (1976) *Freudianism: A Marxist Critique*. Eds I.R. Titunik and N. Bruss. New York: Academic Press.

Voloshinov, V.N. (1986) *Marxism and the Philosophy of Language*. Trans. L. Matejka and I.R. Titunik. Cambridge, MA: Harvard University Press.

14

THE NORMS OF ANSWERABILITY: BAKHTIN AND THE FOURTH POSTULATE

Greg Nielsen

This chapter examines conceptual shifts and interconnections between two of Bakhtin's first essays: *Towards a Philosophy of the Act* (1919–21) and the unfinished 'The author and hero in aesthetic activity' (1920–4). These works are key because they contain three distinct but overlapping problem motifs that combine to constitute the core of his philosophical anthropology: the personalist ethics of Being yourself, the aesthetics of the self–other or author–hero relation, and the normative framework of answerability that would come to define his general theory of the dialogic work inherent to the whole sphere of culture. I am particularly interested in further reconstructing how Bakhtin's thought evolves out of a critical reception of neo-Kantian ideas.

My main argument is that conceptual shifts in the early essays are attempts to move beyond the fourth postulate of neo-Kantian philosophy, that is, the assumption of the existential animateness of other egos and the implications such an assumption has for normative actions. This position is explained in the first section presented below. I examine how Bakhtin absorbs elements of Kant's first three postulates that are presented as necessary preconditions for ethical acts, but also how he rejects Kant's general theory of action. Bakhtin's concepts are presented in a unified theme that I am calling the norms of answerability that come out of this critical reception. In other words, how should I act, not because of the rules or the expectation of my duty (as with Kant), but how should I act given the imaginary but not fictional subjectivity of another who can answer me back – however different that subjectivity might be from my own. Bakhtin's notorious reverence for the most shady characters in Dostoevsky's novels and the most fantastic and twisted bits in Rabelais's version of grotesque realism attest to his sustained interest in this moral privileging of the other as both an individual stranger and potential collective friend. Well before the monographs on the latter artists, Bakhtin defines normative action as the emotionally and volitionally oriented act towards another axiological position that can answer back. Kant's question of 'what should I do?' becomes for Bakhtin 'how should I act' towards this other 'I' – this other emotional-volitional orientation – and in what aesthetic form can we consummate this action?

I argue that the philosophical understanding the young Bakhtin reaches for can only be achieved by balancing the needs of normative authority (consummation of a transgredient intersubjective act between two or more individuals) with the principle of infinite openness (the unfinalizability of self–other relations). To achieve this he develops a series of doubling concepts that are designed to uncover different layers of cross-over or trans-gredient relations. By 'transgredient' Bakhtin means that elements of the self or of culture in general cross-over to other selves or cultures and take on elements from each other as they complete themselves. Each side becomes itself through authoring or taking on aspects of the other side. Examples that Bakhtin works with across these three essays include the transgredience between the self and other, the author and the hero, the image of the inner and the outer body, the representation of the soul and the spirit in works of art and literature, as well as relations between the indi-vidual and the community.

Bakhtin doubles the concept of responsibility into the individual responsibility of being oneself and being in relation with another (Bakhtin, 1993: 3). The deepest expression of the self–other relation is the 'contrapo-sition of I and an other. Life knows two value-centres that are fundamen-tally and essentially different, yet are correlated with each other: myself and the other; and it is around all these centres that all of the concrete moments of Being are distributed and arranged' (1993: 74). Bakhtin achieves the first level of this understanding of intersubjectivity by doubling the relation between consummation or completion and open-endedness in self–other relations. He claims that the whole world is unitary in content when it is correlated with me or with an other. This transcultural meaning of the world is both particular and universal and raises the question of its unity to the level of a unique event.

Before beginning to treat these themes in more depth, I need to better situate the normative approach I claim Bakhtin develops. Bakhtin is very critical of any functionalist or theoretical definition of norms and so we need to provide a wide enough avenue to define the normative in a way that can accommodate his position. Once I have presented the way the fourth postu-late develops in the neo-Kantian context, I situate a discussion of the normative in the second section of the chapter. I have chosen to start with Socrates' original understanding of the norm of the good as that of the virtue of knowing yourself. Even though Bakhtin would only write on Socrates much later, I maintain that his early turn from neo-Kantianism is in part an intuitive extension of Socrates' notion of the good. This discussion emphasizes the importance Bakhtin places on individual responsibility but also of the reliance on the intersubjective relation. Next, I present a brief overview of the most famous neo-Kantian, Hermann Cohen, and review the way in which he understands the question of community. His special geneal-ogy of the concept of fellowship is cited as a possible source of Bakhtin's own sense of the origins of answerability (Nikolayev, 1992: 222). Both Cohen and Bakhtin share an interest in removing the wedge Kant drives between experience and knowledge. There is not enough space to provide a detailed description of Cohen's approach nor to present a full critique of Cohen from the Bakhtin circle that others have pointed out (Bernard-Donalds, 1994; Clark and Holquist, 1984). Instead, I explore how Cohen also looks for a way to join experience with knowledge and account for the unity of the world. The doubling across the body–soul–spirit relations as developed in the Author–Hero essay are presented in the final section below against the background motive of the fourth postulate and as a problematization of the individual–community relation.

How Bakhtin Absorbs Kant's Three Postulates but not His Ethics

It is important to remember that the fourth postulate can be understood as both an addition to Kant and as departure from Kant's original doctrine regarding the impossibility of knowing the 'thing-in-itself' or the neumenon.

Kant argues that three postulates are necessary to serve as a platform that enable us to move beyond the distinction of the norm as being that which is remembered through fallible subjective experience (Kant, 1993: 113–56). He argues that for the norm of the good to be valid we must be able to make some sort of measure against an ultimate form of the ought, that is, the norm that might explain how the thing should be. His first postulate is that for an ultimate norm of the good to exist there must also be some infinite time span in which the norm might occur; hence, there must also be the possibility of immortality. Secondly, God must exist in order for such a measure of the ultimate good to be possible. Without the concept of God, we could have no mechanism for agreeing on what the ultimate good might be like. Finally, Kant's third postulate is that human subjects must be free to choose between good and evil for there to be such a thing as the good in the first place (Kant, 1990: 18, 46, 53).

This question of the free volition of the norm is what sets up the immediate ethical dilemma of how the subject should act in a given situation. Note here, that the dilemma for Kant is not about how the subject should act faced with other subjects in a given situation, a subject whose emotional-volitional or axiological orientation might be in conflict or in harmony, but rather, how the subject should act regardless of other axiological positions provided in a given context. This is the basic groundwork of deontological or duty-bound ethics and the main reason Kant only speaks of ethical acts as duties and not as aesthetic or creative events. Kant's categorical imperative states that we should only ever act on those maxims that we could will to be universal. In other words, the question is not how I should act in a given situation, but rather, what is my duty for the sake of duty. The source of my duty is deduced from universal or transcendental categories and not from the subjective negotiations in actions that struggle over norms.

The return to Kant in German philosophy began after the 1848 revolutions in the context of a collapse of political, ethical and epistemological systems. In philosophy, the movement is understood as a return to the starting-point of critical idealism and not a plea to defend Kant's overall system. Some, like Kuno Fischer and Eduard Zeller, returned to Kant from Hegelian perspectives, while others, like Rudolf Lotze and Albert Lange, were looking for a way out of mechanical materialism and the rising dominance of positivism. In Marburg, Cohen and his students, Paul Natrop and Ernst Cassirer, developed neo-Kantianism towards logic and epistemology as well as social democratic or liberal-socialist political models. In Baden, Wilhelm Windelbaum and Heinrich Rickert were more concerned with defining the fundamental tasks of the cultural sciences and were less concerned with political theory or engagement in praxis. For all, the crises of the epoch set the backdrop for a revival of moral philosophy that developed around highly tentative and experimental interpretations of Kant's critiques (Willey, 1978).

The fourth postulate comes out of this larger context. One of the earliest to argue for the fourth postulate as an addition to Kant was Bakhtin's philosophy professor, Alexander Vvedensky. He claimed that 'the three postulates of practical reason established by Kant are not sufficient for the full understanding of moral behaviour'. Vvedensky formulated the fourth postulate as 'a belief in the existence of other egos, as a morally established faith' (Lossky, 1951: 161). Like Kant, Vvedensky maintains that the other's inner life is unknowable and that one can only ever know oneself. Bakhtin hesitates when confronted with the question of whether we can actually know the other's I-for-the-self. Initially at least, he allows the more neo-Kantian assumption that breaks from Kant by assuming we might completely experience the other's being through empathy (Bakhtin, 1990: 25). But he immediately counters that pure empathy is impossible because it would mean completely giving up on the empathizing individuals once-occurrent-Being (1993: 16). Hence, it would not be correct to argue that Bakhtin's approach is simply the extension and working through of the fourth postulate even though he eventually sees in Dostoevsky's novels an example of an artistic vision that is capable of completely imagining the other as an unmerged voice.

Unlike Vvedensky, Bakhtin shares the more common neo-Kantian suspicion of Kant's doctrine of the inability to ever know the thing-in-itself. At the same time he also distances himself from *Lebensphilosophie* and other intuitivist approaches. He shares several other themes that were common to neo-Kantian criticisms of Kant. In the first essays in particular he relies heavily on Windelbaum's concept of the transgredient relation between subjects as opposed to Kant's transcendental version of normative relations. On the other hand, he embraces Kant's architectonics as a means of constructing the whole from the parts and he privileges moral and practical responsibility over absolutist theories of ethics. Bakhtin never wrote on the fourth postulate and yet his moral privileging of the other remains an outstanding feature across his work. The fourth postulate, therefore, should be understood as a starting-point for thinking through the background motives for Bakhtin's early conceptual shifts rather than as an axiom that explains all of his work. A point to keep in mind is that Bakhtin was not alone in his search to shift emphasis away from the a priori synthesis of knowledge towards an interest in the ethical and aesthetic problems raised by our more direct experience with each other.

Bakhtin is very critical of Kant's formalism. Keep in mind, though, that he does not dismiss the content of the latter's three postulates even though he does not develop his approach in terms of postulates or necessary non-demonstrable principles. As his biographers are continually stressing, and as is evident in his own texts, Bakhtin never left the soul–immortality–individual freedom assumptions behind. On the contrary, he retains and develops the premise of the existence of God (the soul–spirit–body relation), the possibility of immortality (for example, Dostoevsky's capacity to divine aspects of the future from the present and the past) and of free volition (of the normative). In *Toward a Philosophy of the Act* (1993) and 'The Author and the Hero Relation in Aesthetic Activity' (1990), Bakhtin presents the most significant philosophical elaboration of the need for a special effort to reunite the aesthetic (the shaping of meaning in action) and the ethical (a cognitive element of the act itself) into one unified event. Kant, on the other hand, drives a wedge between knowledge and experience that is supported by the further divisions of the separate spheres of possible knowledge (theory, ethics and aesthetics).

One of Bakhtin's points in criticizing Kant's formalism is that as we reflect on the aesthetic representation of another's life through empathizing, or construct a philosophical ethics about how someone should act, we have already left the domain of once-occurrent-Being. This does not signal a post-moralist nor a relativist dilemma. The rules of conduct and the translation of desire into virtuous acts are not separated. On the contrary, once-occurrent-Being is never outside a normative deed. Bakhtin's insistence on the immediacy of once-occurrent-Being is an implicit component of the fourth postulate. Bakhtin argues that any position that does not take the understanding of the other's coeval and equal existence as in itself can only be a formalist understanding of how it should be or what it should be like.

By positing the animated existence of another I, Bakhtin addresses the larger question of the 'consummation' between parts and the whole in the experience of the action itself. Kant's ethics are seen as flawed in that the norm is not defined inside the act but from an appropriate belief system or discipline outside the act that places it into context. 'What is needed is something issuing from within myself, namely the morally ought-to-be attitude of my consciousness toward the theoretically valid-in-itself proposition'. Deontological ethics correctly assumes that the ought is a category of consciousness, 'a form that cannot be derived from some particular material'. But it further 'conceives the category of the ought as a category of theoretical consciousness, and, as a result looses the individual act or deed' (Bakhtin, 1993: 23). For Bakhtin, the ought is not only an element of the act, it is a category of individuality itself. Neither the unique aspect of the individual act nor its universally valid claim can be repeated or performed by someone else. The uniqueness lies in the I's affirmation of the non-alibi in Being.

A Reading of Socrates' Influence on Bakhtin's Version of Knowing Yourself

Socrates, Plato, Aristotle, the Stoics, the Epicurians, and the Sophists all differed over the definition of what it means to live a good life. Martha Nussbaum shows how for the Stoics the good is understood as a virtue that carries multiple meanings only because there is a universal *logos* or reason that each local claim of the good taps into. The highest good is human reason but it needs to be nurtured through dispassionate civic education that allows one to become a completely cosmopolitan world citizen (Nussbaum, 1996: 7–8). Epicurians, on the other hand, had little interest in politics and community and believed that the highest good was that of the highest possible pleasure. This meant that pain had to be eliminated and which implied in turn that the highest good would be to heal pain (Cicero, 1987: 112–13). Epicures thought philosophy should be therapeutic (Nussbaum, 1994: 13). The Sophists, like modern-day relativists, argued that there is no absolute good, nor universal norms. Then, as now, such a position confuses the relation between values and norms. It confuses the relation between ephemeral changing values and fixed ideal rules of conduct (or 'techniques of the self' as Foucault would come to call them) that build values, impulses or desires into good actions or into virtuous public acts.

The contradictory relation between the universal good and the particular value context is not easily solved and is still very much a part of the theoretical paradox of contemporary anthropology, in the sense that the more we think of what might be particular or essential about a given human culture, the more we wonder what is universal or transcultural about it – and vice versa (Bauman, 1973). We might say that for the Ancients, the normative is about appearance but that a norm also mediates the social. Bakhtin defines a norm as 'a special form of free volition of one person in relation to others' (1993: 24). In this sense, norms are both the meditations and breaks of social life. As a voluntary agreement, a norm allows us to interact meaningfully and as a break it allows us to come together without crashing. Free volition does not apply to religious or legal norms but to everyday normative acts. Bakhtin holds no strong versions of either a will to power, or of a utilitarian deduction in which norms are strictly derived through a calculated taking into account of the consequences and the effects of actions. For the young Bakhtin, the social is given form through something like a will to responsibility that actors undertake in intersubjective relations in both existential and instrumental terms. He might well agree with both the classical and the contemporary idea that the social is constituted by a plurality of norms that allow a certain degree of paradox given that inside societies there are disparate views of the good. However, it is not so clear that he would agree with the classical liberal notion from Kant on that the right must prevail over the good. The paradox wherein norms apparently contradict one another is the transcultural source of what Bakhtin calls answerability. The paradox allows differing degrees in which speakers from a given culture do the work of reminding each other about what they already know. In a sense, enculturation means reminding each other about the norm that is aspired to in an emotional-volitional orientation. Hence, the norm is both transcendental or overarching and actual, that is, something that is practised in a transgredient way in the life of speech and action.

For Socrates, one norm for knowledge was that the more you know, the more you know there is to know or be reminded of. We can easily extend this norm to the idea of contemporary transculturalism: the more we know other cultures, the more there is to know. Socrates often insisted he knew nothing. He did not want to instruct people; he simply wanted to learn what they already knew. Instead of lecturing, he discussed. Bakhtin reminds us that anacrisis and syncrisis were his main techniques (Bakhtin, 1984: 110). By confessing ignorance (Socratic irony), he showed that knowledge came from what we already know. Through anacrisis he could provoke words with words and through syncrisis he could juxtapose words and generate new words. In Plato's 'Meno' dialogue, Socrates uses both techniques to draw out the answers to questions about the circumference of a square from someone who has no formal education. Socrates takes the fact that he could get the answer as a proof of the immortality of the soul. Though he claimed he himself new nothing, he also argued that everyone already knows everything before they are born. It is the shock of birth that leads us to forget (Plato, 1963: 370–1). The rest of our lives is spent remembering or being reminded of what we already know. The art of this remembering is imbued with a deeper responsibility, that of knowing yourself.

In *Toward a Philosophy of the Act*, Bakhtin argues for the personal responsibility to be oneself and to resist pretending to be someone else. If it is possible to say that Bakhtin has a notion of the ultimate good, it is this. Another way of understanding Bakhtin's appropriation of Socrates' original maxim, 'know thyself', is to think that humans (wherever they are) must overcome all kinds of diversity and relativity in order to become themselves. He defines Being as singular and once-occurrent and so the event-of-Being is also seen to precede any kind of essence or identity thinking. Here, Bakhtin makes an important point in critiquing those positions that would mistake discourse on identity as somehow representing Being in-itself. Shifting the in-itself existence of identity to the *vita contemplativa* (cognitive and even political thinking on identity) is the most general level of the error Bakhtin calls theoreticism. Yet, it is paradoxical in this text that Bakhtin might also be convinced by Aristotle, and later Hegel, that recognition of the many – of diversity, and by way of extension, the struggles for this recognition – also precedes the recognition of the singular unity of the world.

I should return at this point to clarify something about Bakhtin's concept of holism and what I take to be his understanding of the universal. He defines the whole as containing a 'loophole' that allows a way out of any finalization. In post-metaphysical terms, unity should not be understood as a closed off or finished exercise, but rather as the unique consummation of the ensemble; 'the uniqueness of a whole that does not repeat itself anywhere and the actuality of that whole and hence, for the one who wishes to think that whole, it excludes the category of unity' (Bakhtin, 1993: 37). Unity exists in the answerable act, that is, in the moment of decision and of resolution. Unity is unique and unrepeatable. It is not Being in any omnipresent sense, it is the event of Being for which I take responsibility. 'It is only my non-alibi in Being that transforms an empty possibility into an actual answerable act (through an emotional-volitional referral to myself as the one who is active)' (1993: 42).

The accumulation of each individual act makes up my life history, my 'once-occurrent-life'. 'To be in life, to be actually, is to act, is to be unindifferent toward the once-occurrent-whole' (1993: 43). If I am indifferent towards the once-occurrent-whole, or if I am pretending to be someone I am not, then the fact of my uniqueness and answerability are severely jeopardized. In fact, if I ignore my active self and simply live the passive self (who receives), I am by definition pretending. 'I can try and prove my alibi in Being. I can pretend to be someone I am not. I can abdicate from my obligative (ought-to-be) uniqueness' (1993: 42). But pretending means to risk being chosen by someone else. Even a little pretending, we might say, influences the possibilities of action across one's life. It is this collection of acts that become the content of one's life history. In the sense of unity, life history is a single complex act. Every time I perform a particular act I perform my life history 'and every particular act and lived-experience is a constituent moment of my life – of the continuous performing of acts [*postuplenie*]' (1993: 3).

The unity of the answerable act is derived from its combined claim of objectivity, validity, and sincerity. When we act we take-into-account the consequences of our action. This taking-into-account (objectivity) means imagining or reasoning the valid effects of our action as well as our response to a possible response. Every act is answerable. Emotional-volitional tone (sincerity or, conversely, the lack of sincerity) is where we find the force of active answerability. Being-as-event is measurable by the degree of sincerity indicated in the emotional-volitional tone. When one is describing once-occurrent-Being, Bakhtin employs the term faithfulness (being-true-to). 'The emotional-volitional tone, encompassing and permeating once-occurrent, Being-as-event . . . is a certain ought-to-be attitude of consciousness, an attitude that is morally valid and answerably active' (1993: 36).

The unity of Being-as-event cannot be grasped theoretically but can only be described. A reflection on the representation or the sign of Being can only ever be a reflection on 'once-occurrent-Being'. Something that represents something to someone is also something that means something to someone. Bakhtin's doubling of the symbolic means that I find myself passively in Being but I also actively participate in it. My uniqueness is given and I participate in its consummation or what it has not yet achieved. I am both what is and what ought to be. This moral presence in the act is one side of its answerability whereas the specific content of the act is its other. Two-sided answerability is required to join the individual and the collective or life and culture (1993: 28). 'In all Being I experience only myself – my unique self – as an I. All other I's (theoretical ones) are not I's-for-me' (1993: 46). These are the Is for-the-other or the others-for-me. My non-alibi in Being means to struggle with the seduction of pretending where I imagine how the other might see me or I imagine how I would like them to see me.

One side of philosophy, so it seems, has always theorized that reminding each other about the transcendence of the norm is the best way to live ethically while the other has taught that the only way to live ethically is first to be true to oneself. If we somehow confuse our value relation to the norm as being independent from any transcendence (sophism), or if we pretend that the transcendence of the norm is extra-historical (that is, does not pass through a transgredient relation and therefore is not bound to a value relation – Stoicism, Plato's forms), then we risk giving up on the theory of the good as being plural and multiple as well as unique and universal. In the case of a strongly stated non-separation between norm and value, we end up in a dogmatism that insists no unity or foundation for truth is possible except, of course, the proposal of the one who posits such a statement ('The End of History', 'The Last Man', 'The Death of Philosophy'). In the case of too strong a separation between the norm and the value, we give up the spontaneity and source of diversity that makes the stability of the norm possible.

There is not enough space here to go into all the sociological differences between us and the Ancients, or the history of ideas that distances us from that civilization. Hannah Arendt explains, for example, that our sense of the concept of excellence is measured in terms of productivity and not by the achievement of great deeds achieved through speech and action. Our sense of reason is that it is instrumental and administrative whereas for the Ancients it is the highest virtue. Our sense of equality is about justice and even the guaranteed equality of outcomes whereas for the Greeks it means being among peers. One of the most profound differences Arendt speaks of is the precedent we afford to the private over the public sphere and how the private is seen as the space of unfreedom for them whereas for us it is privileged as a precious escape from the administrative rationalization of our public lives (Arendt, 1958: 22–78). Still, for both civilizations, it is the question of values that gives rise to the problem of the orientation to norms that we call right and wrong. If, with Arendt and Bakhtin, we adopt the neo-classicist position that the ability to choose between right and wrong lies in the transgredient relations of speech and action (*vita activa*) and not in transcendental categories, then we also maintain Socrates' position that suggests people who have good insight will choose the right way.

Hermann Cohen's 'The Discovery of Man as Fellowman'

As we saw in our introduction, a common theme of the return to Kant at the end of the nineteenth century was the attempt to find a way to bring the spheres of human activity back into one unified philosophy. Hermann Cohen became the leading figure in neo-Kantianism and one of the most important influences on Bakhtin and his friends. Cohen's first works were close commentaries on Kant's three critiques. In each work Cohen looked for ways of narrowing the gap between the phenomenon and noumenon until finally in his *Ethic die Reinen Willen* (*The Ethics of Pure Will*) he re-establishes the will of the subject as in-itself, a position that greatly concretizes the categorical imperative (Scharzschild, 1981; Zac, 1984). Cohen establishes a philosophical basis for a theory of law and of binding social relations in practice and not only in transcendental synthesis. As Willey points out, Cohen 'developed the main thesis of Marburg socialism by broadening the categorical imperative into the fundamental rule of society directed by moral reason and constituted under law' (1978: 124). In a sense, Cohen returns us to the older notion of reminding each other about the norm.

While Cohen's 'ethics of pure will' remains partially attached to the philosophy of natural law, a second part of his project is to reduce the gap between the theological understanding of God as a postulate of transcendental reason and the direct experience of God. As Clark and Holquist put it: 'He seeks to reduce the gap between the God of the philosopher and the God of Abraham' (1984: 304). Cohen's philosophy is itself derived from readings of the ancient testament and Jewish theology. For Cohen the problem of the norm originates in the correlation between God and man. The relation itself is defined as the holy spirit. The reintroduction of experience into the relation between 'God' and 'Man' leads to the theoretical problem of man as plurality and man as individual. Out of plurality comes the problem of unity. The unity of man means the extension of the power of the One 'over every individual member of the plurality'. This is a founding question of monotheism: what to do with the foreigners who do not believe in the One God? In fact the problem of the foreigner is a key political problem for all societies.

For Cohen, an individual man is but a unit in a series; he is only 'one man next to another' or just the next man (*Nebenmensch*). The concept of 'the next man' is taken from historical experience and 'poses for ethics and also for religion . . . the problem of the fellowman (*Mitmensch*)' (Cohen, 1972: 114). The next man is not a fellowman; 'he' is not just there innocently or unobtrusively. The correlation of man and God cannot be maintained if man and man is not achieved. Thus, the problem of fellowman becomes the highest problem of morality – it is the problem of the contraposition of the I–other relation Bakhtin defines at the end of *Toward a Philosophy of the Act* (1993: 74). Ethics cannot be possible unless it is attached to the question of the fellowman. If fellowman is levelled down to the concept of the next man, sociability could not arise and normative orientations (meditations and breaks) would be impossible.

Cohen's definition of the fellowman is based on a theological orientation, but it is also situated genealogically. He argues that monotheism, specifically Judaism, gave rise to both the humanist concepts of man as all humankind and man as an individual. But monotheism had to solve the problem of how to deal with the other who would not share the beliefs and customs of the one religion. It solved the problem through the concept of the stranger. The concept of the fellowman has its origins in the older concept of the foreigner, a concept that predates Ancient Greece. The state creates the distinction between the foreigner and the native. Cohen adds that as sociability increases and locals come to know the stranger, he may be elevated to the status of the guest-friend, the immigrant; the one who is invited to eat and to stay and participate. 'The stranger is not thought of as a slave, but as a guest-friend, who requires the piety of guest-friendship. Humanity is already so rooted in the stranger that the slave, as stranger, can be admonished to the bond of gratitude' (Cohen, 1972: 120). The guest-friend may be excused from strict observance of the laws and is not required to believe in the one God. The guest-friend evolves into a more legal status and is called the quest-sojourner. Here, a foreigner-stranger may enter into another's territory and be recognized as having the same legal rights without being expected to observe the same cultural laws or even believe in the one God. Eventually, as enough guest-sojourners begin to immigrate, they eventually take on the status of 'brother' (Cohen, 1972: 127).

It is not difficult to see how the political implies the capacity to shift around the categories of 'just the next man' and 'the fellowman'. But moving from fellowman to just the next man requires some form of community backed by the rule of law (Cohen, 1972: 137). The foreigner, the guest-friend or immigrant, the stranger, and the sojourner-stranger are the release valves and side entrances to the absolute law of community. The political, as well as the ethical, evolve out of the movement between these categories and the interests they get attached to in the social division. As Cohen argues, whereas one cannot be indifferent to the tragedy of the good fellowman it is easier to be indifferent to 'just the next man', or to the fellowman who does bad, but not to the fellowman who does good.

In one sense, for Cohen, social division is rooted in the inability to maintain the integrity of the fellowman (1972: 130). Cohen refers to the biblical example where Cain kills Abel because his brother possessed more than he did. A flash of fratricide became possible at the point where Abel could be levelled down to the status of just the next man. But the question becomes how is social division possible given the necessity of the common good of the community (man) and God? Does not social division create opposition to fellowman? The next man becomes the opposing man (*Gegenmensch*). 'Even more than the question of the stranger, the question of rich and poor is asked in one's native land and among one's own people; this human question is asked with regard to every man, with regard to every fellowman' (1972: 128). Out of the question of poverty and suffering comes the primary emotion of pity, a kind of glue for the sociability of fellowship.

Cohen succeeds in concretizing the categorical imperative by introducing the dynamic between the opposing man, the next man, and fellowman. His sideways shift from a transcendental metaphysics that separates knowledge from experience to a religious metaphysics (from 'the God of philosophers to the God of Abraham'), leads him to theorize an 'ethics of pure will' in itself. However, the shift to religious metaphysics only brings the individual–community problem into sharper focus. It remains a question whether his shift can offer a solution to the normative puzzle that is generated with the fourth postulate. The larger anthropological question of how to approach others as coeval partners whoever and wherever they might be is still not fully answered. The category of the stranger-immigrant solves some of the political dilemma of the one society and the one religion but does not begin to theorize the phenomenological effect the stranger has on the community nor does it answer the question of what effect the community has on the stranger. In a way, Bakhtin's starting-point from the fourth postulate is not how to solve the problem of the stranger but is the more difficult question of understanding the effect of the animated I ('the man in the man') as a more permanent condition of the stranger category. We will explore this argument in the next section before coming to a conclusion.

Body–Soul Cross-over

In *Toward a Philosophy of the Act*, Bakhtin develops concepts aimed at providing a personalist ethics that focuses on the self taking responsibility for action that unfolds as an event of Being. The book-length essay, 'The Author and Hero Relation in Aesthetic Activity', is an expansive theoretical outline of the manifold problems of how the artist might represent or create the animate I of the other as a hero and how the relation between these cognitive and ethical Is are consummated aesthetically. In Bakhtin's I-for-the-self, action takes place as the I 'acts through the deed, word, thought or action. I come to be through my acts' (Bakhtin, 1990: 138). What is added to Bakhtin's philosophy of the act is the I's self-reflection on its act and the way in which the I is consummated aesthetically through the cross-over relation with another.

Like Cohen, Bakhtin attributes the origin of the 'I' to the communities' production of fellowman. But here Bakhtin goes further by reintroducing his theory of the non-alibi in Being under the guise of a theory of alienation. Here the I lives 'in the other and for the other. In my lived life, I participate in a communal mode of existence, in an established social order, in a nation, in a state, in mankind, in God's world'. In each of these contexts, Bakhtin argues, the I lives life in the category of the other. 'I experience, strive and speak herein the chorus of others. But in a chorus I do not sing for myself; I am active only in relation to the other and I am passive in the other's relation to me'. Acts are performed in a context that is relative to day-to-day life, to a universe of social and political values, and of aesthetic and ethical values. In communitarian ('fellowman') action 'I exchange gifts, but I do so disinterestedly; I feel in myself the body and the soul of another. Not my own nature but the human nature in me can be beautiful, and not my own soul but the human soul can be harmonious' (Bakhtin, 1990: 121).

The author–hero essay brackets the 'fellowman' context while it theorizes the cross-over relation between self and other as an aesthetic and ethical problem of the fourth postulate. The author–hero essay is divided in four general sections. Each deals with the perspectival uniqueness of seeing, knowledge, and experience. The first section deals mainly with the problem of the excess of seeing or exotopy, the way in which we perceive more of the other's body than he or she might be able to see of herself or himself as well as the way we perceive our own bodies. He emphasizes that we come to be ourselves through gifts bestowed on us by others, gifts of language and, more importantly, of positive emotional-volitional orientations that anchor the temporal and spatial order of our souls. In the second section he introduces us further to his usage of the concept of transgredience and of the difference between empathetic co-experiencing and sympathetic co-experiencing or how we cross-over into each other's experience without giving up who we are in order to consummate relations aesthetically. The third and fourth sections of the essay ask the question of how to represent the other as an animate other with a soul and not 'just as the next man', to use Cohen's expression. Bakhtin moves us from the problem of reconstructing the transgredient I–other relation in terms of sympathetic co-experiencing to the aesthetic consummation of the other's outer body, and to the I's attempt to represent the Other's inner soul. Both the inner and outer body relation and the inner-soul, outer-spirit relation are transgredient, that is, each are situated in emotional-volitional or axiological normative orientations and each cross-over to other normative positions as they become themselves.

It is important to remember that Bakhtin's construction of the problem of the soul–spirit relation is not theological but aesthetic. It is derived from his understanding of the history of writing and artistic creations in different societies at different times. To dismiss his theory of the artist's representation of the soul as adoration of Christology is to miss the point. His essay on the Author–Hero relation provides a new problem that is emerging in his theory of the aesthetic significance that I am arguing takes-off from the fourth postulate. We could also easily miss an important step in understanding his theoretical shift to the early version of the Dostoevsky book if we were to be sidetracked by a defence of his theory of authorship here.

The issue needs to be bracketed and possibly returned to at greater length in a separate work.

To begin with, then, the artistic act of representing the I-for-the-self turns out to be intrinsically related to cognitive and ethical processes for Bakhtin. The author–artist operates from an excess of seeing much as any subject-actor would. Each of us sees the Other from outside and each of us has the advantage of a point of view above and over that which the Other might have on herself. A simple way of understanding this is to consider that we can see much more of each other's physical exterior than we can see of our own exterior. The author–artist provides the hero's physical or exterior image while the hero herself is in the process of facing the dilemma of how to act, or what to do next. Bakhtin argues that the author supplies the angles from which the wholeness of the hero can be justified, a wholeness the hero cannot see from where she is, a wholeness that is maintained regardless of what the heroine's life might have in store for her (1990: 14).

Exotopy or the ability to see all around is the condition out of which it becomes possible for us to offer a loving axiological position to another; a teacher to a student, a father to a child, a friend to a friend, a lover to a beloved, an author to a hero (1990: 34). This gift is described positively as a loving projection on to the hero that includes a normative orientation that supports the hero who then takes on his or her own axiological position. Only a gift derived from a sympathetic understanding of the hero's 'forward looking life' can free the hero so we can experience her soul and her I-for-herself. Bakhtin asks two questions regarding the problem of how the author can present the hero's soul. First, how is the soul ordered spatially, and secondly, how is the soul ordered temporally.

The hero's exterior is a gift from the author. The outer body of the hero is transgredient with the inner self's 'potential and actual self-consciousness'. The normative principle of 'the other's inward outsidedness and over-againstness' (1990: 101) comes about in the same way as in the inner-body aesthetic – the inner organic sensations gathered around an 'inner centre' that makes my body an inner body and the body of the other an outer body (1990: 48). Ordering, organizing and forming the soul is not a process that is fundamentally different from representing the relation of the soul to the outer body. The soul is transgredient to the self-consciousness of the hero. '*The soul is spirit the way it looks from outside, in the other*' (1990: 100; added emphasis).

The author can order the soul in the hero because the author is capable of both transposing his own soul on to another and of experiencing through imagination what the other might experience. This sympathetic co-experiencing gives order to the spatial aspect of the soul. It is the process by which a transposition of the experience of one's own soul outside oneself in another is rendered possible. Such a transposition or sympathetic co-experience, Bakhtin notes, is not a copy of one to another but 'a fundamentally and essentially new valuation, a utilization of my own architectonic exposition in being outside another's inner life' (1990: 103). The soul in the other as well as my own soul is itself an image of the totality of everything that has been experienced in the dimension of time by me or by the other. The spirit 'is the totality of everything that has the validity of meaning – a totality of all the forms of my life's directedness from within myself' (without detachment from the I). Spirit is set 'at every moment as a task' (1990: 110). Like the problem of meaning in general, spirit has no existence in time but is contextually situated.

Spirit cannot support rhythm or an aesthetic order on its own. Spirit does not order the future and its relation to the past or the present. Rhythm is the emotional-volitional 'reaction to a reaction' and not itself an axiological point of view (1990: 117). Thus it is rhythm that sheds light on the event by changing the future into the present or the past into the future. The temporal ordering of rhythm does not determine the normative 'ought-to-be' but it can distort it by making it conditional: the 'what-is, the what-ought-to be, what-is-given and what is imposed-as-a-task are incapable of being rhythmically bound within me myself from within myself' (1990: 118). The normative grounds of answerability 'confront me from within myself as in another world – it is precisely this moment that constitutes the highest point of my creative seriousness, of my pure productiveness'. Creative acts, acts that represent the animateness of the I-in-the-other, are 'extra-rhythmic' and once the acts are performed they fall away into 'what was' (1990: 119).

Conclusion

To recap, we have reviewed the main concepts that Bakhtin constructs from the motive of the fourth postulate. We saw that Bakhtin's ethics and aesthetics are derived from a critique of Kant's theory of action and yet Bakhtin retains his main postulates. In a similar fashion Bakhtin also draws implicitly on Cohen's theory of fellowship. However, he also contrasts communitarianism with a theory of alienation that is suspicious of any metaphysical conclusion that would ignore the autonomous animated existence of the other.

Bakhtin leaves *Toward a Philosophy of the Act* with the problem of the subject's state of inner responsibility and the effect of the other's reaction back on that subjectivity – the doubling process of answerability. Only aesthetics, Bakhtin tells us, can explore the soul's life as it is in the subject's unique experience. All aesthetically valid determinations are transgredient to lived experience; only this transgrediency provides their power and validity. For the author to form a soul he or she 'must see more than being'. The author gains an excess of seeing only by being situated outside the soul that is being formed. This architectonic privilege is the same as where my experience ends and my seeing the other's spirit or the outer body of her soul begins (1990: 135). In the aesthetics of the author–hero relation we still see the sociological importance Bakhtin lends to the way in which we are authored by our significant others, our communities, our cities, nations and God's.

Finally, we saw that for Bakhtin the open ethical event where questions of 'oughtness' are worked out has no universal (transcendental) grounding. This does not mean that he has no normative theory or concept of the transcultural. Each of Bakhtin's first essays shows him coming to terms with limitations based on a series of conceptual doubling: (i) of the ethics of being yourself through others; (ii) of the inner and outer soul–body aesthetic; and (iii) of the individual while others are discarded or slip into the background. The key definition of varying norms of answerability and the argument concerning the responsibility to be oneself are two core principles that are absorbed in the shift to define the transgredient or cross-over relations between self and other as an aesthetic activity. Bakhtin moves from an existentialist phenomenology to an abstract aesthetics and then back to a more concrete formulation of the individual–community relation. A more complete interpretation of the conceptual shifts across the rest of his corpus, using the fourth postulate as an orienting point of departure, remains to be done.

Note

I would like to thank Tapani Laine for his criticisms of this chapter and for introducing me to 'the fourth postulate' argument. Any shortcomings in the chapter are of course my responsibility. I am also indebted to Aurilia Klimkiewicz who provided me with a 'non-official' rough translation of Pumpyanski's (1924) notes on Bakhtin's lectures on Kant and other topics. Thanks to the students in the Bakhtin graduate seminars over the last few years at York University, University of British Columbia, and Concordia for their insights and will to dialogue.

References

Arendt, Hannah (1958) *The Human Condition*. Chicago: University of Chicago Press.

Bakhtin, M.M. (1984) *Problems of Dostoevsky's Poetics*. Ed. and trans. Caryl Emerson. Minneapolis, MN: University of Minnesota Press.

Bakhtin, M.M. (1990) 'Author and hero in aesthetic activity', in *Art and Answerability: Early Philosophical Essays by M.M. Bakhtin*. Eds M. Holquist and V. Liapunov. Trans. and notes V. Liapunov. Austin, TX: University of Texas Press. pp. 4–256.

Bakhtin, M.M. (1993) *Toward a Philosophy of the Act*. Ed. Michael Holquist. Trans. and notes Vadim Liapunov. Austin, TX: University of Texas Press.

Bauman, Zygmunt (1973) *Culture as Praxis*. London: Routledge & Kegan Paul.

Bernard-Donals, Michael (1994) *Mikhail Bakhtin: Between Phenomenology and Marxism*. Cambridge: Cambridge University Press.

Cicero (1987) 'On Ends', in A.A. Long and D.N. Sedley (eds), *The Hellenistic Philosophers*. Cambridge: Cambridge University Press.

Clark, Katerina and Holquist, Michael (1984) 'The influence of Kant in the early work of M.M. Bakhtin', in *Literary Theory and Criticism, Part I*. Ed. Joseph P. Strelka. Bern: Peter Lang.

Cohen, Hermann (1972) *The Religion of Reason: Out of the Sources of Judaism*. Trans. Simon Kaplan. New York: Ungar.

Kant, Immanuel (1990) *Foundations of the Metaphysics of Morals*. Trans. Lewis White Beck. New York: Macmillan.

Kant, Immanuel (1993) *Critique of Practical Reason*. Englewood Cliffs, NJ: Prentice-Hall.

Lossky, N.O. (1951) *The History of Russian Philosophy*. London: International Universities Press.

Nikolayev, N.I. (1992) 'Introduction' to 'Lectures and reports of Bakhtin (1924–1925) in Pumpyanski's papers', in *M.M. Baxtnh Kak Filosof*. Ed. L.A. Gogotishvily. Moscow: Hayka. pp. 221–52.

Nussbaum, Martha (1994) *The Theory of Desire: Theory and Practice in Hellenistic Ethics*. Princeton, NJ: Princeton University Press.

Nussbaum, Martha (1996) 'Patriotism and cosmopolitanism', in *For Love of Country: Debating the Limits of Patriotism*. Boston, MA: Beacon Press.

Plato (1963) 'Meno', in *Plato: The Collected Dialogues, Including the Letters*. Princeton, NJ: Princeton University Press. pp. 370–1.

Scharzschild, Steven S. (1981) 'Introduction', in Hermann Cohen, *Ethik des Reinen Willens*. Hildesheim: Georg Olms. pp. xii–xxxv.

Willey, Thomas (1978) *Back to Kant: The Revival of Kantianism in German Social and Historical Thought, 1860–1914*. Detroit: Wayne State University.

Zac, Sylvain (1984) *La Philosophie religieuse de Hermann Cohen*. Avant propos de Paul Ricœur. Paris: Librairie Philosophique de J. Vrin.

INDEX